Carnal Hermeneutics

John D. Caputo, *series editor*

PERSPECTIVES IN
CONTINENTAL
PHILOSOPHY

Edited by RICHARD KEARNEY
and BRIAN TREANOR

Carnal Hermeneutics

FORDHAM UNIVERSITY PRESS
New York ■ 2015

Library of Congress Cataloging-in-Publication Data

Carnal hermeneutics / edited by Richard Kearney and Brian Treanor.
     pages cm. — (Perspectives in continental philosophy)
   Includes bibliographical references and index.
   ISBN 978-0-8232-6588-6 (hardback) — ISBN 978-0-8232-6589-3 (paper)
   1. Human body (Philosophy)   2. Hermeneutics.   I. Kearney, Richard, editor.
II. Treanor, Brian, editor.
   B105.B64C345 2015
   128'.6—dc23

                                                              2014040676

Printed in the United States of America
17 16 15   5 4 3 2 1

First edition

Contents

Acknowledgments

A book like this inevitably depends on the efforts of a great many people. The project would, of course, have been impossible without the generosity and enthusiasm of our contributors. A half-dozen translators also worked to make possible the inclusion of so many of the leading lights of French philosophy. And the staff at Fordham University Press efficiently prepared the manuscript for publication. These people, and others, all helped the editors to pull together this remarkable volume, which introduces and develops "carnal hermeneutics" for the first time. We are indebted to them and grateful for the support we've received.

Helen Tartar was an early and enthusiastic supporter of this project—a project that, tragically, she was unable to see into print. As the Editorial Director at Fordham University Press over the past decade, Helen was a great friend to continental philosophy and continental philosophers in the United States and abroad. More than simply an editor, Helen worked closely with scholars—both junior and senior—to actively shape philosophical discourse. She had a fine eye for a good book, a keen sense for the direction in which scholarship was moving, a purposeful work ethic, and a gentle spirit. Sadly, she passed away in an automobile accident just as this project was nearing completion. However, her spirit lives on in the work of the many authors she helped to discover and cultivate, and in the many books that she carefully shepherded to press. This collection is dedicated to her memory and to pressing on with the work that is her legacy.

We also thank Tom Lay, whose steadfast support and assistance saw the project through to publication during a time of transition at Fordham. He closely monitored our progress and was instrumental in keeping things on schedule, moving us to press in an expeditious manner. We are grateful to the rest of the team at Fordham, especially Jack Caputo, editor of the Perspectives in Continental Philosophy series, who has been a stalwart champion of this collection; Eric Newman, Managing Editor of the Press; and Adaobi Obi Tulton, whose copy editing helped to polish the manuscript.

Gitty Amini, Donald Boyce, and Murray Littlejohn all helped in the proofreading and editing of certain chapters. Their diligence and care helped us to eliminate a number of errors in early drafts of the text.

We are especially grateful to the skilled translators whose work allowed us to bring a number of these essays to an English-speaking audience: Carlie Anglemire, Anne Davenport, Scott Davidson, Christina M. Gschwandtner, Anne Bernard Kearney, Simone Kearney, Roxanne Lapidus, and Anne Marsella. Scott Davidson and Christina M. Gschwandtner deserve special recognition for the philosophical expertise they contributed to the project, and the speed with which they responded to numerous requests for clarification.

Finally, we are grateful for permission to include the following edited or modified essays and extracts in this collection: the section on "Motion and Emotion" in Jean-Luc Nancy's "Rethinking Corpus" is taken from the journal *SubStance* 126, vol. 40, no. 3, 2011; Jean-Luc Marion's "On the Phenomena of Suffering" is excerpted from "The Invisible and the Phenomenon" in *Michel Henry: The Affects of Thought*, edited by Jeffrey Hanson and Michael R. Kelly (London: Continuum, 2012); Jean-Louis Chrétien's "From the Limbs of the Heart to the Soul's Organs" first appeared in *Symbolique du Corps* (Paris: Presses Universitaires De France, 2005); Michel Henry's "Incarnation and the Problem of Touch" is excerpted from *De la phénoménologie* (Paris: Presses Universitaires De France, 2003); Julia Kristeva's "The Passion According to St. Teresa" is a modified version of "Saint Teresa of Avila," which was published in *Saints: Faith without Borders* (Chicago: University of Chicago Press, 2011); and, finally, Paul Ricoeur's "Memory, History, Oblivion," which appears here with the permission of the *Fonds Ricoeur*, was delivered as a lecture in Budapest on March 8, 2003.

We would like to add a special word of thanks to the artist Sheila Gallagher for the cover image, photographed by Matthew Littell.

Introduction

Carnal Hermeneutics from Head to Foot

RICHARD KEARNEY
AND BRIAN TREANOR

The essays collected in this volume all address, in one way or another, the theme of carnal hermeneutics—that is to say, the surplus of meaning arising from our carnal embodiment, its role in our experience and understanding, and its engagement with the wider world. The voices represented here are diverse, each contributing to the view that the work of Hermes goes all the way down, from the event horizon of consciousness to the most sensible embodied experiences of our world.

Why Carnal Hermeneutics?

In the first section, *Why Carnal Hermeneutics?*, we show why our project of carnal hermeneutics is central to hermeneutics more broadly conceived, and to explain in some detail why this focus is necessary, productive, and timely.

Carnal hermeneutics, as the opening essay indicates, offers a philosophical approach to the body as interpretation. How do we make sense of bodies with our bodies? How do we read between the lines of flesh and skin? Building on previous hermeneutic models—the "as-structure" of existential understanding in Heidegger, the dialogical play of questioning in Gadamer, the semantic surplus of meaning in Ricoeur—we try to show how the new "carnal" turn in hermeneutics ranges across a wide spectrum of interpretation, from head to toe, from sky to earth, from the most sacred and sublime to the most tactile and terrestrial. What we propose to develop from previous hermeneutic projects are the following basic principles: (1) human existence requires an art of understanding as well as a science of explanation, (2) our understanding involves a finite, spatiotemporal being-in-the-world, (3) our finite experience calls for a phenomenological appreciation of meaning as a projection of possibility and reception of reality, (4) this meaning involves "sense" mediations in a wide arc of signifying ranging from the proto-linguistic domain of corporeal sensation and orientation to the most advanced forms of linguistic articulation, (5) this extended hermeneutic arc transcends the traditional dualism between rational understanding and embodied sensibility, and reverses the prejudicial hierarchy of the senses where sight and hearing trump taste and touch, (6) this reversal—or more accurately redistribution—of our bodily senses enables us to see how the most carnal of our sensations are *already* interpretations: a question of tact and tang (from the same root, *tangere-tactum*); and, finally, (7) this equiprimordial redistribution of the senses invites hermeneutics to go "all the way down," abandoning residual tendencies to oppose language to sensibility, word to flesh, text to body.

Once we follow the hermeneutic ladder all the way from head to foot we find that text is body and body is text. If there is nothing outside of the text it is because there is nothing outside of the flesh. Word *is* flesh. This is the basic lesson of carnal hermeneutics: all experience, from birth to death, is mediated by our embodiment and only makes sense of sense accordingly.

By way of illustrating and substantiating these core principles of carnal hermeneutics,[1] the opening essay charts a hermeneutic genealogy of touch, from Aristotle's discovery of flesh (*sarx*) as "medium" (*metaxu*) to the revolutionary analyses of embodiment in the more contemporary works of Husserl, Merleau-Ponty and Ricoeur. One of its main aims is to show how savvy is as much about savor as *savoir* (from *sapere*, to taste), which means amplifying and deepening hermeneutics to embrace sensory orientation as much as intellectual understanding.

In the second essay, "Mind the Gap: The Challenge of Matter," we suggest that hermeneutics must undertake a Ricoeurian "detour" through carnality in a wide variety of applications, including new philosophical realisms and materialisms and the work of the "hard" sciences from which they often hail. Such a detour is especially important when taking up issues like the environment, neuroscience, health, and more general questions of matter. This means that hermeneutics must be willing to engage modes of thinking that see carnal embodiment as hard, material reality in addition to those that see it as cipher or symbol. Far from attempting to "objectivize" hermeneutics or "subjectivize" science, the essay argues we should take seriously the possibilities inherent in Ricoeur's dictum that "to explain more is to understand better." To this end, we engage with some contemporary approaches in which this might occur, including Michel Serres's recent reflections on the "hard" and the "soft" of reality. We propose that preliminary gestures in this direction can be found in carnal hermeneutics understood in the broad sense of a reengagement with both our human senses (the medium of lived flesh) and the "flesh of the world" (which calls for a new environmental hermeneutics based on eco-phenomenology and extending to nonhuman forms of life).

These two opening essays, which constitute the first section of the book, are intended to serve as overall genealogies and topologies of our two guiding terms—carnal and hermeneutics—and set out some common coordinates for the essays that follow.

Rethinking the Flesh

The next section of the book showcases some major contemporary voices in our conversation: Jean-Luc Nancy, Jean-Louis Chrétien, Julia Kristeva, Michel Henry, Jean-Luc Marion, and Paul Ricoeur.

Jean-Luc Nancy opens this section with an intriguing reflection on what he calls "essential skin." Nancy addresses issues of touch in relation to life and death, taboo and zone. He shows how skin is where inside and outside are related and distinguished. It is where the in-itself finds itself outside of itself in order to be a self. Nancy explores how different languages signify the enigma of skin, exposing the roots of flesh in multiple etymologies besides his native French—Greek and Hebrew, Latin and English—yielding everyday poetries of flowering and fruition, sounding and stitching. In a particularly evocative passage on the caress (echoing several other essays in the volume), Nancy shows how in such moments of intimacy, the body moves beyond functionality, perception, and action—and in so doing, scatters seeds of carnal signification: "Sign, signal, omen, or promise, the skin assures us it will never stop stretching out, being offered, and deepening. It promises that the body is entirely there within it, that it is the body itself and consequently that it is its soul."

In a companion piece on bodily movement, Nancy goes on to offer a detailed investigation of the intimate liaison between carnal motion and emotion, exploring the rich semantic play between the terms *rühren*, *berühren*, and *Aufruhr*. Touching, he says, sets something in motion—displacement, action, and reaction. It begins "when two bodies move apart and distinguish themselves," as in birth. Touch is the first *rühren*, but only comes to fullness with separation/birth—only a separated body is capable of touching. Leaving the un- (or under-) differentiated environment of the fetal-body-in-the-womb, the separation of birth opens us to touch, to contact, to the world, to relationship. This separation is a prerequisite for passion, the essence of which is to touch, contact from the outside. On this reading we are not "in contact"; we are contact itself. My entire being touches and is touched. Thus, being is not separate from relationship and "what we currently call the 'soul' is not different from arousal and receptiveness to motion and emotion. The soul is the body that is touched."

Jean-Louis Chrétien's "From the Limbs of the Heart to the Soul's Organs," provides a hermeneutic retrieval of the carnal language of the *Song of Songs*—a language that gives us a voice to probe regions of experience that would be voiceless without it. Following some of the great classical and medieval commentaries of the *Song*—Origen, St. Augustine, Gregory the Great, and others—Chrétien maps the homonymous isomorphism of the "inner and outer man" by describing the various accounts of eyes, ears, hands, neck, and other bodily "parts" of the heart. As translator Anne Davenport notes, the "body is the word-bearer through which meaning reaches us and in which every possible call is answered"; but we can lose sight of this eloquence when we isolate the body and fail to appreciate it as incarnation of the word.[2] Chrétien's analysis of the encounter with ultimate love in the *Song of Songs* suggests new hermeneutic possibilities for thinking embodiment and spirituality.

Julia Kristeva takes the hermeneutics of the body in a distinctly humanist direction in "A Tragedy and a Dream: Disability Revisited." Here she argues that disability, despite its obvious tragic dimensions, has the power to move us toward a "new humanism," offering itself as a challenge and a complement to the Greco-Christian "ontology of privation" or "poverty"—a standard ontology which can give rise to acts of charity, but which risks turning disabled persons into *objects* of care. Kristeva argues that insofar as disability (physical or mental) reveals the incommensurable singularity (*haecceitas*) of each person—both those with *and* those without disability—it harbors the possibility of restructuring the social bond. Disability is the "difference" that most radically confronts us with mortality and the finite limitations of all incarnate life, and that challenges us with a new "Scotist ethics" of the singular.

Michel Henry's contribution, "Incarnation and the Problem of Touch," directs us to the "phenomenological foundation" of incarnation—the condition of possessing flesh. Phenomenologically, the body can appear in the mode of the world, as an object external to us. But in the mode of "life" phenomenalization is different; here the old opposition between appearing and what allows it to appear breaks down in terms of what Henry calls "revelation." There is no longer separation, no "outside of oneself":

"the revelation of life and what it reveals are one and the same." Flesh is the proper name for this unity and its auto-revelation. Arguing that the traditional phenomenology of the body always presupposes a second transcendental and constituting body—leading to impassible aporias—Henry proposes that we reverse this tradition so that the "original" body is not the mundane body in the world but rather the flesh and its "auto-impressionality." The "arrival in a flesh" is the truer and more radical meaning of incarnation that illuminates our human condition and the archipassibility of life itself. Though Henry himself does not explicitly avow the rich hermeneutic implications of his reading of life (e.g., as a hermeneutic retrieval of Husserl's phenomenology of the lived body and the Christian revelation of flesh), they are strongly present. And a similar point applies to Jean-Luc Marion's subtle reading of incarnation and suffering in the wake of Henry's work—offered here as "On the Phenomena of Suffering"—an interpretation which he explores in his more developed analyses of "flesh" in *Being Given* and *The Erotic Phenomenon*.

In the last essay of the second section, "Memory, History, Oblivion," (published here in English for the first time), Paul Ricoeur picks up the question of lived suffering in relation to history, memory, and history-writing. Although he does not address the question of carnal hermeneutics per se, this late text points toward one of the reasons why such a "carnal turn" is necessary: namely, to address the persistence of what Ricoeur calls "the wounds left by history" and the consequent "call to justice owed to the victims of history." It is interesting to note that Ricoeur wrote this text to highlight the particularity of suffering touched on in his last major work, *History, Memory, Forgetting*. Under a variation of this title, Ricoeur stresses here the moral imperative to reconnect hermeneutic remembering to the concrete "acting and suffering" of living beings. In preparing this paper, he reviewed numerous Holocaust testimonies (including films like *Schindler's List* and *Shoah*). This essay may be read, accordingly, as a call for a new hermeneutics of the suffering body, in continuation with his hermeneutic retrieval of flesh as "other" in study 10 of *Oneself as Another* (discussed in our opening essay). We might also note here that "the wound of history" is an example of a broader concern with suffering bodies shared by other hermeneutic reflections in this volume—we are thinking not only of Julia Kristeva's essay on disability but also of Shelly Rambo's analysis of the scars of trauma, Ed Casey's meditation on the pain of incarcerated bodies, and Anne O'Byrne's essay on the umbilicus. These recurring references to wounding represent an important bridge between standard hermeneutic concerns with writing and reading (texts, narratives, testimonies) and the more carnal significations of the lived body (marked with traces, traumas, scars).

Matters of Touch

The third part of our volume comprises essays by leading contemporary continental philosophers—from both Europe and America—who explore a hermeneutics of body and touch in pioneering and original ways.

In "Skin Deep: Bodies Edging into Place," Ed Casey offers an engaging account of the complex liaisons between body and place. Beginning with a harrowing account of the body in solitary confinement, he proceeds to discuss the notion of "edge" and "skin" in terms of intervals and boundaries. Ranging through a compelling list of descriptions—from prison cells and MRI tubes to living rooms, porches, yards, and landscapes—Casey shows how the "lived body" is both "absolutely here" and yet always edging into place between oneself and another. Drawing from phenomenologists such as Husserl, Merleau-Ponty and Sartre (with the Bachelard of the *Poetics of Space* never far off), Casey proposes an original hermeneutics of skin as the ultimate edge between body and place. "We take in the world as a series of places felt in and through the skin." For skin is the most intimate medium (*metaxu*) which both separates and connects each one of us with the world.

In "Touched by Touching," David Wood reflects on a variety of "quite ordinary" experiences in the course of plumbing "the creative plurivocity of meaning murmuring within the concepts that most fascinate us." Touch, he thinks, is an exemplary case. Wood considers: the stroking, nuzzling, and licking of feral cats turned semi-domestic mousers; the confusing complexities of eroticism; visual and tactile intimacies in the case of romantic partners; the indirect sexuality of flowers via the work of pollinators; literary accounts by Neruda and Hopkins; and, finally, the unwanted "vampire touch" of leeches. Reflecting on these diverse cases, which extend the carnal to include the non-human worlds of animal and plant, Wood suggests that a very fertile site for carnal hermeneutics is the question of boundaries that is disclosed and traversed—willingly or unwillingly, with joy or anxiety—by touch.

In her "Umbilicus: Toward a Hermeneutics of Generational Difference," Anne O'Byrne proposes a hermeneutic circle marked by the umbilical scar, the navel that marks our belonging to another, as vulnerable, and as generated and generational. The navel as the "circular fold of skin at the center of us . . . the place where the hermeneutic circle makes a Mobius twist and interpretation turns inside out." Philosophical and theological traditions touch on the umbilical scar—from Christian monks at Mount Athos to Aristophanes's circular people, and from Greek religion to psychoanalysis—but none plumb the depths of understanding necessary to account for the umbilical relationship. Why does the maternal body nurture and grow the fetal body rather than attack it as foreign? How does the fetus survive inside an immunologically hostile maternal body? Biology tends to get by as if it were "positing epicycles" and turning a blind eye, but some research suggests a new model of immunology in which the notion of a war between the self and all intruders (nonself) is replaced by a model of permeable communities that permit immigrants unless and until they present a danger. The fetus does not cause an immune response because it causes no immunological damage. O'Byrne's umbilical hermeneutics directs us to questions of generational and sexual difference, and asks us to consider *sense* rather than *meaning* as the goal of hermeneutics. Such extended consideration has, needless to say, evident political and social implications for our contemporary world. Which reminds us here, as in other essays, that carnal hermeneutics often calls for an *applied* hermeneutics of lived suffering and action.

In "Getting in Touch: Aristotelian Diagnostics," Emmanuel Alloa brings us back to the beginning of hermeneutics. He argues that while hermeneutics as an art of textual interpretation was born in Late Antiquity in Alexandria, there is a pre- or even non-textual art of distinguishing which has to do with sensible diagnostics. Alloa provides a rich, scholarly overview of this non-textual tradition of *diakrisis* within the Greek world, especially in the medical tradition, and underlines the importance attributed to the different sense organs. In tune with our opening essay and other contributions to this volume, Alloa's account confirms that touch has a peculiar position among the senses, being considered the "lowest" and at the same time the most universal: all senses "touch" their objects. With this thesis in mind, Alloa offers a close reading of Aristotle's *De anima*, showing how it provides both a rehabilitation of touch as a crucial sense for orientation in the world and a strong rebuttal of reductionist readings of touch as immediate. Demonstrating how flesh is not the organ of touch but its medium, Aristotle inaugurated a whole new theory of sensorial diagnostics.

In "Between Vision and Touch: From Husserl to Merleau-Ponty," Dermot Moran explains how Merleau-Ponty reinterprets and transforms the account of "double sensation" (*Doppelempfindung*) discussed by Husserl (and other contributors to this volume). Husserl claims that double sensation is characteristic only of touch, and that this indicates a certain priority of touch over the other senses in the composition of the living organic body (*Leib*). However, Merleau-Ponty argues that the reversibility of sensation is characteristic of all five senses, and that it prefigures and founds the reflexivity of thought. Moreover, this intertwining—which goes by various terms in Merleau-Ponty's work: the chiasm, interlacing, or inversion of the flesh—has *ontological* import. It expresses "the ambiguous character of human embodied being-in-the-world," which is the subject of his late work on *la chair*. Moran carefully charts this key development in the philosophy of sensation, showing how Merleau-Ponty's account of intertwining grows from and significantly develops Husserl's own account.

In the final essay of this section, "Biodiversity and the Diacritics of Life," Ted Toadvine takes up the meaning and value of the much-heralded notion of "biodiversity." Although this term is ubiquitous in both academic (scientific, economic, philosophical) and popular discourse, it is far from clear that it has real empirical or ethical value. Building on Kearney's diacritical hermeneutics, as well as on Merleau-Ponty and his readings of Saussure and Valéry, Toadvine suggests a form of "biodiacritics." He argues that the diacritical perspective captures an insight into the experience of life as difference while preserving our sense of life as unity, and he does so in a way that helps us to explore sense "beyond or beneath apparent sense." The pre-theoretical sense of life that precedes any biological investigation of living things is, Toadvine insists, diacritical: it mirrors the coexistence of unity and difference. On this view, the unity of the different nodes of life is in the intervals and gaps that constitute them; each one "implies the whole and therefore hangs together with the whole insofar as its own identity is the determinate negation of every other moment within the whole." While biodiversity measures a kind of difference, it misses the "intervals, deferrals, and gaps" to which biodiacritics is attentive. Each form of life, each being, is a unique set of historical legacies. And, as Toadvine notes, "it is precisely insofar as life . . . institutes an evolving history or even a figured memory . . . that it commands our respect and hospitality." This essay—along with frequent other references in this volume to matter, earth, animals, sacred bodies, and the environment—suggests how important it is to keep carnal hermeneutics open to extra-human forms of life.

Divine Bodies

The final section, *Divine Bodies*, helps illustrate how carnal hermeneutics can extend to the fullest range of meaning while keeping sight of our inescapably carnal nature. Hermeneutics, including carnal hermeneutics, navigates both the sacred and the terrestrial, ranging up and down, translating messages from "above" and from "below."

In "The Passion According to Teresa of Avila," Julia Kristeva deploys a psychoanalytic hermeneutic to interpret the life of a great woman visionary. She enumerates three characteristics of Christian life highlighted by its mystics: the Ideal Father who, loved, is the foundation of the subject;

the resexualization of this ideal by the mystic (*père-version*); and the oral gratification of the Eucharist that reconciles the believer with the beaten Father. Teresa is offered as an archetypal example of such mystical hermeneutics. In her "incarnated fantasies" the ideal father who persecutes her is transformed into a loving father, "*jouissance* and extreme pain, always the two together or alternating." These raptures are expressed in a unique narrative. Teresa loses her identity, becoming a "psyche-soma" below the threshold of consciousness. Her visions inhabit the entire body and mind, including the philosophically underappreciated senses of touch and taste. They are part of what Kristeva calls the "*sensitive* imaginary" in which water signifies the link between the soul and the divine. The body is earth, which becomes garden at the touch of water. And the divine is brought down from its supersensitive status to become an element that nourishes and touches. Touch—psychosomatic contact—is the mode in which Teresa appropriates the Other. Transcendence turns out to be immanent: the Lord is not above, but within.

In "Refiguring Wounds in the Afterlife (of Trauma)," Shelly Rambo asks the reader to rethink the notion of the "invisible wound" in a manner that would draw on all the senses rather than privileging sight. The double wounding of trauma—the wounding event and its aftermath or scar—is said to result in a wound that does not close; and part of the task of trauma theory and psychoanalysis is to make visible what is invisible in the process of healing. Wounds, of course, are central to the Christian tradition, but Rambo focuses on the afterlife of wounds, the wounds of resurrection, and thinking these wounds in terms of the figure of the scar. Examining the case of the wound/scar associated with Macrina, sister of Gregory of Nyssa, Rambo notes the aporias associated with traditional visual readings of the scar, which she resolves via a multisensory, carnal reading. Macrina's story also complicates the gendered politics of trauma and recognition— insofar as Gregory is displaced by the mother-daughter-maidservants relationships—in a way that reads scars not as a reinscription of wounding, but as a mark of the "complex textures of life." Finally, the story rereads traditional accounts of resurrection by emphasizing the healing aspects of touch. Rambo thus performs a hermeneutic retelling of a story of wounds which is itself a retelling of the Christian story.

In "This Is My Body" Emmanuel Falque considers key elements of the Eucharist—Christ as the "lamb" on the altar, the Eucharist as the "body" of Christ, and what it means to "eat" that body. The "real presence" of Christ in the Eucharistic meal has always been controversial; and understanding it strains the limits of phenomenology: the phenomenological excess of "sense over non-sense"; the increase of "flesh over body"; and the "weakness in the forgetting of force." As translator Christina Gschwandtner notes, Falque's work criticizes the phenomenological distinction between *Leib* and *Körper* for reinscribing a body/soul dualism that downplays the "animality" of our flesh: "[Falque] seeks to recover the 'organicity' of the body (in its concrete 'flesh and bones') and to take full account of its animal nature (the chaos or 'abyss' of our passions, drives and impulses)."[3] Here Falque reads the viaticum as joining in the union of bodies in Eucharistic communion, and concludes with an account of "abiding" in which the real presence is linked to desire. Neither fleeing from humanity, nor falling below its limit, Eucharistic enthusiasm animates the act of communion in the sense that the communicant is "fully incorporated into God" such that his or her animality, corporeality, and desire are made meaningful and converted.

Karmen MacKendrick's "Original Breath" challenges the traditional non-carnal readings of "speaking" in the Genesis creation account: creation *ex nihilo*, God beyond space and time, humans as absolutely distinct from animals, and so on. In MacKendrick's hermeneutic retrieval of this text, God's calling the world into existence takes place in the presence of a "there is" already in creation—formless matter that responds to God's call, the *ruach elohim* (mighty wind, breath). Here "breath is given form by matter and matter its meaning by breath." The chapter follows the Genesis creation narrative, tracing the manner in which the breath of God breathes life into humans and animates animals, challenging us to think of meaning in matter. MacKendrick analyzes the naming of the animals by Adam, questioning the assumption that this task confers some form of absolute dominance, and suggesting that this call must await a response, nonlinguistic but carnally meaningful, from the creature named. Her account offers a richer option for human-animal interaction and relationship, one that, without conflating the human and animal, thinks in terms of a "divine animality" and a "continuous carnal creation."

Rounding out the collection, John Panteleimon Manoussakis's "On the Flesh of the Word: Incarnational Hermeneutics," reflects on the claim by which "Christianity stands or falls": the Word became Flesh. He suggests that a long history of misreading and misappropriation has caused us to think in terms of spiritualizing the flesh rather than incarnating the spirit. Hermeneutics has forgotten the command "take, eat, this is my body" in favor of a textual rumination that results in regurgitation rather than digestion and sustenance. This is reflected in the marginalization of the Eucharist. Manoussakis offers a detailed and original reading of St. Augustine's *Confessions* as an exemplary text of carnal hermeneutics in which he finds a "conversion of the flesh" alongside the more familiar episodes of the "conversion of the mind" and "conversion of the heart." This third conversion is evident in Augustine's reversal of the traditional hierarchy of the senses by giving primacy to touch, in his use of the parable of the prodigal son to emphasize the flesh, and in his extended use of language associated with hunger, eating, and feasting.

The essays of this volume are not conclusions but rather openings to further dialogue and debate. They are signposts of things to come in the ongoing conversation of carnal hermeneutics. This conversation is, we suggest, marked by certain challenging characteristics. First, a radical commitment to interdisciplinary work, opening philosophical hermeneutics to fruitful exchanges with other human sciences such as linguistics, anthropology, theology, poetics, psychoanalysis, and politics. One of the greatest challenges for hermeneutics in the twenty-first century, as Ricoeur has said, is dialogue with the sciences. And for us today this also means expanding the hermeneutic circle—often texts talking to texts—to engage "harder" disciplines such as cognitive science, neuroscience, computer science, and other environmental and life sciences. It is at the limit of phenomenological hermeneutics that we shall find both the task and test of its future. This volume presents itself accordingly as a series of invitations to think "at the edge." And these, taken collectively, suggest a further challenge of carnal hermeneutics: namely, to rethink, in a new key, the enigma of flesh that has so baffled philosophers for centuries and, above all, to realize that flesh can no longer be confined to a phenomenological account of the human body but must also be recognized as a membrane or medium connecting us to "the flesh of the world." Flesh is precisely "the edge" where the human meets worlds that exceed and entreat it—animal and environmental, sacred and profane. It is the site of endless transmissions between selves and strangers where "surplus meaning" comes to remind us that we can never be sufficient to ourselves. This surplus may be of the order of joy (viz. the reflections in this volume on eros, creation, life, and caress) or of the order of suffering (viz the essays on pain, trauma, tragedy, and violence); but both orders serve to instruct us that there is more to flesh than meets the eye—or even the tips of our fingers and tongues. Flesh raises more questions than answers. And that is why this volume is no more than a beginning—a promissory note of work to come.

Why Carnal Hermeneutics?

The Wager of Carnal Hermeneutics

RICHARD KEARNEY

Part One: Making Sense of Sense

What is the sense of sense? How do we read between the lines of skin and
flesh? How do we interpret the world with our bodily senses, and especially
those long neglected in Western philosophy—taste and touch? How, in
other words, do we discern the world *as* this or that, *as* hospitable or hostile, *as* attractive or repulsive, *as* tasty or tasteless, *as* living or dying? These
are key questions of carnal hermeneutics.

A Matter of Taste and Touch

From the moment we are born we live in the flesh. Infant skin responds to
the touch of the mother, hands and feet unfurling, mouth opening for first
milk. Before words, we are flesh, flesh becoming words for the rest of our
lives. Matter, no less than form, is about what matters—to us, to others and
to the world in which we breathe and have our being. The old dichotomies
between "empirical" and "transcendental," "materialism" and "idealism,"
are ultimately ruinous. Life is hermeneutic through and through. It goes all
the way up and all the way down. From head to foot and back again.

Let me explain. I speak of sense in three senses. First, there is sense in
the common connotation of physical *sensation*: sight, sound, smell, taste,
and touch (as in: I have a strong sensation that . . .). Second, there is sense
in the equally habitual connotation of *meaning* (as in: I get the sense of

what you mean). And, third, we have sense in the original etymological connotation of *direction*—as in so many Romance languages, *sensus, senso, sens*—referring to how we orient ourselves in space and time, how we move towards or away from, fore or aft, hither or tither (as in: *Je vais dans ce sens, à gauche plutôt qu'à droite*). These three connotations of sense—as (1) sensation, (2) meaning, and (3) orientation—signify how we make sense of our life in the flesh.

Central to the interpretation of embodied life is evaluation. The ancient term for wisdom, *sapientia*, comes from *sapere*, to taste. *Sapere-savourer-savoir*. This etymological line speaks legions, reminding us that our deepest knowing is tasting and touching. We first sound the world through the tips of our tongues. Discerning between hot and cold, savory and unsavory, course and smooth. Living well is a matter of "savvy," as we say. Ordinary language knows this, and philosophical language is no more than an extrapolation of what we already know "deep down." Wisdom, in the end, is tact. That is what we mean, isn't it, when we say that someone *sensible* is someone *sensitive*: they have "the touch," as healer, teacher, artist, lover. Just as, by extension, they have the eye, the ear, the nose. They are attentive, tentative, in touch with things. They get it. To have the right touch is to touch and be touched wisely. Touching well is living well. Hermeneutics begins there: in the flesh. And it goes all the way down, from head to foot.

Between Phenomenology and Hermeneutics

Contemporary continental philosophy has done much to address this question. But it has sometimes suffered from a tension between two related tendencies—phenomenology and hermeneutics. Phenomenology has done extraordinary work in rehabilitating the body. Think of Husserl's analysis of *Leib* as intentionality, as active and passive synthesis, as primal and secondary sensibility (*Ideas II*). Think of Sartre's brilliant descriptions of the body as caress, desire and possession in *Being and Nothingness*; of Merleau-Ponty's soundings of the body-subject in its sexual being in *The Phenomenology of Perception*; of Levinas's descriptions of eros, sensibility and enjoyment in *Totality and Infinity*; or of Irigaray's pioneering explorations of eros as birth, touch, and taste in *An Ethics of Sexual Difference*.

These phenomenological inquiries opened new doors to a hermeneutics of flesh. And yet when the explicit "hermeneutic turn" occurred in the 1960s—with the publication of Ricoeur's *Conflict of Interpretations* and Gadamer's *Truth and Method* (inspired by Heidegger and Dilthey)—we witnessed an embrace of language at the expense of body. The journey from flesh to text often forgot a return ticket. And so we find the "linguistic turn" of hermeneutics parting from the carnal as a site of meaning, replacing body with book, feeling with reading, sensing with writing. As if the two could be separated. Already in Heidegger's ontological hermeneutics, Dasein was stripped of its sexed, incarnate skin in the name of a quasi-transcendental discourse (*Rede*). Language as the "destiny of Being" came to overshadow the embodied life of singular beings (relegated to the status of "ontic" particulars). The temporality of understanding trumped the spatiality of flesh. And a subsequent veering from carnal experience was witnessed in the hermeneutic orientations of Gadamer and Ricoeur. A veering accentuated as hermeneutics increasingly engaged with structural linguistics and deconstruction. Textuality swallowed the body and turned it into *écriture*. But this did not mean that mainstream hermeneutics ceased to be phenomenological: Heidegger, Gadamer and Ricoeur constantly reminded us that what they were doing was "hermeneutic phenomenology." Granted. Yet there is no denying that the linguistic *turn to the text* was often construed as a *turning away from the flesh*—in practice if not in principle. And one of the main purposes of this volume is to suggest ways of undertaking a return journey. Ways which might help us recover the body as text and the text as body: to restore hermeneutics to phenomenology and vice versa, making explicit what was implicit all along. A step back to step forward.

What we are proposing therefore—at a moment when questions of matter, flesh, and body call out for new thinking—is to revisit the deep and inextricable relationship between *sensation* and *interpretation*. To show how both are, as Aristotle once noted, modes of hermeneutic "mediation" (*metaxu*). Our wager in this volume is that such a move may help us better understand how we are constantly *reading* flesh, *interpreting* senses, and *orienting* bodies in passion and place even as we symbolize and dream. This is the task of carnal hermeneutics.

Discerning among Strangers

So we are concerned with a hermeneutics that goes all the way down. A mode of understanding that helps us "diacritically" discern between diverse kinds of embodied beings. Reading between gaps. Discriminating and differentiating between selves and others—and others in ourselves. Such carnal hermeneutics has a crucial bearing, to cite an example we explored elsewhere, on how we "sense" subtle distinctions between strangers who surprise us (the same term, *hostis* can mean guest or enemy).[1] The first act of civilization is wagering on whether to open the hand or reach for a weapon. Hostility or hospitality is at stake from the outset. What do we make of strangers that arrive out of the blue, walk in from the desert, and knock at our door in the middle of the night? And in this regard, carnal hermeneutics may be said to have two patron saints—the god Hermes and the dog Argos. For if Hermes, messenger of the gods, discloses hermetic cyphers from above, Argos brings animal savvy from below. The former, masked as a migrant, revealed himself to Baucis and Philomen as, arriving from nowhere, he "tasted" their gift of food. The latter, Argos, deployed canine flair in recognizing his master, Odysseus, when he returned to Ithaca disguised as a beggar.[2] In both cases we witness fundamental forms of "tact" in the discerning of strangers; and find a reminder that we often need animal or divine messengers to get us back in touch with ourselves.

What is true of Greek wisdom is equally true of biblical and other cultures. The inaugural act of Abrahamic discernment is, let us not forget, a scene of "tasting" where Abraham and Sarah greet strangers from the desert at Mamre who—in sharing food—reveal themselves as divine and announce an impossible child, Isaac. The subsequent revelation of the name of Israel is through a mutual "touching" of limbs between Yawveh and Jacob (the famous wrestling with the angel). And as John Panteleimon Manoussakis notes in this volume, Jesus came to earth to do two things: to taste and to touch. Both acts of carnal hermeneutics take place at the Last Supper and Emmaus; but they are already in evidence in multiple healings and epiphanies throughout the Gospels (the pasting of mud and saliva on the eyes of the blind man, the bleeding woman touching Jesus's hem, Thomas touching Jesus's wound, the washing of feet at the last supper).[3] And this tradition of transformation through touch and taste—epitomized in hospitality of food and wine—continues down through western literature and art, inspiring such classic scenes as Monseigneur Myriel sharing his best cuisine with Jean Valjean in *Les Misérables* and the miraculous metamorphosis of bodies and minds in Karen Blixen's *Babette's Feast*.

Nor should we forget the rich testimony of non-Western traditions in this regard. Let us recall, for example, how one of the most revered forms of address for Brahman, in the Vedantin tradition, was *Anna* (food). And how the Buddha, when challenged by Mara to reveal by what authority he spoke of suffering, simply touched the ground. His finger touched earth and he felt the sensation of breath. Enlightenment followed.[4]

In short, carnal hermeneutics covers a wide spectrum of sense, both sacred and profane, as it ranges up and down—in ascending and descending spirals—from the most elevated cyphers of the divine to the lowest probings of tooth and claw. From Gods to dogs and back again. While hands reach up, feet reach down. But the point is that no matter how high or low experience goes, it still *makes sense*. Flesh sounds, filters, scents. Between the extremes of hyper rationalism at one end, and blind irrationalism at the other, we find the all too human path of carnal hermeneutics. A middle way. A road less traveled philosophically to be sure. But one that needs to be taken again and again.

It is a journey for which, fortunately, we have wise guides—as we hope to show in what follows in this essay, and in the other essays of this volume.

The First Breakthrough: Aristotle on Flesh as Medium

The philosophical discovery of carnal hermeneutics did not have to wait for the twentieth century. There were significant early intimations, starting with Aristotle. In the second book of the *De Anima*, Aristotle already acknowledged the enigmatic role of touch in his analysis of the five senses. It is a notoriously difficult and dense passage, but its implications are revolutionary—if largely overlooked for two thousand years. I offer some preliminary reflections on this text here before going on in "Enigmas of Flesh" (in the following section) to chart a summary hermeneutics of flesh from Husserl to Ricoeur. My aim throughout is to show how carnal phenomenology is intimately and ultimately carnal hermeneutics.

In the concluding sections of *De Anima*, Book II, Aristotle makes the bold claim that touch is a discriminating sense.[5] Against the common view that touch and taste are the lowest sensations—because unmediated—he responds that these traditionally underestimated senses have their own indispensable form of "mediation." With respect to touch, flesh (*sarx*) is the medium (*metaxu*) which gives us space to discern between different kinds of experience—hot and cold, soft and hard, attractive and unattractive.[6] Or as Aristotle puts it, "touch has many differences."[7] In touch, we are both touching and touched at the same time, but we do not dissolve into sensuous sameness. Proximity is not immediacy. Difference is preserved. "*Flesh is a medium, not an organ.*"[8] And this breakthrough insight means that flesh always harbors a certain distance or interval through which touch navigates. Touch is not fusion but mediation through flesh.

Unlike Plato, who denigrated touch and taste as unmediated senses, helpless before the flux of things, and contrary to materialists who claimed touch brings us into immediate contact with material stuff, Aristotle insists on the mediating character of tactility. To be tactile is to be exposed to otherness across gaps, to negotiate sensitively *between* other embodied beings, to respond to solicitations, to orient oneself. From the beginning, contact always involves an element of tact.

Aristotle places human perfection in the perfection of touch. Why? Because without touch there is no life. All living beings possess touch; which is why it is the most *universal* of the senses.[9] And precisely as the most basic and encompassing of sensations, it expresses the general "sensitivity" of flesh. But the most basic here does not mean the most transparent. In fact, touch turns out to be the most complex and elusive sense (which is perhaps why Aristotle places it at the end of his analysis of the senses in *De Anima*, Book II rather than at the beginning where one might expect to find it). Touch covers up its own medium and it is nigh impossible, admits Aristotle, to actually locate the organ of touch. Touch is "present throughout the flesh without any immediately assignable organ."[10]

But if touch is enigmatic, it is also keenly intelligent. For it is the sense which makes us most "sensitive" to the world and to others, bringing us into contact with things greater than ourselves and thus putting us in question. To learn to touch well is to learn to live well, that is, *tactfully*. "The being to whom logos has been given as his share is a tactile being, endowed with the finest tact."[11] And this is not just in the realm of the tangible, but potentially in all matters of seeing, hearing, tasting, and smelling. For touch crosses all the senses. Its universal presence throughout our entire corporeal experience is what keeps us perpetually in touch with things refusing to allow any sensation to withdraw into itself or close itself off from others. Touch keeps us open to the world—even in sleep (where bodies still breathe and respond to noise or temperature)! Like Hermes it is forever moving and messaging between inside and outside, self and other, human and more than human. Tactility is a medium of transition and transmission. It is always "on."

Let us try to unpack some of these inaugural claims. While I may seem to be immediately present to what I touch and to be immediately touched by what I touch—unlike sight, where I am not necessarily seen by what I see, or hearing, where I am not necessarily heard by what I hear, etc.— there is always something mediate in the ostensibly immediate, something "far" in the "near." In other words, there is *sensing* in sense, a *making* sense and *receiving* sense from someone or something other than myself. Flesh mediates this otherness, crossing back and forth between self and strangeness. And this is where hermeneutics begins. What Heidegger calls the "hermeneutic as-structure" is already operative in our most basic sensations. For since all the senses, as noted, involve touch, and since touch involves mediation, all our sensations involve *interpretation* (albeit in the primal sense of orientation prior to theoretical understanding).[12] This is so even when such omnipresent tactile hermeneutics hides itself, functioning as a carnal medium we see through (*diaphanein*) but do not see. Flesh mediates unbeknownst to us, remaining for Aristotle an enigma describable only in images—e.g., watery membrane, air envelope, slim veil, or second skin. When we try to grasp the medium of touch we find only metaphors in our hands. Flesh is figural from first to last. Literal is figurative. In touching the world we are constantly prefiguring, refiguring, and configuring our experience.

But if touch is something we do to the world, it is also something the world does to us. It works both ways. Touch is what first *affects* us, and does so in the most concrete, singular ways. From the beginning, flesh is charged with issues of attraction and retraction. When the child moves to the touch of its mother or opens its mouth to feed from the breast it is already orienting and interpreting. It is not merely reacting to a stimulus but responding to a call. In the natal contact of flesh on flesh, there are already tiny seizures and exposures of joy and fear, desire and anxiety. With the separation of birth, the mouth ceases to be a buccal cavity and becomes an oral medium.[13] The first cry is a call responding to a call. Or summoning a response. A reaching across distance, a leap over a gap or caesura between self and other. So the first touch is not neutral but already a reading between the lines—of skin and bone, of soft and hard, of hot and cold, of far and near. Or to anticipate the terms of modern phenomenology, we might say that flesh is not a thing—qua object or organ—but a no-thing (like Heidegger's Dasein or Sartre's for-itself) which makes sense of things. It involves a highly sensitive carnal *Befindlichkeit* which evaluates and discriminates in the most concrete of situations. Babies are moody little beings, their babblings and strokings already a play of probing and sounding, testing and tasting.[14] Before we ever actually say the words "here" and "there," "*fort*" and "*da*," our fingers and tongues are figuring things out in terms of this and that. "Touching never does away with the interval between us, but turns the interval into an approach."[15] Touch, like its variation, taste, doesn't simply record sensible properties: "it grasps and immediately feels their noxious or useful character, their relevance to the preservation of our being."[16] If we don't know what a thing is, our first impulse is to touch it. That is why Aristotle says touch is "always true."[17]

If touch was often called a "primitive" sense it was not because it was base or crude but because it was primal for life. For tactility is the ability to moderate and modulate the passion of existence, understood etymologically as *pathos/paschein*—suffering, undergoing, receiving, exposure to others who come to us *as* this or that. (This is what Edmund Husserl terms "passive syntheses" and what Christian Wiman calls "passion of pure attention, nerves, readiness.") To touch and be touched simultaneously is to be *connected* with others in a way that enfolds us. Flesh is open-hearted; it is where we experience our greatest vulnerability. The site where we are most keenly attentive to wounds and scars, to preconscious memories and traumas, as even our navel reminds us (see Anne O'Byrne in this volume). With this goes a deep sense of fragility and insecurity. "Without insecurity no sensation" and vice versa.[18] Through flesh—naked and tactile—we are subject to touch, day and night, even in sleep. Exposed on all sides to great risk and great adventure. Keenly sensitive. We can take nothing for granted. We develop savvy. Flesh is a surface that is always deep. And precisely because it mediates between a self carnally located "here" and an other located "there," it is, at bottom, what allows for empathy. Suffering with, *sym-pathein, Ein-fühlung*. The capacity to feel with others in and through distance. As such, touching finds its social beginnings in the handshake: open hand to open hand—the origin of human community.[19] War and peace are skin deep in the profoundest sense.

This question of pathos is crucial for our consideration of carnal hermeneutics. As the "medium" which enables us to feel with others, flesh filters what is strange and alien. As Diderot reminds us in his *Letter to Alembert*, we do not feel what is the *same* as us but only what is *different*: in the case of temperature, for example, we sense what is hotter or colder than our own flesh. While the organ of smell is odorless and the organ of sound soundless, the medium of touch is always tactile. Unlike sight and sound, touch is touched by what it touches, and can even touch itself touching (as Husserl and the phenomenologists explore in great detail). This reversibility means that I can expose myself to "feel what wretches feel," risk being bare-skinned, feeling the other who is making me feel—from outside, from what is not me. And it is this very sensitivity to differences, opposites, alterities which makes up our original hermeneutic sensibility. Namely, the ability to discern and discriminate (*krinein/diakrinein*) through flesh. "Every sense discerns" (*hekaste ge krinei peri touton*), as Aristotle reminds us. "Touch has many differences" (*he d'aphe pleious echei diaphora*").[20] Which means, at its simplest, that it is through the medium of flesh that (1) we have "contact" with external sensibles and (2) we transmit these with "tact" to our inner understanding. But even to speak in terms of inner and outer is already derivative, for flesh is the membrane that both connects and separates. It is what mediates between internal and external, sensing and sensed. Just as it discriminates tactfully, at the level of value, between eros and thanatos, between what brings life and what brings death.

Here we return to the question of *risk*, the hermeneutic wagering of flesh. For without the sensitivity of touch (exposed, naked, fragile), there would be no resourcefulness of taste or tact. Sensitivity *is* sensibility because it provides the basic intelligence of attention, delicacy, vigilance, finesse. That is why, in most wisdom literatures, the smooth-skinned are deemed intelligent while the coarse-skinned are not. Think of Odysseus and the Cyclops, Jacob and Esau, Jesus (who weeps) and Barabbas (who does not). "Man's flesh is the softest of all," notes Aristotle in *De partibus animalium*. And precisely as the most sensitive of animals, man is the "most sensitive to differences"; and therefore presumed to be of superior intelligence to other animals, whose skins are thick, hairy, hard. "Those whose flesh is tender are more gifted intellectually."[21] Perfection of intelligence comes down, in the end, to perfection of touch. What transpires at the tips of fingers and tongues. Hermeneutics is in the first and last instance carnal. Sensibility of taste and touch.

All this is not without aporias and enigmas, however. Recall Aristotle's claim, for instance, that touch is *one* of the five senses and at the same time the condition sine qua non of *all* the senses. It brings us into intimate contact with particular concrete things while remaining a universal sense which traverses the other four. It expresses body and soul at once. The point is simple and profound, and bears repeating: one cannot live without sensing, one cannot exist as soul without flesh, and every sense requires the ability to be touched—whatever the distance—by what one senses (through eye, ear, nose, or tongue). Touch is the heart and soul of the senses, the intersensorial link and milieu which makes all sensible mediation between the outer and inner world possible in the first place. "Since we touch with our whole body, our soul *is* the act of touch, and only as such can it be a hearing soul, a seeing soul and so on."[22] Touch fosters a synesthetic community of sensing. Or as Octavio Paz put it, "I touch you with my eyes / I watch you with my hands / I see with my fingertips what my eyes touch."

There are also, let it be said, ethical evaluations at stake. And further hermeneutic wagers. A refined sensibility of touch makes for a refined sense of goodness. And this is why in the *Nichomachean Ethics* Aristotle speaks of the importance of distinguishing between (1) good touch which differentiates between various kinds of sense, and (2) bad touch which degenerates into coarse undifferentiated behavior (gluttony, loutishness, perversion). Immorality of the senses comes from *contact deprived of tact*: grasping without feeling, consuming without caressing, swallowing without tasting, gorging without gustation. "Self-indulgent people make no use of taste. The role of taste is to discriminate between flavors (*he krisis tou khumon*), which is precisely what wine-tasters do, as well as those that season dishes."[23] Here lies the difference between the gourmand who ingests and the gourmet who relishes. Between the mouth as cavity (*bucca*) and as palate (*os*). It is all a matter of waiting, withholding, savoring, taking in the fullness of the thing sensed with the fullness of the sensing body. Good taste is delicate, discriminating, integral, free. Bad taste is partial, reductive, unmediated, driven.

This is why touch—as the most holistic of senses—is logically the primal mode of sensibility in both life and judgment. A tall order for the body, which is tactile through and through (with the exception of nails and hair). And it is because touch thus belongs to flesh *as a whole* that it is, we repeat, the *sensus universalis*, capable of touching all things through all the senses. While we can close our eyes, ears, nostrils and lips, we are always touching and being touched. To live fully is to be constantly exposed to the elements, to being, to life, to others; it is to be forever attentive and attuned, from head to foot, to pain and pleasure, to happiness and grief, to good and ill. Touch is a "membrane" sensitive to everything that comes and goes. It feels by feeling what is not itself. It is a portal opening onto a world that can never be shut. The first *topos* of our consent to being, our welcome to the other. And it is also, for these very reasons, the first place of pain and pathos. Being in touch with flesh means being at risk. And without risk no life is worth living.

The Greek Legacy of Touch

In making such startling claims, Aristotle was, as mentioned, combating a number of prevailing prejudices. First he was challenging the fallacy of "sensory immediacy" held by the materialists.[24] In explaining how the senses related to things sensed, influential thinkers like Empedocles and Democritus had promoted a mechanist account of matter directly touching the organs. Empedocles spoke of effluvia, Democritus of atomic pellicles. But both of them agreed, and the "physiologists" with them, that there was immediate contact between sense organs and sense objects. They denied the existence of mediation. The Platonic position was a little more nuanced but still denied the role of medium (*metaxu*) to the more carnal senses. In the *Philebus*, for instance, Plato had distinguished between the "noble" mediated senses of sight, hearing, smell, which perceive things at a distance, and the "animal" immediate senses of touch and taste, which do not. The latter sensations, exposed to pressure from the material world, fell victim to the sway of need and necessity. Plato accordingly privileged intellect (*nous*) and understanding (*dianoia*) over the senses and passions; but of all the senses, sight was deemed the most theoretical in that it allowed for the most distance and detachment. Whence arose what Derrida calls the opto-centrism of western metaphysics, presided over by the "soul's eyes."

Aristotle had to overcome such multiple prejudices, in addition to the common view that touch made us prone to licentiousness and bestiality. For, the old argument went, there could be debauchery of touch but not of sight. (You could not be overwhelmed by what you "see" for eyes keep things at a discriminating distance: if you bring an object right up against the eye it blinds it.) After his careful explorations of animals and plants in *De paribus animalium* and of the senses in *De Anima*, Aristotle repudiated this opinion, advancing a new theory of sensibility beyond both the mechanistic accounts of the materialists and the idealist account of Plato and the Academy. He boldly challenged the opinion that divided the senses into those of immediate contact (*haptomenon*), on the one hand, and of mediated distance (*apothen*), on the other, declaring instead that in *all* the senses, including the so-called lowest ones of taste and touch, there is already a *metaxu* at work. Just as light is the medium of sight and air of smell and sound, in taste we have the medium of saliva—if the mouth is too dry or too wet there is no proper gustatory sensation—and in touch we have flesh. In each of the senses, as we noted, "the reality of an intermediary is necessary."[25] And the intermediary always implies an interval or gap—a spacing which mediates between organ and object. In touch it is flesh which allows for both contact and tact, both a sensing from itself and "through another" (*di' heterou*). Flesh is transmission not fusion. The gap makes all the difference, inviting us to differentiate and discriminate. And so Aristotle replaces the common notion of *sensing through distance*—which denigrated the fleshy senses of touch and taste—with *sensing through mediation*.

Aristotle concludes accordingly that "flesh is the medium of touch" (or in Suarez's rendition: *caro non est organum sed medium*).[26] Flesh is not reducible to either the object or organ of tangibility but remains a highly elusive milieu in which the organ of touch and the object touched are proximate but never in direct contact. The carnal medium veils itself as it enables form to pass through matter and both to mingle and commune. *Metaxu*, in other words, serves as a transmitter between (*dia*) sense organs and material objects, allowing the forms to travel to the soul, thereby bringing perceiver and perceived into community (*koinonia*). This, as Emmanuel Alloa aptly reminds us, is the first great discovery of "difference in co-*appartenance*": the birth of a dia-phenomenology which acknowledges that meaning goes all the way down, to the very lowest of our senses.[27] As such, the carnal *metaxu* is both potency (*dunamis*) and act (*energeia*): a potency which can take on the form of anything *other* than itself without being it; and an act which establishes a continuity (*suneches*) across distance and difference.

Metaxu, in sum, is the spacing of the interval which produces community through the differentiation of the milieu. It both unites and separates at once. It does not preexist the operation of mediation—it *is* mediation. It does not exist in a localizable space—it is the operation of spacing itself. As the very power of transiting between same and other, it makes the sensing of differences possible. Flesh, as medium, is both one and many.

In all of this, Hermes hovers. What these initial probings, dating back to the beginning of philosophy, disclose is the existence of meaning and orientation at the most basic level of our carnal being. The work of Hermes is everywhere—from the inner capillaries of our heart to the nerve endings of our fingers—sounding and coding, ciphering and signifying through skin and flesh. Sometimes this work of mediating conceals itself diaphanously, as Aristotle notes, in which case Hermes proves hermetic. Other times, it serves to transmit between deep and surface messages, translating between inner wounds and outer scars, between secrets and signs, in which case Hermes assumes his hermeneutic task and enlists us in the art of deciphering flesh.

In the second part of our analysis, which follows, I propose to chart a summary trajectory of a contemporary hermeneutics of flesh as it develops from Husserl's distinction between *Leib* and *Körper* to the diacritical and diagnostic accounts of the lived body (*le corps propre*) in Merleau-Ponty and Ricoeur.

Part Two: Enigmas of the Flesh: From Husserl to Ricoeur

*Husserl's Recovery of the Lived Body (*Leib*)*

In spite of Aristotle's momentous insight into the hermeneutic potential of sensation, it was largely ignored for most of the subsequent philosophical tradition. The split between intellect and the senses, pronounced by Plato, prevailed. With some notable exceptions in medieval mystics and romantics,[28] the dominant metaphysical mind-view continued to deem reason the prime agency of interpretation, while the flesh was relegated to an inferior realm to be governed and supervised. In the process, touch was de-mediatized and demoted. To be sensible was to be reasonable rather than sensitive, to be rational rather than savvy. And when it came to adjudicating the role of the senses this meant confirming the Platonic priority of sight and hearing over so-called "immediate" sensations. Already Augustine had noted this hegemony of sight in the *Confessions*.[29] And Kant in the *Anthropology* would copper-fasten this dominion of "knowing" sight over the lower carnal senses of taste and touch. "Sight is what best approximates to intuition," he argued; for it is what is most noble, active and critical in contrast to touch which is passive and subservient to the immediacy of external perception. Moreover, this epistemological depreciation of the "lower" senses had a moral corollary. In sum, the rationalist dualism of reason versus flesh prevailed in the Western metaphysical tradition from Plato to Kant until it was radically challenged when Husserl restored the primacy of the "flesh" (*Leib*) as a living body constitutive of psychic reality.

Let us take a close look at this critical moment in the story of carnal hermeneutics. It was in section two, chapter 3 of *Ideas II*, that Husserl made his phenomenological breakthrough concerning the flesh. Taking the famous example of one's left hand touching one's right, he remarked on the curious phenomenon of "double sensation." "The sensation is *doubled* in the two parts of the Body, since each is then precisely for the other an external thing that is touching and acting upon it, and each is at the same time body."[30] In this bilateral gesture, one is no longer an isolated subject experiencing the body as mere object: one is flesh experiencing flesh, both active and passive, constitutive and receptive, spirit and matter—or to use Husserl's terms, *Empfindung* and *Emfindnis*. When one touches in this double way, announced Husserl, "*one becomes body, one senses.*"[31] In this manner, Husserl reversed the privilege of the visual over the tactile, affording primacy to the latter. "In the case of an object constituted purely visually we have nothing comparable . . . an eye does not appear to its own vision. . . . I do not see myself the way I touch myself. What I call the seen body (*Körper*) is not something seeing which is seen the way my Body as touched Body (*Leib*) is something touched which is touched."[32] Only in the case of touch, Husserl claims, does one have a total sense of flesh as a Janus-body turning both ways at once.

Husserl then makes a second, more complicated, claim. Because flesh is this two-way transmission between inner and outer, it is the place where I enjoy my most primordial experience of the other. My perception of others accompanies my perception of self.[33] Husserl does not develop the implications of this revolutionary insight, alas, but later interpreters of his phenomenology—in particular Paul Ricoeur—will do so in a radical fashion. Ricoeur will push Husserl's insight beyond Husserl to argue that at the heart of an egology of consciousness we find a heterology of flesh: the body curled in the womb of psyche. There is no auto-affection without hetero-affection. For it is my flesh which first opens me to a radical passivity and passion—naked exposition to the other than me, receptive to whoever and whatever exceeds and gives itself to me. As both Ricoeur and Chrétien would insist, my flesh is my wound, my natal pact, my umbilical memory, my vulnerability.[34] For while sight offers me dominion over external persons and things, it is my flesh which inserts me—body and soul—into the flesh of the world. It reveals my radical interdependency as a being who feels both ways—as an embodied consciousness projecting meaning onto others at the same time as receiving meaning from them. Once again, we rediscover Aristotle's insight into flesh as mediation, hyphen, and crossing.

But let us return to Husserl. "The body as such," he says, "can be constituted originarily only in tactuality and in everything that is localized with the sensations of touch."[35] While everything we see is touchable and so always in concrete relation to the body, the same cannot be said for visibility. "A subject whose only sense was the sense of vision could not at all have an appearing Body."[36] This is a radical departure from tradition and Husserl presses his claim. The body can, of course be "seen" like any other thing in the world—as a mere thing among things, as pure external object (*Körper*) determined by mechanical causes—but it only truly becomes a living incarnate Body (*Leib*), by "incorporating tactile sensations,"[37] that is, by touching and being touched. Incorporated as flesh, the Body serves as a precondition for the existence of all other sensations—visual, acoustic, olfactory, gustatory—which participate in it.[38] Husserl is very clear on this basic phenomenological point. It is thanks to touch that the Body—with its various senses—is *here* in relation to someone or something that is *there*.[39]

It is in this double gesture of action-passion that flesh provides the ground for carnal hermeneutics. I do not exist in a vacuum, ex nihilo, neutrally. My simplest sensations are already shot through with all kinds of values and desires, withholdings and yieldings. This is what Husserl means when he claims that "all sensings pertain to my soul";[40] or one might add, to the body-soul as "flesh." For here, he insists, belong "groups of sensations which play a role as matter for acts of *valuing*." These are, he explains, the sensations which form the "material substrate for the life of desire and will, sensations of energetic tension and relaxation, of inner restraint, paralysis, liberation etc."[41] So, where Kant and the rationalists gave primacy to reason as transcendental unity of apperception, Husserl talks here of the "Body as a new sort of unity of apprehension."[42] Aesthesiology grounds gnoseology. We are not, in the first instance, cerebral sovereign egos but sensing incarnate Bodies. "The material Body is intertwined with the soul"; it serves as "an underlying basis of consciousness and undergoes its realizing apprehension *in unity with* this consciousness as soul and psyche."[43]

This unity persists even if the psyche remains for the most part unaware of its natal debt to primordial embodiment. And here Husserl confirms one of Freud's late dictums (much commented on by Derrida and Nancy) that "Psyche is extended and knows nothing about it."[44] And he also confirms Aristotle's observation that carnal mediation remains diaphanous and unknown to us—a fluid second skin which we see through (*dia*) but do not see. Husserl does not quote Aristotle directly, any more than he does Freud, but he is quite explicit: "The 'turning point' which lies in the Body, the point of the transformation from causal to conditional processes, *is hidden from me*."[45]

In paragraphs 43–47 of *Ideas II*, Husserl explores a further dimension of extension and transformation—namely, how the "corporeal body" operates in the "mutual relations and communications between man and man," as well as in questions of identity and other deep "connections" (*Zusammenhangen*) between humans and animals. Moving thus into the domain of the intercorporeal, he makes a crucial distinction between (1) the "primal presence" of our own bodies as lived internally by each person, and (2) the indirect "appresence" of other's bodies. The experience of other's bodies is lived both as an objective external object out "there" (*Körper*) and as a living body like mine "here" (*Leib*)—a double experience of empathy-in-distance mediated by a process of transfer by analogy. Suffice it to say that, for Husserl, our lived flesh "senses" not only bodies as given (presented) but also as non-given (appresented)—or, more accurately, as given in nongivenness. Hence the carnal enigma of presentation-in-appresentation.[46] (We shall return to this important point in our discussion of Ricoeur below).

In this same passage Husserl implies that our embodied relations with others already involve signifying connections before we ever get to explicit verbal language as such. For our intercorporeal relations always entail a primal reading of *signs* which prefigure full language. Even the most basic form of empathy implies a process of pre-linguistic embodied signification.[47] Before we are conscious of ourselves as speaking beings, we are in meaningful corporeal relations with others.

Husserl himself did not, alas, develop the radical implications of this carnal hermeneutics. But he made some crucial observations for others to follow. Subsequent interpreters of his work—from Merleau-Ponty to Ricoeur—would explore how flesh is the source of both our empathy and enmity with others. Edith Stein and Max Scheler would analyze how sympathy exposes us "to feel what wretches feel," while Sartre and De Beauvoir would disclose how flesh is a part of our power relations with others: desire, hate, masochism, and sadism. Flesh, as we shall see, is where the struggle of hearts first takes place—where basic wagers between hostility and hospitality unfold.

Conflict and Caress: Sartre and Levinas

Sartre. Sartre learned from Husserl (and his Paris contemporary Gabriel Marcel) that we do not merely *have* bodies, we *are* bodies. This phenomenological fact of incarnation, which is decisive in Sartre's analysis of relations between self and other, forms the third part of *Being and Nothingness*, entitled "Being for Others." To be my body—or to *exist* my body as Sartre puts it—is at the same time to be exposed to others. And this, for Sartre, means that from the beginning human consciousness is an awareness of what is opposed to it in space and time. Sartre writes: "The body—our body—has for its characteristic the fact that it is essentially that which is known by the Other. What I know is the body of another, and the essential facts which I know concerning my own body refer me to the existence of . . . being-for-others."[48] Simply put, my embodied being is inextricably tied to my being-for-others.

Sartre picks up where Husserl leaves off. He both agrees and disagrees with his mentor. He concurs that while sight offers me an objectively perceived body it cannot allow the body to appear as a subjective body (for me). The eyes are never a seeing-seen as flesh is a touching-touched. Sight does not allow for carnal reversibility. But unlike Husserl, Sartre does not take the next step from sight to touch—from one-way vision to two-way touch. He flatly rejects the phenomenon of "double sensation," refusing the corollary of empathic reciprocity between bodies.[49] For Sartre I cannot "be" my body as both subjective (for-itself) and objective (in-itself) at once. I cannot experience my own body in a reversible lived way, since it is only "by means of the *Other*'s concepts that I know my body."[50] Thus, for Sartre, my carnal experience of myself is *alienated* by its dependence on another's objectivizing grasp of me as external body. I can only know my body in "instrumental concepts which come to me from the other." And thus considered the incarnation of my for-itself is totally dependent on strangers set off against me who seek to determine me with their *regard*. When I experience shame or embarrassment at my own body it is actually my body as it exists *for others* which embarrasses me.[51]

Sartre proceeds, accordingly, to see my relationship with others as one of rivalry and conflict. To be exposed is to be opposed. Lifting the transcendental brackets of Husserl's reduction, Sartre reintroduces the embodied self into the perilous world of power and struggle. His account is dramatic and uncompromising. In so far as the other fixes and constitutes my body in its "look," it affirms its freedom to my detriment. The other sees my body as an instrumental "thing." And I see the other in equally reifying terms without being able to connect with the other's freedom and transcendence. That is why Sartre concludes that "the existence of the Other is my original *fall*."[52] The other is a no-thingness which I can only experience as an embodied—which for Sartre means estranged—"thing" and which can only experience me in turn as a "thing." I cannot, in short, sense my body except through the expropriating look of the other. "We resign ourselves to seeing ourselves through the Other's eyes."[53] My experience of my body is never truly lived by me but only as "extended outside in a dimension which escapes me."[54] And this means passing from the flesh (as mine) to language (as my alienated being with and for others).[55] Flesh and word are opposed.

This alienating fall is particularly obvious in Sartre's landmark analysis of the "caress." Here we reach a point of intimate intersensorial contact where reciprocity between my body and another's would seem to be most possible. But where Husserl saw carnal touch as a reversible mediation of intersubjective human relations, Sartre sees it as the opposite. Why? Writing of carnal desire, Sartre speaks of how it "compromises," "invades," and "clogs" my freedom. In passion we become passive. Carnal eros "takes hold of you, overwhelms you, paralyzes you."[56] Erotic flesh is described by Sartre thus as a contingency which one experiences as "vertigo." "I *feel* my skin and my muscles and my breaths . . . as a living and inert datum . . . a *passion* by which I am engaged in the world and in danger in the world."[57] The mention of danger here is telling, for the ultimate state of sexual desire is a "swooning" where I am swallowed up in the body. There is no trace here of Aristotle's hermeneutic "mediation" or Husserl's "intertwining." "Flesh is a pure contingency of presence";[58] it finds itself at risk of being frozen and fixed in the medusa glance of the other. And if I do allow my consciousness to descend into flesh, it is in order to seduce the other to do likewise, so that I can take hold of her. "In desire I make myself flesh in the presence of the Other in order to appropriate the Other's flesh."[59] In this process I discover my body as the facticity of flesh and either submit (masochism) or use this incarnation as a passing ploy to capture the other in its "contingency of presence."[60] Writing of the movement from sight (*le regard*) to touch (*la caresse*), Sartre offers this vivid description:

> Desire is an attempt to strip the body of its movements as of its clothing and to make it exist as pure flesh; it is an attempt to incarnate the Other's body. It is in this sense that the caress is an appropriation of the Other's body. It is evident that if caresses were only a stroking or brushing of the surface there could be no relation between them and the powerful desire which they claim to fulfill; they would remain on the surface like looks and could not appropriate the Other for me . . .

the caress is not a simple stroking; it is a *shaping*. In the caressing of the other I cause her flesh to be born beneath my caress, under my fingers.[61]

The caress, in short, is not some innocent gesture; it is a teleological ploy which seeks to cut the other's body off from its projects and possibilities, uncovering the "web of inertia beneath the action"; and thereby reducing it to passive "being there," a mere thing-amongst-things. The caress is intentional and strategic. But as I incarnate myself as flesh in order to coax the incarnation of the other, I realize it is a strategy doomed to fail. In my efforts to catch the other by making myself flesh, I end up being caught by the other. My only options are then to accept this (masochism), or to coercively reduce the other to her flesh without solicitation or seduction (sadism). Both are self-defeating. For in exchanging the caress for the blow, the stroking palm for the striking fist, one is equally doomed to failure. In seeking to "ensnare" the other's consciousness in embodiment—where I may take my pleasure or exert my power—I end up not with the other in its freedom (which is what I desire) but merely as a corpse-like shell. Sartre describes this no-win dilemma with customary flair: "Everything happens as if I wished to get hold of a man who runs away and leaves only his coat in my hands. It is the coat, it is the outer shell which I possess. I shall never get hold of more than a body, a psychic object in the midst of the world."[62] No matter how much power I exert over my neighbor, lover, partner, enemy, I can never actually possess their living freedom and transcendence. "I can make the Other beg for mercy or ask for pardon, but I shall always be ignorant of what this submission means for and in the Other's freedom."[63]

Either way, the possibility of reciprocal relation being achieved through a mutual caressing of bodies is annulled. The dream of "double reciprocal incarnation" ends, absurdly, in a form of death.[64]

To put this in terms of carnal hermeneutics, we could say that the ploy of incarnation to reduce others to something "immediately sensible" is forever frustrated by the fact that flesh is always a medium. The carnal contact between self and other remains a mediation attesting to a certain ineliminable gap by means of which the other flees from me and preserves his/her meaning intact. In the nearest touch of the near something still remains far. One cannot possess *la chair* (*Leib*) in immediacy, only *la chose* (*Körper*)—and that is *not* what we seek. *La chair*, as living body, never ceases to operate as a two-way transmission between self and other. It resists reification.

So here is the rub. By resorting to a Cartesian dualism of subject versus object, freedom versus extension, consciousness versus body, Sartre ultimately reduces the story of flesh to a tragedy of fall and failure. In resisting double sensation Sartre refuses the possibility of double incarnation as meaningful human communion. The only options for reciprocal relations remaining are masochism or indifference. A dialectical seesaw of power and paralysis. Hence Sartre's logical conclusion that "man is a useless passion."

In ultimately denying the transformative potential of flesh—as medium of hermeneutic crossing and dialogue—Sartre reduces the body to a thing of nothing. His phenomenology of *la chair* becomes a nihilism of *la chose*. He misses the hermeneutic turn.

Levinas. In Emmanuel Levinas, another early interpreter of Husserl in France, we find a very different phenomenology of the caress. This time flesh is not so much a clogging of consciousness qua thing as a lure of the future. The key passage is located in the final section of *Totality and Infinity*, titled "Phenomenology of Eros."[65] Levinas states here: "The caress, like contact, is sensibility. But the caress transcends the sensible."[66]

From the outset Levinas establishes a paradox whereby the caress is a "non-signifying" touching of flesh on flesh. It is what he calls an "intentionality of search" which goes towards the invisible—and so negates any intentionality of vision. It forages for what is not yet, seizing upon nothing, soliciting what escapes its form toward a "future never future enough."[67] So saying, Levinas admits that the caress "expresses" eros "in a certain sense," but "suffers from an inability to tell it." It is an ineffable expression; a prelinguistic sensing. It searches, but searches what? The feminine, responds Levinas, the inviolate, the virginal.

In a clear departure from Sartre, Levinas declares that the carnal caress is not about trying to capture another in its freedom, in some master–slave dialectic of power and possession. "It is not that the caress would seek to dominate a hostile freedom, to make of it its object or extort from it a consent."[68] No. The caress rather constitutes a "profanation." It brings us to a place of voluptuousity which opens onto an experience of "absence"—absence which is not an abstract nothing but absolute futurity. What the caress touches when it touches the flesh of the naked other is not another person or thing that *exists* out there. What it touches is the "untouchable in the very contact of voluptuousity, future in the present."[69] Thus moving beyond both Husserl and Sartre, Levinas claims that the caress brings us into nonexistence so that something new may be born.

The carnal, the tender par excellence correlative of the caress, the beloved, is to be identified neither with the body-thing of the physiologist, nor with the lived body of the "I can," nor with the body-expression, or face. In the caress, a relation yet, in one aspect, sensible, the body already denudes itself of its very form, offering itself as nudity. In the carnal given to tenderness, the body quits the status of the existent.[70]

What this cryptic phenomenology signals is the caress's entry into the nonbeing of the not-yet. This is the night of the erotic, the mysterious, the clandestine. It dissipates into an anonymous passivity, a passion that is infantile, animal, vertiginous, elemental.[71] Here the flesh of the Beloved is exposed as nakedly vulnerable and mortal, operating in a no-man's-land between being and non-being. As such, the caress is without will or goal. It does not act but swoons, an intention without meaning, an amorphous not-yet-being which overwhelms the "I" of the subject, sweeping it into an absolute future through the suffering of its own evanescence. As Levinas says: "It dies with this death and suffers with this suffering."[72] A suffering transformed, paradoxically, into the happiness of voluptuousity. The caress makes us sick with the joy of love.

But what exactly is the voluptuous? It is impossible to say. We get no hermeneutic hints from Levinas. As we embrace the night of eros, there is no Hermes to guide us. No signs or signals. Only a maze of equivocations. As erotic nudity of flesh, voluptuousity is what "says the inexpressible."[73] But it is a saying which silences and dissimulates—an expression which expresses the impossibility to express. It is not an intentionality which *sees* or sheds light; it does not reveal a face or disclose an object; it is not an I relating to a Thou, nor a consciousness (however embodied) passing into a concept or idea, nor, finally, a touch of reciprocal desire. In revealing the hidden as hidden, the voluptuousity of the caress inverts the orders of signification into blind raillery.[74] Eros inveigles us into the "non-signifyingness of the wanton (*lascif*)."[75]

More simply put: while the face signifies, the flesh does not. The face is about exteriority, society, language, ethics. The caress, contrariwise, is about unspeakable secrecy. The face—which commands as eminent voice of the teacher—comes divinely from above. Voluptuousity murmurs ravishingly from below. "In the face the Other expresses his eminence, the dimension of height and divinity from which he descends."[76] By contrast, the erotic, identified by Levinas with the feminine, is described as a shading of the ethical visage, defying language as it lures us into the "shadow of non-sense."[77] Or again: "The face, all straightforwardness and frankness, in its feminine epiphany dissimulates allusions, innuendos."[78] As such, femininity inverts the face, inaugurating an "asocial relation of eros"—the ambivalence of a silent animality without responsibility. In this impersonal and inexpressive anonymity of night, concludes Levinas, "the relations with the Other are enacted in play; one plays with the Other as with a young animal."[79] As consequence, lovers in erotic nudity cease to exist as individual speaking persons, as moral agents with responsibilities, and embrace, at least momentarily, a closed *egoisme-à-deux*. "The common action of the sentient and the sensed which voluptuousity accomplishes closes, encloses, seals the society of the couple."[80]

Here Levinas discloses what for him is the ultimate paradox of flesh. In the lovers' den of darkness, stripped of society and language, intimacy triggers something ungraspable: the not-yet future of the child. In the obscure "non-sociality of the society of lovers" comes the less-than-nothing, the collapse of the I and thou into a pre-personal play of flesh, a blind interplay of eros with eros, a voluptuousity of voluptuousity, which allows ultimately for the engendering of the child.[81]

Beyond the Caress? So what does all this mean for our thesis on carnal hermeneutics? At first blush, it seems Levinas may be acknowledging the hermeneutic power of the physical caress to open up the future. As such flesh—caressing and caressed—might be construed as a mediation between self and other, leading to the third, the child. But this apparent promise of carnal mediation, as a reciprocal gift, is quickly foreclosed. The ethical separation of face and flesh—and attendant separation between language and sensation, transcendence and profanation—means Levinas neglects the possibility of flesh as reversible signification between myself and another. In Levinas, no less than in Sartre, the mystery of "double sensation" is denied. And by so starkly opposing face (as teaching from above) and flesh (as caress from below), Levinas also misses the hermeneutic turn. He fails to see that a phenomenology of eros and tenderness, of touch and taste, *already* signifies and interprets, already reads the other. In short, he fails to appreciate that face *is* flesh. And vice versa. So when Levinas claims that the face of the other has eyes without color or skin without scars, he is resorting, I submit, to the old metaphysical dichotomy of transcendental versus empirical. His transcendental phenomenology actually ends up, for all its attention to the caress, in excarnating the other, removing her/him from the historical context of concrete spatial embodiment. In a quasi-Platonic move, Levinas thus ultimately identifies ethical (divine) otherness as a category of transcendence *beyond carnal singularity*. And by so denying the possibility of "double incarnation" he equally denies the option of complementarity in sex, love, and friendship. There is no such thing as a carnal I-Thou. (Levinas was no friend of Buber). There is no possibility of hermeneutic "dialogue." Instead, the caress signals a collapse of distinct selves, without recourse to meaningful mediation.

Meaning, for Levinas, only arises at the level of language when the face finally replaces flesh and ethics trumps erotics. And in this passage from carnal eros to the language of transcendence the virile I takes his departure from the feminine—like Aeneas from Dido (a move justly critiqued by Luce Irigaray and other feminists).[82] If carnal erotics has a role for Levinas—and it does—it is in suspending our personal sense of ourselves so that in a profane play of indistinction something new is engendered—beyond all signification or intentionality—namely, the child. Destroying every sense of historical past and present, the caress, in a swooning evanescence of blind love, ejaculates the not-yet of the future. And in this suspension of vision and light, in this dissolution of hermeneutic meaning into the "less than nothing" of lust, the invisible whispers a way out—opens an escape hatch to the exteriority of transcendence. In this sense, we may conclude that Levinas's phenomenology of the face is the impossibility of a hermeneutics of the flesh.

This last point is crucial, so let me be more exact. Levinas equates language with the face. The face, he insists, signifies in so far as it presents itself in person. "The symbolism of the sign already presupposes the signification of expression, the face."[83] Thus, even though Levinas concedes at one point that "the whole body—a hand or a curve of the shoulder—can express as the face,"[84] the body in this exceptional sense is, I would argue, "transcendentalised" rather than touched. It is not body as flesh but a mere pretext for ethical hallowing. The hand or shoulder in question is, in such instances, no more than a surrogate face—a trace of an other who transcends the flesh towards the invisible, the vertical, the infinite, merely leaving its mark, like an evacuation notice, on the finite body. Levinas writes: "In voluptuousity the other is me and separated from me. The *separation* of the other in the midst of this community of feeling constitutes the acuity of voluptuousity."[85]

The operative word here is "separation"—not "alteration" or "differentiation." The rupture between self and other, for Levinas, is absolutely asymmetrical, denying any possibility of reciprocal communion—or, by extension, of hermeneutic dialogue (so central to the thought of Ricoeur and Gadamer). Levinas's ethics of separation tends to equate any notion of symmetry with un-ethical "possession"—a variation on the Hegelian-Sartrean dialectics of power. And that is why, in Levinas, eros never seeks to possess or objectify the other, as in Sartre. "Nothing is further from

Eros than possession. In the possession of the Other I possess the Other in as much as he possesses me: I am both slave and master. Voluptuousity would be extinguished in possession." But, by contrast, the impersonality of voluptuousity "prevents us from taking the relation between lovers to be a complementarity. Voluptuousity hence aims not at the other but at his voluptuousity; it is voluptuousity of voluptuousity, love of the love of the other."[86] Thus, unlike friendship, which goes forth to the other, love for erotic flesh, femininity, nudity, seeks not another existent person but rather "the infinitely future, what is to be engendered."[87] In flesh the same and the other are not reconciled (in some project or meaning) but "engender the child"—the child heralding from that "nothingness of the future buried in the secrecy of the less than nothing."[88] A nothingness, let it be noted, which has nothing to do with anxiety, as in Heidegger and Sartre.

Let me add finally that while the terms "eros," "love," and "desire" are often used synonymously by Levinas, he occasionally uses "eros" as a generic term which can cover both "love" as an enclosing *egoisme-à-deux* (fusion) and "desire" as a metaphysical search for the invisible—as desire of desire, voluptuousity of voluptuousity, infinitely seeking out, beyond totality, a future never future enough. This slippage between terms is, in my view, yet a further symptom of Levinas's inability to fully embrace a hermeneutics of flesh, a lack of proper discrimination and discernment. As is the fact that the greatest of these three terms, for Levinas, is ultimately "desire," understood as a metaphysical yearning for an impossible other beyond the double incarnation of *Leib*.

Double Sensation in Merleau-Ponty

Merleau-Ponty restores the phenomenology of touch as double-sensation and takes it to a new level. He boldly challenges Sartre's dualism between an "objective body" (qua other) and a "phenomenal body" (qua mine).[89] Whereas Sartre had declared that the body touching and the body touched belonged to two "incommunicable levels,"[90] Merleau-Ponty redescribes them as deeply co-implicated in the notion of "flesh" (*la chair*). In *The Visible and the Invisible,* he defines flesh accordingly as a "chiasm" between me and the world—a reversible crossing which precedes all analytic and transcendental divisions between subject and object, consciousness and thing. Flesh is not simply how I as a subject see nor how I as an object am seen; it is the common vinculum of both—and indeed of all other reversible perceptions—tactual, gustatory, olfactory and synesthetic.

Revisiting Husserl's notion of "intertwining" (*Verflechtung*), Merleau-Ponty reinterprets flesh as a mutual interweaving between perceiving and perceived. To say that the body is a seer is, he says, to say that it is visible.[91] Just as to say that it touches is to say that it is tangible. But it is also to say more: that the body is *both* visible *and* tangible. There is not just a reversibility within each specific sense (as with Husserl)—touching and being touched, seeing and being seen—but across different senses. One finds a crossing of the tangible with the visible and the visible with the tangible.[92] And this reversibility is extended not only to all the senses but to language itself. The I which speaks words is the I spoken in words. Sensation and language are isomorphic. But they are also transmorphic. In a radical gesture that brings Merleau-Ponty to the threshold of what we are calling carnal hermeneutics, he speaks about a chiasmus of linguistic and perceptual sense: "the same fundamental phenomenon of reversibility which sustains both the mute perception and the speech . . . manifests itself by an almost carnal existence of the idea, as well as by a sublimation of the flesh."[93]

Flesh is the cradle of both perception and the word. The phenomenon of multi-reversibility extends from touch and sight to language itself, revealing flesh as a shared membrane between body and world. Here Merleau-Ponty rehabilitates Aristotle's ancient insight (without naming him) that all senses involve touch, and brings it to an ontological level. He claims that flesh is both what makes the world appear (as touching-speaking) and what belongs to the world (as touched-spoken). I do not begin with an isolated body opposed to another consciousness; I exist my body because I am already operating in and from the flesh of the world. I touch because I am in touch with the world. I speak because I am spoken to and spoken through. In short, flesh is the pre-existing, pre-reflective chiasm which allows for the mutual insertion of the world between the folds of my body and my body between the folds of the world.[94] It is a twofold ontological texture—feeling and felt—which provides the underlying unity between the becoming-body of my senses and the becoming-world of my body—or, as Merleau-Ponty puts it, between nature and human being. As such, the chiasm of flesh is not reducible to the metaphysical dichotomies of matter and form, soul and substance, consciousness and object, but is to be understood instead as an ontological "element" in which we already find ourselves—sensing and sensed, speaking and spoken at once.

Here the old transcendental problem of intersubjectivity—which bedeviled modern philosophy from Descartes to Sartre—is resolved to the extent that "it is not I who sees, nor the other who sees, because an anonymous visibility inhabits both of us."[95] Husserl's original insight into the implications of double sensation for "empathy"—developed by both Edith Stein and Max Scheler—is here afforded a new ontological depth. Though it has to be said that Merleau-Ponty resists the dialectical temptation—signaled by Derrida in *On Touching*[96]—to lapse into premature synthesis. He avoids, I believe, the lure of "totality" by recognizing that there is always an element of the invisible and the untouchable in the other's life. The reversibility of touching-touched is imminent but never fully realized.[97] There remains a gap. And the gap makes all the difference, preventing fusion and keeping open the task of transit and translation between self and other. The flesh, as chiasmic tissue and texture, allows "ownness" and "otherness" to interweave in multiple carnal reversibilities and doublings; but it never reduces them to the *same*. Were it to do so, we would be deprived of the diacritical role of *reading across difference*, and submit to what Derrida calls "hapto-centric closure."[98] Had he construed flesh in such self-enclosing fashion, Merleau-Ponty would have foreclosed the possibility of carnal hermeneutics. He would have simply replaced Platonic optocentrism with philosophical haptocentrism. Contrary to Derrida's suspicion, we do not believe he did so.

Embodiment and Eros. An initial insight into the potential of carnal hermeneutics can be found, I believe, in Merleau-Ponty's discussion of the caress in the fifth chapter of *Phenomenology of Perception* entitled, "The Body in Its Sexual Being." Here he claims that the best way to understand how things signify in general is to begin by exploring the significance of our "affective life" at its most basic level of "desire and love."[99] Merleau-Ponty affirms that incarnation, as eros, must be understood not just biologically but ontologically. If Freud provided a distinction between the basic drives—eros and thanatos—in *Beyond the Pleasure Principle*, Merleau-Ponty gives phenomenological substance to this claim. He speaks of an "erotic perception" which has a specific "significance," not as a *cogito* aiming at a *cogitatum*, but as an existential body aiming at another in the world.[100] Citing the example of Schneider, a patient deficient in touch and vision and incapable of living in the world in a sexual or emotional way, Merleau-Ponty notes how his inability to read life through touch coincides with the fact that he cannot respond to the world sexually. He cannot make distinctions between one kind of sexual being and another. The impairment of action, cognition, and sex are structurally interconnected.[101]

Psychoanalysis had already shown that libido is not a mere instinct and that even the most basic erotic act has a "meaning." The sexual is not just genital but a general intentional (albeit pre-conscious) way of being-towards-the-world. Eros, Merleau-Ponty observes, is geared toward the whole life of the subject, relating to existential wagers of flight or conquest, desire or recoil, adherence or rejection, seduction or shame, fear or fascination. As such, phenomenology "expands" the notion of sexuality to show how it is both physical and metaphysical, both physiological and ontological. Sexuality must be construed, accordingly, as a distinct sign and symptom of our full existence, in much the way as Gestalt psychology shows that "no layer of sensory data can be identified as immediately dependent on sensory organs: the smallest sensory datum is never presented in any other way than integrated into a configuration and already *patterned*."[102] At the level of the senses (as in the brain or psyche which they embody) nothing exists in isolation, but only in differential relation to other parts and wholes. Biological existence is synchronized with human existence through and through. To live the body (*leben*) is, therefore, already to live this or that particular kind of world (*erleben*). Eating, breathing, loving are always forms of ontological expression, marking out a singular "style" for each living person. "The life of the flesh and the life of the psyche," as Merleau-Ponty puts it, "are involved in a relationship of reciprocal *expression*."[103] Which is not to say that body is the integument of spirit (spiritualism), nor that mind is caused by body (naturalism). The body does not indicate an inner mind as a house number might indicate a home. The body signifies meaning because it *is* that meaning. If I lose my voice (aphasia), it is not because I am withholding speech but because I cannot speak. "The girl does not *cease* to speak, she 'loses' her voice as one loses a memory."[104] Or to take another example, to lose a book given by a friend when one falls out with that friend signifies a general relationship of loss (including both book and friend); just as finding it again when one is reconciled with that friend is a sign of general reconciliation. The one is linked to the other in a single existential sensibility (of losing and regaining, forgetting and remembering). In this sense, we may say that carnal signs are full signs—both signifier and signified at once.

Relating this to other cases of mental illness such as anorexia or frigidity, Merleau-Ponty shows how bodily symptoms are neither simply determined biochemically, nor strategically manipulated by conscious volition, but express a carnal manner of being in the world which is often healed more by the touch of a hand than a disclosure of knowledge. Citing Binswanger's famous version of the "bedside manner," Merleau-Ponty argues that cures often come more from the senses than from will or consciousness.

> In treating (these conditions), psychological medicine does not act on the patient by making him *know* the origin of his illness: sometimes a *touch of the hand* puts a stop to the spasms and restores to the patient his speech . . . the patient would not accept the meaning of

his disturbances as revealed to him without the personal relationship formed with the doctor, or without the confidence and friendship felt towards him, and the change of existence resulting from this friendship. Neither symptom nor cure is worked out at the level of objective or positing consciousness, but *below* that level.[105]

Therapeutic hermeneutics is, at bottom, a carnal hermeneutics that goes all the way down.

Therapy, in this wise, involves a "conversion" through the body-subject in *tactful* contact with other body-subjects. Because our flesh is what constantly exposes us to others—human, animal, vegetal—even its closure in itself (refusing words, food, sex) is never a given. Just as in sleep we are never completely asleep, in sickness we are never completely sick. Qua flesh, the human being is never either a pure "nothingness in the mind" nor a mere "thing" amidst things—it is the possibility of co-existence with other human beings. Healing is thus defined by Merleau-Ponty as a re-opening of self to others *through the body*, a turning from thanatos (death drive of closure) to eros (life drive of communion). I quote again:

Precisely because my body can shut itself off from the world, it is also what opens me out upon the world and places me in a situation there. The momentum of existence towards others, towards the future, towards the world can be restored as a river unfreezes. The girl will recover her voice, not by an intellectual effort or by an abstract decree of will, but through a conversion in which the whole of her body makes a concentrated effort in the form of a genuine gesture, as we seek and recover a name forgotten not "in our mind" . . . but "on the tip of our tongue." The memory or the voice is recovered when the body once more opens itself to others or to the past, when it opens the way to *co-existence* and once more acquires significance beyond itself.[106]

Because our bodily existence inaugurates our primary "consonance with the world," it remains our first line of resistance and openness to others. Existence comes into its own in the body and finds there its originary sense. Expression does not exist apart from the body and the body does not exist apart from expression. What Merleau-Ponty terms the "*incarnate significance*" of flesh is the "central phenomenon" of which the traditionally opposed poles of body and mind are abstract derivatives. Flesh and existence presuppose each other, they *are* each other—flesh as "solidified existence" and existence as "perpetual incarnation."[107] Together they constitute a "woven fabric" of "inter-communication."[108]

Returning to his guiding theme of eros, Merleau-Ponty concludes that "desire and love" are not "bundles of instincts" governed by natural laws nor strategies of some willful mind, but carnal interplays where the self "opens out upon another"—an exposure to alterity which is the beginning of both our physical and metaphysical existence. Indeed, Merleau-Ponty goes so far as to declare that "sexuality is co-extensive with life," comparing it to a particular "atmosphere" or "haze" which hides itself even as it provides the secret means (*metaxu*) through which we see the world. Located in flesh, eros spreads forth like a transpersonal "color" or "sound" between self and other. Merleau-Ponty coins the term "interfusion" to describe this mutual mediation where "existence permeates sexuality and vice versa."[109] That is why there is no explanation of eros which can reduce it to anything other than itself, for it is already something other than itself—a perpetual crossing between inner and outer, nature and freedom, sameness and difference, such that "we never know whether the forces which bear us on are its or ours."[110]

Diacritical Perception. This role of "difference" at the heart of sensation was developed by Merleau-Ponty in his Collège de France lectures in the 1950s, delivered at the time he was sketching his notes on the carnal chiasm for *The Visible and the Invisible*. In one particular lecture series of 1953, entitled *Le Monde sensible et le monde de l'expression*, he offers a fascinating account of what he calls "diacritical perception."[111] This is a new mode of expressive sensibility involving the crossing of sensation and language. Borrowing liberally from Saussure's notion that words only signify by virtue of their differences with other words, Merleau-Ponty argues that meanings are never given as isolated terms or objects but always as parts of a mobile interaction of signs involving intervals, absences, folds and gaps (*écarts*). This is not just a function of language, however, but the very structure of perception itself. Going well beyond Saussure and the structuralists, then, Merleau-Ponty makes the radical claim that because perception is structured like language in its nascent state it is *diacritical*. Here is how Merleau-Ponty puts it in an important note from his 1953 lectures:

Diacritical notion of the perceptual sign. This is the idea that we can perceive differences without terms, gaps with regard to a level (of meaning) which is not itself an object—the only way to give perception a consciousness worthy of itself and which does not alter the perceived into an object, into the signification of an isolating or reflexive attitude.[112]

In a subsequent note entitled "Diacritical perception," Merleau-Ponty adds this intriguing example. To see another's visage is to interpret it carnally *as* this or that form of expression:

> To perceive a physiognomy, an expression, is always to deploy diacritical signs, in the same manner as one realizes an expressive gesticulation with one's body. Here each (perceptual) sign has the unique virtue of differentiating from others, and these differences which appear for the onlooker or are used by the speaking subject are not defined by the terms between which they occur, but rather define these in the first place.[113]

This logic of diacritical perception is alien to the classical presumption that difference presupposes identity. On the contrary, writes Merleau-Ponty, the identity of terms emerges in the tension of their differences, their contours arising from the encroachment (*empiètement*) of things on things. And here he deploys the term "infra-thing" in contradistinction to the old notion of discrete objective substances.

With this move, Merleau-Ponty departs from the classic habit of defining something new in terms of a preexisting genre or foundation. Diacritical perception through gaps reveals the inadequate character of the traditional one-to-one correlation between consciousness and object—showing that such correspondence arises only in retrospect—which ignores the fact that there never was an object in the first place, but only several different infra-things, and at the very minimum a reversible interplay between figure and ground (*fond*). This plurality of infra-things is irreducible to the dualist framework of an isolated mind faced with an isolated object. Diacritical perception is, Merleau-Ponty insists, the sensing of meaning as it expresses itself in the intervals between such infra-things of our experience. It involves our sense of identity through differentiation rather than differentiation through identity.

Our most basic carnal sensations may thus be said to be structured diacritically in so far as they are structured like the phonetic differentiations of language. "To have a body capable of expressive articulation or action and to have a phonetic system capable of constructing signs, is the same thing."[114] Our body schemas, in other words, operate like phonetic systems which function according to principles of which they are not conscious (e.g., *parole* is not conscious of *langue*, just as touch, as Aristotle noted, is not conscious of its *metaxy*). But to compare carnal sensation to linguistic structure in this way is not to reduce the latter to the former (naturalism), nor to reduce the former to the latter (structuralism). Nature does not make the body any more than it makes phonetic systems. And it would be a mistake to construe the perceptual capacity to play with principles of which it is not immediately aware as some kind of "unconscious." Perception of figure is not simultaneously perception of ground—but rather "imperception": the sensing of the invisible in and through the visible, a "*sentir en profondeur*," by negations, absences, *écarts*. Or as Merleau-Ponty puts it in Gestalt language: "consciousness of the figure is consciousness without knowledge of the ground (*fond*)."[115]

We may say accordingly that diacritical perception (or more broadly, sensation) witnesses the birth of expression, against an unformed background, as a meaning which begins and re-begins, an awakening which takes the form of a figure that is prefigured and refigured again and again, now fore, now aft, now here, now there. Hence the importance of Merleau-Ponty's metaphor of modulation: "Consider sensation itself, the act of sensing (*le sentir*), as the intervening of a figure on a *fond*. Modulation. As a sound modulates silence. As a color modulates an open space by varying it. Every sign is diacritical."[116] And Merleau-Ponty adds significantly, "This is Valéry's idea," thereby indicating that his attempts to describe the hidden "diacritical" function are as indebted to literary poetics as they are to structural linguistics. (Once again we note the recourse to poetics when it comes to naming or expressing the enigma of signifying flesh—Aristotle's recourse to tropes of membrane and water, Merleau-Ponty's to figures of modulation and chiasmus.) Either way, this sensory birth of meaning occurs not in the manner of a foundational cause (as in standard metaphysics) but as a diacritical play of visible and invisible, tangible and intangible, an embodied vigilance capable of signaling and resuscitating "full being" (*l'être total*) on the basis of a fragment.[117] This diacritical interplay between *figure et fond* represents an endless reversibility—for what is one perceiver's *figure* is another's *fond* and vice versa. The diacritical art of sensing ultimately amounts, in Merleau-Ponty's view, to the displacement of natural cause by cultural expression.

In the same 1953 lecture course, Merleau-Ponty offers one further noteworthy illustration of the diacritical isomorphism of perception and language. He compares the perception of movement to the comprehension of a sentence. We only understand the beginning of a sentence from its end, he says, just as we only perceive movement in light of its goal. Perception does not follow something as it displaces itself from one fixed place to another, as if one solid object succeeded another; it proceeds rather as a wave which stretches back and forth across distances in the same manner as a sentence circulates through a whole linguistic field.

Carnal sensation is, therefore, best depicted as a fold (*pli*) in the moving flesh of the world; there is no world without it and it cannot be without a world. "Like signs in language," writes Merleau-Ponty, "the points traversed in movement have only a diacritical value; they do not function in themselves as places but rather as passages in the same way as words of a sentence are traces of an intention which (invisibly) transpierces them."[118] Or to put it another way, perception operates like language in that it does not confront an object head on, but senses things which speak to it laterally, on the side, provoking one's "complicity" in the manner of an "obsession." Less objective than obsessional, then, the thing perceived "solicits" us (Valéry). Like an epiphany that calls for remembrance (Proust); or a naming which invites co-naissance (Claudel); or a pregnancy that yearns for birth and rebirth (Bachelard); or a frosted branch whose every crystal signals a whole order of emergent meanings (Stendhal). With all these literary analogies, Merleau-Ponty is suggesting that each carnal perception of the world constructs itself on the basis of an emerging part which solicits our co-creation of this world; just as language constructs itself in terms of a circular movement between a present part and absent whole. (Merleau-Ponty also uses here the analogy of a film montage where each frame functions in the movement between gaps across an invisible background.)

But it is important to remind ourselves here that the diacritical model of carnal interpretation is not a matter of voluntarist invention (à la Sartre). It is not a question of reading *into* something but of reading *from* (*à partir*) something. We are solicited by the flesh of the world before we read ourselves back into it. Carnal attention is as much reception as creation. It precedes and exceeds transcendental idealism. And this is why I think Merleau-Ponty insists that the solicitation of our body schema functions symbolically, obliquely, indirectly, like a sexual or ontological *surprise*. Diacritical sensation, across distances and intervals, comes not just from us but from another person or thing that meets us "like a stranger in the dark." Merleau-Ponty again cites Valéry to make his point. "A man is nothing so long as nothing draws from him effects and productions which surprise him."[119] But to be surprised one must be ready to receive, open to solicitation and seduction, prepared to partake of the thing sensed and symbolized. Every sense, as Merleau-Ponty concludes, has its own *symbolique*. Every carnal act and organ inscribes its own *imaginaire*. From sexual expression to the act of eating itself. Nature is already culture as soon as we sense it *as this or that* (however mute or self-concealing this hermeneutic-as may be). Sensation is expression and expression sensation. Flesh is word and word flesh. Hence the significance of Merleau-Ponty's description of sensation in terms of a diacritical Eucharistic communion:

> Just as the sacrament not only symbolizes, in sensible species, an operation of Grace, but is also the real presence of God, which it causes to occupy a fragment of space and communicates to those who eat of the consecrated bread, provided that they are inwardly prepared, in the same way the sensible has not only a motor and vital significance, but is nothing other than a certain way of being in the world suggested to us from some point in space, and seized and acted upon by our body, provided that it is capable of doing so, so that sensation is literally a form of communion.[120]

Here we find yet another, deeper meaning to double sensation and double incarnation. We are far from conceiving the flesh according to the logic of "possession" (Sartre) or of "separation" (Levinas). Merleau-Ponty resorts to an Aristotelian logic of "analogy"—more precisely, of proper proportionality: A is to B what C is to D. Namely, the sacrament of transubstantiation is to the responsive communicant what the sensible is to the attentive sensor. He delineates this quasi-Eucharistic power of the sensible as follows:

> I am brought into relation with an external being, whether it be in order to open myself to it or to shut myself off from it. If the qualities radiate around them a certain mode of existence, if they have the power to cast a spell and what we called just now a sacramental value, this is because the sentient subject does not posit them as objects, but enters into a sympathetic relation with them, makes them his own and finds in them his momentary law.[121]

In other words, each sensory encounter with the strangeness of the world is an invitation to a "natal pact" where, through a form of "diacritical sympathy," the human self and the strange world give birth to one another. Sacramental sensation is a reversible rapport between myself and others, wherein the sensible gives birth to itself through me.

What a fine example of carnal hermeneutics. Everyday sensation as exquisite empathy.

Between Phenomenology and Hermeneutics: Ricoeur's Wager

Paul Ricoeur, the final figure I consider here, also developed a phenomenology of flesh inspired by Husserl in the 1950s. But while this early phenomenology was developing strongly in the direction of a diagnostics of carnal signification—in tandem with Merleau-Ponty—once Ricoeur took the so-called "linguistic turn" in the 1960s he departed from this seminal phenomenology in order to concentrate more exclusively on a hermeneutics of the text. There are, however, some fascinating reflections in Ricoeur's final writings which attempt to reanimate a dialogue between his initial phenomenology of the flesh and later hermeneutics of language. I will take a look at these by way of suggesting new directions for a carnal hermeneutics—directions which might bring together the rich insights of a philosophy of embodiment (developed with Husserl and Merleau-Ponty) and a philosophy of interpretation (deriving from Heidegger and Gadamer).

Before looking at these later reflections, however, let me say a few words about Ricoeur's early "diagnostics" of bodily expression. As I have written on this elsewhere, I will confine my remarks here to a few summary points.

Diagnostics of the Body. Ricoeur's main contribution here comes in the form of three important sections of his first major work in phenomenology, *Freedom and Nature: The Voluntary and the Involuntary*, published in 1950, five years after *The Phenomenology of Perception*. The sections in question are entitled, "Motivation and the Corporeal Involuntary," "Bodily Spontaneity," and "Life: Structure, Genesis, Birth."

Ricoeur sets out in this work to explore the life of the "incarnate cogito," drawing on the phenomenological notion of the *corps propre* (announced by Husserl and Merleau-Ponty), Gabriel Marcel's notion of incarnation, and Maine de Biran's analysis of the embodied *cogito* (as touch, effort, and resistance). From the outset Ricoeur proposes an account of the body as a dialectical rapport between the voluntary and the involuntary in direct opposition to naturalism. Starting with the phenomenon of "affectivity," he notes that "*sentir est encore penser*," understanding *sentir* no longer as a representation of objectivity but as a revelation of existence.[122] Carnal affectivity is thus seen as a mediating bridge between (1) our flesh and blood existence and (2) the "thinking" order of interpretation, evaluation and understanding. But if "incarnation" is the first anchor of existence, it is also the temptation of betrayal—for the affective body lends itself to reductive objectifying accounts.

Ricoeur takes up the challenge, beginning with "need" as something to be phenomenologically experienced not as a natural event from without, but as a lived experience from within. It is here, right away, that Ricoeur proclaims his diagnostics of the lived body: "the diagnostic relation which conjoins objective knowledge with Cogito's apperception brings about a truly Copernican Revolution. No longer is consciousness a symptom of the object-body, but rather the object-body is an indication of a personal body (*corps propre*) in which the Cogito shares as its very existence."[123] Affectivity and thought are thus connected from the outset by a tie of mutual inherence and adherence. The two bodies (inner and outer) are not separate realities but two ways of "reading" the same flesh—externally (as nature) and internally (as incarnation).

Ricoeur then goes on to show how need relates to pleasure in terms of various "motivating values and tendencies"—evaluative discriminations that are not imposed by consciousness or reason but are already operative in our most basic affective relations. Nor is need to be reduced, naturalistically, to a mere reflex sensation translating an organic defect in the form of a motor reaction. It is not a "re-action but a pre-action"—an "action towards. . . ."[124] Otherwise put, need reveals me not as a mechanism of stimulus-response but as a "life gaping as appetition for the other."[125] To have needs does not mean being *determined* by them; we are continually *discerning* between needs and pre-reflectively evaluating when best to realize or suspend them. "It is because the impetus of need is *not* an automatic reflex that it can become a *motive* which inclines without compelling and that there are men who prefer to die of hunger than betray their friends."[126] As Gandhi's hunger strikes or the sacrifice of countless heroes and saints attest, "man is capable of choosing between his hunger *and* something else."[127]

Need is thus revealed as a primordial spontaneity of the body where will mixes with a "first rank of values" which I have not engendered but which mobilize my feelings. The existing body as living flesh is the original source of carnal hermeneutics; it is what makes our first *savoir* a *savoir-faire*, a savvy of life. "Through need, values *emerge* without my having posited them in my act-generating role: bread is good, wine is good. Before I will it, a value already appeals to me solely because I exist in flesh; it is already a reality in the world, a reality which reveals itself to me through the lack. . . . The first non-deductible is the body as existing, life as value. The mark of all existents, it is what first reveals values."[128] It is at this crucial point that Ricoeur addresses the role of carnal imagination at the crossroads of need and willing. He explores how we imagine a missing person or thing (which we need or desire) and the ways towards reaching it. But the corporeal imagination is not just about projecting possibilities from within; it is equally a means of reading the "affective signs" of real sensible qualities out there in the world. The carnal imagination—witnessed in need, pleasure and desire—is already a diagnostics in which primal judgments become both affective and effective. Imagining the world in the flesh is a matter of feeling, valuing, and doing. "We must not lose sight of the *sense* quality of imagination," insists Ricoeur, "for it is in our imagination mobilizing our desires and discerning between good and bad ways of realizing them that our life can be *evaluated*."[129] Values mean nothing unless they *touch* me. Contrary to Kant and the idealists, ethics requires the mediation of flesh. Ricoeur concludes his reading of the body as primal field of evaluation with this manifesto:

> The body is not only a value among others, but is in some way involved in the apprehension of all motives and through them of all values. It is the affective *medium* of all value: a value can reach me only as dignifying a motive, and no motive can incline me if it does not *impress my sensibility*. I reach values through the vibration of an affect. To broaden out the spread of values means at the same time to deploy affectivity to its broadest span.[130]

Ricoeur spends the rest of his phenomenological analysis exploring this claim for affective sensibility as "medium" of evaluation. Suffice it for now to note that his initial sketch of corporal diagnostics offers what we might call a proto-hermeneutics of the flesh.

The Textual Turn. In spite of this promising early diagnostics of the body, however, Ricoeur was soon to abandon this trajectory. After the "textual turn" in the 1960s, we witness a surprising (and I believe regrettable) rift between a hermeneutics of texts, on one hand, and a phenomenology of affectivity, on the other. He now looks back on the whole emphasis on sensible experience as susceptible to the lure of "immediacy, effusiveness, intuitionism," contrasting this with the more authentic "mediation of language."[131] And he even commends the later Merleau-Ponty—in an obituary homage—for moving beyond his initial phenomenology of "incarnation" towards a "second philosophy" of language as a privileged medium of "distance" and "reflection."[132] A commendation which, one suspects, is curiously applicable to himself.

This tension between flesh and text is nowhere more evident than in the 1964 essay, "Wonder, Eroticism, Enigma." Here Ricoeur speaks of sexuality as contrary to language. He starkly opposes what he calls (1) the "immediacy" of the "flesh to flesh" relationship and (2) the "mediations" of language and interpretation. Simply put: "Sexuality de-mediatizes language; it is eros not logos."[133]

Eros in our contemporary culture, Ricoeur argues, has lost its old cosmic force in sacred mythology and assumed the form of a "restless desire." It becomes a "demonism" that resists both the logos of understanding and the logic of instrumental rationality. "The enigma of sexuality," he claims, "is that it remains irreducible to the trilogy which composes human existence: language, tool, institution."[134] And if at times it articulates itself, it is "an infra-, para-, superlinguistic expression." Eros "mobilizes language," admits Ricoeur, but only in so far as "it crosses it, jostles it, sublimates it, stupefies it, pulverizes it into a murmur."[135] Utterly de-mediatized in this manner, eros cannot be reabsorbed either in an "ethic" (like marriage) or a "technique" (like pornography); it can only be "symbolically represented by means of whatever mythical elements remain."[136] Left to itself, in short, the "flesh to flesh" relationship defies the order of logos: "Ultimately, when two beings embrace, they don't know what they are doing, they don't know what they want, they don't know what they are looking for, they don't know what they are finding. What is the *meaning* of this desire which drives them towards each other?"[137] Sexual desire does not, claims Ricoeur, contain its own meaning but gives the impression that it participates in a network of powers whose cosmic connections are forgotten but not totally abandoned. Eros shows us that there is *more* to life than life—"that life is unique, universal, everything in everyone, and that sexual joy makes us participate in this mystery; that man does not become a person . . . unless he plunges again into the river of Life—such is the truth of sexuality."[138] But this River of Life has, Ricoeur notes, become obscure and opaque for us today. Like a lost Atlantis sunk within us long ago, it has left sexuality as its "flotsam" (*épave*). Hence the enigma of eros. The meaning of this submerged, dislocated universe is no longer accessible to us in terms of immediate participation, but only indirectly "to the learned exegesis of ancient myths." There is no straight route to eros—only hermeneutic detours.

So Ricoeur concludes that the best means to interpret the enigma of sexuality is a hermeneutics of ancient texts which record and represent this forgotten world of cosmic eros. The opposition between flesh and text could not be more explicit: "It lives again only thanks to hermeneutics—an art of interpreting writings which today are mute. And a new hiatus separates the flotsam of meaning which this *hermeneutics of language* restores to us and that other flotsam of meaning which sexuality discovers *without language*, organically."[139] On the one hand, *textual reading*, on the other *organic feeling*. Two forms of flotsam at the limits of reason. A dualism of logos and eros.

Between Flesh and Face. But this was not to be Ricoeur's last word on the matter. Fortunately, he returns to other options for a hermeneutics of flesh in one of his last major works, *Oneself as Another* (1990). In a section of the final chapter, entitled, "One's own body, or the Flesh," Ricoeur defines flesh as "the mediator between the self and a world which is taken in accordance with its various degrees of foreignness."[140] As such, it reveals a certain "lived passivity" where the body, in the deepest intimacy of flesh, is exposed to otherness. How to "mediate" between this intimacy and this otherness, between the immanence of Husserl's *Leib* and the transcendence of Levinas's *Visage*, becomes a key concern.

This dialectic of passivity-otherness signals the enigma of one's own body. Or to put it in phenomenological terms: how can we fully experience the human body if it is not at once "a body among others" (*Körper*) and "my own" (*Leib*)? We need both, suggests Ricoeur. We require the experience of our lived flesh to provide us with a sense of our individual *belonging*. This is what gives a corporeal constancy and anchoring to the self.[141] Flesh is the place where we *exist* in the world as both suffering and acting, pathos and praxis, resistance and effort. Combining the pioneering work of Maine de Biran with the phenomenologies of the *corps propre* in Husserl and Michel Henry, Ricoeur shows how it is through active "touch, in which our effort is extended, that external things attest to their existence as much as our own." It is the "same sense that gives the greatest certainty of one's own existence and the greatest certainty of external existence."[142] In the pathos of passivity and passion, "one's own body is revealed to be the mediator between the intimacy of the self and the externality of the world."[143]

Here Ricoeur makes the interesting point that it is not, as we might expect, in Heidegger—who ostensibly existentialized the phenomenological subject—that we discover the greatest ontology of the flesh.[144] It is rather Husserl, in retrospect, who offers the "most promising sketch of the flesh that would mark the inscription of hermeneutical phenomenology in an ontology of otherness."[145] Ricoeur's hermeneutic retrieval of Husserl runs as follows. In the *Cartesian Meditations*—written ten years after *Ideas II*—the founder of phenomenology had argued that in order to constitute a "foreign" subjectivity, one must formulate the idea of "ownness"—namely, flesh in its difference with respect to the external body (of others seen by me or of me seen by others). Flesh opens up a realm of *Leibhaftigkeit* (immediate embodied givenness), excluding all objective properties. It is the pole of reference of all bodies belonging to this immanent nature of *ownness*. And it is by pairing one flesh with another that we derive the notion of an alter ego. But here we return to the deeper paradox: flesh as a paradigm of *otherness*. Flesh is what is both most mine and most other. Closest to me and furthest from me at the same time. This enigma of far/near is revealed most concretely, once again, as *touch*. As center of pathos, our flesh's "aptitude for feeling is revealed most characteristically in the sense of touch."[146] It precedes and grounds both the "I can" and the "I want." Indeed, it even precedes the very distinction between the voluntary and the involuntary. "I, as this man," explains Ricoeur, "is the foremost otherness of the flesh with respect to all initiative."[147] Or to put it in more technical language, "flesh is the place of all the passive syntheses on which the active syntheses are constructed, the latter alone deserving to be called works (*Leistungen*); the flesh is the matter (*hule*) in resonance with all that can be said to be *hule* in every object perceived, apprehended. In short, it is the origin of all *alteration of ownness*."[148]

Ricoeur concludes accordingly that flesh is the support for selfhood's own "proper" otherness. For even if the otherness of the stranger could be derived from my sphere of ownness—as Husserl suggests—the otherness of the flesh would still precede it.[149] This paradox of flesh as ownness-otherness reaches dramatic proportions in a crucial passage from Husserl's "Fifth Meditation," where flesh is claimed to be a primordial space of immediacy prior to all linguistic or hermeneutic mediations:

> Among the bodies . . . included in my peculiar ownness, I find my *animate organism* [*meinen Leib*], as *uniquely* singled out—namely as the only one of them that is not just a body but precisely an animate organism [flesh]: the sole Object within my world stratum to which, in accordance with experience, I ascribe *fields of sensation* (belonging to it, however, in different manners—a field of tactual sensations, a field of warmth and coldness, and so forth), the only Object "in which" I "*rule and govern*" *immediately*, governing particularly in each of its organs.[150]

It is only on the basis of this primordial spatial materiality of immanent flesh—as a "pre-linguistic" world of I can—that we are able to construct a genuine semantics and hermeneutics of action. But it is here that phenomenology reaches its limit, and Ricoeur departs from Husserl. In seeking to derive the objective world from the "non-objectivating primordial experience" of flesh, Husserl went too far. He ignored that flesh is not just mine but equally a body among other bodies—both *Leib* and *Körper* at once. In order to make flesh part of the world (*mondanéiser*) one needs to be not just oneself but oneself as another—a self with others. And this means that the otherness of others as "foreign" relates not only to the otherness of my flesh (that I am) but also exists prior to any reduction to ownness. For the flesh can only appear in the world as a body among bodies to the degree that I am myself already an other among others—a self-with-another "in the apprehension of a common nature, woven out of the network of intersubjectivity—itself founding selfhood in its own way."[151]

So Ricoeur concludes this highly intricate analysis by observing that while Husserl recognized the primordiality of subjective flesh and the necessity of intersubjective language, he could not reconcile the two. "It is because Husserl thought of the other than me only as another me, and never of the self as another, that he has no answer to the paradox summed up in the question: how am I to understand that my flesh is also a body."[152] In short, Husserl could not adequately account for both the flesh's intimacy to itself (in the absolute immediacy of immanence) and its opening onto the world (through the mediation of others). He had a carnal phenomenology but lacked a carnal hermeneutics. Only the latter could provide a full account of the ontological relationship between flesh and world.

One's Body and Another's. In correcting Husserl it is important, however, not to go to the other extreme. And this is, according to Ricoeur, where Levinas erred in traversing flesh too quickly towards alterity. Identifying the carnal caress with a play of feminine immanence, Levinas, as we saw, redirected the virile self in the direction of an ethics of vertical transcendence in which the face trumps flesh. In contrast to both Husserl and Levinas, we might say (with Ricoeur and Irigaray) that if flesh needs the other to save it from fragmentation and inner collapse, the other needs flesh to save it from Platonic moralism and paternalism.[153] And here we return, finally, to the realization that we need to combine sensibility (flesh) and language (face) in a new carnal hermeneutics. The ultimate question stands: how to make sense of sense by making flesh a body in the world.

Let us recap. In order for my flesh to engage upon an intersubjective world with others and empathize with them, I must have both an intimate body for me (*Leib*) and a physical natural body among other bodies (*Körper*). This involves a complex intertwining (*Verflechtung/entrelacs*) whereby I experience myself as someone in a shared world. Thus Ricoeur, challenging the Sartrean dichotomy of flesh versus body, asks: "To say that my flesh is also a body, does this not imply that it appears in just this way to the eyes of others? Only a flesh (for me) that is a body (for others) can play the role of first *analogon* in the analogical transfer from flesh to flesh."[154] And this reveals in turn that intentionalities that are aimed at the other—as strange and foreign to me—go beyond the sphere of my immanent ownness in which they are rooted and given. The other is revealed to my flesh as *both* inscribed in my embodied relation through flesh *and* as always already transcendent. Or to put it in more precise terms, the other is not reducible to the "immediate givenness of the flesh to itself" in originary presentation, but only in appresentation. The gap can thus never be bridged between "the presentation of my experience and the appresentation of your experience."[155] And this interval is revealed in the fact that the pairing of your body over *there* as flesh with my body *here* as flesh always retains a certain distance. The analogizing grasp between two embodied selves is never complete or adequate. Total assimilation is impossible. "Never will pairing allow us to cross the barrier that separates appresentation from intuition (immediate presentation). The notion of appresentation, therefore, combines similarity and dissymmetry in a unique manner."[156] It is this double fidelity of flesh to both near and far that is captured in Ricoeur's felicitous formula, "oneself as another." And it is precisely because of the irreducible distance of alterity at the very heart of our flesh that hermeneutic mediation is always operative. This is where phenomenology reaches its limit and calls for more. Where the analogical transfer of flesh to flesh, through an intersubjectivity of bodies, "transgresses the program of phenomenology in transgressing the experience of one's own flesh."[157]

So what does all this mean for the hermeneutic relationships between self and other? It means, first, that the other who is stranger is *also* my "semblable," a counterpart who, like me, can say "I." The transfer of sense shows how "she thinks" signifies "she says in her heart: I think"; and at the same time it reveals the inverse movement of "she thinks and feels in a way that I can never think or feel."[158] I am called by the other who comes to me in a way that I cannot assimilate to my immanence. I can only respond by "reading" their transcendence in immanence, across distance and difference. Ricoeur actually speaks of a hermeneutic interpreting of the body by the body which precedes the work of inference through formal linguistic signs. He refers to it as a primal "relation of *indication* in which the interpretation is made immediately, much as the reading of symptoms." And the "style" of confirmation to which this reading of indications belongs involves, says Ricoeur, "neither primordial intuition nor discursive inference."[159] It entails a special grammar of carnal hermeneutics across distance, gaps and differences. Carnal hermeneutics as diacritical hermeneutics.[160]

With this final intuition, Ricoeur retrieves some of his most radical early insights into a diagnostics of affectivity. He charts a middle way between Husserl's phenomenology of carnal immanence and Levinas's ethics of radical transcendence. While the former addressed the movement of sense from me to the other (through analogy, transfer, pairing, appresentation), the latter addressed the movement of the other towards me. But in Levinas, as we saw, the other goes too far in instigating a rupture of separation: the face of the other is one of radical exteriority to the exclusion of all mediation. "The Other absolves itself from relation in the same movement by which the Infinite draws free from Totality."[161] So if Husserlian phenomenology veers at times towards an excess of egology (the haptic circle of the hand touching its hand, critiqued by Derrida in *On Touching*), Levinas veers toward the opposite extreme of heterology. The ultimate "evincing" of the Levinasian face, as Ricoeur notes, lies apart from "the vision of forms and even the sensuous hearing of voices."[162] To the extent that a call remains, it is the voice of the Master of justice who teaches but does not touch. For Levinas there is no primacy of *relation* between the terms of flesh and face. No communication or communion possible. No *metaxu*. "No middle ground, no between, is secured to lessen the utter dissymmetry between the Same and the Other."[163] Put in more affective terms, the Levinasian other persecutes, summons, obsesses, offends, but does not love. And it is against this paroxysm of absolute separation that a diacritical hermeneutics of dialogue proposes itself. "To mediate the opening of the Same onto the Other and the internalization of the voice of the other in the Same, must not language contribute its resources of communication, hence of reciprocity as is attested by the exchange of personal pronouns (I, you, he, she, us)?"[164] And must not this basic linguistic mediation call in turn for an even more radical hermeneutic exchange—"that of question and answer in which the roles are continually reversed?" In short, surmises Ricoeur, "is it not necessary that a dialogue superpose a relation on the supposedly absolute distance between the separate I and the teaching Other?"[165] And is it not precisely the task of carnal hermeneutics to do this by finding a just balance between the movement of same toward other and the other toward same? A balance which would not only bridge the divide between Husserl and Levinas, but also, by extension, between Merleau-Ponty's reversible *chair* and Derrida's irreversible *différance?*

The answer, I submit, is yes and raises further on-going interrogations. For what kind of language are we talking about? One not only of words and writing, surely, but also of sensing and touching. And what kind of dialogue? One not just between speakers but also between bodies. And what kind of sense and sensibility is at issue here? One not only of intellectual "understanding" but also of tangible "orientation." Thus does the simplest phenomenon of touch lead to the most complex of philosophies. Because the simplest *is* the most complex and remains the most enigmatic. In posing such questions, Ricoeur opens a door where phenomenology and hermeneutics may cross in the swing door of the flesh. He marks a new beginning. But much work remains to be done.

Concluding Remarks

By way of conclusion I would like to note four further orientations for the continuing conversation of carnal hermeneutics.

First there is the *deconstructive hermeneutics of touch*, sketched out by Derrida in *On Touching* and developed by Jean-Luc Nancy in a number of powerful recent works from *Noli me Tangere* to *Corpus* I and II. The contributions of Anne O'Bryne, David Wood and Nancy himself in this volume show the rich potential of this itinerary.

Second, there is the *feminist hermeneutics of the body* inaugurated by thinkers like Julia Kristeva and Luce Irigaray, drawing from psychoanalysis, semiotics and phenomenology, and represented here by Kristeva herself and a new generation of feminist thinkers like Shelly Rambo, Anne O'Byrne, and Karmen MacKendrick. Recent work by Judith Butler, Susan Heinamaa, and Susan Bordo also moves in this direction.

Third, there is the *theological hermeneutics of incarnation* inspired by the phenomenological retrieval of Christian mysticism and exegetics and represented in this volume by some of its major proponents—Michel Henry, Jean-Louis Chrétien, Jean-Luc Marion, Emmanuel Falque, and John Panteleimon Manoussakis. One might also mention here the recent writings of Virginia Burrus, Caroline Bynum, and Catherine Keller.

Fourth and finally, there is a *diacritical hermeneutics of flesh*, represented in this volume by the eco-phenomenology of David Wood and Ed Casey, the bio-diacritics of Ted Toadvine, and the dia-phenomenology of Emmanuel Alloa and Brian Treanor (the latter in dialogue with the new realist and materialist movements, the recent findings of cognitive science, and the growing challenge of environmental ethics).[166] In addition to these projects, I would add the importance of diacritical hermeneutics engaging more specifically with the carnal "signs" of our particular time, as evinced in the increasing digitalization of the body and the virtualization of our means of communication and community. Here "medium" takes on new connotations unknown and unknowable for Aristotle when he first wrote about *metaxu* two thousand years ago; and scarcely imaginable for the major phenomenologists discussed in this essay. This diagnostic task will be a major challenge in the coming age of excarnation.[167]

Mind the Gap

The Challenge of Matter

BRIAN TREANOR

> Let us settle ourselves, and work and wedge our feet downward through the mud and slush of opinion, and prejudice, and tradition, and delusion, and appearance, that alluvion which covers the globe, through Paris and London, through New York and Boston and Concord, through church and state, through poetry and philosophy and religion, till we come to a hard bottom and rocks in place, which we can call *reality*, and say, This is, and no mistake . . .
>
> —Henry David Thoreau[1]

> Truth is not that which is demonstrable, but that which is ineluctable.
>
> —Antoine de Saint Exupéry[2]

Why Carnal Hermeneutics?

Why "carnal" hermeneutics? Don't we already talk enough about the body? After all, the body has, since the dawn of philosophy, been a topic of concern in one form or another. Plato talks about embodiment in the *Republic* and *Philebus*. Aristotle takes up the subject in *De Anima*, the *Nicomachean Ethics*, *De Partibus Animalium*, and other works. Augustine, Aquinas, Descartes, and others all write about the body; it has hardly been ignored. And don't we already have enough flavors of hermeneutics? The latter half of the twentieth century was dominated by hermeneutics: Heidegger, Gadamer, and Ricoeur; the radicalization of these thinkers by Derrida; the expansion of "postmodern" hermeneutics into religion, feminism, political philosophy, psychoanalysis, and myriad other fields. One might legitimately wonder about the usefulness of yet another subfield, another niche in an oversaturated philosophical landscape. Nevertheless, a book on carnal hermeneutics—the hermeneutical engagement with the body as a lived, sensuous, carnal reality—is compelling and, indeed, timely for at least three reasons.

First, the body is, or ought to be, a core topic of philosophical concern. The injunction of the Delphic oracle looms large in the history of philosophy: *know thyself.* Socrates opined that, until one is able to adequately respond to that injunction, "it seems ridiculous . . . to inquire into extraneous matters."[3] Sound advice. And, while it may not be fashionable in academic philosophy, I'm happy to think of myself as a philosopher in the Socratic mold: I'm interested in myriad philosophical questions, but my main concern is understanding how I ought to live.[4] However, since all that living is done "in," or "through," or "with," or "as" a body—choose your preposition—it seems worthwhile to reflect on the nature of our embodiment, to understand what it is like and how it shapes our capabilities, powers, and limitations, and to appreciate the ways in which it determines our engagement with ourselves, with others, and with the world.[5]

Second, although continental philosophy has long rejected both the Platonic view of the body as a "prison house" for the soul and Cartesian dualism, which relegates the body to a mechanistic and subordinate position vis-à-vis the soul, those developments do not generally bring us around to reflecting on, much less living through, the *carnal* body. With some notable exceptions, when continental philosophy has addressed the body it has done so in terms of the body as signifier or transcendental abstraction rather than the body as carnal, sensuous, lived reality.[6] This is part of a larger trend in which materiality has been occluded, marginalized, or downplayed in "postmodern" thinking, which tends to focus on the constructed nature of the world. As Stacy Alaimo points out, the "enormously productive" turn to "culture, discourse, and language" in postmodernity has led to a situation in which there is a high degree of suspicion associated with materiality.[7] Because the material seems fixed, and tends to imply connections to concepts like "reality" and "truth," postmodern thinkers have generally steered the ship of philosophy clear of the shoals of materiality.

Finally, the tendency to think of the body in terms of symbol, signifier, trace, or construction points to a third reason that carnal hermeneutics suggests itself as a timely topic: hermeneutics, the philosophy of interpretation, finds itself under increasing pressure from a number of quarters. Cosmology, biology, psychology, and other disciplines, as well as various schools of philosophy, are calling into question both the primacy and the inescapability of the hermeneutic circle. By critiquing "correlationism," "constructivism," or even "language" itself, these thinkers—some of whom I will group under the banner of "new realism" in what follows—either deny the primacy of hermeneutic engagement with the world or, more critically, dismiss the entire project as unsound.[8]

In what follows, I hope to present carnal hermeneutics as a counterpoint of sorts to the "hermeneutics of texts" that dominated late twentieth century philosophy, and which tended to overlook the role of the carnal body and material world, but also as a rejoinder to the "reductive real" evident in the work of those who, reacting to the aforementioned hegemony of texts, have gone too far in the opposite direction: ignoring, minimizing, or dismissing phenomenological hermeneutics; downplaying the significance of meaning and value; and suggesting that a single bandwidth, however significant it may be, represents the full spectrum of reality. Thus conceived, carnal hermeneutics addresses both the material lacunae associated with much contemporary continental philosophy and, in addition, the overenthusiastic backlash that tends, in certain instances, to lead back to the natural attitude or scientism.

This view, which engages both the carnal and the imaginative, realism and interpretation, the animal and the angelic, is prefigured both in certain hermeneuts of the text, notably Paul Ricoeur, and in some philosophers of the real, such as Michel Serres; however, neither of these thinkers—nor, until recently, any others—has made fully explicit *both* the inescapable nature of our hermeneutic condition *and* its ineluctably carnal character. So while carnal hermeneutics is, in a sense, nothing new, insofar as it is prefigured in other philosophers; it is, in another sense, a refreshingly new endeavor, one that returns us to thinking about the lived body but with all the resources of phenomenology and diacritical hermeneutics.

Of course, on the ground, hermeneutics has always been, and will always be, carnal. It is in the halls of the academy that philosophers are tempted to transcendental abstractions and self-referential webs of signification, where students get the idea that hermeneutics is something esoteric: the province of bookish academics, scholarly exegetes, those initiated into the mysteries of the cult of Hermes. Nothing could be further from the truth. At the most basic level, hermeneutics, like the cautionary announcements on the London Tube, enjoins us to "mind the gap" (*écart*, *metaxu*). These gaps evident, to be sure, in texts and in language: the spacing of plots, the *différance* in words and meanings, the fracture or betrayal in translations, the difference between the saying (*le dire*) and the said (*le dit*), the contrast between *parole* and *langue*, the silences in speech, the gaps in narratives, and so forth. However—and this is critical—gaps are also carnal, material, and earthy: the synaptic gap between nerves, the gaps between sense organs and the objects sensed, the distinction between body (*Körper, la chose*) and flesh (*Leib, la chair*), the fold of proprioception, the reversibility or "intertwining" (*Verflechtung, entrelacs*) of sensing and sensed, the distance of alterity between the self and the other (*autre* or *autrui*), the spaces between bodies in the world, the shift of stellar parallax, and so on.

In short, hermeneutics has to do with a way, the human way, of being in the world. It is concerned with the "surplus of meaning" found in all these multifarious gaps and, therefore, my own view is that hermeneutics is best thought of in very broad terms indeed.

The "New Realism(s)"

Today, realism is, so to speak, in the air. It travels under many guises: the speculative realism of Quentin Meillassoux, the object-oriented philosophy of Graham Harman, the material feminisms of Stacey Alaimo and others, Timothy Morton's hyperobjects and ecology without nature, Jane Bennett's vibrant matter, Ray Brassier's transcendental realism, Michel Serres's philosophy of the hard and the soft, Catherine Malabou's materialist neuroplasticity, Bruno Latour's "realistic realism," and others.[9]

True, many of these thinkers have substantially different agenda, and some are fairly sharp critics of others: process- or activity-oriented critiques of Harman's account of objects by Ian Hamilton Grant and Elizabeth Groz;[10] Harman's critique of Meillassoux's residual anthropocentrism and idealism;[11] and, perhaps most famously and sensationally, Brassier's dismissal of speculative realism itself as the product of "a group of bloggers" pushing "actor-network theory spiced with panpsychist metaphysics and morsels of process philosophy . . . a 'movement' whose most signal achievement thus far is to have generated an online orgy of stupidity."[12] Nevertheless, the notion of a "new realism"—or, better, given the diversity of these thinkers, "new realisms"—captures something significant about the philosophy of the past several years, something in the air that distinguishes the dawn of the twenty-first century from the dusk of the twentieth. There is a feeling among some philosophers that philosophy has lost itself in a linguistic hall of mirrors in which nothing is really real and we are left with only simulacra of simulacra *ad infinitum*. We've strayed too far from experience, from science, from nature, from reality. This wandering—or, worse, errancy—makes it exceedingly difficult for postmodernity to engage science, medicine, biology, ecology, and similar disciplines in "innovative or productive ways—the only path available is the well-worn path of critique."[13] We've had quite enough denaturalization; at this point we are in need of some renaturalization.

Whether or not the new realisms prove to have staying power remains to be seen, and here I am not concerned with a direct engagement with any one of them insofar as each represents one of a variety of potential detours or explorations through which hermeneutics might engage realism and materialism. Other scholars are busy debating the details of their philosophies. Here I am more concerned with the spirit which animates all of the new realists to one degree or another: a reaction against the *zeitgeist* that seemed to dominate late-twentieth century continental philosophy. Some critics peg the decisive turn as far back as the critical philosophy of Kant, others in the rise of phenomenology or in the radicalization of phenomenology and hermeneutics in deconstruction. However, in each case the criticism is the same: philosophy has lost sight of reality, "the problem of matter," and of "the existence of a real beyond the human's consciousness and control . . . ."[14] We've replaced things with words, and in so doing posited an unbridgeable chasm between the real (which we cannot grasp) and the perceived (which is all we can access). We've become so thoroughly committed to the perspectives through which we view reality that we've completely abandoned the quest for, and even the idea of, an Archimedean point. The so-called "Copernican" revolution in philosophy is in fact nothing more than a doubling down on Ptolemaic subjectivism and anthropocentrism.[15]

Correlationism/Realism

A central critique of the new realisms is the rejection of "correlationism." Different thinkers phrase their criticisms in different ways and, in fact, not all of them employ this specific term; however, a number of people have adopted the definition put forward by Meillassoux: correlationism is the claim that "we only ever have access to the correlation between thinking and being, and never to either term considered apart from the other."[16] As a consequence, philosophies of correlationism—beginning with Kant and exacerbated by phenomenology, hermeneutics, and deconstruction—only engage with what is "given to thought, never an entity subsisting by itself."[17] Correlationism obscures reality in favor of a misguided focus on our perception and interpretation of it:

> Contemporary philosophers have lost the *great outdoors*, the *absolute* outside of pre-critical thinkers: that outside which was not relative to us, and which was given as indifferent to its own givenness to be

what it is, existing in itself regardless of whether we are thinking of it or not; that outside which thought could explore with the legitimate feeling of being on foreign territory—of being entirely elsewhere.[18]

The correlationist cannot think that which is not given to thought—for example, those objects Meillassoux identifies as "ancestral": objects existing prior to thought itself, prior to the evolution of life or the accretion of the Earth.[19]

Correlationism comes in different strengths, but according to the new realists they all make some version of the following claim: "there are no objects, no events, no beings which are not always-already correlated with a point of view, with subjective access."[20] The result?

> Ever since Kant, to think science as a philosopher has been to claim that science harbors a meaning other than the one delivered by science itself—a meaning that is deeper, more originary, and that furnishes us with the truth of the latter. And this more originary meaning is correlational: it construes those elements that seem to be indifferent to our relation to the world in terms of that relation itself.[21]

But, counter the new realists, reality is not a text fashioned by the demiurge of language; it is something that existed, exists, and will exist independent of human perception, description, experience, and understanding—and science can access it. We can, we do, have reliable knowledge of reality independent of human thought, including ancestral objects. Thus, Meillassoux argues for an absolute realism that we can access literally and without the correlationist codicil of ". . . for humans."[22]

A number of thorny and intriguing issues arise in the wake of the rejection of correlationism; but surely two of the most significant for hermeneutics are non-anthropocentrism and materialism, both of which deserve a brief word here.

Anthropocentrism/Non-Anthropocentrism

Several among the new realists are keen to undercut belief in human superiority, to reject the idea that humans are special in an ontological sense, and to deny notions of teleology and progress.[23] They insist that non-human nature has meaning and value independent of any interaction with humans, and that we would do well to recognize our finitude, contingency, and insignificance in the cosmic scheme of things. This is most evident in the Spinozist arguments of "object-oriented" philosophers like Harman and Morton, but is also in Jane Bennett's Deleuzian account of "assemblages" of "distributive agency" and Brassier's transcendental nihilism. Harman, for example, argues in Levinasian language that the alterity of objects is just as significant, and just as absolute, as the alterity of other persons, and therefore speaks in terms of "doing justice to objects."[24] And Morton writes:

> I see no inherent reason why what I called the strange stranger in *The Ecological Thought* should not apply to any entity whatsoever: fireplaces, the Oort Cloud at the edge of the Solar System, flamingos and slices of pork rotting in a garbage can. Since lifeforms are made of nonlife, and since what counts as a lifeform is very much a performative act down to the DNA level, I see no big reason not to extend the concept of the strange stranger to cover all entities . . . .[25]

In a world where *tout autre*—*every* other: person, dog, tree, rock, nebula— *est tout autre* in the most far-reaching and homogenizing sense, thinkers like Harman and Levi Bryant insist there is only one type of being: objects.[26] This sort of realism is committed to radically flattening out the differences between humans and other entities. And, at least for Brassier, letting go of teleology and human exceptionalism—acknowledging "a mind-independent reality, which, despite the presumptions of human narcissism, is indifferent to our existence and oblivious to the 'values' and 'meanings' which we would drape over it to make it more hospitable"[27]— leads not only to a stark realism, but also to nihilism.

Idealism/Materialism

The rejection of correlationism also leads a number of new realists to embrace some form of materialism. This is most evident in the work of thinkers working on human consciousness and the brain, including Brassier, Johnston, and Malabou. Malabou, for example, "insists on materiality" and immanence in order to speak of the "real without the human subject":[28] "The only valid philosophical path today lies in the elaboration of a new materialism . . . ."[29] She seeks to replace the "motor scheme" of writing with one of neuroplasticity as a model for a "plastic ontology" in which the organization of the brain is a model for understanding all kinds of organization.[30] This commitment to materialism leads her to a "closed totality without any kind of transcendence."[31]

Of course, there are various types of materialism, just as there are various sorts of realism—and, frankly, on those two distinctions hinges the notion of a materialist hermeneutics or a realist hermeneutics. However, while not all of the new realists go so far as to embrace the eliminative materialism most notably associated with Paul and Patricia Churchland—and a few explicitly reject it—at least some see, in the work of Thomas Metzinger and other neuroscientists, a project well on its way to explaining human consciousness, including statements of meaning, purely in terms of the natural sciences.[32] Science—"the measure of all things, of what is that it is, and what is not that it is not"[33]—will allow us access to even "noumenal" realm.[34] If such projects were ever to fully eliminate the subjective ghost in the material machine, as least some speculate about the distinctly nonhermeneutic possibility of an exhaustively objective "view from nowhere."[35]

Paul Ricoeur: Detour and Return

Regardless of the particular critic or specific charge, hermeneutics needs to address questions about realism, anthropocentrism, and materialism in making its own "carnal turn." How then should hermeneutic philosophers respond to these provocative—and potentially damning—critiques?

Well, they should not respond with an indifferent silence. The new realists are diverse, but a number of their arguments are well worth considering. Moreover, materialism and realism are at stake in hermeneutics whether or not one is in dialogue with the new realists. Neither should hermeneutics respond with a condescending dismissal of new realism. None of these thinkers are unsophisticated realists, and the common rebuffs to naïve realism will not suffice as a response to their concerns. But, finally, hermeneutics should not pull up stakes or cede the field, both because there are problems of various sorts associated with new realist positions and because hermeneutics has an enormous amount to contribute to discussions of the carnal body and the material world.[36]

The proper response, I submit, is to follow the lead of one of the great hermeneutic thinkers of the twentieth century in charting a path for the twenty-first. Paul Ricoeur was also faced with a number of hostile interlocutors, including those who, dismissive, would not even deign to enter into dialogue with him. However, in each case, he responded by engagement—not in the spirit of belligerence that is, alas, all-too-common in academic philosophy, but in a spirit of dialogue characterized by intellectual hospitality, open-mindedness, and a willingness to listen.

Ricoeur consistently and scrupulously engaged other perspectives as part of his commitment to dialogue, willingly subjecting his own hermeneutic convictions to repeated critiques. This strategy is most well-known as the pattern of "detour and return" through which he explored other traditions and perspectives.[37] However, one can also view this approach in terms of a dialectic between "critique and conviction" in which one's convictions are repeatedly subjected to critique, and these criticisms lead to new forms of conviction.[38] Or, finally, we can think of this strategy in terms the triad of "first naïveté, doubt, second naïveté," in which our beliefs, understanding, and perspective are subjected to the crucible of doubt, the proverbial dark night of the soul.[39]

The image of detour and return may bring to mind the common criticism that hermeneutics is circular: one begins with a certain perspective that colors one's interpretation of the world in such a way that the interpretation confirms the original perspective. Hermeneutic philosophers themselves are fond of reminding us there is "no escaping the hermeneutic circle." There is no "innocent eye" or "view from nowhere" uncolored by one's perspective, a perspective that is itself shaped by culture, history, narrative, and the like—as well as by body and place. But this objection misunderstands both Ricoeur's hermeneutics and the structure of detour and return. For Ricoeur, the hermeneutical journey is not the circular path from A to A of an opinion looking for reasons; it is rather a helical or spiraling one from A_1 to A_2, A_3, . . . A_n in which each "return" also brings us to a new landscape with a new perspective. With Elliot, Ricoeur suggests:

We shall not cease from exploration
And the end of all our exploring
Will be to arrive where we started
And know the place for the first time.[40]

The helical rather than circular pattern that characterizes Ricoeur's way of proceeding is, I submit, among the most significant of his many philosophical contributions.[41]

Ricoeur engaged in a number of detours on his philosophical path: through structuralism, psychoanalysis, social sciences, analytic philosophy, and more. These detours did not end because he lost faith in the practice, or because he had taken all the detours that needed to be taken. Far from it. Toward the end of his long career Ricoeur was still challenging himself and critiquing his own convictions: beginning new dialogues, starting new detours, and charting new paths on his philosophical itinerary. Apropos to the engagement with realism—and the development of carnal hermeneutics, environmental hermeneutics, and similar lines of inquiry—Ricoeur himself remarked that hermeneutics must embrace dialogue with the hard sciences during a conference marking his eightieth birthday in 1993, although he was never able to embark on this detour himself.[42] Those of us thinking in his wake must complete these detours, as well as imagine, plan, and embark on others yet to be conceived.

Michel Serres: The Hard and the Soft

If hermeneutics is to take a detour through the new realisms, I'd suggest that one useful landmark en route is to be found in the work of Michel Serres. Despite holding a seat on *L'Académie Française* and enjoying significant popularity in France, Serres is something of an obscure figure for Anglophone philosophy. Certainly his thought is relatively unknown in North America compared to contemporaries like Jacques Derrida and Gilles Deleuze. Nevertheless, his work offers points of contact with—and therefore potential sites for bridges between—hermeneutics and science, interpretation and realism, and metaphor and materialism.

Serres began his studies as a mathematician engaged closely with the sciences before turning his attention to the humanities and, although he is not allied with the core group of new realist thinkers, his education—along with problems he saw in the philosophies dominant during his studies at the *École Normale Supérieure*—left him an unapologetic realist:

> Without being able to prove it I believe, like soothsayers and haruspices, and like scientists, that there exists a world independent of men. No one knows how to demonstrate the truth of this proposition, which we might like to call realist, since it exceeds language and thus any utterance which might demonstrate its proof. [However,] realism is worth betting on, whereas idealism calls for demonstration.[43]

This commitment to realism is combined with instances of fiery assaults on language that would please any of the critics of correlationism. An example relevant to carnal hermeneutics can be found in his reaction to the *Phenomenology of Perception*, at which he recalls "laughing":

> [Merleau-Ponty] opens it with these words: "At the outset of the study of perception, we find *in language the notion of sensation . . .*" Isn't this an exemplary introduction? A collection of examples in the same vein, so asture and meager, inspire the descriptions that follow. From his window the author sees some tree, always in bloom; he huddles over his desk; now and again a red blotch appears—it's a quote. What you can decipher in this book is a nice ethology of city dwellers, who are hypertechnalized, intellectualized, chained to their library chairs, and tragically stripped of any tangible experience. Lots of phenomenology and no sensation—everything via language.[44]

Why this animosity?

One of the key distinctions in Serres's thinking is between "the hard" (*le dur*) and "the soft" (*le doux*).[45] By the hard, he means the domain of nature, the given, the physical, the world of objects, reality independent of human perception of it. By soft he means culture, concepts, ideas, signs, meaning, and, generally, human accounts of reality. Serres claims that language initiates the inexorable drift from the hard to the soft. And philosophy, especially in its idealistic or quasi-idealistic manifestations, accelerates and exacerbates the tendency to equate things with words: "when [philosophies] come across an object, they change it, by sleight of hand, into a relationship, language or representation."[46]

Among his numerous spirited criticisms of language, perhaps none are as sharp as those found in *The Five Senses*, especially in the third chapter, "Tables."[47] Here language is referred to variously as an enormous burden, a prison, a numbing agent, a narcotic, an addiction, poor, suspicious, dull and insipid, interfering with or killing the senses, and so forth. When we cocoon ourselves in language, we veil, overwhelm, and ultimately lose the things that, in their hardness, make up the world.[48] True, the hard reality remains—as any victim of a significant fall will tell you, gravity takes no holidays—but we increasingly find ourselves detached from that hardness, which is veiled by the words that cover and obscure the thing, drowned out by the noise of chatter, or obscured in its unique particularity by the application of a general name or genus.

But if Serres sometimes criticizes the soft, he is no naïve realist with respect to the hard. Nor is he an unambiguous champion of science, which is neither an all-purpose solvent to dissolve the accreted *doxa* covering reality nor a skeleton key—whittled down, no doubt, by Occam's Razor—to the truth. Although he criticizes the pervasive influence of language, it seems clear, in other passages, that language itself is not *malum in se*.[49] After all, Serres himself argues as a philosopher, using language that is often praised for its subtlety, nuance, and beauty. And, most importantly, like hermeneutic philosophers he operates under the guidance of Hermes, patron of transport and messages.[50]

Serres's critiques of language are more nuanced than they might appear at first blush. The historical drift from the hard to the soft is perhaps inevitable for *zoon logon echon*. And observation, which Serres allies with science rather than epistemology (the social sciences and philosophy), "cannot be detached from interpretation"[51] But if softening, so to speak, is in some measure inevitable for humans, we nevertheless "live in hope of returning to a state of trust without deception or cheating [i.e., realism that does not cheat the hardness of objects]."[52] What is this if not a second naïveté in which we "remember hardness,"[53] so as not to lose sight of "the given which resists being named by language and is still without concept"?[54] And it is here, on the topic of the integration of the soft and the hard, that *the body* plays a critical role.

Seraphic Bodies

Although Serres allies himself with Hermes, he notes that angels perform a similar function.[55] What do angels do? They too are messengers (*angĕlŏs*: messenger or envoy); they transport, they travel between different worlds or spheres. Or, hermeneutically, they translate between different idioms. This is important for carnal hermeneutics because Serres often describes the *body* as angelic.[56]

What does the body, as angelic, translate? It travels between, translates, or otherwise mediates, I'd suggest, the hard and the soft. The body is a carnal seraphim or ishim,[57] an envoy between the hard and the soft, between nature and culture, between the world and language. This carnal translation is described by Serres in terms of the "black box" of the body: the hard enters in one side and the soft exits the other, but what takes place within remains obscure.[58]

> The box transforms the world into coloured pictures, into paintings hanging on walls, changes the landscape into tapestry, the city into abstract compositions. Its function is to replace the sun with heaters and the world with icons. The sound of the wind with gentle words.[59]

The body receives the hard given from the world and, in the act of processing that given, names and labels it, replacing the thing with a word, concept, or idea. This substitution is problematic on its own, but the distance between the hard and the soft is further exacerbated by the clumsy use of language. For example, we tend to label in broad, undetailed, and nonspecific ways (e.g. "flower") rather than in a manner that is attentive to the particularity of the real (e.g., "Hochstetter's Butterfly-Orchid" or, better, a detailed description of *this particular* Hochstetter's Butterfly-Orchid).[60]

So the body is the bridge between the reality of the hard and the construction of the soft; and it is the nature of this bridge that is a key concern for carnal hermeneutics. Transmuting the hard to the soft is commonplace, and easy. Numerous examples and images suggest that the softening of reality is, for humans, both a historical fact and an unavoidable fate: as *zoon logon echon*, we effortlessly replace hard reality with soft language, and as *zoon thnēton*, mortal animals, we, like Eurydice, die and become "shades," soft shadows of the hard reality we once were. It is precisely the ease and ubiquity of the first kind of softening (hard reality to soft language) that gives rise to the objections of the new realists; and the second sort of softening—the inevitable loss of order and organization—is so powerful it is enshrined in scientific law: the second law of thermodynamics, which predicts the heat-death of the universe in thermodynamic equilibrium, and which gives rise to Ray Brassier's nihilism.[61]

But perhaps we ought not think of the black box of the body as a system with a single operation: the transmutation of the hard to the soft. Perhaps through some subtle alchemy the body can transmute the soft to the hard as well. If so, we ought to think, not in terms of the absolutely hard or the absolutely soft, but rather in terms of softness and hardness. Here, I think, is the opening for a thinking that is *both* carnal *and* hermeneutic.

This second transmutation, from the soft to the hard, is no doubt more difficult, as Serres suggests in his reading of Orpheus's attempt to restore Eurydice's shade to life.[62] Moving from softness to hardness requires conscious effort, while moving from hardness to softness does not. Nevertheless, "hardening" can and does take place. One of the most beautiful passages in *The Five Senses* describes in glowing detail sharing a 1947 Château d'Yquem with two friends, an example that points toward a commonplace transformation of the soft to the hard.[63] In cooking, raw nature is compacted, concentrated, mixed, and blended to produce food—the mysterious transubstantiation of nature into our daily bread. Under the influence of skilled hands, the hard and the soft combine to make the softhard/hardsoft of *cuisine*, expressed uniquely by each culture. Here the hard is indeed softened, as the physical reality of digestible calories (hard) becomes palatable food associated with a certain culture (soft)—the same hard reality of a duck's carcass is transformed into an expression of French-ness (*canard a l'orange, cassoulet*) or Chinese-ness (*Yātóu, Běijīng Kǎoyà*). But it is equally true that the soft is hardened in the same process, as specific cultures (soft) become expressed in material reality (hard): Frenchness made manifest in material form and then, completing the circle, quite literally transformed again into a material body in the act of consumption and digestion. This "sublime alchemy"[64] both intermingles the soft and the hard, and produces a concentrated form of sensual, empirical knowledge (*sapience*: wisdom; *sapere*: to taste, to know).

Cooking, vinification, lacto-fermentation, and similar processes are perhaps the most common examples through which we turn culture (soft) into something hard(er), but they are far from the only cases. Other examples abound: all forms of material culture, any new invention that modifies material based on an original idea, diverse forms of art, and so on.

Or, reversing both sorts of softening—linguistic and entropic—consider the conscious decision to create and nurture new life. Here, as with other examples, a soft idea (love) is given hard material form (a child). Moreover, this act actually *reverses*—however temporarily and locally—the inexorable increase in entropy. To make love and create life is to spit in the face of death, disorder, nihilism, and thermodynamic equilibrium.[65]

Such incarnational, creative labors of love, which accomplish what we are calling the transmutation of the soft to the hard, can take various forms. However, in each case the transformation moves from a general idea to a particular hard reality, reversing the softening process by which we replace unique hard realities with general soft ideas. As Erazim Kohák—whose work in environmental phenomenology and hermeneutics prefigures carnal hermeneutics—reminds us: "The miracle of incarnation is not abstract; it is as tangible as the labor in which love becomes embodied and comes to belong, from eternity to earth, but not just earth in general . . . to *this* spread of land, to *these* boulders, to *these* trees, to *this* river."[66]

But if our angelic bodies transform, transport, or translate from the hard to the soft and from the soft to the hard, we should be thinking in terms of degrees of hardness—and, consequently, degrees of softness—rather than in terms of the purely hard or purely soft. Serres suggests as much when he notes that empiricism, like the cook, "learns not to abhor impurity, puts its finger in the soup. It learns about mixtures."[67] The problem is not that there are harder and softer realities, nor the obvious fact that some realities lend themselves to certain approaches rather than others; the problem comes when, blinded by the idea of purity we lose sight of complexity and mixture, pursuing a rigid dogma of the hard or mindless ideology of the soft that forces us to imagine hard(er) objects in soft(er) terms or, it's worth emphasizing, vice versa.[68] Science may be *primus inter pares* in accounting for and describing certain hard realities or in answering certain sorts of questions, and philosophers and humanists should recognize this; but the world is made up of more than hard objects, and scientists and engineers should recognize this.[69]

Carnal Hermeneutics: Moving Between the Hard and the Soft

Paul Ricoeur was a hermeneutic philosopher of detour and return who, despite wide-ranging interests, never quite followed through with certain detours: through the carnal body, through the sciences, through material place and environment,[70] through "hard" reality. Here we have a hermeneutics that is not quite carnal—like a seed lying dormant for years, waiting for the right conditions to burst forth into new growth. Michel Serres's work, on the other hand, is deeply engaged with the carnal body, action, lived experience, and empiricism, but in a philosophy that feels, at times, too severe and uncompromising in its treatment of language. One is left with the impression that his account of black boxes is perhaps too critical and one-sided; he overlooks or minimizes some of the salutary aspects of language, despite his gestures—certainly underdeveloped by comparison—regarding the transmutation from the soft to the hard. With Serres we have, so to speak, Hermes without the hermeneutics.[71]

What we need, however, is philosophy informed by both these insights: one that is *both* carnal *and* hermeneutic.

It is true that the model of detour and return offers us a general rather than detailed itinerary, and that the specifics of the engagements with hard sciences, materialism, and realism will be worked out in the course of performing them. Will they unfold in terms of realism and idealism? Neo-Lockean accounts of primary and secondary qualities? Non-reductive materialisms? Or something entirely unanticipated? These questions and others cannot be answered in advance of inquiry, reflection, and, most importantly, dialogue.

A hermeneutic detour through the hard sciences and the new realisms is precisely in line with Ricoeur's dictum, conceived when engaging the social sciences, that "to explain more [e.g., in this case, scientifically, objectively] is to understand better [i.e., existentially, in terms of meaning]."[72] Scientific explanation and existential understanding need not be at odds; they should be engaged in a collaborative dialogue. The aim here is not to "objectify" philosophy or to "subjectify" science—a hermeneutics of the body and a biology of the body ask related but distinct questions—but rather to enrich our understanding by drawing on both. This process of dialogue and cross-fertilization is already taking place in carnal hermeneutics, environmental hermeneutics, and similar fields.[73] Indeed, I argue that carnal hermeneutics and environmental hermeneutics are two expressions of the same desire: to return hermeneutics to material reality—carnal, sensuous bodies and wild, material earth. The hermeneutics of *humus*: human and earthy.[74] The flesh of the body and the flesh of the world are two parts of one flesh.

Serres suggests that we must navigate a path between "a stable apex of trust" (hard, scientific, and realist) and "a maximum of distrust" (soft, correlational, associated with the suspicion of constructivist thinkers).[75] In this I hear echoes of Ricoeur's "critique and conviction," the interplay of the hermeneutics of suspicion and the hermeneutics of affirmation, which is central to the method of detour and return. For his part, Serres advises us to err on the side of trust in the real: "a little bit of naivety is better than [too much] suspicion."[76] Hear! Hear! We are all in favor of the real—lovers of the good, the true, and the beautiful. And there is something to be said for waxing interest in the carnal and material in light of recent intellectual history. But if, as Serres suggests, realism is worth "betting on," worth believing in even when we might doubt it or when we cannot fully grasp it,[77] we might ask ourselves just what sort of wager, belief, or conviction he has in mind. "A little bit of naivety" about reality is a good thing, better than a skepticism that burns everything to the ground and salts the fields, better than nihilism or relativism. But what kind of naïveté is he talking about here? Certainly not the naïve or direct realism of "what you see is what you get," especially given that so much of what we know about reality relates to things we cannot see or grasp, as suggested by the examples of astrophysics and the ancestral so dear to the new realists. Perhaps, then, this commitment to the real is not so far from a form second naïveté, a point on the helical journey of understanding, and a commitment to "remember the hard" in the wake of the hermeneutics of the text.

There is no escaping either the hard or the soft, the material or the hermeneutic. Indeed, it is only through abstraction that we can even pretend to disentangle them. Complete understanding is, and always will be, conditioned by both. We are *zoon logon echon*, the linguistic animal, the animal that softens the hard, the subject caught in the hermeneutic spiral. And we are *zoon thnēton*, the mortal animal, the animal that succumbs, along with everything else, to entropy. As a consequence, we never get *pure* hardness: we soften things, and we ourselves are softened. But we never get, and should not want, *pure* softness either—we cannot escape materiality and mortality, chemistry and physics. We want, we long for, hard(er) reality: carnal bodies, material places, wild nature, real life.[78]

If pure hardness or pure softness are not on offer, what we are left with is impure hardness and softness—a chiaroscuroed, resonant, piquant, fragrant, textured landscape made up of and populated by: (1) harder, demonstrable realities, about which science can tell us a great deal, with a great deal of certainty and precision; (2) softer realities that we understand and appreciate hermeneutically, which are ineluctable, if indemonstrable (and thus, as Saint-Exupéry suggests in the epigraph to this chapter, real); and, finally, (3) the innumerable variegated mixtures of the two.[79] Traversing this landscape, a responsible hermeneutics will both "remember the hard" (as carnal) and "mind the gap" (as hermeneutic).

Hermeneutics is the philosophy of gaps, the philosophy of the gap (*écart*), of the between (*metaxu*), and of the movement across these intervals and interstices. It is the gap that opens, that calls for, that *requires* hermeneutics—interpretation, translation, transmission, mediation, dialogue, discernment, *phronesis, sapience, savoir-faire*—because, paradoxically perhaps, where there is a gap there is a surplus: something more to be understood. It is the movement or transition back and forth across these gaps that constitutes the work of hermeneutics, as the work of Merleau-Ponty, Kearney, Alloa, and others suggests. These gaps are innumerable and are present, in varying degrees to be sure, in all human experience; they go all the way down: to the "nerve endings, organs, and sensations"[80] of our carnal embodiment and to the very earth that sustains us and in which we are, inextricably, rooted.[81] Carnal hermeneutics is not a narrowing of focus, as if we were undertaking the hermeneutics of some specific object, like clothing; it is a widening of focus, as expansively as possible, to encompass the fullness of the human experience of reality, textual and material: environmental hermeneutics; implacement and displacement; nature and culture; natality, vitality, and mortality; human bodies and animal bodies; active bodies; wounded bodies; disabled bodies; divine flesh; and much more.

That there are gaps all the way down, across these diverse fields, does not, I believe, suggest that we cannot get to some truth, or that all truths must be qualified by the parenthetical codicil ". . . for humans." Hermeneutics is, Kearney notes, "far from idealism."[82] It does mean that our experience and understanding are diacritical, that the lacunae, folds, and gaps in our experience and understanding are structurally present and that they tell us as much as the terms, points, or nodes that they separate. It is precisely because the gaps go all the way down that a sound hermeneutics must start from the ground up. Carnal hermeneutics—as well as associated fields like environmental hermeneutics—is a step toward such a grounded philosophy.

Rethinking the Flesh

Rethinking Corpus

JEAN-LUC NANCY

I: Essential Skin

"To Have Somebody's Skin"

The meaning of this idiom is "to kill someone," or metaphorically speaking "to reduce someone to nothing," "to settle the score." Life escapes through skin that's been pierced by a weapon. Skin that is intact protects life, holding it together, but in order to do this, it has to tie itself together; it has to tie a knot in the cut umbilical cord. The cord is an extension of skin in the nourishing mass of placenta, but all the while it's distinct from the mother's body. It penetrates the placenta with tiny ramifications, but it is formed as an organ "independent in its interdependence," to use an expression once common in politics. Placenta leaves both the mother and the child, but it doesn't have an existence that is all its own. It disappears once it has fulfilled its function (in the case of many mammals, the mother eats it, taking it back into her own substance).

The belly button is the signature or seal of propriation: from now on there is a body entirely distinct—and that was never really indistinct, since from the beginning it was formed as autonomous. When the skin is knotted, this reenacts the tying together of the two chromosomes. It is truly a knotting; the belly button looks like a knot, but it's actually a suture, the type of welding that we call a "scar." It is fibrous tissue that extends into the body with several ligaments, vestiges of the vessels that once passed through the umbilical cord.

Being tied to oneself, and the scar from the cut: these two motions, impulses, and emotions are always already preceded by their complementarity and distinction. The skin closes over itself, inscribing itself as the trace of the other, visible on the outside and attached to the inside. It is precisely here that the outside and the inside are distinguished and completely separated. There are two distinct areas, but at the same time they're not simply separated like places in space; they define themselves in relation to each other. What's enclosed beneath the scar excludes the rest and is defined as a relation to the self, exactly as each living cell is defined. However, this relation to the self is implicated in the relation to the other on the outside. Skin combines the two, and is the intermingling of the one and the other, or signals that even the "in-itself" is found "in" an outside-of-self in order to be a "self."

Hence how "to have someone's skin" can mean "to kill someone" (one might also say "to want to have someone's skin"). "To have" takes on a violent and antiphrastic meaning: to seize, undo, injure, and destroy the skin insofar as it is an envelope that protects one from another and is a demarcation. To do away with the boundary; to make what's not, properly speaking, an opening, but is an injury, wound, gash, or breach.

Blood immediately flows, circulating in the skin itself, just beneath the last layer exposed to the outside. The blood that spurts from a wound has a specific name in Latin, *cruor*, which is distinguished from *sanguis*, the blood that circulates in the body. *Cruor* first referred to bleeding flesh, what is called *meat* and is thereby distinguished from *flesh*. Meat is dead and can be eaten either raw (or "rare") or cooked (the word "*viande*" coming from "*vivenda*," what serves to help us to live). Flesh can be used to qualify meat ("tender flesh"), but the word primarily designates the integrality and the integrity of the living body, according to the Latin translation *caro* of the Hebrew *basar* (which primarily designates the body's soft substance, and then also the bodies of creatures as such, in their fragility).

Skinned

Skin is usually separated from dead flesh that becomes meat. Removed, it is leather, sometimes decorated with its own fur. What appears beneath the skin is given the anatomical term "skinned" (*écorché*), a word derived from "bark" (*écorce*): the exterior part of a tree that's separable from it (the outermost layer of the brain is called the "cortex"). Technical English uses the word *écorché*, but in its verb form, "to skin." The skin itself becomes the action of detaching the skin or "taking the skin off" (*dépiauter* in colloquial French). Similarly, the verb *peler* or "to peel" (to remove the skin from fruit) is related to the old French word *pel*, which means *peau* or "skin" (*pellis* in Latin) but comes from the word *poil*, "hair" or "coat" (in Latin this is *pilus*, another word). Skin here becomes the action of its removal and separation.

Skin has a virtuality of separation, a capacity to be removed from the flesh that it covers. What's skinned holds the complete shape of the body and retains all the characteristics of its living activity. However, we know that it's a sort of monster, a robot, or a disquieting, if not repulsive, mutant, because it shows us what isn't meant to be seen. It's not only what lies hidden under the skin, but what is only hidden because all this machinery is supposed to animate the skin beneath which it moves, palpitates, breathes, and metabolizes.

The tendentious detachment of the skin answers to its essential being, which is not simply to envelop but to develop what it envelops, to expose it, place it outside, and give it to the world. The mythical skinned figure is Marsyas, a satyr Apollo skins to punish him for wanting to rival him. Apollo plays the lyre, and Marsyas the flute, having taken up the instrument when Athena gave it up because it ruined the shape of her cheeks. The satyr doesn't worry about his swollen cheeks, and he plays admirably well. According to certain versions of the myth, although his skin is skinned, it continues to resonate with music that doesn't come from the lyre.

Apollo's instrument is in tune with harmonious and precise values, while the flute is passionate and quivers when blown into, like a voice, the wind, or thunder. Moreover, prostitutes played the flute at banquets. Thus, Plato condemns the flute and favors the lyre.

Skin develops the breath, élan, push, and vibration of the body. If the soul is the form of a living body, the skin conforms to this form: it turns pale or blushes with it, it's made smooth or rough, it shudders, its hairs stand on end, and it's shaped by its inclinations, elevations, and folds. The skin tightens, relaxes, creases, and toughens. It is modified, varies in thickness and suppleness, tends to be more like leather or integument, like a film (thin skin) or a membrane (the envelopment of a limb or a part of the body). It becomes humid and full of mucous and invaginates, lips giving way to a gorge, a trench, an access road or exit. The "skinned" is developed by its envelopment; its nostrils breathe, its pores perspire, its sphincters tighten and loosen, its eyelids disclose or conceal the world, the cartilage of the ears vibrate, and the sex swells and reveals intimate flesh, without being skinned, without cruelty, raw and smooth.

À Fleur de Peau: *On the Surface of the Skin*

Fleur or "flower" designates the extremity of the plant and in Latin means "the finest part," like flour, salt, or copper. The flower is foam, a flake, powder, or even perfume, the fragrance of the surface. It is light and soft, and while it's barely palpable, it shows the most delicate, refined, subtle, and sensitive side of the substance that shows its face or makes its appearance. In the flower, there's also color, the intensity of the substance shooting out of itself. The flower is excitement or arousal: a call to the outside, a call from the outside.

À fleur de peau, or "on the surface of the skin," is a light touch: the closest possible movement, the lightest contact there is, just shy of being out of touch. It is touching without pressing down, touching less the skin than its "flower," its downy hair or itself insofar as it is turned toward the outside, the exceedingly thin film of its exposed and weightless surface, the sign of an infinite depth. Sign, signal, omen, or promise, the skin assures us it will never stop stretching out, being offered, and deepening. It promises that the body is entirely there within it, that it is the body itself and consequently that it is its soul.

The body blooms, it opens through its skin, and the skin is its opening. It's what one calls soul, life, mystery, presence, and appearance. It's also its color, countenance, behavior, character, its thinking, and its truth. The flower is the harbinger of the fruit, and the fruit is the response to this announcement, the swelling of new flesh beneath new skin, another chromatic intensity (*chrôma* first designating the color of the skin) and the immanence of fragrance and juice, a liqueur issuing from the flesh.

Comparisons between the skin and fruit are common, such as in phrases like *peau de pêche* or "skin like a peach," *joues comme une pomme* or "cheeks like an apple," *tes seins sont les grappes de ma vigne* or "your breasts are like the grapes on my vine," and all of the magic of the masquerade of strawberries, kiwis, avocadoes, and oranges . . . The skin announces and promises fruition, a word that is dead in French but exists in English and is the equivalent of enjoyment or *jouissance*. As in enjoyment or *jouissance*, fruition is given over to the ambivalence—or simply to the *ambitus* in the musical sense—that is in play between possession and rejoicing. However, this ambivalence and this *ambitus* are given right at the skin: one takes, seizes, and abandons oneself to it, rejoicing in it.

The caress lightly touches and makes its response known; the skin quivers in reply. The simple contact of skin already implies the agreement of proximity, or at least the assurance of kindness: a handshake, embrace, *abrazo*, or *hongi* (the rubbing of noses among the Maoris), not to mention greetings that involve bodies that don't touch each other but instead touch themselves (the hand over the heart, bowing toward the ground . . .). But the caress initiates both more and less than contact; it is moved, and if the caress is well received, it is moving. This is why it moves and repeats its movement. It touches in the sense of rattling, disturbing, agitating, or shaking, arousing and sating itself as well as the skin of another.

The Taboo of Touch

There's no taboo more widespread than the taboo of touch, from the many rules and hang-ups of certain rituals (touching the dead, touching religious objects, parts of the body, clothes, etc.) to current rules of contact (for example, the simple, fortuitous touching of hands in a crowd). Generally speaking, one might say that "taboo" means "do not touch." It was no accident that Marcel Duchamp entitled a picture of a breast in relief on the cover of an exhibition catalogue "Please touch."

"Touching" always implies both more and less than what is evoked by the word "contact." Why more? Because contact is reduced to a connection—that's why the term can have a technical or practical meaning—while touching is a commitment to or an evocation of intimacy. Contact guarantees transmission (of information or energy), while touching doesn't communicate anything determinate: someone approaches, tries something out, gropes, and feels around. "To feel around" means both "to feel by touching" and "to touch delicately," while "to grope" refers to the hesitant touch of someone who tries to get his or her bearings without being able to see.

Touching sinks into the darkness. Beneath my fingers, the clarity of another's body transforms into the night that is created between our two skins. The night is what we have in common and what both joins and separates us. Touching never does away with the distance between us, but it changes the interval into an approach. It isn't changed into contact, but an arrival, not a presence but an appearance, not a "being there" but a way of "passing through," a haunting, or frequenting. What a strange word, this French verb *frequenter* (also in Spanish, Italian, and sometimes in English, "to frequent"), whose meaning changed from "a large number, a crowd, an assembly" to "relations that are repeated and regular," and finally designated (in outdated language) the approach of a lover (between "courting" and "going out with," as people today put it).

Touch "frequents" the skin: it approaches, visits, and observes it—both in the sense of "seeing and examining" it and in the sense of "respecting and complying" with it. Touch is a gaze that completely conforms with its object and for this reason removes it from the objectivity of the visible. It no longer places it before itself but against itself. Skin is against skin, marrying it, attaching it to itself, converging with its lines, conforming to its patterns and to its light and volatile thoughts, whose scent lingers on the skin. Taboo is here, in the delicate interval of skin, in the "between the two of us" where the high frequency of intimacy continues to quiver. This superlative of interiority trembles, and nothing can exceed it but an impossible definition: *interior intimo meo*. This is the God of St. Augustine, but it's an expression obviously discovered in a caress.

The taboo says: Don't touch me; touch what in me is far away from me. This is what Proust meant when he wrote: "My gaze fell on her skin, and my lips could hardly believe that they followed my gaze. But it was not only her body that I wanted to reach; it was also the person who lived in it and who I only sort of touched to try to get her attention, or to penetrate her, to awaken in her an idea."[1]

Zones

As Freud remarked, the entire body—and all of the skin—can transform any part of its surface into an erogenous zone, a zone whose sensitivity is open to sexual desire. The entire body is carried away by this desire, especially the body insofar as it is skin and is distant from its organs and functions (the reproductive function is present, even though it's not always sought out—perhaps this indicates that reproduction is itself more than and something other than a function). A body beyond functionality, a body that no longer belongs to the world of perception and action but is a skin in the world of another skin.

A zone is not actually a place, nor is it a region, space, or ground. It is rather deterritorialization right up against territory, or territory as a division from itself and a dehiscence. The Greek word *zonè* means "belt," and belts in antiquity often served to make the fabric of clothing gather above them and then drape down, falling to various lengths and creating many different folds. Just as in contemporary French slang, *zoner* means "to loiter or bum around," and *zone* refers to a stretch of sparsely populated suburban sprawl; similarly skin that is "zoned" is skin that's eroticized, dissociated from its dermic or dermatological functions and is instead related to the finality without end of sexuality, whether the finality of coming in the sexual sense or of reproduction. Reproduction only entails the end that is the arrival of a being who is open, beyond any end; and coming is similarly its own unending end. While coming can be related to conception, what is opened up is the coming of the being yet to come, first its arrival and then its own coming.

Zones represent the distinction and differentiation not only of the body's extension but also of its purpose and structure. They are a sort of deconstruction, an access to the structure, but an access to a chaotic heap rather than a coherent framework. Each zone has its own particular type of pleasure. When it comes to the genital zones, there's a return to function and to organs, as excitement escalates and leads to an outflow. There are alterations in the skin's tissue that are called "mucocutaneous" in the poetic language of anatomy. Even when it is just cutaneous or dermal, a zone already entails a variation in the skin's regular patterns or behavior. The skin no longer envelops (the role of the cutaneous, the Greek *kutos* giving us *cyto-*, a prefix referring to the cellular), and it no longer protects (the role of the dermal, *derma* initially meaning skin that has been detached, such as leather or a pelt): instead it opens up and exposes itself. People speak of "epidermal reactions" in a way that's both completely psychological and completely physiological, precisely because as it is a matter of skin, the two registers are, perhaps in this case more than in others, two forms of the same being. The epidermis is the skin rising from its own surface, bristling or blushing, shivering or shrinking away from something. It is where the skin enters into *mimesis* and *methexis*, reproducing signs (such as goosebumps) and being stirred up.

A zone sets up the possibility for disturbance. It is the sea rocked by gusts of wind, the ground that dancers stomp on, a cloud pushed together or stretched out, a flight, beating, or palpitation. When it's grasped, skin is as dissociated as it possibly can be from its nature as a sort of envelope or boundary: instead it has the appearance of dough, paste, or mortar, of ribbons, laces, straps, bands, or liana, or of banners, and sails that are unfurled, along with the rigging used to haul them down. Skin soars and is heaped up; it is lustrous, creased, and moist.

"I've Got You under My Skin"

It is once again Proust who writes that dreams "satisfy what is vulgarly called the desire to have a woman under one's skin."[2] Edith Piaf sings "*je t'ai dans la peau*," and Virginia Bruce "I've got you under my skin." This turn of phrase is different from "stepping into someone else's skin," where it is more a matter of slipping into an envelope, a costume, or a role. "Having someone under my skin" means, as Bruce puts it: "I've got you deep in the heart of me / So deep in my heart, you're really a part of me."

The other is driven deeply in and becomes integrated, spreading throughout the skin, being incorporated into it, and then trembling and living with it, as it. The other seeps in like a dream: without mediation, transition, or translation, without delay, instantaneously, seized in a present that does not flow out, in this copresence that gives dreams their force and makes them what they are. Like scenes and figures that we dream of, the beings who we have under our skin—things, plants, animals, people— are phantoms, spirits that haunt, occupy, obsess, and possess us.

We don't only desire subjects or objects, and it's not only striking forms or substances that make us catch our breath or arouse our fantasies; things that are trifling, like a coffee bean or chiffon, can also get under our skin, their appearance making an impression on us. Without us even realizing it, roughness, softness, jerking, striations, vapors, urges, and murkiness all enter into our skin. The skin feels, handles, gathers, and deals with everything that we see, hear, and breathe.

"The immediate return of the exterior organism into itself is the skin, in which the organism becomes a relation to itself,"[3] Hegel writes. He considers the skin to be the first differentiation of tissue, from which all the other differentiations within an organism derive.

What's under our skin is not what it covers but what it is: it's the integument whose texture makes us what we are, exfoliated phenomena, things in themselves whose profound nature is to appear and expose themselves with all their pores, to exhale and inhale all along the stretch of skin with its many zones, in ways that are infinitely supple, nimble, and sensitive.

Coda

The skin of the two sexes—the sexual organs but also the bodies of people who are of a different sex—is hardly different. Perhaps right at the skin, sexual difference is the least different when there is intense touching, rubbing, pressure, and an outflow. There's a sexual porosity, an indefinite play between surfaces, creases, cavities, erections, projections, and openings. The skin, all skin—that of the eyes, the tongue, the hair, the teeth; the skin that is kneaded and the skin that bristles; the skin that doubts itself and the skin that flatters itself; the fine skin of the lips, the scrotum, the ears, and the nostrils; the robust skin of the shoulders and buttocks; the skin that quivers and the skin that sags; the skin that is dry and taut and the skin that sweats—all of these share a difference that's not one of type but is rather difference in itself, which makes the skin skin, through and through.

II: Motion and Emotion

Rühren, Berühren, Aufruhr:[4] The German language allows us to place in the same semantic family of *ruhr* three notions that in French would correspond to *bouger* (move), *agiter* (agitate), *toucher* (touch) and *soulèvement* (uprising), each understood in all the diversity of their possible meanings. *Move* and *agitate* are taken in their physical senses as well as their moral/emotional senses, as are *touch* and *uprising*. The latter orients its moral value in a socio-political direction.

This semantic family is that of movement that is neither local (in German, *Bewegung*) nor a movement of transformation (*Verwandlung*—metamorphosis, for example generation and decay, growth and decline). Rather, *ruhr* designates the kind of movement that might best be called "emotion," a term that stems from *motion*, the closest transcription of the Latin *motus*, from the verb *movere*, which persists in French as *mouvoir* and *émouvoir*, both understood in the English *move*—both physically and emotionally.

The French *toucher* and English *touch* are semantically disassociated from *movement*, whereas in German they are linked. In French and in English, *touch*, *tact*, or *contact* seem to arise from a more static than a dynamic order. Obviously we know that we must *move* in order to *touch*, that we must "*come* into *contact*," as the saying goes, but touch itself seems to designate a state rather than a movement, and contact suggests a firm adhesion rather than a mobile process.

Nevertheless, the French and English languages also acknowledge the mobile, moving and dynamic value of touch, apparent when we say that a person or a work of art "touches us," and when we speak of a pianist's or a painter's "touch," as well as the notion of being "touched" by divine grace.

To touch sets something in motion. As soon as I approach my body to another body—be it inert, made of wood, stone, or metal—I displace the other—be it ever so slightly—and the other displaces me, while holding me in some way. Touch acts and reacts at the same time. Touch attracts and rejects. Touch impels and repels, pulsion and repulsion, rhythm of outside and inside, of ingestion and rejection, of self and nonself.

Touch begins when two bodies move apart and distinguish themselves from one another. The baby leaves the belly and becomes himself a belly that can ingest and regurgitate. He takes in his mouth his mother's breast, or his own finger. Sucking is the first touch. This suction of course ingests the breast milk. But it does more: it attaches the mouth to the body of the other. It establishes or re-establishes a contact that reverses the roles: the child that was contained now in turn contains the body that contained it. But he does not enclose it within himself; rather, he simultaneously holds it in front of himself. The movement of the sucking lips never ceases to alternate between proximity and distance, between penetration and exit—the same movement that presided over the events leading to the womb and culminating in the exit of this new body finally ready to separate itself.

In separating himself, he conquers this new possibility that he had only vaguely known: the possibility of rapport and contact. The vague knowledge was mainly auditory, and hearing itself was diffracted by the prism of the tiny body immersed in the liquid resonator with which the other body enveloped him. The sounds of this body, of its heart, of its intestines, and the sounds of the outside world simultaneously touched his ears, his closed eyes, his nostrils, his lips and all of his infused skin. Nevertheless, "touch" would be saying too much. Every possible sensation was still diluted in an indistinct sense, in a permanent exchange, quasi-permeable, between interior and exterior, as well as among the different routes of access to the body. "Touch" would be saying too much, and yet it is already there: it's the first *rürhen*, the first flow and the flutter swaying the as-yet unborn.

Once he is born, he will separate himself. But he will remain that thing—he or she who floats deep within an element, within a world in which everything is related to everything else, everything tends toward everything else and distances itself from everything else—but this time according to the multiple scansions of all the insides/outsides of separated bodies.

Only a separate body is capable of touching. It alone can entirely separate its touch from its other senses—that is, attribute to one autonomous sense that which nevertheless traverses all the senses, as though differentiating in them while distinguishing itself as a kind of common reason. Reason or passion, drive, motion.

Where he once was immersed, floating and enveloped in an indistinction between his outside and his inside, intermingled in the common balance of the two bodies, sucking his own finger, now he detaches himself, and once outside, he finds himself confronted with this outside. In other words, he is no longer inside the inside, nor in the immanence. In the most proper sense of the word, he *transcends*—he passes out of the being-in-itself.

His mobility leaves behind the suspension, the near-weightlessness and the viscous indifference to direction. It's now real movement, based on withdrawal from other bodies. Rather than seeking a return to immanence and immersion, his gestures affirm his distinction—a separation that is by no means a privation or an amputation. His mobility is an opening to relationship. Relationship does not seek to restore indistinction; it celebrates distinction; it heralds encounter—that is, contact.

Actually, contact begins when the unborn child begins to occupy nearly all the space in which he is floating. He begins to touch the walls, and his movement becomes one of slow reversal, which prepares him to exit, to allow himself to be pushed from within and to breathe the outside—that is, definitively to espouse the order of inside/outside. Touching the limits of the vase and the womb, he himself becomes simultaneously like another wall and like a wave ready to assert itself and flow between the lips that will separate for it. This flowing gives its ultimate form to the passage from floating to rubbing, from immanence to transcendence, and in opening the vulva it also opens all the gaps that its separation will create, and across which contact will become possible, itself gap and adherence, intimate extremity.

Contact does not cancel separation, far from it. All metaphysical or psychological logics that posit the primordial attraction of a supposedly lost unity and the necessity of resolving the constraint of separation (of cutting the umbilical cord, of sexuation, of the plurality of the senses, of bearing, of appearances) are the logic of a kind of morbid monotheism or monodeism. These are pathological, but are not the logic of *pathos*, nor of the *dunamis tou pathien*, which is the power to receive, the capacity for being affected. Now affection is above all passion and the movement of passion—of a passion whose very nature is "to touch"—to be touched, to touch in return, to touch oneself with the touch that comes from outside, of she who touches me and of she through whom I touch.

To be affected does not mean that a given subject, in a given circumstance, succeeds in receiving affection. How could he receive without being capable of it? But this very capacity must be a capacity in the strictest sense—potential to receive. To be able to receive implies already receiving, being affectable. To be affected requires having been so, already always having been so. This is why there has always been some "outside," and an opening toward it.

When that vase releases its contents, the water pours out, and the little one emerges from it, all wet. His entire body—for the first time entire and detached—bears the damp imprint that becomes his skin, that melts into the design of his skin but which makes this skin always capable of receiving the outside, of being bathed and rocked, lulled by the undulations of the outside.

Thus touch is first and foremost this rocking, this floating and rubbing that is repeating in sucking, renewing, and replaying the desire to feel touched and to touch, the desire to be affected by the contact of the outside. More than being "in contact"; we are contact itself. My entire being is contact. My entire being touches / is touched. Which is to say, also, open to the outside, open by all my orifices—my ears, my eyes, my mouth, my nostrils, as well as all the channels of ingestion and digestion, as well as my humors, my sweats and my sexual fluids. The skin's role is to surround all these openings, these entrances and exits, as an envelope that not only situates and specifies them, but itself develops the capacity to be affected, and to desire it. Each of the senses specializes the route of affection according to a strict system—seeing, hearing, smelling, tasting—while the skin continually links these systems, without mixing them up. The enveloping skin itself is the development and exposition of the entire circumscription of the body (of its entire detachment). In French we could playfully say *ex-peau-sition*. In German, we could play with *Aus-sein/Haut-sein*.

But in any language, what matters is that the exposition, the *Ausstellen* that is the body and its *Ausdehnen* ("*Psyche ist ausgedehnt*," wrote Freud) does not consist of a fixed movement, like a painting in an art gallery. On the contrary, this display can only be understood as a permanent movement, like an undulation, a deployment and a replacement, an ever-changing motion in contact with all other bodies—that is, in contact with all that approaches and all that one approaches.

As has been acknowledged since Aristotle, the identity of that which is felt and the one who feels is similar to the identity between that which is thought and the thinker in the act of thinking, implying at the point of sensation (vision, hearing, smell, taste, touch) a kind of copenetration of the two in the act, and as that act. According to the Aristotelian concept of the act as *energeia*, the sensory act creates the current effectivity, where the event springs from the sensation. The soul that feels is itself feeling, and hence feels itself feel. This could not be clearer in the sense of touch. Neither the eye nor the ear nor the nose nor the mouth is aware of its own sensations in the intense and precise way that the skin is. The image, the sound, the smell, and the taste remain in some way distinct from the sensory organ, even when occupying it entirely. No doubt it is likewise with touch if I *describe* to myself the substance touched ("this cloth is rough"; "this skin is cool"). Though impossible to verify, it could be said that representation is less immediate than touch. As for the other senses, it is more obvious, though differing according to the case (the image coincides with our apprehension of it; likewise for melody or timbre, though to a lesser degree; taste is even more distanced from tasting, and an odor is even farther from the sense of smell, to the point of being more along the order of touch).[5]

However, this identity between the toucher and the touched can only be understood as the identity between a movement—a motion—and an emotion. Precisely because this is not the identity between a representation and what it represents. The cool skin of which I speak is not first and foremost "a cool skin" in the act of my hand that touches it. The cool skin "is" my gesture, it is my hand, and my hand becomes it because my hand is its contact or its caress (except for medical contact, no contact with the skin is without the potential for a caress). Motion and emotion (which are themselves one single thing) envelop the act—the sensory *energeia*. And this *energeia* is none other than the effectivity of contact, the effectivity of an approach to a receptiveness, hence a double quality of exchange: I approach the skin that accepts me; my skin welcomes the approach of the other. The approaches of both intersect at a point of quasi confusion. And this point is not fixed; it is only a "point" via image; its reality is motion and emotion, movement, traction and attraction, while also being interrupted variation, fluctuation. It is simultaneously vibration, palpitation of one against another, oscillating from one to the other, and therefore an "identity" that does not identify itself, even though it resembles the one and the other and shares their presences in a common venue.

Such is the *rühren* of touch. The liquid movement of a rhythm, of a wave, the backwash of the ex-istence that is "being outside" because "outside" is the inflection, the curve and scansion of the floating and rubbing that makes my body bathe among all bodies and my skin rub along other skins.

The movement of touch is thus not that which goes by another term—*tasten* in German, *tâter* or *palper* in French, *palpate* in English—which could seem more proper. To palpate, in fact, is a cognitive act, not an emotional one. One palpates in order to recognize or evaluate a surface, a consistency, a density or a suppleness. But that is not the way one caresses. Touch caresses, is essentially caress—the desire and pleasure of coming as close as possible to a skin—human, animal, textile, mineral, etc.—and to use this proximity (this extreme, superlative approach) to make the skins play one against the other.

This play reprises the rhythm that is essentially and originally the play of inside/outside—perhaps the only game, if all games consist of taking and abandoning places, of opening distances, of occupying and abandoning places and compartments, of timing. Touch is movement in the sense that it is rhythmic, not in the sense that it is a process of exploration. Here "approach" does not mean to come into an area, and "contact" does not mean the establishment of an exchange (of signs, signals, information, objects, or services). Approach here is the superlative movement of proximity that will never disappear into an identity, since "the closest" must still remain infinitesimally distant in order to remain what it is. Contact means an extreme, superlative vibration of sensitivity, of that which gives the ability to receive, to be touched. (*Rühren* can have the sense of playing an instrument, as in French one used to say "*toucher le piano*," or in English one might "tickle the ivories"—it's always a matter of awakening, of making vibrate, of animating.)

This play and this rhythm of contact are the *rühren* of a desire. Perhaps desire itself, for is there a desire that is not a desire to touch, since touch gives the pleasure of desire itself—the pleasure of desire oriented toward the proximity of relationship, since relationship is the first step toward the sharing of an inside and an outside.

The first and formerly most widespread meaning of *rühr* is romantic and sexual pleasure. The rhythmic movement and the overflowing, the surge that is not simply fluids but that of entire bodies that spread against another, one within the other, and one and the other pulling apart in order to gather themselves and come together again, in the succession of waves that they become, one via the other. This movement belongs to no process of action or cognition; we're not talking here about the end that is procreation, leading to a new body, for sexual pleasure is without finality; it has no other end but that which suspends it above the overflowing that exhausts it and opens it beyond itself.

Of all the senses, touch is the one that is subject to the most taboos. Freud notes this, and it is borne out by ethnology, anthropology. The importance of this taboo in our own culture is obvious: we know exactly where touching is allowed, be it only the hand of someone else, not to mention the rest of his body, and up to what point it is acceptable to kiss on the cheek, to hug, to caress.

We know almost scientifically to what extent touch engages the being, and consequently, how the being cannot be disassociated from relationship. There is absolutely no case of "being" first, followed by relationship. There is "to be," the verb whose action and transitivity are formed in relationships, and are only formed in this way. Descartes's "*Je suis*" does not contradict this, nor does the "I" of Kant, Fichte, or Husserl, or Heidegger's "*Jemein*." Every "I" is and is only the act of its relationship with the world—toward what is termed "the other," whose difference is revealed in touch or as touch.

However touch (which not by chance has given its name to a mode of divine intervention in the soul), when taken as motion and emotion in the other, consists in both the point of contact and in the reception or acceptance of its pressure or its trespass. It grazes, pinches, penetrates, or seizes, undiscernably, in a vibration into which it immediately withdraws. It is already its own trace; it effaces itself as a mark, as a point-like imprint, all the while spreading its effects of motion and emotion.

Saint John of the Cross writes of "touches and feelings of union with God" and adds "nothing is better suited to dissipating these delicate knowledges than the intervention of the natural spirit. Since we are dealing with a supernatural intelligence, it is useless to seek to actively understand it; this is impossible. The intelligence has only to accept."[6] Not "to actively understand" is to understand passively—it is to hear an odor, to smell a touch. Mysticism does not have a monopoly on this kind of metaphoric transfer—if in fact it is one. A painter's "touch," a pianist's "touch" (and the "*touches*" [keys] of the piano itself, which could also be said of the computer's keyboard), and the "touch" that one can add (of fantasy, of melancholy, etc.) to a project or a text, share the same focused and vibratory quality as erotic touch.[7]

However, it is never a question of metaphor. It is always a matter of sensory reality, thus material and vibratory. When the soul trembles, it does indeed tremble, just as much as water does when it approaches the boiling point. What we currently call the "soul" is no different from arousal and receptiveness to motion and emotion. The soul is the body that is touched, vibrating, receptive, and responding. Its response is the sharing of touch, its awakening to it. It rises up, as the German *Aufruhr* indicates, like sociopolitical upheaval. There is insurrection—and sometimes erection—in the motion of touch. A body rebels against its own closure, against its enclosure in itself, against its entropy. It rises up against its death. It is perhaps not impossible that the very touch of death unleashes a last *surrection*, both heartbreaking and uninhibited.

Whether it is a question of the approach of another person or even of the approach of the absolute otherness of death, it is the body that opens itself and extends itself to the outside. This is its pure act; just as Aristotle's Prime Mover is pure *energeia* in which there is no "potential" (*dunamis*)— nothing to wait for, nothing that can come from outside, so likewise when I am *touched* I have nothing to wait for: touch is all in the act, in its mobile, vibratory, and sudden act. And as with Aristotle's God, this act brings with it its own excess that is its pleasure—the pleasure that is the flower or the climax of the act—sun or shadow—always an abyss toward which surges the *rühr* of *berühren*.

—*"Essential Skin" translated by Carlie Angelmire;*
"Motion and Emotion" translated by Roxanne Lapidus

From the Limbs of the Heart to the Soul's Organs

JEAN-LOUIS CHRÉTIEN

In the interpretation of the *Song of Songs*, according to which each one of us is the Beloved's spouse, at least potentially, the soul, or "inner man," is what receives the praises that the Beloved heaps on the spouse's beauty, limb by limb. The soul is said to have a mouth, teeth, hair, cheeks, and so forth—all of which are immaterial limbs corresponding to the soul's faculties, operations, and possibilities. Although these immaterial limbs are named in reference to the limbs of our carnal body, they are distinct from them and stand apart from them. At the very start of his commentary on the *Song of Songs*, Origen states the principle clearly: "We will see that the names of bodily limbs are transferred to the limbs of the soul (*transferri ad animae membra*) or, rather, to the soul's agency and affect (*efficientiae animae affectusque*)." After citing a number of Scriptural examples, he adds: "In short, as these examples show, a similitude of vocabulary is drawn between both (sc. between the external man and the internal man), yet the proper meaning of each reality remains distinct. What is corruptible is assigned to what is corruptible, and what is incorruptible is assigned to what is incorruptible."[1]

Someone who encounters a language of this kind for the first time is likely to find it strange, artificial, or even comical.[2] It has the bizarre effect of making a second, invisible man appear behind the ordinary visible man of flesh, endowed with the same anatomy as he. In the case of the *Song of Solomon*, some may be tempted to conclude, rashly, that the whole idea is a subterfuge, aimed at rescuing a highly erotic celebration of the body by hiding it under a spiritual meaning. Nonetheless, there is a logic to this way of speaking about the soul—a special force, as well as a long history and a necessity. Thanks to its flexibility and heuristic power, it allows us to "make sense." It helps us to articulate regions of our experience which would remain voiceless without it. The goal of this chapter is to bring to light its basic architecture without attempting to be exhaustive about its origin and genesis. At stake is not only a new access to the authors. More especially and essentially, what is at stake is the body's meaningfulness, which is to say its propensity to "signify."

We must start at the beginning, namely with the Bible and with the *heart*. Both in the Hebrew Bible and in the Greek Bible, the word *heart* plays a key role. It is featured in a hundred places, used in a hundred different ways and in a wide variety of contexts, bearing a meaning, or meanings, that pagans never knew.[3] Far from being reduced to the bodily organ, the heart forms the very place of our identity, of our *ipseitas*. It is what we most properly *are*, which means that it is also the very place where we might successfully avoid being ourselves since an abyss of irresponsibility is opened to us precisely where the highest responsibility is bestowed. What exactly does the heart do in the Bible? It rejoices or weeps; soars or falls; hardens or stiffens; opens up or slams shut; expands or contracts; turns away from God, neighbor, and task, or turns towards these; trembles or firms itself up. It whispers, cries out, sings, scolds, praises, renders grace, whimpers, speaks, and speaks to itself. It seeks and knows; it loses its way. It attaches and detaches itself; it forgets and remembers; it hides or shows itself. It is faithful or unfaithful, twisted or straight. It purifies or sullies itself, turns old and brittle or renews itself, overflows generously or remains stingy, appeases itself or makes itself anxious, hears or not, understands or not, decides or remains undecided. Nor is our list complete. Most often, we could simply replace "my heart" with "me," whereas I would never confuse myself with my physiological heart.

We must emphasize, as a matter of contrast with other languages, that the heart is also the center of thought and volition, or at least of resolve and affect. In the sixteenth century, Suarez makes a point of it: "By the name *heart*, Holy Scripture typically signifies the intellect, not just the will."[4] Pascal, as well, remembers the same idea a generation later, even though he also opposes heart and reason, since he writes: "The heart senses that there are three dimensions in space and that numbers are infinite."[5]

While Biblical anthropology is rich and diverse, the Bible itself, except for some very rare exceptions, treats the heart as an undivided whole and does not parcel it out into distinct organs, which will happen at a later date. Among the rare exceptions to this are Jeremiah and St. Paul. Evoking the notion of spiritual circumcision, Jeremiah says: "Remove the foreskin of your heart,"[6] which is to say injustice and sin. St. Paul, in turn, writes to the Ephesians: "May he (sc. God) open the eyes of your heart, that you may be allowed to see what hope his call opens up to you."[7] As important and profound as these words are, they remain exceptional and do not form a system. We may add another expression used by Jeremiah, at least according to the Septuagint, where, speaking of a suffering that penetrates into our innermost depth, Jeremiah evokes the "senses of the heart" (*ta aisthètèria tès kardias*)[8] which modern translations render instead as "walls" or "fences." Jeremiah does not, however, mean to proffer a doctrine about the constitution of inner man; what he means to describe is simply extreme, lacerating pain. The heart is every bit as carnal as it is spiritual, indivisibly so, yet it does not have organs or members. The same holistic view is maintained in the work of Philo Judaeus.

Philo preserves the heart's Biblical importance and meaning. Taking his inspiration from a phrase in Deuteronomy, he repeatedly presents the heart as part of a triple set that allows him to analyze the structure of human action, good or evil. His set consists of heart, mouth, and hands. The heart is considered chiefly as the place where reasoned decisions are taken. The Good, Philo explains, is not at the other end of the world, nor is it in the highest heaven. It is neither the final goal of some laborious quest nor the distant haven where a winged spirit eventually finds its rest. Rather, "it is within reach, nearby. It is captured within the three organs with which we have been provided, namely the mouth, the heart, and the hands, symbols of speech, thought, and actions."[9] In order for human conduct to qualify as good, there must be a concourse of all three elements, converging in righteousness. The absence of any one of them, Philo says, does not merely abrogate the action's goodness, it "destroys it completely."[10] This lesson, Biblical and Mosaic, is found in Philo often: the Good is near, very near to us.[11] This is not to say, as Hölderlin would put it, that the Good is easy to grasp! It is only our human imagination that depicts what is near to us as easy and what is far away from us as difficult, sometimes as a pretext to laziness, sometimes as an incentive to adventure. True thought knows that what is hardest to grasp is what lies within our immediate reach. True thought knows this indeed by learning it, since the idea itself is right within our reach. Be this as it may, the heart is no more possessed of organs in Philo's triple scheme than before.

In a beautiful passage where Philo speaks in the first person and in which we seem to discover a "consolation of philosophy" before Boethius's celebrated text of the same title, the expression "the eyes of the soul" is used: "Half-opening the eyes of the soul, which I thought had turned blind from despair of attaining a noble ideal, I am illuminated by the radiance of wisdom. I have not been handed over to darkness for the whole duration of my life."[12] The expression is Platonic, but the context is soundly Jewish since the phrase follows a prayer of thanksgiving toward the one and only God followed, in turn, by a statement announcing a vigilant exposition of the Mosaic laws. What is significant is that Philo does not speak of the "eyes of the heart" but of those of the soul. Antoine Guillaumont has shown that a number of Greek-speaking Christian mystics had already sketched a doctrine of the heart's organs, such as the heart's "eye," or the heart's "sense," as we find in Diadochus of Photice.[13] Conspicuous as the doctrine may be in the history of spirituality, Philo's own phrase does not include the organic differentiation that interests us.

The first formulation of such an organic differentiation as a matter of principle is found in the writings of Origen. Origen also states the founding linguistic law of the principle. He takes the Pauline distinction between outer and inner man as his point of departure. Assuming that this distinction merely clarifies what occurs throughout Scripture, Origen writes: "I have noticed that non-corporeal things are denominated by means of corporeal homonyms. Corporeal things describe what belongs to outer man, while their homonyms describe what belongs to inner man."[14] The same exact words have a double meaning and denote a double intention, depending on how they are deployed. Origen does not set out to launch a new language but to provide a key to decipher a language that is already in place, namely the language of the Bible. What is chiefly involved is a hermeneutic method, granted that there is a need in the background to justify the language theologically and philosophically by showing that there are real features in things that call for us to use the words that we use. Origen, in short, starts with a "fact of speech" (just as Kant appeals to a "fact of Reason") and this fact is the language of the Bible.

Having stated his principle, Origen applies it: "Just as outer man has inner man for a homonym, so do his members. One can say that every limb (*pan melos*) that is possessed by outer man is found again, with the same name, in inner man."[15] Origen does not speak of this in terms of metaphor, but in terms of homonymy. Implicitly, there is a root equivocity in language, which allows the same terms to refer to two distinct realities. Origen considers next, in succession, the eyes, ears, nostrils and odors, taste, touch, the hands, feet, the head, entrails, bones, the heart, the hair, blood.[16] Saint Gregory of Nyssa will follow his lead.[17] I will skip the detail of Origen's and Gregory's doctrine of inner organs. It matters, however, to discuss Augustine's differentiation of organs now because of Augustine's overarching importance for the Latin tradition.

The approach that Augustine uses in his Treatise XVIII on the Gospel of John to establish that the heart has senses and to outline their characteristics is particularly interesting. He starts with John's affirmation that "the Son cannot do anything of himself unless he sees the Father do it."[18] Saint Augustine is eager, first of all, to rule out a naïve, imaginative, and overly human interpretation of these words, namely that the Verb is some kind of apprentice watching the actions of a master in order to reproduce them. In what sense and in what way can we say that the Verb sees? In order to answer, or to begin to answer, such a question, we need, not to pile up arguments and construct hypotheses, but to consider what it means for us to see. We must probe the many possibilities of our own gaze. An *exercise* in seeing, in effect, is required for us to be able to speak about seeing. What use is there in discussing sight blindly? "You have a corporeal eye with which you see the craftsman, but you do not yet have that eye of the heart (*nondum habes oculum cordis*) with which to see God. This is why you wish to transfer to God what you are used to seeing in the craftsman. Leave what is earthly to the earth, turn your heart upwards (*sursum cor*)."[19] What is required first is that we purify our heart, which is to say that we render our spirit more rigorous and clear, sharpening our desire and our quest. In other words, if man has any hope of grasping the possible meaning of John's words, he must start by grasping himself, by seizing his own proper possibilities and learning to exercise all of the modes of seeing that are available to him.

In his analysis of sense experience, Saint Augustine starts by pointing out that the differentiation of organs throughout the body is precisely what provides the body with its unity: "What a given member is able to do, another member is not. Yet because the body is one, the eye sees for itself and for the ear, the ear hears for itself and for the eye."[20] He then goes on to cite a psalm in order to assert that He who has given us sight cannot be blind, nor deaf He who has provided us with hearing. Since, however, the divine Word is not corporeal, the divine senses cannot be situated in different places but must be wholly in Himself, Saint Augustine shows, so that the divine Word is "wholly vision" and "wholly hearing." To the Word, "hearing is not anything other than seeing" and "hearing is vision and vision is hearing."[21] The Word's eye listens, the Word's ear sees. Does this not attest to the abyss that lies between man and the Word, as well as to the misunderstanding that we have of our own powers, we who are made in God's image?

"Return to the heart," Augustine says next, then "return to your heart," moving from the plural to the singular. He pursues: "Return to your heart and see in it what you must perhaps think of God since it is there that

God's image is found."[22] The heart has vision, hearing, smell, yet one cannot point to the heart's "eyes, ears or nostrils"; they are not "different organs." "In your heart, you hear where you see."[23] The Biblical heart thus differentiates itself into many senses: it sees, hears, smells, tastes and touches. Strictly speaking, the heart's sensorial differentiation is not organic, since the heart as an undivided whole is each time the one and same organ of its different senses. As we know, however, the organs of the body serve by way of metonymy to speak of organic functions as such. We say that the eyes see and that the nose smells, when we should really say that the whole living body sees and smells through its organs. In short, the claim that the heart is endowed with senses is clear, yet it raises a number of puzzling questions.

To see *where* we hear—is this to say that we see the same *thing* that we hear? What does it mean exactly to say that seeing, for the heart, is the same as hearing, that both take place in one and the same organ taken as an undivided whole? Does it mean that the heart is the one and only organ of a plurality of different operations, the sole agent of a plurality of acts that are really distinct from one another, but which occur together and overlap in a continuous spiritual synesthesia, as though the heart saw by hearing, by touching, etc., grasping various aspects of a same thing through different simultaneous sensations? Or, by using various names which are borrowed from bodily sense, do we mean to describe a single and perfectly simple act of intuition on the heart's part as it grasps its object? These two interpretations are indeed possible. Moreover, is it not possible to conceive that the heart has a sixth or seventh sense without any analog sense in bodily man? If we deny such a possibility, must we not, in turn, draw the immediate conclusion that there is something final about our bodily senses? These subtle questions force us to turn to further writings of Saint Augustine in search of an answer.

The second question is less challenging. On the one hand, it is not unusual for Saint Augustine to draw a contrast between "bodily sense," taken in the singular, and another kind of sense, namely "the inner man's sense," through which "we sense the Just and the Injust: the Just because of its intelligible beauty, the Injust because it is bereft of such beauty."[24] On the other hand, whenever he writes about the different modes according to which objects are grasped, he always observes a strict parallel between inner and bodily senses. The famous passage of *Confessions* Book X attests it, which describes God as "a light, a voice, a perfume, a meat, an embrace of the inner man," even though God transcends bodily sense.[25] The five bodily senses each have an analog in the heart and are presented progressively, according to an order of increased intimacy: sight, hearing, smell, taste, touch. The order in itself is not in doubt since Augustine, in a sermon urging us to love Justice above all things, deploys it explicitly, illustrating each inner sense with a Biblical citation: "If indeed you have inner senses, all of your inner senses find delight in the pleasure of Justice. If you have inner eyes, gaze upon the light of justice. . . . Similarly, if you have inner ears, listen to justice."[26] And he pursues by evoking smell, taste, and touch. Thus, there are five *bona fide* inner senses, analogous to the five bodily senses in a way that remains to be examined. The inner man, in other words, is still very solidly *a man*.

The fact that the inner senses lend themselves to an orderly progression that implies a spiritual journey of increased closeness to its object already sheds some light on our second question. Indeed if all of the inner senses were to be reduced to a single act of sensing, if their difference from one another were merely nominal, wouldn't their order be arbitrary? Would it even be possible to evoke them by evoking the distinction of their objects, light, sound, or smell? The senses of the heart, in almost all of the ways evoked by Saint Augustine, are turned towards God, God's Word and Revelation. The inner senses may be open or closed, yet they cannot be opened through our own initiative, as is the case with bodily senses. To open them is God's work. It is God who unlocks in us the space and the channels through which he will be welcomed. Such a dis-closing of the heart does not involve the creation of a new inner sense which we lacked until then. Every human heart is provided with sense, or senses—yet Grace is required to make them active and capable of reaching the goal to which they are destined. While we do not have the power to open them, we have the power to shut them up and thwart them: "Do not be vain, oh my soul, do not let the ear of your heart be deafened by the roar of vanity! Listen, heart: the Word Himself calls you to come back."[27]

A second major difference between man's inner and external senses can also be brought to light. Through the latter, we have pleasant or unpleasant perceptions, yet a great many of our bodily sensations are without much impact. Many are actually neutral in how they affect us—fortunately, since we would not be able otherwise to think of anything except what we were in the very act of sensing here and now. Typically, a beautiful shape or a charming sound stands out against a background of indifferent and banal sensations. In contrast, when it comes to the senses of the heart, their activity always matters absolutely since it results from a divine initiative and puts us in some kind of relationship with God. Every sensation of the heart constitutes an event—which means that it transforms us in some way or another. Nor does this imply that we are purely and simply passive, since we speak of *sensing* through the heart. It is *we*, in the most proper sense of the term, who actually exercise our faculties of inner vision, hearing, and so forth. Moreover, we can (and must!) dispose ourselves actively to sense through the heart, even if we are powerless to start the process: "Tell my soul: I am your salvation. Tell it in such a way that my soul hears it. Here are the ears of my heart before you, Lord: open them and tell my soul: I am your salvation. I want to run after this word and seize you. . . . Too narrow is my soul's house for you to take up residence."[28] Augustine's lines are important in a number of respects. They bring out the whole issue of what we might call the *prolepsis*, meaning the anticipatory grasp of the heart's hearing. In order to speak and to speak to God, we must have listened beforehand and already listened to God in some manner. In order for us to ask that our ears be opened, it must be the case that they have already heard.

Our *prolepsis* is not a vicious circle: how indeed could we desire something that is without proportion to our own being? To turn our ears to God—to "lend our ears" to God—is already to listen to the sound of his silence and to make ourselves available to the sovereign freedom of his manifestation. But what does it mean to present God with ears that are still closed? It means to stand before him in an attitude of obedience even before the gift of a specific calling. With regard to this anticipatory listening and to what distinguishes it from the other senses of the heart, there is a clear and explicit passage in *Questions on the Heptateuch*. Saint Augustine comments as follows on a statement by Moses in *Deuteronomy*:[29] "Until now, God had not given us a heart in order for us to know, eyes in order for us to see and ears in order for us to hear." In this context, where what is involved is what has been seen through fleshly eyes but not understood, Augustine interprets the senses of the heart to mean the heart's attention to God's Word and actions. What role must the inner eyes and ears play? "Understand and obey (*intelligere et obtemperare*)." He adds: "Moses shows them, by the same token, that they cannot, without God's help, either understand or obey (*intelligere et obedire*) with the eyes of the heart and the ears of the heart; yet if God's help is lacking, man's depravity is still to blame."[30] Indeed *we* do everything in our power to keep them closed. It follows that, even if it is the undivided heart that performs them both, the act of seeing and the act of hearing do not have the same object. We see and hear simultaneously because we must understand what we obey and obey what we understand. The eye sees for the ear and the ear hears for the eye so as to bring about jointly the perfection of a human action, each sense making its own contribution. Augustine interprets the eyes of the heart to be the "eyes of Faith." As for the ears, they loosen up my being and make my activity pliable in order to make them conform to what I have heard and agreed to obey.

While the eyes and the ears of the heart are mentioned more often than the other senses with regard to understanding God's Word, they are not mentioned exclusively. Drawing on a passage of the *Book of Wisdom* that describes anthropomorphic idols whose eyes are blind, whose hands have no touch, whose nostrils detect no smell, and whose feet cannot walk,[31] Saint Augustine argues that we ourselves risk becoming such inanimate statues with inactive and closed senses, not according to the flesh of course, but according to the "inner man." Consequently, he expands the idea to all of the senses: "Of what use are their nostrils if they cannot detect the sweet odor of Christ?"[32] Who would fail to see the long and powerful history of what is involved here? We routinely speak of having "flair," of having "a nose for things," and when Nietzsche says that his "genius lies in his nostrils" (*Mein Genie ist in meinen Nüstern*), he does not claim to have a perfumer's or a hunting dog's talent (although the latter is not without nobility) since he specifies that the object of his keen sense of smell is truth and mendacity.[33] Granted that they are used for purposes that are quite opposed to Augustine's purposes, Nietzsche's nostrils are of the same nature as the nostrils described by the saint. And while Saint Augustine himself says relatively little about the inner man's sense of smell, other Christian thinkers will be more effusive.

There is also a "mouth" and a "palate" of the heart. Such expressions and others of the same kind may be surprising, amusing, or even shocking. Is it really necessary to describe the anatomy of the inner man in every lowly detail? Does it not involve an overly naïve, even vernacular vision of the "heart" and of its actions? The answer is to turn to the important hermeneutic principle that Martin Luther states in his commentary on *The Song of Songs*. It summarizes clearly what was presupposed by the whole of the tradition before him: "It must be noted," Luther says, "that the Holy Spirit in using allegories focuses on how a thing is used rather than on its form." "Allegory is connected to usage rather than to form."[34] Whether an object is involved, or an organ, we must first consider what it is able to do, what it serves to accomplish or allows us to perform, rather than its visible appearance. "To stand vertically is the purpose of a column. The use of a cup is to contain drink." The heart's "anatomy" is nothing other than the system of its functions and potential acts.

Saint Augustine appropriates for himself the Biblical idea that the Word is nourishment, indispensible for us to pursue and sustain life. We thus must eat, drink and ruminate the Word.[35] There is a mastication of the Word and there is a savoring of the Word. The terms "mouth" of the heart and "palate" of the heart aim at these two notions. "With our bodily mouth, we eat and drink. Just as we use the bodily mouth for the restoration of the body, so we use this other one for the restoration of the heart (*ad refectionem cordis*)."[36] The very first function of the mouth of the heart is thus mastication of the Word. Indeed how could anyone who had never eaten words ever be able to produce words and proffer them? If this is the case, we must ask right away what distinguishes the mouth from the ear, according indeed to Novalis's deep insight: "Is the mouth not an ear that moves and answers?"[37] The mouth and the ear are not related in the same way to the Word that they receive. The ear obeys, the mouth drinks or eats: the mouth internalizes, assimilates, but also tastes, masticates, and transforms what it absorbs before ruminating. The mouth turns the Word into an element of our very being and life. The activity of the mouth is thus not of the same nature as the activity of the ear. As far as the mouth is concerned, the Word presents itself under two forms, liquid or solid.[38]

Reminiscing in the *Confessions* about his first encounter with Ambrose of Milan, Augustine remarks: "I yet had no idea, no direct experience of the delightful pleasures that he felt in the secret mouth that was in his heart (*occultum os ejus, quod erat in corde ejus*) as he ruminated over your bread."[39] A few lines later, we learn that the inner mouth that Ambrose exercises through his silent reading and which feeds him with God's Word, is what allows him to become a great preacher because it has the capacity to feed itself. In the same context, Augustine specifies that Ambrose, burdened by a myriad tasks and duties, devoted the little time that he had for leisure to "restoring his body with indispensable nutrients and his mind with reading." The two are explicitly parallel. The only difference is that, while it is sometimes meritorious to impose a fast on the body, it is always dangerous to impose a fast on the mind!

In yet another famous page of the *Confessions*, Saint Augustine describes his and his mother Monica's attitude in the pursuit of divine Truth: "We kept the mouth of our heart wide open to the waters that flow from your wellspring, from the source of life that abides with you, in order to be watered according to our capacity and to be able in some way to conceive of your grandeur."[40] Unlike what happens in the case of the ears, keeping the inner mouth open is not simply a matter of focusing one's attention and of making oneself available. It is the open mouth of desire—of a desire that strains towards what is for the heart a question of life and death, an essential thirst. It is hardly surprising that food is given here in liquid form, which is to say in the earliest and most easily absorbed form, since the passage describes the very infancy of a journey. Elsewhere, Augustine apologizes for the length of one of his sermons by appealing to "the greed of our inner mouth."[41] The hunger and the thirst for Justice that make up one of the Beatitudes[42] are often associated with this mouth of the heart. And whoever says "mouth" implies lips, teeth, tongue, palate, and throat. Unlike commentators of *The Song of Songs*, Saint Augustine does not exploit these possibilities, however, at least not in the case of the heart.

While he speaks more than once of the teeth of the Church, taken as a collective body, Augustine does not mention, it seems, the teeth of the heart. In commenting on a psalm that speaks of the jubilation of the lips, he remarks that "lips are typically said both of the inner man and of the outer man," then rules in favor of the former as the proper interpretation, given the context. Yet he does not give the "lips" a more precise meaning than what he gives to the mouth itself.[43] Later, Cassiodorus will identify mouth and lips with one another: "*Lips* signify the inner man's mouth; the spirit indeed also has a voice, with which he silently cries out to the Lord."[44] On the other hand, the palate of the heart, *palatum cordis*, receives important elaborations as the organ of taste. One of the psalms speaks of the great and bountiful sweetness that is in God. "Here, if someone without piety asks 'where exactly is this bountiful sweetness?' I will answer 'How can I show it to you when you have ruined your palate through the fever of injustice? If you had had no experience of honey, you would not be able to attest to the sweetness of its savor without tasting it. You have lost the palate of the heart that is needed to taste all of these good things. What can I do for you? How can I show you such sweetness?'"[45]

By means of these simple words, two crucial lessons are given. Our desperate quest for objects, for quantity, and the bitter suffering that we feel in their absence, forget that everything that matters is perhaps right in front of us, within our reach, but that we have mutilated and ruined the organs with which we are provided in order to reach them and even just to perceive them. A violent person might believe that gentleness extended to him would appease and calm him, without recognizing that we must provide access and doorways of our own if something is to reach us and penetrate us. There must be some sort of intelligence in us, however elusive, in order to receive what presents itself from elsewhere. Moreover, since we eventually become incapable of doing what we initially simply refused to do (like those doors that remain shut for so long that they become deformed and can no longer open), we must start by asking God to liberate our heart and set its faculties into motion, rather than ask for all sorts of things that we are not yet in a suitable state to receive. Even when he moves the heart, God does not compel us to hear, he only makes it possible for us to do so.

Our analysis so far has been limited to the face, namely to the eyes, ears, nostrils, mouth, and palate of the heart. In his celebrated discussion of memory in *Confessions*, Book X, Augustine now risks a "hand of the heart." When we search for a memory, it sometimes comes to us right away. It also happens, however, that a longer search is required and that all sorts of other memories come to mind instead, more or less akin to it, such as happens when we try to remember a forgotten name. "Some assail us like hordes, asking 'maybe *we* are what you are looking for?' when in fact we are seeking for something else. Then I sweep them away from the face of my memory with the hand of my memory (*et abigo ea manu cordis a facie recordationis meae*) until the one I desire steps out of the shadows under my eyes and leaves its hiding place to present itself."[46] The heart's hand, in effect, scatters unwanted memories in the same way as a bodily hand serves to scatter insects from our face. Although the phrase is full of charm and nicely captures the sense in which attention requires a sort of active inattention, which is to say a capacity to dismiss whatever is not the object of our focus, it does not have the same Biblical roots as our earlier terms or the same force.

After Saint Ambrose, who had spoken of the "feet of the spirit," (*animi pedes*),[47] Saint Augustine, in turn, speaks of the "foot of the soul," (*pes animae*). We move from the sensorium to the motorium—to the register of gate and gesture, which implies moving through time as well. "The foot of the soul is rightfully understood to be love: which love, if bad, is called coveting or appetite (*libido*); but it is called charity and delight if it is righteous. Indeed it is through love that a thing moves, as to a place where it tends."[48] The soul's place is not spatial, Augustine explains, but coincides, rather, with the place where the soul finds delight and self-fulfillment. The idea is utterly Biblical: where my treasure is, there is my heart also.[49] I am not where I am, I am where I am headed, I am where I tend, where I aspire to be. The better known image of *weight*, borrowed from ancient physics, is replaced here by the image of the foot or of its gate: my love is my special gate, which is to say my direction and my distinctive way of walking. Elsewhere, Augustine speaks of our feet, in the plural. Love indeed subdivides into two precepts of charity, namely love of God and love of neighbor. If either one of these is defective, our gate will be crippled, tardy and slow.[50] What does it mean, Augustine asks, to say that we approach nearer to God or move away? We do so through resemblance and dissemblance. "Indeed in this journey our feet are our affections (*affectus nostri sunt*)."[51] Spiritual mobility is not a function of space but of affect. According to the pilgrimage paradigm that is so dear to Augustine, we must walk without ceasing in the transient journey that is our temporal life.

The meaning of the body takes on a very different character depending on whether we view it in its motions and acts or statically as a shape that gives itself to be seen. It is thanks to its feet that the body as a whole moves from place to place and progresses, so that the inner man's feet are not only affections but also what decides, in many ways, what direction we take and, therefore, our ultimate end. There will be many who will remember Augustine's teaching in this regard. Conversely, it may happen that the body, taken from its feet up to its head through a collective symbol, is viewed as an ascending motion from a lower to a higher order. Thus Honorius Augustodunensis, in the twelfth century, commenting on the *Song of Songs*, saw in the feet a symbol of the "first order of the Just," namely the lowest, which is to say the "tillers of the earth who, like feet, bear the (whole) body by sustaining the Church with the necessary things that they provide."[52] We have here a very different perspective on the body.

After Saint Augustine, the "blazon" of the heart, namely of the inner man, in the old sense of a formal praise of the Beloved's body limb after limb, grew progressively richer over time. What follows gives only a few examples aimed, still, at tracing its emergence. The Bible turns the notion of a stiff neck that refuses to bow or to bear a yoke into the very symbol of pride, rebellion, and insubordination towards God: "I have seen this people: it is a stiff-necked people"; "Circumcise your heart and do not stiffen your neck"; and also: "They have stiffened their neck so as not to listen to my words."[53] Saint Jerome explains the expression by evoking "those who reject the yoke of the law and, metaphorically, are like wild animals."[54] Rabanus Maurus (d. 856) says, more broadly, that Scripture substitutes "neck" for "pride" (*superbia*).[55] It thus seems only natural that Saint Gregory the Great would eventually speak of the "neck of the heart" (*cervix cordis*), urging us to incline it and bend it.[56] Because of the ubiquitous importance of Biblical language, English has even developed the routine expression "stiff-necked" to mean "obstinate." Saint Gregory also elaborates on the theme of the heart's ear, seeing in it the origin of confessional speech. Whoever preaches speaks only to the extent that he listens and only as long as he listens. "He who preaches properly first inclines . . . the ear of the heart (*aurem cordis*) towards the Word that sounds in his innermost intimacy so that he can then open the mouth of the body (*os corporis*) and issue admonitions."[57] The mutual dependence of listening and speech, so dear to Heidegger, has deep roots in the Biblical and spiritual tradition.

Saint Gregory the Great has even stronger views on the spiritual nose and sense of smell. It is "by smell that things that are not seen are known." The spiritual sense of smell is the sense of what is hidden—a way of paying attention to what does not yet appear but already acts and, therefore, already emits an odor. Spiritual smell anticipates what might happen. It detects dangers and threats before they come to light and manifest themselves to the eyes.[58] It is "a fore-sighted discernment." Like Augustine before him, but now in a positive mode, Gregory connects the hand of the heart with the activity of memory: "The saintly man, filled with the spirit of eternity, firmly fastens to his memory all that constantly flows away by means of the hand of his heart."[59] The expression articulates the Gregorian idea of a "duty of memory," which stems from the awareness that a large part of human history is doomed to be erased.

Because it repeatedly evokes several parts of the body, the *Song of Songs* will lead its commentators, first in the patristic age then in the medieval era, to widen, sharpen and multiply the symbolism and language of the heart. It matters to see that this language is not created as a matter of expediency to meet new needs, or forged artificially. Rather, it possesses deep and definite roots in the language and anthropology of the Bible, even though the terms "heart" or "inner man" oftentimes give way to the terms "spirit" and "soul." A few examples borrowed from Wolbero, who was a medieval German commentator of the *Song of Songs*, will suffice to illustrate both the continuity and broadening in question. Wolbero likes to evoke the "palate of the heart," still in connection with the sweetness and savor of God's Word. "The usefulness and savor of his precepts (i.e., of the Spouse that is Christ) are sweet and pleasant to the palate of my heart and the capacity of my spirit (*mentis*)."[60] What is involved indeed is a "repast" of the soul. As the passage clearly shows, the idea is that the wisdom of God's Word is savored. Tasting, here, is not viewed as some dark sensation that inhibits the exercise of our intelligence. The palate discerns and exquisitely analyzes the diverse flavors of the Word and, therefore, the heavy bundle of life and future that these flavors bear. Further on, Wolbero evokes "the beloved who has listened to the voice of her Spouse exhorting her and who has tasted, with the palate of her heart, the sweetness of his precepts" to the point of reaching the vigilant intoxication of plenitude.[61] Elsewhere, "this sweetness so delights the palate of her heart" that she does not want to keep it to herself or to be the only one to benefit from it but wants to communicate it to others and make them experience it as well.[62] The "ear of the heart," in turn, undergoes the trial of sweetness.[63]

In these evocations, Wolbero does not simply interpret the Biblical expressions, he also describes the activity in which he himself is engaged. A fine palate is required in order to read and transmit the sense of what one has read and tasted. How many writings leave us with a bitter taste, acrid and rough, which makes us want to rinse our mouths out, simply because the author was unaware that the heart has a palate! Wolbero brings the purpose of this palate to light. The commentator is a *praegustator*, he is the first to taste the wine of the Word and learns to acclimatize it properly and to serve it. Wolbero commands a wide register. He describes the Beloved, wounded by a celestial desire as "she read or listened to writings," and letting her spirit flow out into "a fountain of tears, like a sort of blood of the soul (*quasi quidam animae sanguis*)."[64] The soul's hemorrhages are neither red nor scarlet but lucid and clear. And whereas the body is weakened by a loss of blood, the soul garners strength from the tears that it sheds while listening. To Wolbero, the spirit (*mens*) also has a navel, which is nothing other than "holy charity"—the center towards which all virtues fix their gaze and without which they would not be, or would be nothing, and upon which they depend ceaselessly.[65] The spirit of the commentator also has fingers (*digitos mentis*), which prepare themselves, with the help of the Holy Spirit, to pluck the "ultimate chord" of the *Song of Songs* in order that the whole of its harmony reach the readers.[66] Here, the interpreter's touch takes on a directly musical sense.

Before pursuing our investigation further into the history of the heart's limbs, let us pause to reflect on its meaning, legitimacy, and relevance from a philosophical point of view. First of all, is it appropriate to speak of metaphors? The question lends itself to a number of viewpoints. With regard to Biblical expressions about the heart, Antoine Guillaumont has remarked that the physical and the spiritual are so utterly interlaced and blended, even fused, that "it is difficult to say with any certainty when we are in the presence of a metaphor" since metaphors presumably require that there be two distinct registers allowing the transfer of terms from one to the other.[67] Yet Guillaumont sticks with the notion of metaphor, even if this means watering it down. In sharp contrast, Charles Péguy adopts a principled position. Speaking of the soul's death as a "hardening," he writes: "We must guard ourselves here from seeing a metaphor. In truth, there never are any metaphors."[68] Then he goes on to describe the "very real phenomenon of the soul's gradual hardening" through habit, as the soul becomes its own hard overcoat. Rediscovering the insight of an ancient idea, Péguy goes so far as to speak of a "spiritual matter, so to speak," a "matter of the soul" that hardens. The question is philosophical and spiritual, not simply linguistic and rhetorical. The tropes are proportional to our own mobility or flexibility, not the reverse. In his *Essays and Conferences*, Heidegger focuses on the sense of hearing but shows, in the process, what is true of all of the senses: "We listen when we are 'all ears' (*ganz Ohr*). Yet the 'ear' is not the mere appliance of the acoustic sense. What anatomy and physiology know as ears never produce, *qua* sensory organs, an act of listening (*ein Hören*) . . . .

We wrongly take the activity of the bodily organs of hearing to constitute listening. We must regard listening, in the sense of attention and obedience, as the spiritual transposition of hearing properly speaking."[69]

As far as Heidegger is concerned, to analyze what is involved as metaphor and transfer is to look at it upside down. "We do not listen because we have ears. We have ears, we are endowed with bodily ears, because we listen." A deaf person has not stopped listening, or stopped hearing himself in the act of listening. Conversely, my ears may be in perfect health without my having the slightest suspicion of what listening is. Sartre says the same thing about sexuality: "We say that man is a sexual being because he has sexual organs. What if the opposite were true? What if he possessed sexual organs only because he is fundamentally and radically sexual?"[70] Such a "reversal," mind you, does not boil down to affirming the "primacy of the spiritual" in replacement of the "primacy of the corporeal," since this would mean that the same hierarchy and terms of opposition are maintained. Nothing would be changed fundamentally. What is brought into question here is the very way that the terms of opposition are defined: the way that they are shared and connected, under the figure of reversal and inversion, which makes it accessible for discussion—but for discussion only.

What is clear from the onset is that we cannot reduce expressions about the limbs of the heart to a metaphor if this means a neutral description. This would be tantamount to embarking on a philosophical thesis without securing its foundations, or begging the question and thus stating a simple opinion. No X-ray of the neck will bring to light humility or pride, submission or rebellion, yet we recognize them right away in the body language, posture, and gestures of others, sometimes even before seeing the person's actual body, such as when a strange gesture glimpsed confusedly in passing forces us to look back to see if there is some kind of threat. We have no need of explanations to know what it means to keep one's head high, or to stiffen one's neck, or to appreciate the difference between the two. The stiffness of the neck expresses and manifests the stubbornness of pride. It is not some kind of conventional sign, more or less arbitrary, which we have imported from outside. It is not an "image" of pride; it *embodies* pride. We must add what the ordinary usage of this kind of organic language reveals. Except in the (obviously quite frequent) cases in which an author merely applies ready-made formulas unthinkingly, without reviving their descriptive powers, such a language is not ornamental but *heuristic*.

The point of such a language is not merely to illustrate or add pictures to theses about the heart or the inner man after the theses in questions have been framed in purely conceptual terms. What this language does is allow a rich, intricate and varied description of the interplay of the inner man's powers, as well as their mutual articulation and the acts, initiatives, and operations. Rather than serve as a source of possible metaphors where one would find embellishments for one's discourse, the body, with its limbs and motions, serves as a *schema* (taken in an analogous sense as the one that Kant gives it.) The body allows us to *construct* figures and images of what otherwise would remain for the most part unimaginable. The *schema* of the body, moreover, is a dynamic one, a source of ever new figures, but also of new questions and possibilities. More often than not, what comes to appear thanks to this language is given to us with clarity and precision only because of it. This explains why such a language cannot be fixed in a final lexicon, even though a number of stable expressions have emerged historically. The language is supple, labile. It never ceases to renew itself because the body itself contains latently an inexhaustible power of figuration and of figure-ability. The aim is not to reach some kind of emblematic encoding of the heart in which every symbol has its own univocal meaning. This would be no more than a spiritualist and poetic form of phrenology. The whole power of our language lies in its schematizing flexibility.

In his preface to the *Mystical Declaration on the Song of Songs*, Saint Francis de Sales wrote: "Not even the properties of God or of the soul are mentioned in it; instead, however, eyes, hair, teeth, lips, necks, clothes, gardens, ointments and a thousand such things (are mentioned), causing great confusion in expository texts through the license of commentators who have taken it upon themselves to match each element with one of the senses and, worse, who have taken the unfortunate liberty of interpreting identical expressions on a given page in diverse ways to mean diverse things."[71] Francis de Sales then solemnly declares that he will interpret each term consistently with regard to its symbolism: "Once we have given a meaning to a term, we have not ever changed it." The fluidity of the language, however, is assessed differently depending on whether one adopts a spiritual or a hermeneutic point of view. When it comes to interpreting the Bible, it is obvious that using symbolism inconsistently risks plunging us into complete arbitrariness. By interpreting hair and cheeks to mean one thing in one passage and another thing in another passage, we can make any given Biblical verse say whatever we want. Nonetheless, even if we are mindful of the problem, the poly-semiotic character of symbols lends itself to being established rigorously. Even the most conscientious interpreter and the most faithful to context cannot avoid seeing a multiplicity of meanings attributed by the Bible to a same given body part, more or less convincingly. This is what Rabanus Maurus does in his treatise on the parts of man, which is to say on the human body: he classifies various Biblical passages by assigning them to their physical subject matter.[72] If we adopt a different perspective, however, must we bemoan or praise the perpetual renewal of this language? Its renewal is not a form of hermeneutic artifice, it stems from the inexhaustible significance of the body and of the blessing that the body is for speech and for life. The body's significance cannot be locked up into a "key," or into a final dictionary, like the so-called lexicon of Melito of Sardis, where one reads, for example: "Knees, confession of humility," or "kidneys, inner spaces of the heart," along with a Biblical reference for illustration.[73]

It is only thanks to its flexibility and fluidity that the symbolism of the body does not become a stultifying yoke for the life of the mind. By definition, our schema remains a source of new figuration only to the extent that figures remain susceptible of changing. Profusion is part of its strength. Once we have addressed these issues, we are now free to return to the genealogy of the limbs of the heart, then of the soul, in a clearer light. The exegesis of *The Song of Songs* did not give birth to it but vastly contributed to its elaboration and depth. By evoking all sorts of bodily parts, including parts that have no major role in the rest of the Bible, the *Song* invited commentators to complete, so to speak, the organic nature of inner man. Inner man, like outer man, has a face. Thus Gilbert of Hoyland writes: "Just like the body, the mode of being and of conducting oneself has, in a way, its cheeks." These "inner cheeks of the soul" are "part of the face of conscience, where God's eye alone sees, not indeed of the man's face. Each person's conscience has something like a face. Its cheeks become dyed in red, the chaste color of humility, if one refuses, in one's innermost being, to boast of one's actions."[74] This whole mystical tradition culminates in the seventeenth century in the fact that the mystic poet Claude Hopil is able to speak very naturally of the "eyes of the soul" (which no contemporary reader would question) but also of the "hair of the soul" and its "lips," which might surprise even the seventeenth century reader.[75] Our language is a language for the long-term.

In the passage cited earlier, Saint Francis de Sales gives an extended, even complete, picture of it. At stake is what he calls the "mystical parts" of the soul. These are, he says, "the eyes, which is to say the intentions that move the soul; the hair, which is to say the affections, hatred, love, desire, and so forth, which are like hair insofar as they are not good or bad in themselves but depending on whether they are used for good or evil; the teeth, meaning the senses that chew the food that must enter into the stomach of the understanding; the lips and speech, meaning the thoughts that produce insensible discourses by way of inner words; the cheeks, which are the two rational powers of understanding and willing; the neck, which acts as an irascible force to overcome obstacles; the breasts, which are the two actions of the force of concupiscence, namely to embrace the good and to shun evil. All of these parts must be groomed and beautified if God is to love the soul and be able to say: *How beautiful you are, my beloved, how beautiful you are!*"[76] As we see, Francis de Sales introduces concepts drawn from Greek philosophical anthropology into the Biblical language, especially from Plato, with "the irascible" and the force of "concupiscence," which are the Latin forms of Plato's *thumos* and *epitumia*. He is not the first.

A key place, for our purposes, where the two languages meet, is none other than the *oeuvre* of Pseudo-Dionysius the Areopagite, so crucial for the history of mysticism generally or at least for some of its currants. There are two pages in which Dionysius articulates with great precision how to use a symbolism of the body for what is not corporeal. The first is found in *Celestial Hierarchy*, where Dionysius presents his angelology and where he justifies in his own way a Biblical language that sometimes speaks of angels anthropomorphically.[77] Like Dionysius, and unlike many others, we must go to the trouble of distinguishing between two different types of anthropomorphism: the first expresses the actions or operations of superior beings by citing those of the human *mind*; the second, by considering those of the human *body* or its limbs. This is why historians of religion, drawing on the language of Church Fathers, speak of *anthropopathism* (e.g., God's "wrath"), which they distinguish from *anthropomorphism* (e.g., God's "arm"). After invoking the first, spiritual type of analogy, Dionysius turns to the second type: "We may, moreover, or so I think, find adequate images to represent celestial Virtues in each of the many parts of our body," namely speaking of angels. The order adopted by Dionysius progresses from top to bottom and combines the notion of bodily organs with the notion of bodily states. He starts with the eyes and eyesight, then moves down to smell, then to hearing, to taste, and then to touch. Next, he turns to eyelids and eyebrows, adolescence and youth, teeth, shoulders, arms and hands, heart and chest, the back, and feet, before moving on to a new theme, namely the symbolism of clothes and of utensils. Since his concern is to describe angels, we do not need to study his symbolism here in detail, yet it confirms, in the case of an author who is not especially focused on the body and for whom the body does not occupy an exalted rank, that the body's significance possesses extraordinary power. Not only do the organs of the human body provide a way to symbolize spiritual powers, as they do in Dionysius's other passage, but they also, as they do here, serve to symbolize the actions of higher, simpler beings than man.

By way of example, let us cite the way in which smell is extended. Its powers of discernment and receptivity signify "as far as possible the welcome that they [sc. the Celestial Virtues] extend to the odorous transmission that transcends the mind (*huper noun*)." Let us also cite the beautiful Neoplatonic interpretation of the teeth, which anticipates a number of medieval developments: the teeth "divide up the perfect food that is given to them—indeed each and every intelligent essence, thanks to a providential virtue, divides and multiplies the unifying intellection that is bestowed upon it by the more divine essence, so that the inferior essence is able to rise up as far as its forces allow." In other words, these spiritual teeth are not so much what angels use to feed *themselves* as what they use to prepare and make available what they have received from higher up so that lower intelligences may, in turn, receive and assimilate it. These teeth chew for the benefit of others. From a unique ray of light that would, in itself, be blinding, they make, with their teeth, mouthfuls of light that are more numerous but less intense, adjusted to souls with less acuity. What Dionysius says about angels, the Latin tradition will say about human interpreters of Scripture, who cut up the continuous flow of meaning (upon which we would choke) into intelligible morsels that we are able to savor one by one.

Commenting on Dionysius's page, John Scotus Eriugena will write in the ninth century: "If the divine mysteries have not been cut up into pieces beforehand by masters thanks to their intellectual teeth (*intellectualibus dentibus*), they cannot be of any use to disciples or help them grow in life."[78] In the twelfth century, Hugh of St. Victor will again paraphrase our Dionysian page with lovely remarks about the intermingling of the visible and the invisible.[79] Moreover, with regard to the same symbolism, John the Scot will add that, not only do "the different members of the human body" lend themselves to signifying angelic properties, but also to signifying those of the cause of all things, God himself,[80] which Biblical language confirms.

The second passage in which Dionysius evokes the human body is more succinct. It is in his treatise on *The Divine Names* and constitutes a sort of methodical exposition of his reflections on the symbolism.

The multiplicity of images that we use with God as our aim, Dionysius says, must not lead us to attribute a similar multiplicity or any diversity to God. "Similarly, if we reasoned about the nature of the soul by representing it in a bodily manner and made an image of the parts of the body to correspond to what is in itself indivisible, we would have to understand the symbolism of these parts in a new way, taking into account the properly indivisible character of the soul."[81] This is where he relates the parts of the body and the powers of the soul in the way that Greek philosophy has conceived of them. "Thus we might call head the mind (*nous*), neck opinion (*doxa*)—as an intermediary between the rational and the irrational—chest the irascible faculty, stomach the faculty of concupiscence, thighs and feet nature, applying symbolically names taken from the parts of the body to psychic powers." Such a correspondence, drawn from Plato, is more Greek than Judaic and diverges from the Biblical meaning of bodily members. It will have its own posterity.

While this symbolism has its own rigorous and principled logic, it evolved progressively as a function of time, through various authors and exegeses. The synoptic view that Dionysius adopted is partial and limited. The view that Saint Francis de Sales adopted results from a very long development, of which we have only considered the start. Commentaries of *The Song of Songs* constitute the focal center of this development. In order to conclude our preliminary sketch, however, and limiting ourselves to Christian literature, we must mention two works of an encyclopedic scope that will be prominently used by medieval authors. The first is the section of Book XI of the *Etymologies* of Saint Isidore of Seville (d. 636) that is devoted to man and his parts.[82] As the title indicates, a limitless "Cratylism" reigns in the work, and the meaning of things and beings is derived from etymologies that are generally discarded today even though they were long backed by tradition. Two very opposite perspectives may be endorsed of this work, which enjoyed such considerable importance, historically speaking. We may view it as a mass of assertions that are as arbitrary as they are obsolete, or we may view it as an extraordinary verbal playground, poetic and attentive to the symbolism of signifiers to the point of offering a feast of language. Based on alliterations, similar consonances and "paronomases," on loose and imaginative associations of ideas, the work contains many a gem. Organs are oftentimes supposed to derive their names from their function. Thus for example eyelids (*palpebrae*) "derive their name from palpitation, since they are in constant motion," while "eye-brows" are so-called because they "adumbrate" the eyes and protect them. The name "mouth," in turn, *os*, is "like the entrance (*quasi ostium*) of the body" (which means that Isidore inverses the direction of the etymological derivation, since it is, rather, the entrance of a house that is its "mouth"). Isidore's delightful and poetic playfulness is, nonetheless, regulated by a medical as well as lay knowledge of the body that directs the interplay of signs.[83]

A single striking example will suffice to show it. The example concerns the cheeks and knees, which in Latin are *genae* and *genua*. "Knees are called *genua* because they are placed *in utero* against the cheeks. There, indeed, they are stuck together face to face, parents of the eyes, which signify tears and compassion." It is the bulge of the knees that dug out the cavities of the eyes in our face when our body was being formed in our mother's womb. "This explains why men burst into tears as soon as they bow down on their knees in prostration. Nature indeed wants them to remember the maternal womb where they remained in darkness before coming into the light."[84] The humility of a posture of adoration is not directed at the divine eternity alone, which gives itself to us as a future, but also at the immemorial past of our life *in utero*. It is not through an effort of the mind, moreover, that we elicit this memory from before birth, it is our body that remembers for us, retrieving in its bodily posture the brotherhood that once existed between our knees, cheeks and tears. Rabanus Maurus appropriates and pursues this idea on his own account.[85] Rupert of Deutz copies the same lines in his commentary on *The Song of Songs*,[86] but he does not limit himself to copying. He also draws his own teaching: "Surely, whoever focuses on this cause with the right attention correctly and knowingly praises and approves the custom of saints and of those who are purified in thought, namely to kneel down and bow frequently to God on High and to apply their cheeks full of tears to their bent knees, so that the Creator in heaven is reminded of the way in which he formed us in the uterus and reflects on it." Bodily gestures in a state of prayer follow no arbitrary code: they are the carnal memory of our human condition and of the poverty or impotence that mark its origin. By adopting a position that is all at once fetal and supplicatory, I inscribe in my very body the cry that I make to God on high about my distress and weakness. So far, only the knees of the body are involved, but the knees of the heart also have an ancient history. An apocryphal text that is often appended to the Vulgate, *The Prayer of Menasseh*, says: "*Et nunc flecto genua cordis mei . . .* (And now I bend the knees of my heart)." Origen, in turn, remarked: "What profit will I gain if, when I come to pray, I bend the knees of my body before God but bend the knees of my heart before the Devil?"[87]

As for Rabanus Maurus, who was surnamed *praeceptor Germaniae*, his treatise on the parts of the body, which is one of the sections of his impressive encyclopedia, is far more directly Biblical than Isidore of Seville's treatise, granted that it also includes much compilation. Rabanus Maurus follows a descending order that goes from the top of the skull to the soles of the feet. It is much more detailed, moreover, than what is found in other authors. With regard to the parts of the body, his project consists of collecting and classifying their many Biblical uses and meanings in order to frame a symbolism, both individual and collective. He thus elaborates an orderly repertory of the Biblical meaning of the parts of the body, even though he also calls upon etymologies and medical notions borrowed from the Greco-Roman tradition. The result, however, is not a "key" to be applied extrinsically to the *Song of Songs* since the *Song* plays a direct role in the initial elaboration. Approximately fifteen citations from the *Song* can be counted in this section of Rabanus Maurus's book, which is a lot. The symbolism of the body and the interpretation of the *Song* cannot avoid coalescing.

Let me conclude with two remarks. As Antoine Guillaumont has nicely shown, the heart does not have the same meaning in the Bible that it has in Greek or Roman literature and philosophy. The same is true for the rest of the body. Whereas Patristic notions of anatomy and physiology depend on Greek science, more or less well transmitted, the case is different for the symbolism of organs and gestures. Its Judaic character is conserved throughout the developments and extensions wrought in it by Christians. The case of Rabanus Maurus, as we saw, amply shows this. My second remark is that Rabanus Maurus, even though he draws analogies between a given bodily member and a given faculty or activity of the inner man, chiefly applies the symbolism to the collective body that is the church. A bodily member corresponds to a given category of faithful.

—Translated by Anne Davenport

A Tragedy and a Dream

Disability Revisited

JULIA KRISTEVA

No one has yet determined what the body can do.
—Spinoza, *Ethics*, 3, Proposition 2, Scolie.

The financial, economic, and political crisis that is spreading throughout Europe and the world today is showing itself to be an existential crisis in which we are lacking a new humanism. "New humanism" is humanism that is capable of recognizing its source in Christian humanism and its debt towards this tradition, notably Catholic, and at the same time taking account of new disciplines at the heart of new historic and social conditions.

In this spirit the extreme states of human life, such as those of disability, are a testing experience and a possibility. This is my claim, which I make drawing on my living with disability as a woman, mother, philosopher, psychoanalyst, and writer.

To begin, I wish to highlight two aspects of the challenge that surrounds disability.

The first aspect is the link between disability and mortality. For me, disability represents the modern face of the tragic in that it confronts us with mortality (both individual and social), which we are incapable of thinking about, even today. This mortality is not only unthinkable on the occasion of a crime or of a war, but is even more so when it is foundational, present throughout human existence.

However, this tragedy—and this is the second aspect of my proposal—*can* become an *opportunity*. How? By mobilizing an exceptional creativity in each of the protagonists of the challenge; indeed, the situation of disability allows a revelation of the *irreducible singularity* of the "speaking being" that we are. It is around this opportunity that we might reconstruct our social bond.

"Why are you interested in disability?" I hear your question; and I am often asked this. Generally, I satisfy such curiosity, but not without having noted that the simple fact of asking this question already reveals the particular exclusion which strikes persons in situations of disability. Indeed, after two centuries of struggle for human rights, and whatever may be the inadequacies of what has been achieved in this area, we find it normal that somebody is committed to fighting against racism, anti-Semitism, or other discriminations because of ethnic origin, social class, race, religion, or sexuality. It is not the same, however, when it is a matter of disability: this does not confront us with a difference that is the same as these others, or even with a fragility or a vulnerability like others. And this explains the persistent surprise: "Hey, are you interested in that? And why?" I hope to contribute to explaining something of this particular discrimination, and what is at stake.

Living with the neurological difficulties of my son David, for which he followed an atypical schooling, means that I have come to know all the variants of disability: motor neuron, sensory, mental, and psychic. In response to the working project "Disability," which President Jacques Chirac launched, I wrote an "Open Letter to the President of the Republic on Citizens in the Situation of Disability, for the Use of Those Who Are and Those Who Are Not" (2003). I then organized the General Assembly at UNESCO in 2006. Anxious to address all the sensibilities of the nation, I invited the Unified Jewish Social Fund (*Fond Social Juif Unifié*), the Great Mosque, and Jean Vanier, the founder of *L'Arche*. Vanier accepted to participate on the theme of family, affective, and sexual life.

My experience with disability has in reality not only transformed the intellectual in me—I was more abstract in my thinking, and on the way to being a psychoanalyst—into a novelist, writing with a less conceptual and a more sensitive language; it also got me involved, as a mother, in a gigantic task, the urgency and utopian character of which I measure in every moment. Because through this task, it is a matter, in reality, of no more or less than refounding humanism.

How does disability change our experience, and with this, our idea of human being? Can we, from this upheaval, build bridges between Christian humanism and the humanism that stems from the Renaissance and the Enlightenment? This was the implicit issue—beyond and through the concrete narrative and the day to day of our living with disability—that I dealt with in my correspondence with Jean Vanier, published under the title *Their Look Cuts Through Our Shadows* and now translated into several languages, including Italian, with a remarkable preface from Cardinal Ravasi, President of the Pontifical Council for Culture.

Secularization and Humanism

An event occurred in Europe—and, incidentally, nowhere else—during the Renaissance and the Enlightenment: given that the "machine for fabricating the beyond no longer functions" (Philippe Sollers), men and women have "cut their connection with (religious) tradition" (Tocqueville, Hannah Arendt). By rebelling against dogmas so as to liberate their bodies and their minds, and to become the only legislators of social bonds, men and women have rejected the idea of God. From agnosticism to atheism, there exist diverse variants of secularization. And far from being a nihilism that leads automatically to the Shoah and to the Gulag, as is often too easily claimed, secularization shows itself to be quite capable of combating obscurantism and religious fundamentalism. In his book, *Do Not Forget to Think of France*, Gilles Bernheim, the Chief Rabbi of France, affirms that "Religion has entered henceforth into the field of the human sciences" to the point of these sciences "having access" to "that which appeared impossible," namely, to "the word of God." This is to say that secularization is connected again to the "broken thread of tradition," so as to tame the complexity of the continent of religions, to reevaluate it, to "transvaluate" it (Nietzsche), by clarifying both the limits and the benefits of their incontrovertible contributions. In the course of our correspondence, both Jean Vanier and I—modestly and in complete sincerity—tried to hold to this great challenge, which the human and social sciences, psychoanalysis, and philosophy are following. Today, and I say this without affectation but in measuring rather the length of the path that remains to be traversed, it appears to me that our exchange is one of the rare concrete examples, perhaps the only one, in the debate on secularism that is not taking place.

As a continuation of this initiative, I participated in the recent interreligious meeting, which took place at Assisi on October 27, 2011, when, for the first time, the Roman Catholic Church invited unbelievers. In concluding this event, Benedict XVI told believers not to consider themselves as the only "possessors of truth," but to take as a sort of example those who do not believe in an absolute truth, but who "look" for it as a "path of being," a "questioning," and an "interior struggle."

How did the experience of disability lead me to this refounding of humanism which passes by way of a new secularism (*une laïcité nouvelle*)? A secularism for which the era of suspicion is no longer enough, because in the face of threats and of the escalation of crises, the time has come to wager on the possibility of men and women believing and knowing together. Why is disability not an exclusion, or a fragility like others, and why from this fact does it call us to revise fundamentally the model that we use when thinking about it—a model that is inherited from Greek philosophy and, under certain aspects, from Christian humanism?

Before presenting you with some philosophical considerations, let me first tell you about some stages of my personal journey, by evoking three examples—John, Claire, and a woman seen on television—three different ways of sharing the challenge of disability. These three cases have marked me, and I am sure they will not leave you indifferent.

John, Claire, and the Woman Seen on Television

John

"People Say I'm Crazy": This is the title of a television documentary that was broadcast in the United States and which I saw during a recent stay there. The program claims to teach us how one might succeed in "curing" someone with schizophrenia by "integrating" him. The hero, full of various medicines that are making him obese—and about which he complains—is saved by his sister, an improvised filmmaker, who has the good idea of filming this poor man John, who fortunately adores and practices drawing and engraving. Thanks to the documentary, John's works are soon made public; he gets the chance to have an exhibition, and plenty of sponsorship follows. The "madman" is from now on "a disabled artist," an "entertainment worker" (as we would say in France), a worker like everyone else, in modern art.

An immense sadness would not allow me to applaud this documentary. Something essential seemed to be missing from the integration that made up the presentation and the documentary. I had been the witness of a *process*, perhaps even of a *procedure*, but not of a *personal renaissance*; I had seen an exhibition and a commercial transaction, but not an interaction between healthy persons and a disabled person. This person was certainly helped, but it was to help him include the objects that he produced in the circle of consumption, the success of which was being measured by his access to the television screen. The person, the *subject*, was absorbed by his objects, and his psychic life was taken as healed because it had simply disappeared.

Claire

I would also like to tell you of my meeting with a "Mother Courage," Claire. Doubtless you know many; there is always a quality of courageousness in the mother of someone with disability. Right from the birth of her daughter Marie, "they" noticed some undefinable motor neuron difficulties, before "they" announced that three-year-old Marie was *autistic*. At the time Marie's father took refuge in his work. He seemed to be saying, "With disability, you can do nothing," without saying it. It was a way of disappearing to protect himself from depression. This man's pain weighed heavily on him. Sharing it was inversed eventually into flight. There was nothing else for Claire, the mother, to do but *take everything on herself*. She became an activist, then president of an association. In response to the father's rejection, her slogan was: "You must just face things, as if there was nothing else." Claire found salvation in the bandage of renunciation, in denial. She tried to persuade herself that nothing was lost, that her daughter was not deficient, if only both of them could get something, from assistants, to a subsidy, a place in a day nursery, a small school, a CAT (which is a place in a work center for those with disability), and so on. The list is infinite. Claire's struggle kept her going. She converted all her energy into demands on public authorities which she rightly considered indifferent, arrogant, and hostile. Since Marie's birth she lived in another world, an antiworld, the world of the disabled that is cut off from the "world of others," which Claire refused to call "normal," not knowing what to make of this revolting word. She was at her wits end and she came to me to ask for psychoanalysis. I sent her to a colleague who is an analyst.

As chance would have it I met her three years later. During her analysis, Claire had taken time to lose herself and to find herself with a third party, to cry and to share her anxiety first with her analyst, and then with her work colleagues—work which she had resumed thanks to her therapy. "I isolated myself," she told me. "With Marie, we are not a single body for two. And besides, Marie found a job, she does some photocopying in a solicitor's office, where everybody respects her as she is. She speaks about her angers and about her loves, because Marie now even has a partner."

I shared her joy knowing all too well, as Claire did, that in the end, nothing was settled. And I wondered if it would always require psychoanalysis and the help of a fine solicitor to demarginalize disability? Would it be possible that the democracy of proximity and solidarity, about which so much is said, but which is slow in coming, would realize that the *respect of rights* first requires and before anything else *the recognition and the respect for the singular person?*

The Woman Seen on Television

The disability that engenders fear also gives rise to shame—and this is the last observation that I would like to share with you. I saw recently in a television program a mother *admit her shame.* She had failed her child, and, not being able to bring him back to his health, always felt guilty (as did the father, even though a man's defenses prevent him most often from admitting shame and culpability).

In the face of this kind of trouble (such as autism, and this despite recent campaigns), in the face of such sufferings and such wounds, one feels the urge to hide oneself. How can one not understand this mother, these parents? And yet, in listening to her, I heard the pride, the unconscious need for parental power in the maternal sobs! Because culpability is the daughter of the all-powerful. This tragic and courageous confession touches all parents of children with disability and reveals, at its foundation, the archaic weight of a culture with which we find it difficult to engage: the culture of a theomorphism, of a theomorphic humanism, that presents human beings as excellent, enjoying, and performing creatures, in the image of an all-powerful Creator. When it does not exclude it, this culture of the absolute power of parents makes vulnerability guilty: it is the culture of the "perfect child," who is to repair parental discontent. Perhaps it is the mirage of the Man-God that is hidden in it, but decked in the Greek and Renaissance cult of beautiful nature, and also by a certain rationalism, Christian then republican, which responds perfectly to our narcissistic fantasies, and which continues to live on in us without our knowing.

Singularity

I am taking up this debate on the "life of disability," therefore, so as to insist on the right to *irreducible singularity*, because I am convinced that modern and collectivist humanism failed when it turned its back on singularity. This was the case in the totalitarian regimes. And this could now be produced in different forms with the trivialization of the human species, which certain advances of the sciences, techniques, and hyperconnectivity are preparing.

In this context, the person in the situation of disability is in this sensitive place in the human chain where the "care by integration / collectivization at all costs" (as the examples of John, Claire, and the woman on television show) can lead to an unprecedented automatization, at the very moment when one hopes that it will bring reparation and relief. We know today that if the modern sense of happiness is freedom, freedom is not necessarily integrative, collective, and standardized, but that *it is concomitant with the singular*. Duns Scotus had already maintained this against Thomas Aquinas: truth is not in the universal idea, nor in opaque matter, but in a "this one," *this man here, this woman there*; hence his notion of *haecceitas*, of *hoc, haec*, or again *ecce*, "this," the demonstrative indexing an unnamable singularity. The discovery by Duns Scotus goes back to his reading of the words that God addresses to Moses: "I am *The One* who is." The unpronounceable calling of the name would be the index of utter singularity.

Why take up this biblical and Scotist dream today, and place utter singularity at the heart of the social pact?

We all sense that a new historic period is beginning: the good having lost its bearings in spectacular globalization, evil is set over against it, or rather the axis of evil, against which a terrified humanity is asked to mobilize. Others, when they are not striving to reconstruct or deconstruct the divine, are in search of a new founding myth. And yet, "on the ground," as we say, in the daily experience of all those outcasts in their unlimited diversity, never has humanity had an ambition so rebellious, so free, so human. It is not about a new mythology of love. I would see in it, rather, a challenge to nature and to the tragic. The acceptance and the accompaniment of the person in the situation of disability expresses the desire of men and women, together, to overcome the most insurmountable of fears—the one that confronts us at our limits as living beings. I distrust the term "integration" of the disabled: it smacks of charity to those who would not have the same rights as others. I prefer to it "interaction" which expresses a politics that has become ethics, in expanding the political pact as far as the boundaries of life. And it is not surprising that one finds a majority of women on this new political front of interaction (and perhaps this is the occasion to deculpabilize the part of the feminine in men?). Could this be because after years of feminism and in prolonging its best ambitions, they seek to renew the age-old capacity of women to care for psychic and physical life in making a political act, a political philosophy?

Mortality

Let us try to approach more closely the singularity of disability. As regards the disabilities (motor neuron, sensory, mental, and psychic) which appear in a specific way in every person who is affected, we might ask if it is a singularity like the others, a solitude like the others. On this point,

Jean Vanier and I had diverging opinions at the outset of our exchanges. I maintain in effect that disability cannot be reduced to the category of "difference." I reject portmanteau words, holdalls such as "we are all different," "all others," "all vulnerable," or "all fragile." No, we are not "all disabled." And this perhaps even less so than us not "all" being "gay" or "German Jews." Why?

Let me repeat this: disability differs from other "differences" in that it *confronts us with mortality.* The nonconformity to the norm, which is the matter at hand in the singularization of disability, is at the crossover with biology (a biological deficit) and with the social response to this deficit: biological and social, nature and culture. But even more than sexual transgressions for example, the distance vis-à-vis the biological and social norms that disability represents is perceived as a *deficit* (I will come back to this), which—although repairable in certain cases and within certain limits— lets me die if I am alone (*me fait mourir si je suis seul*), without prosthesis, without human help.

The fear of death, of human finitude, even of the limits of the human (in the face of certain severely polydisabled) are the dark side of this iceberg—an insurmountable block as disabled persons and their families know too well—which is often the attitude of those who are not disabled in the face of disabled persons, a mixture of indifference, shame, and sometimes arrogance. Certainly, all human beings know that they are mortal, but we prefer not to think of this, some even place their hope on the eternal. However, biology has discovered that cellular death (*apoptosis*) is at work at the same time as growth from conception, and it is this that sculptures a living organism. The person in the situation of disability lives with the work of mortality in him or her; it is the companion of his or her solitude, as Baudelaire says of his pain: "My pain, give me your hand; come this way." The so-called solitude of the disabled person has inevitably an absolute companion, a permanent body double: the pain of mortality. Even if this person is not sick, even if they do not feel specific pains, their disabilities remind them permanently—them or at least those around them if the deficit deprives them of this consciousness—that they are not like others who are able to live in denial about their mortality.

Religions and diverse spiritualities introduce this dimension of mortality to the minds of their adherents, although many of those who claim to follow them oppose it in their daily practice through a defensive denial. Secularization, on the contrary, did not construct a discourse on the mortality that is in us. I am not speaking of death: we are experts in celebrations of it. Nor of dependent old age: the longevity of parents and grandparents has us contributing without skimping, because there is a good chance that this disabling "great age" will strike us one day too. I am speaking of the "mortality of life," from birth or following from these "unpredictable biological genetic variabilities" that can generate disabilities: this mortality that one calls "crippling" is for us still unthinkable. Consequently, a radical change of mentality is needed so that the ordeals of disability might invite us to better assume and accompany the human condition as far as its limits and in its finitude. The consciousness of our finitude and its accompaniment are in effect fully a part of human singularity.

Norms

Disability has led me, thus, to mark in the unicity of the human person its finitude and the fear of death. But still another revision of our tenacious prejudices is needed with regard to disability: that of the norm. Can we approach it without a romantic refusal, without a servile submission, and with all the seriousness that it requires? The norm is not only a discriminating social, economic, and moral constraint; it is written into the social contract right from language. As soon as I begin to speak, I in fact accept and share norms. To speak is to submit to grammatical norms, and the speaking being does not escape common rules, without which there would be no exchange. The compassionate refusal of norms seems equally to ignore the *fundamental biological laws* which command living organisms (even if our current knowledge in this domain is insufficient and that there exists an unpredictable biological variability). The idea of a norm, of a typical form, of a suitable rule is indispensable in biology as it is for the social bond.

However, biopolitics advances another understanding of the norm, in the face of the development of democracies and also the achievements of the life sciences. In effect—thanks to their active adaptation, that is to say rebellious and creative with regard to norms—new political subjects are emerging, among them persons who are in the situation of disability, who push back the limits of former norms and engender new ones. Thus, it becomes normal that disabled persons lead a social, family, and love life. The norm is no longer an a priori fixed concept but a dynamic one. Where is the mainspring for this mutation? What is it that allows singularities to tear down norms and permit them to develop?

Possession versus Privation: "To Have" or "To Be"

Activists for the rights of persons in the situation of disability reject even the term "disability." Among the numerous reasons of this criticism, I would like to highlight one: our model of disability stems from an Aristotelian conception of human capabilities which supposes a universal form-type (an archetype) for which "diverse situations" or "cases" deviate by default through the *privation of having (steresis)*. I am blind, because I am deprived of the sensation or the capacity of seeing. In *Physics* and the treatise *On the Soul* Aristotle with finesse details these variants, their power and their impotence. In Matthew's gospel, the Aristotelian *steresis* will give the category of "poverty" (Matt. 25): "because I was hungry and you gave me something to eat; I was thirsty . . . ; I was a stranger . . . ; naked . . . ; sick . . . ; in prison. Every time you did this to the least of my brothers, you did it to me." Listen to these: various "steriles," defective or poor, share powerlessness in suffering and passion, and in our compassion with the lack of being we establish good living, the ethics that will be Christian humanism.

Without being reduced to an *ontology of negation*, this *ontology of privation* finds echoes in the entire history of philosophy, be that of "Being" and "beings" in their "finitude," from Descartes and Hegel right up to the "ontological difference" in Heidegger.[1] It is of note that the philosophy of privation includes without distinction the poor, the sick, the lepers, the drifters, and the disabled, all struck by a *lack* or a *defect*. Magnificent works of charity are inspired by it: the foundation of Christian humanism and of the Church understood as "a community of the suffering servant" who goes out "to complete," "to give" to those who "have not."

This model of solidarity by means of *poverty/privation/"lack in being"* has not ceased to show its efficacy. Not only through charitable works, but also on the level of knowledge: is it not often through the study of the "empty" (pathologies) that the sciences appropriate the complexities of the "full" (normal functioning)? It is, for example, in studying aphasias that one can better understand the mechanisms of language. Therefore, it is not a matter of ignoring the pathological and even less of abolishing it—the inevitability of the norm prohibits us from doing this—but rather of completing it.

The *paradigm of the lack*—with its counterpart *com-passion and/or tenderness*—also has its limits, even its defects, as I did not hesitate to indicate to Jean Vanier in our correspondence. His theorization is of a Greco-Christian origin, but the model is from then on unconsciously universal. As it is, it risks enclosing the disabled subject in a position of being the "object of care," of being "taken care of," at best by *tenderness*, often in *neglecting scientific knowledge* which succeeds in identifying and in treating specific symptoms, and through a self indulgence that ends up in *infantilization*. Indeed, the intrinsic logic of this model slows down the disabled subject: it prevents them from being open to their "powers," that is to say to their *sin-*

gular potentialities, and prevents them from turning their solitude, always irrevocable, into its *singular creativity*, to its initiative which can be shared within its appropriate limits. When it does not incite to "integration" at all costs, the logic of this model nourishes the fantasy of an ideal pleasure, a claimed fusion-confusion of healthy "possessors" with the "bereft/needy," a supposed communion where religious sects easily do business.

I maintain, on the contrary, against the paradigm of "having" and of "steresis," that *the singularity of being*—which goes as far as including the deficit itself, in as much as it is revelatory of the finiteness and the boundaries of living being—is not a *privation, a failure, or a sin*. The contingency of the *singular is positive*, in it "Being" and "beings" are conjoined. The contingency of the disabled singular reveals to me my own singularity of possessing, called "healthy," that I do not domesticate for the good, beginning with the singularity of the one who lacks. It is mortality on the march which touches me in him or her, I am there, it falls on me, I accompany him or her, I love him or her as he or she is. Through my love for the other singular, I carry him or her to their specific, singular, development—and to mine, equally specific and singular.

Certainly, we no longer, or rarely, associate disability with fault. But spontaneously, automatically, normally, we continue to exclude, to isolate, and to ostracize. It is only in a second phase that one claims to integrate, but always with the idea of a privation, of a fault in the background that we others, the possessors, could not essentially have. "We possess (aptitudes, powers), but he (she) does not have; he is lacking": this model of lack remains the implicit and indelible allusion of our humanist, Christian, and secular philosophy. It is no surprise that the poet sometimes rebels: "No worse deaf than those who possess," says Michaux. But it would nevertheless be false to say that we are all deaf, because we all possess. As long as we distinguish *essential Being* from an *inessential being* in *want*, we will be tempted to segregate the living. The essential Being is perhaps no longer the Divine, but we have replaced it with Biology, when we understand the disabled person as lacking certain biological aptitudes (Biology, with a capital letter, takes then the place of the essential Being: could our "divine" have become the postmodern bioscientific "being"?); or when we understand the disabled person as lacking in cultural and social capacities (Society, always with a capital letter, assuming here the role of our integrative *being*).

On the contrary, in leaving behind this paradigm of poverty and of fault, and in substituting that of the *incommensurable singularity* of each person, disabled persons included, we are getting closer to what I will call a Scotist ethics. What is a Scotist ethics? That is *the* question to ask at the crossroads of theology and of philosophy. Is it a more mystical ethics (some, such as Gilles Deleuze, have said "atheist"), while that of Thomas Aquinas would be more social? In an ethics of a Scotist inspiration, at any rate, singularity could be thought of as the only *positivity*, the only *value*. Beginning from the positivity of *beings*, Duns Scotus extended it to *Being* itself, to God, as the *causa singularitatis*. God would be singular, and Christ quite particularly, because the God-Man develops the density of his singularity through the test of his passion unto death, and as far as his *glorification* as a wounded-crucified survivor, since this is neither a *reparation* nor a *satisfaction* but precisely the evidence of his singularity.

An activist for the rights of disabled persons in the United States, Nancy L. Eiesland, takes up, without knowing it apparently, this Scotist idea in her book *The Disabled God*, when she describes Jesus as the only "disabled God." Does he not appear to his apostles, even in his glory, with an "impaired body," a damaged body? Here, the wound is not a lack, because it is an integral part of the Glory, itself given and perceived as a singularity.

Diderot had taken up for himself this "positive singularity"—in another way, which is that of modern humanism—when he undertook to transform the *disabled person* into a *political subject* for the very first time in the world. In his *Letter on the Blind for the Use of Those Who See* (1749), he basically suggests that disabled persons have all the rights, "are born free and equal in rights." And the *Declaration on the Rights of Man* will need a lot of time to put into practice this principle, which transforms finitude in act in the disabled person. The right to "personalized compensation" in France, enacted in law in 2005, is an outcome of this.

Nevertheless, to achieve this ambition of modern humanism, political will and jurisdiction are not enough. It would be necessary to reinvent this *corpus mysticum* that Kant himself evokes at the end of the *Critique of Pure Reason* (1781) in order that the singularity of the person with disability would be able to transform the norms into a dynamic, progressive concept: to reinvent love as the union with the singularity that is completely other. In other words: *for the inclusive solidarity with the weak, it is a matter of substituting the love of singularities*. What love? Love as desire and will so that the singular might be clarified, be recognized, and develop in sharing its own singularity. Much more than solidarity, which itself has great difficulty in existing, it is only this love that can lead the positive singularity (and not "deficient") of the-one-who-testifies for mortality to blossom in a society that is founded on the norm, without which there is no bond, and lead to the evolution of norms.

By bringing up the question of love, "continuously clarified transfer" in the accompaniment of the disabled person, I am thinking of the *formation of the intervening personnel*, and to the place of psychoanalysis in this complex and polemical domain. Please allow me to conclude on a more personal note, in recalling the maternal role in this ordeal.

Maternal Reliance

"I want that you be," says the mother to the child. *Volo ut sis*, says Scotist ethics. I say to David: "I love that you be." My empathy, my loving fusion with him, has thus allowed me to discover that, with his absolute pitch, he is able to make music despite his neurological deficits. However I only really accompany him in giving him the means of separating himself from me, in individualizing to the maximum his languages, his means of expression, and/or the bond with others. He will make music, multimedia, we shall create an artistic ESAT, he will participate in it in his own way, not as *I* want it, but as *he* wants it and is able. We shall open a new working space: that of sexual and affective life with his friends and those who accompany him, whose training will need to be refined. He is joining a personalized living space: thanks to Jean Vanier, it is called "Simon of Cyrene." He will fall in love; it is difficult, it is possible. I doubt it, and I say to him: "David you are dreaming." "But mum, I dream, therefore I am," he replies to me. And the norm itself is beginning to be adapted to his being. It is even becoming normal that it is spoken about at UNESCO, at Maynooth.

Jean Vanier is pioneering this central role of *empathy*, and of this *love, that is continuously clarified and questioned*, which, for my part, I call *vigilant transfer*. We have recently seen a secular version, which honors republican secularism, in the film *Untouchables* (produced with the support of the association Simon of Cyrene). The love, with the humor and gaiety that result from it, this roar of laughter which breaks through pain, this joyful alchemy, all this embodies marvelously the philosophy of sharing in the singular, which I am exploring with you. It leaves behind a certain postmodern and gloomy humanism that, when it is not exalting the theomorphism of its integrative all-powerfulness, wallows in a depressive and protesting despair. We can see an example of this in another film that is also instructive: the Iranian cinematic saga *A Separation*, the anti-*Untouchables*.

We are, therefore, in the process of substituting another mode of life for the *habitus* of the compassion of the well-off with and in the powerlessness of those who are without: going beyond the deficient self through the *corpus mysticum* of singularities. You know it: the capacity for survival of these disabled bodies is extraordinary, when they are revitalized and jubilant in the transferential encounter. This reminds me of Spinoza's surprise: "no one has yet determined what the body can do . . ." (*Ethics*, 3, Proposition 2, Scolie).

Incarnation and the Problem of Touch

MICHEL HENRY

I: Incarnation

Incarnation, in the first place, refers to the condition of a being who possesses a body or, more precisely, a flesh. Are the body and the flesh thus the same thing? Like every fundamental question, the question of the body—or of the flesh—points back to a phenomenological foundation on the basis of which it can be elucidated. A phenomenological foundation should be understood as a pure appearing that is presupposed by everything else that appears to us. This pure appearing must appear first in order for anything else to appear and to be shown to us. Phenomenology is not the "science of phenomena" but of their essence, that is, of what allows a phenomenon to be a phenomenon. It is not the science of phenomena but of their pure phenomenality as such, in short, of this pure appearing. Other words can also express this theme that distinguishes phenomenology from all other sciences: demonstration, disclosure, pure manifestation, pure revelation, or even the truth, if it is taken in its absolutely original sense. It is interesting to note that these keywords of phenomenology are also for many the keywords of religion and theology.

There are two fundamental modes of appearing—two different and decisive modes through which phenomenality becomes a phenomenon: the appearing of the world and the appearing of life.

In the world, things are shown to us from the outside; they are shown as exterior, other and different. These properties of things—of beings—do not belong to things themselves. It is only because a thing is shown in the world that it is presented to us in this way. Because the world understood in terms of its pure appearing consists of a primordial exteriority—an "outside of oneself" as such—everything that is shown in the world is always already cast outside. It is given in front of us and outside of us, as an "object" or as "facing us." By appearing in the world, the body is something that can only appear to us as external and with all of the properties that result from this exteriority; our own body is like this as well. A body is only possible in a "world": every body is an "external body." If the world is no longer considered naïvely as the sum of things or beings—as a collection of "bodies"—but in terms of their mode of appearing, then the world is illuminated in the opening of this horizon of pure exteriority that Heidegger calls an "Ek-stasis." In this way, it is the arrival from the outside of this Outside that produces the space of light in which everything that we can see becomes visible for us, whether this is a sensible or an intellectual seeing.

In life, the difference between appearing and what it allows to appear—between pure phenomenality and the phenomenon—does not exist. The condition for establishing this unusual identification between phenomenality and the phenomenon is to understand life in its proper sense. Instead of taking it as a "thing" or, in terms of modern biology,[1] as a set of inert material processes, life must be understood as phenomenological through and through, as pure phenomenality and as the most originary mode in which phenomenality is phenomenalized. Life makes every other form of phenomenality possible. Yet, even though life founds phenomenality, its mode of phenomenalization differs fundamentally from that of the world. In order to avoid this equivocation, we will refer to it in terms of revelation.

The revelation of life can be contrasted point by point with the appearing of the world. Whereas the world is disclosed "outside of oneself" such that everything disclosed there is external, the key feature of the revelation of life is that it does not have any separation within itself and never differs from itself. It only ever reveals itself. *Life reveals itself.* Life is an autorevelation. On the one hand, it is life that carries out the work of revelation; it is anything but a blind entity. On the other hand, what it reveals is itself. This is why the revelation of life and what it reveals are one and the same.

This extraordinary situation is encountered everywhere that life exists, even in its simplest modality: the impression. Consider an impression of pain. In the ordinary sense, a pain is initially taken as a "physical pain," which refers to some part of the objective body (a headache, a backache, a stomachache, etc.). For this reason, let's perform a reduction of pain that only keeps its pure impressional character, the "painful as such." This is the purely affective element of suffering pain. This pure suffering "reveals itself," which means that *suffering alone allows us to know what suffering is* and that what is revealed in the revelation of this fact is suffering itself. In this autorevelation of suffering, there is no world "outside of oneself." This can be recognized by the fact that there is no gap that separates suffering from itself. Riveted to itself and crushed under its own weight, suffering does not allow one to establish any distance from it. There is no route through which one could escape from oneself and what is oppressive about one's own being. Without any ability to put suffering at a distance, there is no possibility of directing one's gaze toward it. No one has ever seen his or her own suffering, pleasure, or joy. Pain is invisible, and this holds for every impression.

The invisible is not a negation. It should not be thought of based on the visibility of the world or in a purely privative way, since it is totally foreign to visibility and owes nothing to it. It refers to the primal and positive way in which the impression is experienced in an insurmountable passivity toward oneself, and thus as it is, in the reality of its impressional immediacy. Yet, it is never through itself or its own force that a particular impression is revealed in this way. It is only through the autorevelation of life carried out in its absolutely originary immanence that every conceivable impression is placed within oneself. It is thus impressed on oneself as being what it is. For this reason, the autorevelation in which each impression is experienced passively is not specific to any particular impression but concerns them all; all our impressions are, truly speaking, only the changing modalities of one and the same life.

This ever-changing impressional totality is our flesh. For our flesh is nothing other than what suffers and undergoes, and supports itself and thus experiences itself and enjoys itself through continually renewed impressions. Yet, like each of the impressions that comprise it, this flesh is only possible in life. Life's unity in its immanent autorevelation is equally the autorevelation of all these impressions; it is what makes them one and the same flesh.

Body and flesh are thus distinguished through the radicality of an originary phenomenological dualism. The body lacks the power to make manifest; it has to seek its manifestation in the world outside-of-oneself and is thus constituted as a mundane body. The forms of the intuition of space and time along with the categories of representation under which it is subsumed are the modes of the process of externalization through which it becomes a phenomenon. The flesh, by contrast, is an auto-impression in the process of the autorevelation of life. Its revelation is derived from life and from it alone. Bodies are possible in the world, whereas a flesh never occurs elsewhere or otherwise than in life. Before inquiring further into the phenomenological properties that the flesh acquires through its arrival into life, it is first necessary to analyze briefly the relationship between the body and the flesh from a phenomenological point of view, that is to say, to ask *which of these two realities is the most essential in the sense of providing access to the other one.*

In the world, the body appears as an extended body, with forms and figures that allow it to be known geometrically. But, a worldly body is not only an extended body owing its exteriority to the world outside-of-oneself. It is also a sensible body. It has an impressional texture—it is red, dark, sonorous, painful, nauseating—which cannot be explained by exteriority alone. According to Galileo's analysis, which was repeated by Descartes in his famous analysis of the piece of wax in the *Second Meditation*, the extended body has no color, sound, or odor on its own; it is neither agreeable nor disagreeable, neither beautiful nor ugly. Its sensible, axiological, affective layer comes from somewhere else than its ek-static structure.

This points out the following fact. Every sensible body that is seen, smelled, heard, touched, or moved presupposes another body that sees it, smells it, touches it, or moves it. The operations of this second body constitute the former and make it possible. In other words, it presupposes a transcendental and constituting body, a subject-body or a "subjective" body without which the former, the body-object-of-the-world, would not exist. This transcendental body is a principle but not the object of our experience and thus the following question can be raised with respect to it: what mode of appearing ultimately gives rise to it?

In contemporary phenomenology, especially Husserl and Merleau-Ponty, the nature of the transcendental body still remains silhouetted against the horizon of the world and remains tacitly subordinated to it. This body, to be sure, cannot be reduced to an object of perception, since it is instead what produces them. This corporeal subject has taken the place of understanding in traditional thought. However, as long as the transcendental body is interpreted as an intentional body that casts us into the world and as an appearing whose phenomenality emerges along with the arrival from the outside of the Outside, then nothing has really changed from the traditional conception of phenomenality or from the conception of the body which results from it. Quite the contrary, our body is now "of the world" in the sense that it is no longer merely an object situated in this world but also opens onto the ek-static appearing of the world. It thus still belongs to the world and remains submitted to it in a radical way.[2]

Is this not actually how it is, one might ask? The acts of the transcendental body give colors, sounds, odors, etc.; these are the acts of our senses. The "distance senses" join us to things and can only do so to the extent that this "transcendence" of the Ek-stasis of the world operates within them.

It is here that the aporia of every mundane theory of the body blocks the road. In the world "outside of oneself," no impression or flesh is possible. The flesh can only be experienced in the immanent autorevelation of life. Our body can indeed reach out toward the world, and this bundle of intentions can go out toward the sensible qualities of things. But the acts of the transcendental body—in this case the acts of our different senses— *can be carried out only because they are impressionally given to themselves in the self-givenness of life and only to the extent that they are given there.* How would we be able to see anything outside ourselves, if our vision were nothing in itself, if our hearing were, as such, only a phenomenon, if touching and taking were not living operations experienced in themselves, capable of guiding themselves in their concrete performances?

The aporia of the mundane theory of the body is thus only another name for the aporia that confronts intentional phenomenology in general: if intentionality is what reveals everything, then how is it revealed to itself? Husserlian phenomenology was only able to avoid the spiral of an infinite regress by delivering transcendental life over to the anonymous.

But there is still more. Our transcendental body cannot be limited to our senses; they are not all that intentionally reaches out toward things. The body is also the seat of originary, immanent movements. They are more than the movements that orient our senses and are indispensible to their effective functioning. *This body originally moves itself within itself.* This is how what appears to us from the outside in the external world—for instance, the objective movement of our hands—is in itself the self-movement of a power to grasp that remains in oneself when it is accomplished. It is given to oneself in the impressional self-givenness of life. If one considers this transcendental body more closely, it should be recognized that, instead of being reducible to an intentional body, its own intentionality presupposes—*a fortiori* in its self-movement that moves in oneself—this primal self-impression that excludes all exteriority. Moreover, this is the condition of the possibility of any power whatsoever—as impressionally given to oneself in the same way as pain or suffering, it must be one with itself, never separated from itself, and in possession of itself. It is in this way and in it alone that it can deployed by oneself and act.

But if the powers of our body are only able to act in life, we need to carry out a complete reversal of the tradition. The original reality of our body is not our mundane body that is situated in the world and opens onto it, instead it is our flesh in the auto-impressionality though which all powers are placed in themselves and thereby able to be exercised. The flesh provides our access to the body—whether it is to sensible bodies in the world, our own objective, sensible body, or even the intentional body itself. Yet, *our flesh can only provide access to this body and through this body to the world, because it first provides us with access to itself—because it is impressionally given to oneself where all self-givenness occurs, namely, in and through life.* Therefore, if it is no longer a question of examining the characteristics of the mundane body but rather of *the essential phenomenological properties that our flesh derives from life*, we must return to our initial question.

But, from what Life is it derived? Neither our impressions nor the flesh that they compose can bring themselves into the self; they are only given to the self through the self-givenness of life. Likewise, this life itself—to the extent that it is ours—does not bring about the self-givenness that makes it a life. While our own life happens to lack this ability, only an absolute Life contains this ability within itself, namely, the ability to bring oneself into oneself and to generate oneself in and through the process of its self-revelation. It alone can make life exist somewhere. All other lives are only alive in it—in this unique and absolute life that alone has the power to live. Only the properties of this absolute Life—not as contingent properties but as transcendental possibilities included in the process of self-generation—can account for the phenomenological properties of all conceivable life, including the essential phenomenological properties of our own flesh inasmuch as they come from life.

We thus need to inquire into this absolute process through which Life comes into oneself, even if we can only do so briefly. To live means "to experience oneself." Life comes into oneself, engenders oneself through the experience of oneself, and reveals oneself to oneself. This absolute process is tied to the principle of ipseity. Without ipseity, no experience of the self would be possible. Life is not initially a concept; it is first a real life that is phenomenologically actualized. Ipseity, in which life experiences itself, is also real and phenomenologically actualized. It is a real Self, the First living Self in which Life reveals itself to oneself, its Word (*Verbe*). Because the Self is the most radical possibility of life and its Word, a Self is also connected to every conceivable life. And at the same time, a Self also belongs to everything whose condition of possibility is found in the autorevelation of life—to every flesh and every impression. There is no flesh that does not have a Self within itself, such that this Self, which is implicated in the givenness of this flesh, turns out to be the Self of this flesh just as much as it is the flesh of this Self. There is no flesh that would be an anonymous, impersonal flesh: the flesh of the world. There is no such impression either:

there is no pain, suffering, or joy that would be the pain, suffering, or joy of no one!

We have used the words "flesh" and "impression." But why must the self-givenness of life within us, in our finite life, occur in the form of a flesh as well as in the multiple impressions that form its continuous thread? Haven't we said that all the characteristics of our flesh come from life, ultimately from the absolute Life that is the only Life that exists and from which no life, considered rigorously, can be separated? Without it, one would cease to experience oneself and also cease to be alive. How, then, does the absolute Life enter into oneself in such a way that it can be the origin of our flesh and all its properties?

We can answer in its own immanence because Life, in the immanence of its auto-revelation, remains in the self in a ceaseless auto-affection. This is also a property of our flesh. Nothing can ever separate us from it. It is an unbreakable thread without any fault line or rupture. Yet this immanence of our flesh should not be posited speculatively, like substance in Spinozism. It needs to be understood phenomenologically: how can we experience it in such a way that it is nothing but the revelation of absolute Life in us, as it is experienced in our flesh, and as our flesh, in turn, is only ever experienced in this Life?

Affectivity, or as it could be said, a pure pathos is an experience of oneself without any distance or gap, without the intermediary of a sense. Suffering is given to oneself through affectivity. As we have seen, it does not exist in itself, nor in ourselves, but in the affectivity of absolute Life. Through Affectivity, absolute Life comes into oneself, is experienced and enjoyed. Affectivity is not a fact or a state; it is not one property among others. Instead, it is the ultimate possibility behind a process that continually occurs and is never undone—the eternal process in which Life experiences and loves itself eternally in its Word that is experienced and loved eternally within itself. *This Archi-possibility is an Archi-passibility whose phenomenological actualization is the pure phenomenological matter of absolute Life*—every auto-affection and every possible life exists in this originary Affectivity. And consequently, every flesh exists in it as well. It is only because our own life, in its finitude, does not itself have an *Archi-passibility, which is to say the ability to bring itself into itself through a phenomenologically actualized pathos*. It is because our own life is only given passively to oneself through the Archi-passibility of absolute Life that we have a flesh like ours. *Every flesh is possible in the Archi-passibility of absolute Life, and every flesh is only possible through it*. Truly speaking, our flesh is nothing other than that: the passibility of a finite life drawing its possibility from the Archi-passibility of infinite Life.

We asked the question: what phenomenological properties does our flesh derive from life? We can see the answer better now: it does not entail any particular properties or any group of properties, however essential they may be. What the flesh derives from life is precisely its condition as flesh, that is, the auto-impression of suffering and joy that constitutes the pure phenomenological substance of every conceivable flesh. But, this flesh—which derives its condition as flesh from life—cannot be limited to a multiplicity of impressions or specific sensations, nor to a set of powers. The preceding analysis of these powers forced us to change direction. We had to abandon the phenomenological status of intentionality for that of self-givenness. To the extent that none of the powers of our flesh brought themselves into oneself, they were delivered to the self without being willed and independently of its power. *Each of these powers thus collides within itself with something that it has no power over or against; it collides with an absolute nonpower.* For it is not through itself but only through the heightened power (*hyperpuissance*) of absolute Life that each of these powers is given to itself, like the flesh for which it has become a power. Consider Christ's brutal response to Pilate who displayed his power to either release or crucify him: "You would have no power over me, if it were not given to you from above" (John 19:10–11).

Here again, we can see that this "givenness from above"—the Archi-givenness of life to every life—carries within itself the Archi-passibility to which every self-givenness of a life owes its ultimate possibility. What is given to every power through this Archi-givenness is not the semblance of a gift, nor the semblance of a power; it is not a particular power, such as the power to take something or to move. Instead, this Archi-givenness is what places this power in itself, puts it in possession of itself, and makes it into a true power—a power to be able (*pouvoir pouvoir*). It can then be used *freely*, as often as one wants. For freedom is not an idea but the actual exercise of a set of concrete powers. In the end, no power derives this power to be able from itself, and no human can claim it as his or her own.

If the self-givenness that makes every power a true and free power remains an Archi-givenness, how can we recognize that this Archi-givenness itself derives its phenomenological actualization from the Archi-passibility of absolute Life? Affectivity provides the phenomenological matter for this self-givenness that is constitutive of every power to be able. In modern philosophy, two admirable analyses provide evidence of this decisive situation. Maine de Biran interprets the cogito as an "I can" whose phenomenological possibility refers precisely to pathos, if it is the case that every actual action is an effort and that every effort is a "feeling of effort." This is the ultimate phenomenological condition of all action, itself considered not as the exercise of a power but explicitly as *a possibility of power*. It is Kierkegaard who carried this intuition to its full radicality. In the crucial proposition from *The Concept of Anxiety*, he calls this—"the anguishing possibility of being able"—a proposition on which the Kierkegaardian theory of eroticism and of sin is based.[3]

The Archi-possibility of absolute Life is not a concept that one can freely introduce whenever it would be useful. It must be understood where it is located, that is, in the absolute process through which Life enters into oneself and as the ultimate phenomenological possibility of this process. In the pathos of its auto-impressionality, our flesh becomes possible through this Archi-possibility of absolute Life. *That is what leads any phenomenology of the flesh back to a phenomenology of Incarnation in a radical sense.* Incarnation thus can no longer signify merely the incarnate condition of the human being, with the constellation of problems tied to it: the problem of the body, of its relation to the flesh, of all the behaviors in which this flesh is involved, of action in general with its various affective "motivations" (which are its essence), eros, etc. In-carnation no longer refers to this actual flesh which is considered to be the paradigm of all facticity. *It refers to the arrival in a flesh*, to the process from which it came and in which it remains. In the extreme passivity and possibility of its finitude, it constantly experiences itself as being unable to give itself to itself and thus necessarily refers to the process of the Archi-givenness of absolute Life in its Archi-possibility.

There is thus a "Before-the-flesh"—a Before In-carnation—which resides in the Archi-possibility of Life. Through its reference to what is Before In-carnation, our flesh displays a strange affinity with other essential features of living beings. It ceases to seem like a mysterious and contingent addition to the condition of a living being, as if it were a sort of empirical appendix like our objective body. Instead, it becomes integrated into a network of properties that derive from an *a priori* that is older than the world. How can one fail to notice that the flesh's secondary situation in relation to the Archi-possibility of Life runs parallel to the secondary situation of the Self (thus of "me" and of the "ego") and of living beings in general? In any case, the intelligibility of what is in question—the living being in its ipseity and its flesh—implies that one must be situated prior to them in an original dimension. *This is precisely the same for each of the realities under consideration*, if it is the case that life can only exist in absolute Life, that the Self can only exist in the ipseity though which this absolute Life comes into the self, and that the flesh can only exist in the Archi-possibility through which absolute Life's arrival in the self occurs. Life is thus a pathos, and in its originary enjoyment of itself, it is a Life of love.

"Before the Self" and "Before the flesh" are one and the same. They both refer to the Archi-possibility of Life because that is how Life is experienced in the ipseity of the Self, and thus in every conceivable Self, just as it is through this Archi-possibility that every flesh is joined to the self. This sheds a different light on the human condition. If the same experience of pathos makes the Self into a Self and the flesh into a flesh—*the ipseity of the Self and the auto-impressionality of the flesh*—then the Self and the flesh go together. The human is thus a *carnal living Self*. But, this has nothing to do with the definitions that construct the human as a compound of spirit and matter, of soul and body, of "subject" and "object." Such constructions do not help us to understand anything whatsoever, today no less than in its first instances in Greece or elsewhere.

For the Archi-possibility of Life does not only illuminate our human condition, it also illuminates this Archi-possibility of Life itself. This is because our condition can never be explained on the basis of the world but only on the basis of Life. These premises of the human condition find their most striking expression in the Prologue of John. At the center of the Prologue, there is the Word. It is introduced in two ways, first in its relation to life and second in its relation to flesh. The unconditional affirmation of this dual relation overturns the horizon of Greek thought, which is also largely our own way of thinking today. The relation between *Logos* and life was only envisioned in the Greek world as an opposition. This was decisive due to the paradoxical fact that it provides a definition of the human being. Animals are distinguished from humans by their lack of a *Logos*. Here *Logos* signifies both Reason and the ability to speak, that is, to form ideal meanings. If one adds to this the fact that we, humans, can only speak about things and predicate various things about them to the extent that they are shown to us, then one can discover an original connection by which the Greek *Logos* is joined to the appearing of the world (or of "Nature") and is identical to it. In spite of its apparent positivity, however, the history of Western thought will discover that this specific distinction between the *Logos* and living beings contains an insurmountable difficulty within itself.

Greek thought reveals this difficulty when it encounters—or better, enters into a Titanic struggle with—Christianity. Christianity does not know this aporia inasmuch as its Logos is no longer the Logos of the world but the Logos of Life, and its conception of the body is no longer the Greek conception of a mundane body but precisely the conception of a flesh that only exists in life. Ultimately, it exists in this Logos of Life that is the Word of God.

Two brief statements convey the initiatory revelation transmitted by John: "In the beginning was the Word," "And the Word made flesh." We have already accounted for the former statement, if it is the case that the process of God's self-revelation (explicitly defined by John as Life) in His Word is not generated at its end but in itself, as that in which this process consists: "In the beginning." As for the second proposition in verse 14, it too is illuminating if it is the case that a flesh can only have an auto-impression through the Archi-passibility of the Word of absolute Life. If the ultimate condition of possibility of the flesh is derived from the Word of Life, then the notion of the Incarnation of the Word is not absurd, as it would have seemed to the Greeks. Instead, it is rooted in the basis of things. Conversely, it founds the flesh's ability to receive the Word from which it is derived. In the insightful words of St. Irenaeus: "God can give life to the flesh," "The flesh can be given life by God," and "The flesh will be able to receive and to contain the power of God."[4]

Was the Incarnation of the Word necessary? Was it so admirable that it would have taken place without sin? All finitude presupposes the infinite, but the infinite owes nothing to finitude. The arrival of the Messiah can only be a gratuitous act by the power that governs everything. The Incarnation of the Word is not connected entirely to the historical arrival of Christ, however. For the Word that becomes flesh in Christ is the eternal Word of God. It is in Him that everything was created. This includes not only the world but also everything that is foreign to it: our flesh, the ipseity of our Self, and our life. When God breathed his life into dust from the ground, he turned it into the carnal living transcendental Self that makes up each human being. The body was only matter or dust, but the flesh was wholly alive. The arrival of each living being into its own carnal ipseity is part of the immanent generation of life. Incarnation, understood in terms of this generation, can help us to understand creation. It allows us to distinguish in creation between the process of externalization in the world and the embrace of the pathos of Life. It is through the dazzling light of John's Prologue that the book of Genesis is illuminated.

Christ's own words about himself, "the Incarnation is the Revelation of God," were repeated by his disciples. How this thesis came to be reiterated by the Church Fathers and thus by "Christianity" is the result of an unforeseen Archi-intelligibility, if the Incarnation is no longer understood naïvely as the arrival into an opaque body but into a phenomenological flesh. In the possibility of its unbearable finitude, the flesh is not merely experienced through the play of its ever-changing impressions (which are, in this respect, always the same). The flesh comes into oneself, as an auto-impression, only in the Archi-passibility through which the Word of Life eternally embraces oneself. In the flesh, then, at the bottom of its Night, the Eyes of God are watching us. Every flesh will be judged. That is the reason why with a unique lucidity—following after Paul and John, it is true—the Church Fathers understood the flesh as both the site of perdition and of salvation. The perdition of the flesh occurs when it becomes idolatrous of itself, takes itself as the source of its pleasure, and adores itself in terms of this principle as well as its effects. The salvation of the flesh occurs when it is given to itself through its generation in the Word, no longer loves anything within itself but the Word that connected it to itself in the beginning, and that it receives as its essence in the Eucharist.

We called this an Archi-intelligibility, because the power of revelation at work here is foreign to any form of vision or "e-vidence," whether it would be sensible or intellectual. The latter allowed the Greeks (as well as the Moderns) to adequately apprehend the content of the sensible. There are many degrees of this knowledge that can be divided into different "kinds" and evaluated in terms of their pertinence. That is the knowledge of the wise and learned. But, here is what is new: the power of revelation is conferred to the flesh and this carnal power is the absolute. The pathos of life is vested in every living being as a privilege that no one can ever take away; it is the sign of one's election and the reality of life. This invincible revelation is inscribed in fiery letters in the invisibility of our flesh; it is given in each of the flesh's impressions, in each of its powers, in a "givenness from above."

II: The Problem of Touch

The problem of touch leads us back to that of the other senses according to a dual relationship of similitude and differentiation.[5] Each sense is specific, although they all appear as functions of the same body. The status of every sense is derived from this body—the living individual's own body. Since the question of touch leads us back to the question of the body, it's this that we should first interrogate from a philosophical and general point of view.

The first philosopher I appeal to is Descartes. It is to him that we allegedly owe the dualism of body and soul that still today governs the way in which we most readily conceive our relation to the body, and this not only in relation to philosophy, but also in the domain of psychology, medicine, psychoanalysis, and common sense. In this schema of things, the human is dual, soul or spirit on one side, body as material thing on the other—the difficulty being then, how a spiritual "thing," without volume or physical dimension, such as the soul, can act on the material body or inversely.

And yet Descartes asserted another very surprising proposition about the body that could call in question this dualism which modern thought has not yet escaped. Gassendi wrote, in his *Objections* to *The Meditations*—you say "I think therefore I am, why could you not just as well say, I am walking therefore I am."[6] To this, Descartes unexpectedly responded that it is altogether possible to say "I'm walking, therefore I am," on the condition that one understands by this the immediate experience of the walk, the walk reduced to what it really is for the one who is walking, the pure subjective experience of the act of walking. Reduced to this pure experience, walking is nothing other than a *cogitatio* and, thus, is fundamental to what I am, to the *sum* as well as to the "I think." It is only a modality of this "I think" itself in the Cartesian sense, understood as that which is experienced immediately in and of itself.[7] With this idea of walking, i.e., of a corporeal experience as *cogitatio*, Descartes has an astonishing intuition of an idea of the subjective body that overturns the traditional conception of the body as an object. Unfortunately, Descartes did not develop this completely new point of view of a subjective body. On the contrary, he held fast to the idea of a body-thing, more precisely to the idea of the body as an extended thing—*res extensa*. This conception was taken from Antiquity and reintroduced a few years earlier by Galileo, which he used as a foundation of his physics. This would become the foundation of modern physics as well as of science in general. If the body is in fact an extended thing, endowed with forms, it is knowable by geometry. Hence, the knowledge of the material world must be geometric, and once Descartes lent a mathematical formula to geometric knowledge, the physicomathematical approach to material nature, i.e., modern science, was founded.

And yet our body as we live in it—this body that walks, feels, desires, labors in pain or joy—has nothing to do with the body of physics, nor with its material particles. It has nothing to do either with the biological organism that is made up of molecules, chains of acids, neurons, etc. It is for this reason that the decisive intuition of a subjective body, which was only glimpsed by Descartes, will be taken up again by another great French philosopher, Maine de Biran. In the early years of the nineteenth century, Biran explicitly developed a very in-depth theory of the subjective body. It is by meditating on Descartes's *cogito*—abandoned by all the great metaphysicians after Descartes (Spinoza, Malebranche and Leibniz)—that Maine de Biran makes his incredible discovery of the body as pure subjectivity. For him the *cogito* is not an "I think" in the way we understand it, i.e., an "I think something, I imagine something," but an "I can." I am a kind of primordial force, a power I exert with each action, whether it has to do with mobility like the action of grasping with the hands, of standing up, of walking, or even of the action that dwells in each of our senses, through which, for example, I move my eye in order to direct my gaze in the way that I would like. It is precisely in relation to touch that this force at work in the deployment of each of our senses can be recognized by what is inherently essential to it.

We should now mention the admirable critique that Maine de Biran launched against the theory of the knowledge of one's own body (*le corps propre*) proposed by Condillac. For the great empiricist of the eighteenth century, our body can be reduced to a set of subjective sensations, but it is touch that invites us to traverse this purely subjective layer of impressions in order to experience, in some way, what is behind it. The real being of our body is touch. Concretely, it is the movement of the hand over one's own body (*le corps propre*) that grasps the body as something that resists its pressure. In this way, the hand that moves in a continuous way over our body makes its reality emerge. Its structures and its forms emerge in the same way that it will lead the forms and the structures of external bodies to emerge.

This extremely interesting description of the genesis of the knowledge of our own body implies in fact a dissociation between two bodies, a known body and a knowing body. The known body is this real being whose contours and configurations are traced and recognized bit by bit by the hand as it is moving. It is the body that is touched and grasped by that hand. The body that knows is this hand, inasmuch as the succession of its movements profile the body that is the object of its touch. This act of touching is promoted to the rank of a fundamental power of knowledge, relative first to our own body and then to the external bodies of which the world is composed.

But if we examine the relationship between the knowing body and the known body, this relationship is revealed to us as internal to touch itself. For it is introduced between the touching touch and the object touched— an object that appears to be first and foremost my own body, specifically as the object of my touch. And, if we delve even further and ask which of those two bodies, the body that touches or the body that is touched, is the more fundamental, then we are obviously brought back to the former, to the touching touch without which nothing touched would ever exist for us. *Thus, by virtue of this inescapable subordination, the body-object points back to the body-subject, which always founds it.*

The discovery of a subject whose essence is touch itself—as touching touch and, more generally, as the subjective body and the power that dwells in each of its senses, including touch—is certainly essential. With this corporeal power, we are faced with a subject totally different from the one that classical philosophy had placed at the origin of our experience. That subject was consciousness; but in that consciousness it is understanding that appeared as the fundamental capacity of the mind. The world, correlative to this rational subject, is interpreted as a world made intelligible by the mind, structured by rules that are themselves rational and to which sensible phenomena are subject. A more or less strongly affirmed hierarchy between the intelligible and the sensible traverses Western thought from Greece to the present day.

The establishment of our own body as the principle of our experience of the world and thus as the true subject completely modifies the classical notion of the subject of knowledge. In addition, it changes the world itself. Since its structures depend on the nature of the subject, it thus finds itself transformed at the same time. It becomes the world-of-the-body, the world-of-life, or, as Husserl says, the *Lebenswelt*. This means, first of all, that it is a sensible world and that the conceptual rules by which it is governed (notably, scientific idealities) necessarily refer to the sensible layer of this world that is already given passively, and without which they would not have any meaning. This incarnate subject related to a sensible world is the concrete situation that phenomenology, and Merleau-Ponty in particular, will constantly oppose to the classical description of an intellectual consciousness dominating a world of scientifically known objects.

However, these apt analyses of the world as bound to a carnal subject leave open a wide question that only Maine de Biran had the genius to perceive. If we refer to his criticism of Condillac and to the problem of two bodies united by touch, to the hand that moves over our own body in order to progressively decipher its shapes, an enormous difficulty presents itself. For it is not a question anymore of describing or understanding how the body-subject knows, by the touch of the hand, the body-object whose parts it circumscribes; it is rather a question of knowing beforehand how the touching touch, that is to say the power of movement and of the grasping hand, is originally in possession of itself, in order to be able to move around, to take and to touch. The decisive problem is no longer to understand how the body-subject relates to the body-object by grasping it, touching it, and knowing it in this fashion, but how this touching body is linked to itself and experiences itself as touching, given that the knowledge of this experience is a very particular knowledge, no longer a knowledge but a power. How can the subjective power of the grasping hand be in possession of itself in such a way as to be able to do everything it does, to be able to take, move, and act?

The genius of Maine de Biran is to have understood that the kind of experience through which touch is in relationship with itself, as touching touch, has nothing to do with the experience through which the touching touch enters into relationship with everything else it touches.

The touching touch is in contact with what it touches through an intentionality. It goes beyond itself towards what it touches and reaches it as what resists it. In this way, what resists stands outside of the power that breaks up against it. On the contrary, in the relationship of the touching touch to itself, this touching touch is able to be in possession of itself and act; there is no intentional relation, no relation to exteriority. The touching touch experiences itself immediately. The experience that it has of itself is a pathos without distance, a pure affectivity. Analogously, each feeling relates to itself in this way; every fear and every anguish is immediately aware of itself, in and through its affectivity. Thus the body-subject, the touching touch, is intentionality linked through an external aim to what it touches, while in its internal relationship to itself there is no longer any intentionality, nor any exterior aim (*visée*). There is only this pathos, crushed against itself, immersed in itself, in which the touching touch is one with itself. And it is only this condition that the body-subject is in possession of itself, capable of acting, of moving and of touching.

The relationship of the touching touch to itself enables us to understand our relationship to our body in general, no longer how it gets to know by motricity or through its senses, but precisely its relationship to itself—what I call originary corporeality. Originary corporeality designates the way in which the body inhabits itself; it coincides with itself and thus with each of the powers that compose it. This is what makes it able to exert those powers. The touch knows everything it touches by touching it in the act that stumbles upon what it touches as something exterior to itself. This act is a form of intentionality. But the touching touch does not touch itself. *It is not by touch that we come to know touch.* How do we come to know it then? Through this silent experience in which it experiences itself immediately. The phenomenological matter of this experience is pure affectivity. Life is what experiences itself immediately, without distance, in a "feeling of oneself" whose stuff is pure affectivity, an affective flesh. This is not the life described by the biologists, whose different elements—molecules, particles, etc.—belong to the world and are objectively and scientifically known. The life of the living body, of this body that is ours and with which we coincide, is a phenomenological life, the absolute phenomenological life whose whole essence is to experience itself. It is this life that dwells in touch, the touching touch, which makes it what it is, a power within our reach and that we use in this feeling of effort of which Maine de Biran speaks. This is the mode in which our body is given to itself—our original corporeality.

One last word on this touching touch. We should not interpret it as a singular act or as a series of particular, consecutive acts to which its exercise would be limited. Each act of touching, of grasping with the hands, etc., is nothing other than the actualization of a force, of a prior capacity to grasp. Our problem was to understand how this capacity to touch and to take is in our possession, as a capacity that we can put to work at any moment. It is precisely because this capacity is in our possession that we can use it. That is why the problem of touch is a problem concerning this permanent capacity, this being-constantly-in-possession that resides in our originary corporeality and defines it. This capacity governs time. There is an Archi-Presence of the body to itself. As a result of this originary presence, my body is always already there, as something with which I coincide and that I can put into operation at any moment. This immersion of each of us in our own body comes from the immersion of life in itself. For the living, life is never past or future or even present in the way we say that an object is present to us. It escapes this past, this future, as well as any objective present, precisely because it is always there. It embraces itself in the pathos of an embrace that no force can break.

Because the subjective originary body is constantly present to itself in this Archi-Presence of life to itself, the world to which it opens us through each of its powers, and notably by touch, is a world that also surpasses the actuality of the perception that I have of it at any given moment of my experience. It is a world that is potentially given to me because I can deploy the powers that give me access to it, because the paths that lead to the world are pre-delineated in me and I can follow them whenever I wish. I can touch things at any moment. This power is one with me and thus all of the things that compose the world are accessible to me in principle, inasmuch as I carry this power within me and coincide with it.

The reflection on touch thus leads us to a series of problems of both the greatest interest and difficulty, as soon as we stop considering touch naively as an objective behavior that takes its natural place amongst worldly phenomena. Understood in its subjectivity, and thus as an inner possibility that inhabits our original body, touch refers to a constellation of fundamental phenomena that concern us in the core of our being, as much in our relationship to ourselves as in our relationship to the world and to others.

—*"Incarnation" translated by Scott Davidson; "The Problem of Touch" translated by Anne Bernard Kearney and Simone Kearney*

On the Phenomena of Suffering

JEAN-LUC MARION

Life only lets itself be said in a negative mode, despite the fact that it precisely has the privilege of negating any negativity. For my life only conceals itself, withdraws and flees far from me as inaccessible and foreign, because it happens to me so intimately that I cannot *watch it come* to me, nor establish the least gap between it and me—this gap without which transcendence, intentionality, and horizon cannot operate or let anything show itself. I do not see my life, because I am it—or more exactly, because I am only within it. Life is that *in* which we live.[1]

Hence my life cannot be seen, because it will not let itself be aimed at, even under the exact account of the face.[2] In short, the "facelessness" of essence means ultimately that "life does not have a face," it is "faceless."[3] "Life is invisible,"[4] not because it withdraws and conceals itself, but because it moves so far into me that it coincides with me and that I have no means of aiming at it in distance from myself. Invisible because in-visable—since we can only aim at what belongs to the world and is open to it. And yet I have access to it, since it phenomenalizes itself for the same reason as it does not show itself. Must one conclude that what does not show itself could nevertheless phenomenalize itself? Without doubt, for "life senses itself" and "the essence of life resides in self-affection," because it "constitutes itself the content that it receives and which affects it."[5] I can never doubt what I sense inasmuch as I sense it: as long as I do not relate it to an external object, but assign this feeling to what gives and gives itself, to sensing as such. "No one has ever seen a feeling, a feeling has never caused anything to be seen," simply because "a feeling cannot be perceived."[6] No one has ever seen a feeling, especially not myself—but that is also the reason why I remain alive and am not dead. Similarly for suffering, the sensed (and the feeling) par excellence: "No one has ever seen his or her suffering, anguish, or joy. Suffering, as any modality of the world, is *invisible*."[7] And under this connection also, one would not be able to avoid comparing life to God, as Henry does not hesitate doing as early as 1963: "This is why the absolute permits itself to be understood by starting from this hidden state or as that which maintains itself in this state; this is why 'No one has ever seen God,' and finally why God is the 'hidden God.'"[8] Yet this coming together (what those who denounce it do not see) teaches us precisely as much if not more by a gap it crosses in silence, it seems to me: I die if I see God (and this justifies why we compare God to death or to the sun), while to the contrary I live life as long as I do not see it, precisely because it phenomenalizes itself inasmuch as it remains invisible and, if I pretend to see it—that is, objectify it as a being which would show itself in the world—not only will I not see any of it, but I will possibly substitute a corpse for it. And if this corpse was mine, I would already be dead.

The reason which led us to introducing the "paradox whereby ultimately every fundamental phenomenological inquiry bearing on the essence is gauged,"[9] namely the paradox of an invisible phenomenality, is hence proven correct in strictly phenomenological fashion. There are indeed certain phenomena—and the most indisputable, for they are the only ones which coincide immediately with myself (life, suffering, pleasure, joy, and the like or more exactly, my life, my suffering, my pleasure, and my joy)—that can only phenomenalize themselves by remaining invisible and must manifest themselves by the feeling in which I experience them. These phenomena are manifested without being aimed at, hence without visibility, but by the affection of original feeling. To pretend to make them visible would amount to killing them. Life remains a phenomenon of the night. The distinction between the invisible and the visible according to their respective phenomenalities hence results from a purely phenomenological decision, not metaphysical, not religious.

Is it not possible that . . . certain phenomena cannot appear, not by a defect, but because they cannot do so in principle? Does the method of phenomenology (unveiling, putting into light) always and necessarily coincide with its "object" (the phenomenon to manifest)? Or, is it not possible in certain cases that the "identity between the object and the method of phenomenology loses its evidence"? For example, when it is a matter of phenomenalizing life. "If, to the contrary, life . . . escapes in principle from the domain of the visible . . . then the identity between the object and the method of phenomenology is broken abruptly. It would give way to a heterogeneity so radical that it is first presented to thought as an abyss."[10] *Here* there is not refusal (as by bad will) of phenomenalizing itself at stake but of the work of a phenomenality that does not arise from the open, from evidence, and from visibility, because it does not give itself to be seen but senses itself by self-affection. Not to respect this phenomenality of the invisible as invisible, in another presence than that of the day, goes back to not respecting the things themselves, by imposing on them a phenomeno- logical indifference. "The appearing which unveils in the Difference of the world . . . is in principle totally *indifferent . . . indifferent to all that which it unveils*."[11] The right of the invisible to the difference of its phenomenaliza- tion is only captured *against* the univocity of ontological difference, which remains obsessed with remaining by the ecstasis of the opening.

This question does not lack radicality since it puts into question the univocity of the horizon of the phenomenality of being, to the point where it maybe also puts into question the concepts of the horizon and of being- ness themselves, thus of being. The long polemic of Michel Henry, which put him in opposition not only to Sartre and Merleau-Ponty, but especially to Husserl and Heidegger, was nevertheless doubtless not solitary: Em- manuel Levinas, in his own fashion, shared the same quarrel—to measure which phenomena phenomenalize themselves according to the invisible, and solely under this nocturnal light. After all, the face is not seen any- more than the saying is heard; the call does not depart from the invisible more than the hearing. And, if only what gives itself can show itself, then givenness itself, which thus makes possible all showing, would never be able to show itself, nor to convert its invisibility into visibility. It is not the least legacy of Michel Henry to have so forcefully and clearly posed this question—a question of *method*.

—*Translated by Christina M. Gschwandtner*

Memory, History, Oblivion

PAUL RICOEUR

Enigmas of Memory

What I offer here is not a mere survey of my three-part volume *Memory, History, Forgetting*, but a kind of critical rereading proceeding from a reversal of standpoint. In what sense? The leading thread in my book is the *writing of* history in accordance with the lexical definition of history as historiography. Hence the ordering of the thematics: first, memory as such, then history as a human science, and finally oblivion or forgetting as a dimension of the general historical condition of human beings. Memory, according to this linear construction, was held merely as a matrix of history, whereas historiography displayed its own stages beyond memory: from the level of written testimonies stored in archives, to the level of explanatory proceedings, and from there, to the elaboration of the historical document as a literary work. Forgetting, then, was treated mainly as a threat to the central operation of memory, recollection, the *anamnesis* of the Greeks, and, by implication, as a limit to the claim of historical knowledge to provide a reliable account of past events. From the standpoint of history writing, the notion of historical past appears as the ultimate and irreducible reference of the whole process of historiography.

What I am proposing today is a shift in the prevailing standpoint, a shift from writing to reading, or, to put it in broader terms, from the literary elaboration of the historical work to its reception, either private or public, along the lines of a hermeneutics of reception. This shift would provide an opportunity to extract, from their linear treatment in the book, some crucial problems that clearly concern the reception of history rather than the writing of history and to emphasize them. The issues at stake concern memory, no longer as a mere matrix of history but as the *reappropriation of* the historical past by a memory taught by history and often wounded by history.

As we shall see later, such problems as the duty to remember and other controversial issues calling for a policy of memory—amnesty versus unprescribable crimes for example—fall under the heading of the reappropriation of historical time by memory as taught by history.

My purpose here is to draw the most interesting consequences of this shift of standpoint concerning the relationship between memory and history. Treated in a nonlinear, circular way, memory is allowed to appear twice in the course of our analysis, first as the matrix of history from the standpoint of history writing, second as the channel of the reappropriation of the historical past such as it is conveyed by historical accounts. But this shift of standpoint does not imply that we put aside the phenomenological description of memory dealt with for its own sake, whatever this connection to history may be. We could not even talk seriously of the *reappropriation* of the historical past by memory if we had not previously taken into account the *enigmas* plaguing the process of memory as such.

The basic enigma at stake has to do with the very idea of representation of the past as memory. As Aristotle says in the short treatise *On Memory and Anamnesis*, memory is "of the past." What does this simple preposition "of" mean? We can present the difficulty in the following way: a memory occurs in the mind as an image that gives itself spontaneously as a sign, not of itself, but of something else actually absent yet held as having existed earlier. Three traits are paradoxically put together: presence, absence, and anteriority. To put it in other words, the memory image is present in the mind as representing something which is no longer there, but which has been. A metaphor, which keeps playing an important role in the treatment of this enigma, may be helpful for a while: that of the imprint, like that of a seal imprint in the wax. The notion of trace belongs to the same set of helpful metaphors; but the same enigma remains: the imprint or the trace is fully present but, through its presence, refers back to the shock of the seal or to the initial inscription of the trace. In addition, the notion of absence has more than one meaning: the unreality of fictional entities, fantasies, dreams, utopias. The absence of the past is something quite different. It includes the sense of temporal distance, of remoteness, marked in our language by verbal tenses or adverbs, such as "before" and "later." Such is the initial enigma that history will inherit from memory: the past is, in some way, present in the image as the sign of its absence, an absence which, though no longer being there, is held as having been. This "having been" is what memory tries to recover; memory claims to be faithful to this "having been." The thesis is that the shift from writing to reception and reappropriation does not abolish this enigma.

Confronted with such an enigma, memory is not deprived of resources. Since Plato and Aristotle, we have spoken of memory not only in terms of presence/absence, but of recovery, recollection, which they called *anamnesis*. And when this search succeeds, we speak of *recognition*. We owe it to Bergson to have brought back *recognition* to the center of the problematics of memory. In connection with the difficult concept of the *survival* of the images of the past—whatever the conjunction between the notion of recognition and survival of the past—*recognition*, taken as a phenomenological datum, remains a kind of wonder, "*un petit miracle*" as I like to say. No other experience gives the sort of certitude of the actual presence of the absence of the past. Though no longer there, the past is *recognized* as having been. Of course, such a truth claim may be challenged, but we have nothing better than recognition to make us believe and assert that something happened before we remember and tell it. Such is both the enigma and its fragile resolution, that memory transmits to history, but it transmits also to the reappropriation of the historical past through memory because recognition remains a privilege of memory that is missing in history. But it will also be absent from the reappropriation of the historical past by memory. History may, at best, provide constructions claiming to be reconstructions. But between reconstructions, as accurate and close to the facts as they may be, and recognition, a logical and phenomenological gap remains. We may already anticipate the conflicts proceeding from the claim to faithfulness of memory, too easily assimilated to an ever enduring recognition, against the long and tricky strategies of history.

The Writing of History

Let me say a few words about history as the writing of history, epistemology. We cannot skip this stage to the extent that the reception of history as a mode of appropriation of the past by memory constitutes the counterpart of the whole process of historiography. The test of the distinction between the two approaches may be found in the possibility and the claim to reduce memory to a mere object of history among other cultural phenomena. This reduction is one of the most striking effects of the reversal of roles generated by the emergence and the rise of history as a human science. The earliest potential break between history and memory can be assigned to the invention and the expansion of *writing* as a way of inscribing human experience on a material support distinct from the body: brick, papyrus, parchment, paper, compact disc, to say nothing of inscriptions which don't transcribe the oral voice: marks, drawings, play of colors in clothing, gardens, steles, monuments, and all kinds of archeological remains.

We could follow the progression of the break with memory along the stages of historical knowledge, as an epistemology of history may order them, but this survey does not belong to our topic today. Nevertheless, I want to make an exception for the sake of some critical procedures with which the reappropriation of the historical past by memory *hic et nunc* may have to come to grips. I will limit this incursion into the process of historiography to three major phenomena. First, the place and role of testimony at the stage of documentary investigation. Testimony is, in a sense, an extension of memory taken at its narrative stage. But there is testimony only when some narrative held about events is made public: the subject, in front of somebody else claims that he has been the *witness* of something that happened. The witness says: "I was there, believe me or not." Someone else receives his testimony, writes it, and keeps a record of it. The testimony is reinforced by the promise to testify once more, if required, which engages the reliability of the witness and gives to testimony the gravity of an oath. The fiduciary dimension of a variety of human relations is thus brought to the forefront: treaties, pacts, contracts, and other human interactions relying on our confidence in the word of another. But testimony is at the same time the weak point in the establishment of the so-called documentary proof. It is always possible to oppose testimonies one to the other, either concerning the related facts or the reliability of the witness. A great part of the historical fight for truth proceeds from this confrontation between testimonies, mainly the written ones; questions arise: Why were they preserved? By whom? For the sake of whom? This conflictual situation cannot be kept within the boundaries of history as a science; it emerges at the level of our contemporary conflicts between living and sometimes collectively organized pleas for a tradition of memory at the expense of other traditional memories.

A second set of features related to the explanatory phase of the writing of history will find a specific counterpart at the stage of reading and reception. It has to do with the mixture of casual and intentional procedures. In this regard, there are in historical knowledge no recognized constraints concerning the various uses of the term "because" as a reply to the question "why?" Some uses of causal connection in history are very close to the uses in natural sciences; such is the case in economical history, demography, linguistics, and even the treatment of recurring cultural configuration.

They are explanations in the terms of reasons, reasons for acting in such and such a way. In this case we should be allowed to speak of comprehension rather than explanation. Historians are not dogmatic concerning the boundary between explanation and comprehension. Add to this complex architecture of the so-called historical explanation the ability of historical knowledge to change the scale of the phenomenon and to move from one scale to another concerning stretches of time: the *longue durée* of Braudel, short intervals of time in the kind of *microhistory* practiced by the Italian school. This *jeu d'échelle*—scale game—is only one example of the entanglement of interpretation in the process of explanation, either causal or intentional. With interpretation, the personal implication of the historian comes to the fore. Without overestimating the prejudices, the passions, the partiality of commitment of the historian, it is enough to underline its intervention in the choice of his preferred topic, including the choice of his field of research, of his familiar archives, even the choice among causal or intentional explanation. Interpretation is not a distinctive phase within the whole process of historical knowledge, it is at work at all levels, from the testimony and the establishment of archives, to explanation in causal or intentional terms, from the economical sphere to the cultural one.

With cultural history, the claim of history to annex memory to the cultural sphere reaches its climax. From memory as the matrix of history, we have moved to memory as an object of history. With the development of the so-called history of mentalities—the word being today more or less discredited—this inclusion of history among some other cultural phenomena, which may be called representations, is in principle legitimate. It is even helpful for the sake of the self-critique of memory, mainly at the level of collective memory. The selective character of memory, with the help of narratives, implies that the same events are not evenly memorized at different periods of time. For example, in France after 1945 the public discourse was focused first on the alleged facts of collaboration or resistance. Only later, with the Barbie Trial, was the specificity of the ordeal of the Jews, through the narrative dealing with deportation and extermination of several million persons, acknowledged as a distinctive crime. Here, the boundary between memory as an object of history and memory as an actual capacity or ability of individuals and communities, which may be called communities of history, is crumbling. The case of the narratives told by survivors is, in this regard, exemplary: they belong to history as a cultural phenomenon among others.

With this quandary I move to the topics that, at the beginning of this talk, I put under the heading of memory as *taught* by history. This teaching occurs at the meeting point between history as literary work and reading as a privileged kind of reception, in the sense of a hermeneutics of reception. Writing and reading constitute the two sides of teaching. We would miss this basic connection if we did not take into account the last stage of the process of historiography, namely the production of a literature of its own. Of course, the historical enterprise relies on writing, and the role of written testimonies in our archives confirms it; we dared even say that history was born at the same time as writing. But history generates new written works: published books and articles, accompanied by maps, images, photos, and other inscriptions. At this very stage, historiography, in the full sense of the word, may teach memory. The conjunction between writing and reading is furthermore channeled by the shared experience of telling.

History, as it has been said, is a province of story; even economical or demographical history describes changes, cycles, and developments that are told. This shared experience of telling implies narrative constraints that, from the perspective of the historian, provide readability to the text and visibility to the events related at the expense, sometimes, of the complexity and opacity of the historical past. Add to these narrative constraints the more hidden play of rhetorical constraints that some critics may have over-emphasized by assuming the risk of bringing history close to rhetorics rather than to science. Without returning to a pessimistic standpoint, the idea of historical objectivity deserves to be vindicated against some forms of relativism which would deprive historiography of its main claim, namely that of offering a reliable representation of the past. This claim must be reasserted not only against a rhetorical treatment of historical knowledge, but also against some alleged claims on the part of some supported communitarian memories. If there were no truth claim in historical knowledge, history would not play its role in the confrontation between history and memory to which I will devote some careful consideration in a while. Of course history is deprived from the "blessing" of recognition, which provides to memory a kind of illumination. This lack causes its malaise, but not its doom; we may only expect from its constructions that they be held as reconstructions according to logic of probability in the terms of Carlo Ginsburg's model of historical truth. Without this minimal confidence none of the problems that I intend to consider in the last section of my lecture would occur.

Memory and History

In the last part of my paper, I will focus on three critical issues related to the topic of memory taught by history: the potential misunderstanding between historians and the advocates of memory; the controversial issue of the duty to remember; and finally the use and abuse of forgetting.

The first one deals with the potential clash between the aims of historical knowledge and those of memory, either personal or collective. With history, the horizon of past events is wider than that of memory; the short span of remembered events is swallowed within the broad scope of historical time. Furthermore history brings within the field comparisons that tend to relativize the unicity and the non-comparable character of painful memories. Add to that the plurality of perspectives—economical, social, political, and cultural—opened by history on the same set of events. At last, the attempt to understand may seem to prevent one from judging and condemning. The historian is not even compelled to conclude, unlike the judge or the common citizen; the historian's concern is that of comprehension, explanation, discussion, and controversy. For all these reasons there may be a lasting misunderstanding between historical knowledge and memory. Collective memory is not deprived of critical resources; the written works of the historian are not the only ways of representing the proximate past. They compete with other kinds of writing, in the broad sense of the term, such as fictional accounts, theatrical transpositions, essays, pamphlets, and nonwritten modes of expression: photos, painting, and above all films (think of Claude Lanzmann's *Shoah*, and Spielberg's *Schindler's List*). Furthermore the retrospective kind of discourse proper to history competes with prospective discourses, projects of reform, utopias: in a word, with discourses directed towards the future. Historians should not forget that the citizen is the one who makes actual history—the historian merely *tells* it—and that they, historians, are also citizens responsible for what they say, especially when their work deals with wounded memories. Memory, then, was not only taught by history but also wounded by it.

This last remark brings me close to the second critical issue, that of the duty to remember, as it is called, the duty of not forgetting, to anticipate our last consideration. The duty of memory is often a claim raised by victims of a criminal history; its ultimate justification is the call to justice owed to victims. With this claim the misunderstanding between advocates of memory and supporters of historical knowledge reaches its peak, to the extent that the heterogeneity of intentions is made acute: on the one hand the short scope of memory in comparison with the broad horizon of historical knowledge, on the other hand the persistence of the wounds left by history; on the one hand the use of comparison in history, on the other the claim of unicity of the sufferings endured by a particular community or a whole people. For the historians, the incomparable dimension of an event can be asserted only as the conclusion of the rating of similarities and differences. To arbitrate between these competing claims, it may be useful to turn to some psychoanalytical concepts. In a short essay called *Erinnern*,

Wiederholen, Durcharbeiten (*Remembering, Repeating, Working Through*), Freud introduces the notion of *Erinnerungsarbeit*, to characterize the fight against the confinement in repetition under the pressure of entrenched resistance. Something may be preserved and transposed in the field of historical memory, especially if you complete the notion of the work of memory with that of the work of mourning, borrowed from another essay devoted to "mourning and melancholia."

I suggest we bring together the notion of the duty of memory, which is a moral notion, and those of the work of memory and the work of mourning, which are merely psychological notions. The advantage of this rapprochement is that it allows us to include the critical dimension of historical knowledge within the work of memory and mourning. But the last word must remain to the moral concept of duty of memory which refers, as we said, to the notion of justice owed to the victims.

Our third and last issue, concerning the place of forgetting within the common field of memory and history, derives from the previous evocation of the duty of memory, to the extent that such a duty may be expressed in terms of a duty not to forget.

Now, forgetting is a topic of its own. It has to do with the notion of trace that we introduced at the very beginning of this lecture; and we made room for a great variety of traces in relation either with the brain, or with psychic impressions, or with documents stored in our archives. The first and obvious connection between traces, in whatever sense, and forgetting is provided by the notions of fading, or deleting, or blurring out of traces. But the unavoidable process of blurring out does not exhaust the problem of forgetting.

Forgetting has also an active side linked to the process of recollecting, as a search aiming at the recovery of lost memories, of memories that are not actually blurred out, but only made unavailable. This nonavailability has, to a certain extent, its explanation at the level of unconscious conflicts. In this regard, it is one of the precious teachings of psychoanalysis that we forget less than we think and fear. Traumatic experience in childhood may be recovered with the help of specific procedures proper to the so-called talking-cure. In Freud's essay, *Remembering, Repetition, Working-Through*, he assigns to deep-rooted resistance the compulsion to repeat instead of remembering. Remembering, then, consists in a kind of work, and close to it the work of mourning, to which another important essay, *Mourning and Melancholia*, is devoted.

But this approach through psychoanalysis to the ambiguities of forgetting should not prevent us from exploring some other forms of forgetting for which we may hold ourselves accountable. Let us start from the simple remark that memories are a kind of narrative and that narratives are necessarily selective. If we are unable to remember everything, we are still more unable to tell everything. The idea of an exhaustive narrative is sheer nonsense. The consequences as regards the reappropriation of the historical past are tremendous. The ideologizations of memory, and all the kinds of manipulations akin to it, rely on the resources of variation linked to the procedures of emplotment providing configuration to our narratives. Specific strategies of forgetting can be grafted directly from this art of telling—such as avoiding, eluding, flighting. We wanted to speak of the reappropriation of the historical past, but we also have to speak of dispossession of social agents from their originary power to tell themselves. It is a difficult enterprise to disentangle the personal responsibility of individual actors from the social pressures at work under the surface of collective memory. The dispossession of which we are now talking is responsible for the mixture of abuses of memory and abuses of forgetting, which allows us to speak of too much memory at times, and too much forgetting at other times. It is the responsibility of the citizen to arbitrate between such hazardous assessments.

I should not like to close this set of remarks devoted to the tricks of forgetting, without mentioning the juridical and political dimension of the problem. The practice of amnesty comes to the forefront here. It has a long history which brings us back to the famous decree issued at Athens in the year four hundred and three B.C., forbidding the mere mention of the crimes committed by both parties, which were called "misfortunes." Hence the oath required from each citizen: "I shall not recall such misfortunes" (*mnesikakein*—memory against).

Most modern democracies make a large use of this kind of commanded forgetting, for honorable reasons related to the preservation of social peace. But a philosophical problem keeps recurring: isn't the practice of amnesty harmful both to truth and to justice? Where does the dividing line run telling amnesty from amnesia? The answer to this question cannot be found at the political level, but rather in the will and the heart of private citizens. Thanks to the work of memory, completed by that of mourning, each of us has the duty not to forget, but to recall the past, as painful as it may be, under the guidance of a pacified memory.

To conclude, let me quote the poetic sentence we owe to Isak Dinesen, and that we can read at the top of the chapter devoted to the concept of action in Hannah Arendt's *The Human Condition*: "All sorrows can be borne if you put them into a story or tell a story about them."

Matters of Touch

Skin Deep

Bodies Edging into Place

EDWARD S. CASEY

Some places are hard to bear—to bear bodily. For example, solitary confinement. It has been realized, much too belatedly, how devastating being kept alone in a prison cell continuously—for days, months, even years—can be for human beings. Lisa Guenther opens her recent book *Solitary Confinement* with the statement that "there are many ways to destroy a human being, but one of the simplest and most devastating is through prolonged solitary confinement."[1] The effects studied so far have been mostly about the psychological impact of living in an entirely isolated way: it is known that many prisoners will go psychotic if strictly confined for a period as short as 48 hours, suffering from "insomnia, anxiety, panic, withdrawal, hypersensitivity, ruminations, cognitive dysfunction, hallucinations, loss of control, irritability, aggression, rage, paranoia, hopelessness, lethargy, depression, a sense of impending emotional breakdown."[2] The effect is that of "living death," which Guenther analyzes into *civil death* and *social death*. Indeed, it can be argued that one's entire being is changed by this form of extreme isolation: as one victim of solitary confinement put it, "Solitary confinement can alter the ontological makeup of a stone."[3] At the very least, there is a destruction of one's *world*—one's coherent, customary world. Another prisoner reports that "you feel as if the world has ended, but you somehow survived."[4]

Guenther herself concludes that prisoners in solitary confinement "have the very structure of their Being-in-the-world turned against them."[5] Her remarkable book focuses on this world-loss with all its implications. Here she picks up where Elaine Scarry left off in *The Body in Pain*, a profound study of torture that argues that what is destroyed in extreme physical torture is one's world—an effect confirmed by Jean Améry in writing of his own experiences in a Nazi concentration camp. For Guenther, however, solitary confinement is "the worst form of torture and the principle upon which all more determinate forms of torture are based."[6]

All of this is doubtless true—and indicates just how serious the situation of solitary confinement is: especially in view of the fact that it is so widely deployed in American prisons, themselves the most populated prisons on earth, both in absolute numbers and in percentage of the population (especially among minority groups). In supermax prisons, inmates are locked up 23 hours every day and have virtually no human contact; even the one hour of exercise allowed each day is carried out while alone. Such drastic isolation is a key factor for Guenther, who considers the lack of intersubjectivity as the most critical loss of all, the most deeply undermining.

In the literature on solitary confinement—increasingly dramatic as its baneful effects have become more widely known—one special dimension has gone neglected: what it's like *bodily* to be subject to solitary confinement. In what follows, I shall pursue a carnal hermeneutics of body and place in terms of their intersecting edges by focusing on the bodily experience of being held alone in a prison cell.

Nowhere to Go

Let us imagine for a moment what solitary confinement must be like. One's body, often exhausted by inadequate sleep, has virtually *nowhere to move* and certainly *nowhere else to go*: you might be able to take two paces in one direction and three in another—if there is space enough even for this. The cell space itself is crowded with the minimal furniture allowed to prisoners in this situation: a bare bed, a simple sink, a toilet bowl. Possibly, if one is so lucky, a small window.

Otherwise, one's body is in a forced circumstance of being *up against walls* at all times. One is not just hemmed in by these walls: this locution implies that one might *not* be hemmed in; that one might go outside the walls—precisely what is forbidden. Instead, one is required to live and move in ways that are limited at all times by four unyielding walls (also by the ceiling and the floor: but the upright walls confront the prisoner most starkly at every minute of the waking day—and are even felt at night as dark presences bearing down upon one's recumbent or pacing body).

In this circumstance, bodily movement is not just limited but *forced to stay put* within the severe enclosure realized by the cell walls. Even if one does not bump or butt against the walls literally—as in extreme fatigue or in a fit of rage in which one pounds the walls: futilely, of course—one is aware at all times of the walls as present and as inhibiting any motion through them, much less beyond them. This is the very converse of the cozy domesticity of one's original home-place as described by Bachelard in *The Poetics of Space*—a comforting space in which one can experience "intimate immensity."[7] Neither intimacy nor immensity is felt by the solitary prisoner: quite the opposite.

How is experience in solitary registered *in the body of the prisoner?* So far, I've been talking about the prisoner as an anonymous "one." But the real victim of solitary confinement is an embodied person—a human being *in his or her own body*.[8] Whatever the effects on the mind of that person (and they are immense), the body is the primary suffering subject, and is the source of suffering in very particular ways that tell us a great deal about the basic relationship between body and place. Let us consider, then, what the primary forms of the lived body of the prisoner in solitary confinement must be like, focusing on the relationship between this body and the walls of the cell in which it finds itself. I here aim to do a phenomenological analysis of this situation rather than a scientific study.[9]

First of all, there is the brute fact of the walls' presence to vision: whenever one's eyes are open, *there they are*—right where they have always been and, so far as one knows, may always be.[10] The walls are here and nowhere else: right ahead. But also behind and around; my body is literally cornered by the cell walls. This soon becomes known by my habitual body, so that I do not even need to turn around to verify it: it is felt in my bone and very marrow. But what I see is only part of what my body knows if I have been in captivity for more than a day or two. We can call such knowledge *visual plus*—my vision plus what the other bodily senses deliver. It is a specification—and a cruel reduction—of what Merleau-Ponty calls the "knowing body" (*le corps connaissant*).[11]

Reinforcing all this is the gritty *body memory* of having been continually, inescapably, in this very place: seemingly endlessly. Such memory is not of the body itself, its states of well- or ill-being, but of *the body-in-place*: *this* body in *this* place. My body and no other ("mine to be" in Heidegger's phrase); this place and no other (my place to be). The singularity of one is conjoined with the singularity of the other; not just in immediate perception but in primary memory (taken as the remembering that clusters closely around the present moment). Secondary memories emerge intermittently: memories of earlier experiences of being in that same cell or perhaps of comparable experiences elsewhere. Or of happier times elsewhere and elsewhen, though these are likely to be increasingly dim or unreal. What is brutally insistent are the body memories of being in that cell, day-to-day, so closely conjoined that before long they meld into one continuous body memory: that of being interminably in that place. If held in a single cell long enough—Nelson Mandela was in such a cell in the prison of Robben Island off the coast of Africa near Cape Town for almost 20 years—the effect is to lose track of time. As he writes of this experience, "each day [was] like the one before; each week like the one before it, so that the months and years blend[ed] into each other."[12] Different times lose their difference; they all merge into one undifferentiated memorial mass.

Notice that these memories are *in* the body but *of* the place to which the prisoner in solitary confinement has been restricted. They are felt in the flesh yet remain intentional in being directed onto the cell walls as their fiercely repetitive content and their closed-in horizon. Although they stem *from* the experience of confinement, they are *about* the feeling, the sense of confinement itself. This content is not merely cognitive—and is not literally locative (the prisoner may not even know where his cell is found within the prison complex, or where the prison itself is located in the larger surrounding world)—but is *memorial-placial*: the memories are held in the body but bear mainly upon the space where they have taken place, that very space. Or more exactly, they are of bodily-being-in-place, a commixture of both with one pole predominating at one time and the other at other times. If one is exhausted or sick, the bodily pole will be emphasized; otherwise, the focus will be more fully upon the cell itself. The modalities of such bodily-placial memories are multi-sensory, ranging from the comparative objectivity of the visual to the diffuse subjectivity of smell. They are also interlarded with elements of emotion and belief (and disbelief: that one will ever find an exit) in complex commixtures, of which the body is at all times the privileged carrier.

Running like a *basso continuo* throughout is the ongoing experience of cell walls as defining the limits of one's fate. These walls act as the condensed core, the obsessive focus, of the entire experience. They bear on body not just as inescapable but as having an immovable being of their own, an undilutable otherness. They are characterized by sheer Secondness in Peirce's term for that which we encounter as a brute presence, what is entirely oppositional: that *against which* we find ourselves cast. Walls of every kind are the epitome of such Secondness; but border walls and prison walls are most graphically exemplary of this aspect of the body's experience of walls. Both kinds of wall are, after all, constructed so as not to be passable by unassisted bodily motions—to be "impenetrable," as we say revealingly. They enter the lives of those whose movements they forbid as that up *against which* one is thrust, as if they are ultimate forms of Heideggerian thrownness.[13]

Of all the properties of cell walls and border walls, this last one may be the most decisive, since there is nothing more definitive in human experience than the experience of being a human body—with all its inherent weaknesses, its susceptibility to exhaustion and disease—confronted with the impassivity and impassability of a strongly reinforced wall. Not even the strongest male physique can prevail against the resistance of such a barrier: it is altogether formidable.

The difference between prison walls and border walls is evident: in the case of border walls, one's body remains mobile (at least up to the moment when one is apprehended and arrested) whereas the prisoner's body is radically demobilized, limited to a few steps back and forth in one's cell or a few yards of walking in the significantly named "prison *yard.*"

When Sartre claimed famously that one remains free even when in prison, he did not mean *as a* body in that prison. He meant something rather more Stoic: the freedom to *think* broadly and freely even in such a circumstance, and in particular to give or find meaning in that situation.[14] But this is an entirely *mental* freedom, and it overlooks the full significance of the physical unfreedom of being a body in a cell—in effect, a body-in-a-box. The experience of Stoic freedom is itself exceedingly rare: Nelson Mandela, Jack Henry Abbott, several exceptional prisoners cited by Guenther and other authors, and the rare political prisoner whose sense of mission sustains him. For the most part, after a certain period of time in solitary, the prisoner's mental freedom is seriously eroded: this is the properly *psychical* damage of solitary confinement that I mentioned at the start. But I would maintain that severe bodily constriction is not collateral to such damage, or a mere material condition of solitary confinement; it is the central fact of the devastating deprivation which this cruelest form of punishment wrecks upon human beings.

The Body in Place

What is the prisoner in solitary confinement being deprived of? The answer is painfully evident: *a more open, spacious placement of the human body*. Such placement is so common, so continuously experienced by so many outside of prison (except for the severely physically disabled or the sick who are bedridden), that we rarely reflect on what it means and in what it consists. My yoga instructor Heather recently requested our class to move into the final posture of savasana such that each of us should take a certain distance from the wall (where we had been doing various exercises), adding: "let it feel spacious . . ." At the time I took this instruction for granted—I had heard it many times before—and did not reflect on how fortunate I was in comparison with those in solitary confinement: if *they* were to lie down on the floor of their cells and take the same physical distance from the cell wall as I took from the friendly wall of the open space where I practice in Santa Barbara, you can be sure that they are very likely not to feel themselves to be in a relaxed relationship with their cell wall—given its oppressive and confining character. Instead of feeling something spacious, they are much more likely to experience an uncomfortable, even an unbearable, constriction. The same basic human body is at stake in both circumstances, taking the same distance from a perpendicular wall, but we are talking of two radically different experiences.

In both situations, body and place serve as covariables, intimately intertwined, so much so that we can formulate this approximate rule: *Change the place and there will be a corresponding change in the body in that place.* A change in place of residence in particular—somewhere one occupies for any considerable length of time—brings with it a change in the bodily experience of the new place, and ultimately a change in the very constitution of that body (as indicated by posture, health, and in general, the body's role as the agency of the person-in-place).

Other examples of a more spacious relation between bodies and places come to mind. Being in a living room with sufficient space in which to "stretch out" and to be seated in several chairs or couches, perhaps facilitated by more than one doorway in or out: all this we take for granted, without imagining what its removal might mean for us. The word "room" of *living room* is derived from the German word *Raum*, signifying space in the sense of "open space": *raümlich* means "roomy." This is why the living room in most Western architecture—and its equivalent in other styles of building: the courtyard, the veranda, etc.—are characteristically spacious (or as spacious as we can afford). In visiting Goethe's self-designed house in Weimar, Germany, one first enters into an enormous reception room, suitable for gatherings of several dozen people (Hegel was among them, on several occasions). But as one penetrates further into this residence the rooms become increasingly smaller; the bedrooms are notably cozy, and the kitchen is tiny—as is Goethe's own personal study in the back of the house. In one coherent domestic place, then, Goethe planned a series of places calibrated for their comparative spaciousness. Even the least spacious—the kitchen and study—lack any oppressiveness. One could call them "cells" (in the tradition of "scholar's cells"), but there is a world of difference between these small spaces and those of solitary confinement.

I say "a world of difference" intentionally: for we are here talking about decisive differences in *place-worlds*. Place-worlds designate the uniquely configured worlds that places induce and sustain. A place-world is an avatar of "being-in-the-world" in Heidegger's original sense of the term. Heidegger's locution was notably formal in character, and it conspicuously lacked two concrete factors: the *lived body* and *place*. This body is the primary occupant of place, and its presence infuses elements of orientation, memory (again, a specifically *bodily* memory), sensory perception, and personal agency into what would otherwise be an empty shell of space—a room devoid of animating forces. Whereas what we call "the physical world" amounts to a collection of lifeless objects, the body—as Merleau-Ponty insisted—is no object at all but "a natural myself" who is "the subject of perception"[15] and as such bestows upon the places it inhabits direction, history, sense, and meaning. This is so whether the physical space in which it exists is vast (recall E.E. Cummings's *The Enormous Room*) or is "cabined, cribbed, confined" (in Macbeth's words for a very uncomfortably constricted space). One instance of the latter is the prison cell, another is Goethe's personal study. The study might even have the same dimensions as the prison cell, but it is very differently animated by and for the scholar/scientist/poet who was Goethe than is the cell occupied by the hapless victim of solitary confinement. Not that the latter cannot write and think there—as both Mandela and Abbott managed to do—but it is very unlikely that the prison cell will be a supportive place for thinking or writing in genuinely new ways. The root reason is that the prison cell is differently configured and lived in by its occupant's body. No matter how resilient that body might be, and how determined the prisoner's mind is, there are limits to what a human being can do in a severely constricted space—in the place-world to which he is confined without the prospect of release.

Given the choice, human beings seek the spacious wherever they live. They flourish from a sense of *leeway* in their immediate surroundings. The cultural confinements of late-nineteenth century life in the United States—typified by the "stuffy parlor rooms" of that era where more topics of conversation were forbidden than were allowed—were such that even the living room did not supply sufficient leeway. No wonder, then, that the open porch became such a coveted feature of middle-class houses. I recall the way in which after a family dinner in Abilene, Kansas—a dinner with as many as fifteen participants—my relatives sought the large, wraparound porch at my grandparents' house, walking right through the large living room in order to enjoy the open space of the porch where one could talk more freely (or listen more carefully, as I did when I was younger).

The love of "wide, open spaces" that was part of frontier mentality—in which, however, it played a darkly compromised role as justifying the outright stealing of Native American and Spanish lands—is not peculiar to the United States. Romans living inland already sought the seashore in the summer, living in vacation villas designed for this very purpose. The inner courtyard of much architecture in the Mediterranean world—Muslim as well as Greco-Roman—provided an open space comparable to that of the American porch two thousand five hundred years later. At play here is not just *open space* (empty space as such) but *space that opens out*—out into the open vistas of a larger landscape world. The very concept of "landscape," a creation of early modernity in the West (though part of ancient Chinese and Japanese culture long before), embodies a fascination, indeed a longing, for space that is not too crowded: a space comparatively unpopulated by human beings, opening onto horizons that are themselves openings to still other worlds beyond the world of one's current prospect.

All these modes of open and opening-out place-worlds stand in stark contrast with the cell of solitary confinement. Here nothing is open, much less opening-up or opening-out. All is *here*, just Here; even the There is limited to bare indications of what lies beyond one's cell walls: random noises give the barest clues as to what is happening outside the cell in the immediately contiguous hallway; voices of other prisoners may manifest, but then only fragmentarily, what is on their minds or in their emotions. Otherwise, all that is happening is happening *just here* and nowhere else. And Here means a very delimited parcel of space, with no outlook, no vista beyond the cell walls themselves. A yoga mat is also a very small extent of space, but *from* the mat the practitioner is always free to look around—to *look out*. There are no walls at the literal edge of the mat.

In the prison situation, then, we witness the actualization of *confinement* in its most intense state, and we see starkly displayed what *solitary* means in its extremity. Ultimately, the two are closely related: only such confinement could bring about such isolation, and this same isolation is the effect of being so severely confined. When those outside prison seek isolation, it is for the sake of savoring the solitude it brings: the "labyrinth of solitude" in Octavio Paz's phrase.[16] As Guenther puts it strikingly, "solitary confinement makes even solitude impossible; isolated from social life, even one's sense of individuated personhood threatens to dissolve."[17]

Embodied here as well is the intimate interplay, the *intermonde*, of body and place themselves. It takes a sensate body to experience what the place of solitary confinement is like; left empty, the prison cell cannot realize the function for which it was designed—to sequester human beings not only from the open society outside the prison but even from the place-world inside the prison itself. Violent and cruel as the latter may be, it allows for a certain freedom of movement and a minimal social life in the yard and in the dining hall which are not possible inside the cell of solitary confinement. If not forced to live in such a place as a solitary cell, the human body characteristically seeks alternative experience in other places: "other voices, other rooms." But *in this place*, the cell of solitary confinement, the body leads a drastically curtailed life which is like a dark parody of Husserl's otherwise unimpeachable phenomenological point that the lived body is always "absolutely Here."[18] This is certainly true, but the Here that accrues to a body forced to live in a prison cell has no compensatory There—no alternative but to be brutally, savagely stuck with a Here that is starkly foreclosed and unendurable in its sheer monotony.

Dimensions of Place

You will have noticed that I have been talking about the body-place dyad with regard to one parameter only: comparative room or spaciousness. There are many other dimensions at play, and a more complete analysis would discuss such things as cultural parameters (rendering some places intelligible to those in their midst, others unreadable), historical and institutional specificities of the sort that fascinated Foucault, as well as elemental aspects such as humidity or temperature (not a matter of indifference in the case of prison cells), and so on. Even so, solitary confinement, though differing in detail from cell to cell and prison to prison, has about it a grim generality—a stark sameness—given the simplicity of the basic circumstance of being locked into a single small space. The dire fact is that the prisoner has no choice whatsoever regarding the space to which he or she is consigned. Differences, especially a choice between differences, become more prominent as we move into more open-ended places: architectural differences in the provision of domestic leeway, differences in the style of representing landscape in painting or poetry. In all such cases, cultural and historical differences proliferate, and those not imprisoned have varying degrees of choice to make between them.

Edging into Place

In moving to a close, I want to consider the *edge-structure* of solitary confinement. If body and place are as closely related as I've been arguing, they have to be contiguous with each other in, at, or through a particular space that is the arena of their interconnection. In that arena, body and place connect through the edges of each as these two elementarities come close to one another. Sometimes the contiguity is uncomfortably tight—certainly so in the cell, but also in such otherwise different circumstances as the machine in which I recently underwent an MRI: my recumbent body was ensconced not just snugly but painfully in the long tube to which I was confined (painful because I had to hold my arms above my head throughout, though I was suffering from frozen shoulder); but it remains that I was free to walk out of the clinic after the test.

We can distinguish two kinds of zones in which body and place interact via their respective edges: the *interval* and the *skin*. Most often, both are at play, with the exception of those cases in which the flesh presses directly up against the particulars of the place, leaving no intervening space at all, as in the case of the MRI tube.

Intervals involve a special kind of space: empty of anything but air, they serve as an intermediary domain between body and place, their shared medium as it were. The larger this domain, the more extensive the leeway a given body has in which to move freely in a given place or between places. The open porch affords opportunities for mobility among those conversing there: I remember rocking back and forth gently in the swing on my grandmother's porch as I listened to my great uncles debate politics, glad to be at the edge of their conversation. At the dinner table inside, there were limited intervals for moving about: once I assumed a position at the table, I was expected to stay there for the entire meal. In the cell of solitary confinement, there is much less *Lebensraum* still: this is itself part of the punishment of being forced to live in this space. Nelson Mandela describes his situation in prison in this way: "I could walk the length of my cell in three paces. When I lay down, I could feel the wall with my feet and my head grazed the concrete at the other side. The width was about six feet, and the walls were at least two feet thick. . . . That small cramped space was to be my home for I knew not how long."[19]

The interval between body and place—anticipated in the ancient idea of the *diastéma* that exists between atoms—has little character of its own, being the direct reflection of the relationship between body and place themselves: it is the very space of their dyadic relationship. *In* and *through* this space, they relate to each other by way of their edges—as if these edges, though not in direct contact, were reaching out toward each other. The interval as described here is akin to Platonic *chora*, which has no qualities of its own but that exists by necessity. Both the interval and *chora* are what they are because of the work they must do, which is to locate *other* things: body and place in our case, items of Becoming in Plato's.

It ensues that the body/place interval has *no edges of its own*: any edges it succeeds in relating belong to the very body (or bodies in more complex cases) and place (or places) it serves to situate. As the two members of the dyad shift their position—one or both—so the diastemic interval between them changes in extent and shape. We might say that body and place are modally attuned across the interval they share at their edges. This means that an interval's configuration can be described as having a certain characteristic *contour* that is the joint product of the interaction of body and place in or across the interval. This happens so often in the lives of sentient bodies that we take it for granted and rarely attend to it as such; it characterizes the space of the Santa Barbara Roasting Company café in which I am now writing these words: my bent-over body and the open place of the café articulate with each other in the same space. In this space, there is room for considerable displacement as I change positions to avoid the more talkative customers; I take advantage of a certain "give" in the interval I occupy in the café—an elasticity that is markedly absent in a prison cell.

The interval here at stake can be thought of as a *boundary* between body and place—where "boundary" does not indicate a barrier but rather a permeable membrane through which body and place seep, sometimes close to each other, sometimes drifting apart. Such a boundary is a zone of connectivity. Separative zones I designate as "borders," and they are exemplified in such things as border walls, "no mans' lands," and the like. They include regions of no trespassing, like the infamous "dead zone" that lay between the two parallel walls of the original Berlin Wall: anyone seen running through this zone was immediately targeted and shot. Or they take the form of a constructed object that materializes the border: hence the massive walls that include the ancient Great Wall of China, Trajan's Wall, and the contemporary Separation Wall between Israel and Palestine. And here too is found the wall of the cell of solitary confinement. In all these instances of sheer separation—different as they may be in their construction and practical purpose—humans (and all too often animals) are confronted with a veritable *non plus ultra*: Beyond Here no movement is allowed to go Over There. In the case of such strictly exclusionary intervals as these border-structures represent, there is both a reduction and a restriction of the space of the interval between bodies and places: reduction in that the actual breadth of such structures is never immense (often being no more than several feet in width or thickness), restriction in that free movement over them is prohibited by these same structures. Intervals that are genuine boundaries offer the exact converse, being open to free movement—indeed, inviting such movement in and through them (and not just around them or under them as in the case of border walls).

Skin is something else. Here body and place relate to each other by a factor that belongs properly to the lived body and in particular to its skin. "Skin" is not just the tissue that covers the body; it is the very medium through which the human person, in and through her living body, relates to her surroundings and most notably to place. If interval can be reduced to a zero point—as when there is sheer contiguity between body and place—skin is not eliminable: it is indispensable for the body/place relationship. It is not just always present on the side of the subject (we take in a place from the skin outwards: it is the carnal this-side of every placial that-side); it is the source of this subject's acute sensitivity to the place it finds itself in or has found its way to. For as bodies we *experience a place through our skin*: we feel it, we know it, in our skin. (Even when we "feel it in our bones," this bone-sense is transmitted to us by our skin, along with other more external features of a given place such as its temperature, relative aridity, and other "atmospheric" factors.)

Skin is still more peculiar—and still more important—than we suspect from its role as the enacting agent of the body-place dyad or as the site of the sensitivity that is integral to it. My main title "Skin Deep" is meant to reflect this more profound dimension—really, a double dimension. On the one hand, it is on and in the skin that various depths of human experience and thought are felt and registered: *the depths are on the surface*, a principle pursued by such diverse thinkers as Freud and Wittgenstein, Hillman and Merleau-Ponty. There is no other way for depths of various kinds—psychical, organic, cognitive, emotional, linguistic, etc.—to become manifest as *phenomena* than to appear on the surface of the skin. It is on this surface that the depths come to expression, thus to our notice; but the same skin surface, precisely because of its acute sensitiveness, is vulnerable to exploitation by others—to their unwanted incursion in situations of trauma or torture: or solitary confinement.

Various depths quite literally *show up* on the surface, that is to say, *in the skin*, which is the effective surface of the lived body. They become evident there, even if sometimes requiring interpretation as to their sense or meaning. Where else will they manifest themselves? Where else will they make meaning? Where else can they be interpreted? Clearly, it is in and from the skin that carnal hermeneutics takes its rise and to which it returns, time and again, never straying far from it. The gestures in which so much of our affective and memorial life are expressed occur through the mediation of skin; and the very words by which we articulate our thoughts call for the skin—of the tongue and mouth in the case of speech; of the fingers if we are writing out our thoughts as I have done in composing this essay.

If this first dimension of "Skin Deep" is one whose axis runs from within to without—from within the body, its organic innards, to the skin of that body—the second dimension bears on the way that the without itself, the very surface of the skin, moves outward from itself and links up with the surrounding world in the form of the particular locales that make it into a place-world. What Merleau-Ponty first identified as bodily intentionality—building on Eugen Fink's earlier notion of "operative intentionality"—is here at stake. For it is the skin of our lived bodies that convey our thoughts and wishes onto and into the places that we inhabit at any given moment. The "intentional threads" that bind us to the place in which we are located or through which we are moving extend from our skin onto the very particular structures that places proffer to us as their occupants and animators.[20]

We can think of these threads as spun by our bodily histories and current intentionalities and reaching out to whatever "hooks" that places provide—making them the effective *catchment* areas that draw and capture the outgoing ventures of an enskinned body—not unlike the *points de caption* by which Lacan designated the nodal points that pin down otherwise floating signifiers.

Clearly, with this second axis we are talking about a very special edge-to-edge relationship whereby the outer edges of our lived bodies that are situated in the skin and that allow this skin to bear outward join forces with the outer edge of the things and events that make up a given place. One kind of outer edge, that of our flesh, links up with the other, that of the place in which our flesh is situated; not because they always match (often they do not, and we have to maneuver our bodies in special ways to insure the connection), but because it is thanks to this edgewise relation that the body comes to be in a place and to know it intimately. "Skin deep" signifies the process by which from the depths of our skin-being—from its personal or shared history, including whatever joys and miseries to which it has been subject in the course of its life until then—we are able to link up with the surfaces and depths of the places we are in, and to do so by moving from edge to edge throughout.

If the first axis has an ineluctably inner-to-outer vector, the second dimension moves from outer to outer: from the outermost edges of our body to the equally (but differently) outermost edges of places. It is in the experience of place that the internalism of the first sense of Skin Deep rejoins the externalism of the second sense—each being a necessary component of a complete body/place dyad.

Formal as this analysis may seem to be, it holds true in the most diverse circumstances. It is at work as I write at the Santa Barbara Roasting Company: my fingers at my computer tapping out the words you are now reading, with my body as a whole seated in a place that has become familiar to me in recent years. It is operative in the rally against mass incarceration I plan to attend later on today—when my body will link up that of others in an entire city-place as we march down State Street in Santa Barbara.

And it is an ingredient in the loneliest cell of those who suffer from solitary confinement. For it is the very skin of the incarcerated prisoner that receives and registers the cruelly confining place that is his cell. It is in that skin that the confinement is felt most acutely. More radically, it is *as that skin* that it is experienced. For everyone—philosopher and prisoner alike—takes in the world as a series of places that are felt in and as, by and through the skin. Our knowledge of the place-world is skin-deep, deep in the skin, and we edge into it with the skin we bring to bear upon it.

We end where we began: the solitary prisoner in his (or her) designated cell.

The body of that prisoner is forcibly constrained to be in that place, and experiences the relation between them in the depths of skin, which is at once the outward expression of current rage and frustration as well as of a lifetime of supremely difficult choices. Such skin, in such depths, is the irremissible channel by which a prisoner undergoes a life within the unforgiving walls of the cell into which that person has been locked.

Try to imagine what it would be like to be there, in your body and in that place, felt in your very skin—to be caught in that iron and concrete cage of constraining edges. Then ask yourself: is this anything you would ever want to experience yourself, or to inflict on another human being?

Touched by Touching

DAVID WOOD

> Weren't you asking, even before the beginning, whether we could caress or stroke each other with our eyes? And touch the look that touches you?
> —**Jacques Derrida**[1]

> I understand hermeneutics to be the task of interpreting plural meaning in response to the polysemy of language and life.
> —**Richard Kearney**[2]

In this paper I take select concrete "instances" as opportunities for reflection, openings for imagining a broader practice of carnal hermeneutics. These instances include snatches of conversation, experiences, and works of art. The general assumption is that these cases exhibit many "thinks at a time," that philosophical reflection can bring this out, and that such reflection feeds back into deepening the original experience. After years in the deconstructive trenches, I have been recently influenced by a certain strain of Wittgensteinian practice. I have come to think that the point of philosophy is to encourage and inculcate dispositions that take up the constitutive complexity of often quite ordinary experience. An indispensable dimension of such a practice is to be open to the creative plurivocity of meaning murmuring within the concepts that most fascinate us. Touching is exemplary in this respect, and all the more intriguingly so in the light of the concrete immediacy that seems to be its privilege.

"They Are Feral Cats; They Will Never Let You Touch Them"

Derrida is standing naked in his bathroom.[3] Mary, his female cat, is looking at him, taking in, it seems, his private parts. He cannot know what the cat sees. He cannot appropriate the gaze of the feline. Yet he feels shame.[4]

This feels like an extension, a twist on Sartre's account of the Medusian Look that would turn one to stone. A strange action at a distance. But how much of this story is tied up with the eyes? What if the eyes themselves were touched? Elsewhere I have spoken of looking at the sun, taking in the fact that these very eyes that can see the sun are children of the sun. Without its heat, no life. Without its light, no vision, no eyes. The flesh of the world, as Merleau-Ponty might say. Look directly at the sun and your retina will be burned, touched by fire. But are they not already touched, shaped indeed, by what they seem merely to be looking at? What happens if Derrida touches his cat, or is touched by it?

I had responded to an ad for mousers, feral cats taken off the streets, neutered, given their shots, and then farmed out to people with barns who needed feline death squads to deal with mice. I took three siblings. I was warned: they are feral—they will never let you touch them. Not that they would mistake me for a mouse. It's rather that I should not mistake them for warm, furry pets, no matter how endearing they might look. They are natural-born killers, not cute kittens. Look them in the eye—black holes from which light does not return. Four-legged psychopaths. Mice in the barn will be history.

But they did need feeding, as mice were at first thin on the ground. Over time they got used to the routine, and crowded the bowl. They did not bite the hand that fed them—in time they touched it. The hand made innocent stroking gestures. The next day, the boldest cat was coiling herself around my neck, purr crazy. The rest is history. Perhaps a cat survivor of trauma would never let me touch her. For these cats, touch was just a strange intoxicating magic waiting to happen. What do we learn here?

Wittgenstein says that if a lion could speak we could not understand him. Is nuzzling, purring, coiling, licking—are these not speaking? What is it about her rolling over on her back to expose soft fur to stroking that I don't understand? Am I saying I know what it is like to be a cat? Isn't that an anthropocentric presumption? Doesn't a cat live in a different world, if it has a world at all? Or do we meet, if meeting is ever at all possible, at this carnal level? Suppose the cat licks my finger with a gentle rasping action. My pleasure comes from the edge of roughness of its tongue (a lion's tongue would probably take off my skin). And from the wet warmth, the recognition of the cat's pleasure, and the pulsing rhythm of the licking. I am aware that the cat may be in regressive mode, reverting to its time as a kitten. But are not all these times locked up in each of us, hopefully available for deployment at appropriate times? Anthropocentric presumption? How about carnally crossing the mammalian bridge? We may be human, as we say, but do we not sport other bodies too, ones we share with cats, and one, they say, we share with reptiles? There is difference, there are strange gaps. Even stroking is not always plain sailing with cats. An excess of pleasure and the claws involuntarily come out, pierce through my jeans, and into the skin. But there are just such gaps and strangenesses in our sensuous and sensual relations to the opposite sex, indeed to the same sex, to children, even to ourselves. The problem with the charge of anthropocentrism is that it oversimplifies the anthropos, strips us of our layerings and differentiations. Man is a species that is not one.

What can we learn from such an encounter with a cat? Before language, within language (I am thinking of Kristeva's semiotic here), there is rhythm, pulsation, touch, difference, perhaps even desire of a sort. This is true whether or not these domestic lions can speak. The touch of my cat does not conform or fail to conform to Heideggerian prescriptions about world-disclosure. She touches off questions about the categories I would like to think were more stable—about species distinctness, sexuality, the erotic, language, and indeed, touch and the carnal. But, to make sure we are not falling into a trope of political correctness, she (and her two brothers) also confirms suspicions about multi-stranded commonalities, not just differences.

"My Breasts Are Too Small"

[T]he appearance alters, and from being obscure, small, and faint, grows clear, large, and vigorous.

Berkeley[5]

The magic and the most powerful effect of women is, in philosophical language, action at a distance, 'actio in distans,' but this requires first of all and above all—distance.

Nietzsche[6]

You say your breasts are too small. What are the hermeneutic stakes here? You confess, lament, admit, protest, worry, disclaim, that your breasts are too small. Do you mean as eye candy? To the touch? Too small for what? For whom? Where did you get this idea from? Why do you say this to me? For words of reassurance, consolation, admiration? Anyway, I am touched.

What are the hermeneutic stakes here? This real world example captures in words the interweaving of the multiple dimensions in which we find ourselves living, moving, and having our being. A woman identifies her breasts as sites of anxiety with respect to her desirability to a man or to men, despite having successfully nourished and pleasured an infant. She projects onto her lover, or prospective lover, a culturally specific preference for larger breasts. She may be right about that. But does this preference apply to her lover? And where would this general preference come from? Are we driven by visual images in their own right? Or do we associate the visual with the tactile? Does the man who sees the larger breast imagine a tactile corollary significantly more strokable, or kissable? Is this anticipated pleasure *just* a memory of the suckling delights of infancy? And what's with this "just"? Are adults deceived by the illusion of renewed lactation? Or are the various promises constituted by the warmth of the flesh, the scent and taste of the skin, the sound of the heartbeat, the vibration of the speaking chest, the safety in being held—are these not quite enough even without milk? If so, is not the anxiety about size misplaced? Does he really think of her as a bearer of breasts of a certain size, or does he want to touch and stroke *her* breasts. Does not singularity trump size? And does he bring lips, tongue, and hands to the scene, or *his* lips, *his* fingertips? Is there such a thing as the pleasure of intimate touch in general, or is it utterly dependent on the answers to all these questions? Is it perhaps not that her breasts are too small, but that our questions are too small? Or is desire simply not to be second-guessed, explained, justified, etc.? If she opts for surgical enhancement, is she not just playing the odds? When she says to me that her breasts are too small, she may be making a move in a game, soliciting a response that would repudiate all comparisons. But is she then entrusting her fate to language, to conversation? And will this quell anxiety, or just restage it at another level. ("Does he really mean it when he says I'm perfect?") Can language speak or speak of the singular? And who is speaking? Would her breasts speak like this? And when? Only when neglected? Or even with happy, erect, flushed nipples? I look at you and say, "Your breasts are perfect."

"Two Calla Lilies on Pink"

I am looking at a painting by Georgia O'Keeffe: "Two Calla Lilies on Pink" (1928),[7] which teeters on the edge of plant porn: waving erect yellow stamens set off against flowing light pink petals. The allusions are obvious, for some, too obvious. And yet if we allow ourselves to slow down the imaginative drama of looking at such a painting, there is much to be said. At one level, only a minimal analogical transfer is needed. For these are indeed the sexual parts of the lily. But consider the reflective experience this opens up. Both male and female "parts" are depicted. Does it matter whether the viewer is a man or a woman? Do we understand ourselves as gender-positioned? Does it matter that the artist is a woman? How does it affect our experience that there are two phallic stamens? What does it mean that we can be aroused, or we can imagine being aroused, by a painting of a plant? Is the painting doing something that the actual lilies could not do? After all, there is a stylization in the painting that could not be there in the flower. The petals are like the flowing lines of a dress . . . Or we could say that the painting bears witness to graceful curves, lines that give onto interiority, a topology of surface and depth—that teaches us something of the fundamental shapes of tactile desire. They solicit our imaginative touch. This raises another thought—there is something missing from this painting—the pollinating insect, the bee. Yet if it is missing from the painting, it is not missing from the experience of the painting. For it is precisely positioning us, the viewer. It is then worth noticing that the pollinating insect does its work indirectly, attracted by nectar, and moving pollen around on its feet. At the heart of sexuality is something not essentially sexual at all. The touching degree zero of material transfer. At the heart of meaning, an abyss?

For Heidegger, it is "only because the 'senses' belong ontologically to a being which has the kind of being attuned to being-in-the-world, can they be 'touched' and 'have a sense' for something so that what touches them shows itself in an affect . . . ."[8] There would be no resistance if things did not matter to us. For Heidegger the chair cannot "touch" the wall because it is not a site of disclosure. But what if mattering itself had its dark roots in matter?

Is this a carnal bridge too far, or does it (merely) take us further into the territory already opened up by stroking the cat? If sexuality is something at some level we share with plants, does not that fact make sexuality all the more puzzling? What would it be to understand it better? Could that involve accepting limits on understanding? And what kinds of limits would they be? Is it that whatever else, our sexual being is our incompletely thematizable ground, driving us in ways we cannot wholly explain, and accounting for our existence and the shape of our dwelling in the first place? (Dependent on and typically growing up with more than one parent.)

"The Pleasures of the Text"

A carnal hermeneutics of language can perhaps learn something from Roland Barthes's *The Pleasure of the Text*.[9] In a note, Richard Howard writes:

Perhaps for the first time in the history of criticism . . . not only a poetics of reading . . . but a much more difficult achievement, an erotics of reading. . . . Like filings which gather to form a figure in a magnetic field, the parts and pieces here do come together, determined to affirm the pleasure we must take in our reading as against the indifference of (mere) knowledge.[10]

In this book, Barthes argues that writerly texts (as opposed to readerly texts, which give pleasure) give bliss (orgasm, *jouissance*), by exploding the reader's sovereignty, breaking the codes. Consider on the one hand Pablo Neruda, and on the other Gerard Manley Hopkins.

I am reading a thoroughly readerly poem by Chilean poet Pablo Neruda: "Carnal Apple, Woman Filled, Burning Moon."

Full woman, carnal apple, hot moon,
Thick smell of seaweed, mud and light entwined.
What dark clarity opens between your columns?
What ancient night does he touch with your senses?

Oh, love is a journey of water and stars,
Of suffocating air, and brusque storms of flour:
Love is a battle of lightning
And two bodies—lost by a single drop of honey.

Kiss by kiss I travel your little infinity,
Your margins, your rivers, your tiny villages,
And the genital fire transforms, delicious,

Running through the narrow streets of blood,
Until pouring out as a carnation at night,
And being and not being is but a flicker of shade.[11]

I cannot judge the Spanish original, but Kline's English translation sparkles. Neruda is clearly writing from a male perspective, even as he embraces woman. It is the play of sound, sense, and the sensuous that I want to bring out. My hands assured me that stroking and caressing give shape to skin with the pulse of primal rhythm, that we are as far away from language as we could possibly be. Stop talking they say; just let me touch you. Words melt away.

But an erotic poem like this gives the lie to this thought. Even the fingers light up in a new way. Images, allusions, the sounds, shapes, and rhythms of words create a simulacrum of an erotic encounter, and themselves touch and move the reader. Paint the bird with a fine enough brush and it will sing. Where words break in new things may be.

What are we that we can be touched by words? Neruda's imagery is of the ocean, the sky and then the countryside and streets. The charge of these images comes in the ways they animate without objectifying the woman's body. We know how a landscape can be erotically charged, how we can caress the hills with a distant hand. Here the compliment is being returned, fully charged. Carried by words. Words of movement and flow that already mark the ways things melt in the heat of passion: entwined, opens, touch, journey, battle, travel, transform, running, pouring out and flicker. And the flicker happens between being and nonbeing, as if ontology too is being melted by love.

Pursuing Roland Barthes's distinction, Hopkins is a more writerly poet. His "Pied Beauty"[12] is an ode to difference, what cannot be captured in language: "All things counter, original, spare, strange." At the same time, he reinvents English by dipping back into the layer of sound and rhythm from which language is born. The writerly induces a disruption in the reader's relation to language, taking him or her out of himself, opening up something akin to what Heidegger calls "listening to the voice of language." What is the "I" that is touched, moved, by Hopkins? It is the "I" at home with the middle voice, or with a certain creative dwelling at the margin of words. It is essentially liquid, and embodied.

More generally, who or what are we that we can be moved by words? A carnal hermeneutics would find ever new ways of showing how the imagination inhabits our bodies, from the pores of our skin to the ways we schematize our dynamic corporeality and our engagements with others. The erotic spawns some of the most telling ways, but there is no place for correctness here. The flesh is equally a site of lawless excitation and incitement—pain as well as pleasure, excess, and violence. If it has a transcendental face, a carnal hermeneutics would ask the question: how is all this possible? Perhaps taking a cue from Freud, it would ask about the drive to destruction, death, security, release from stress (even anesthesia), as well as the search for pleasure, thanatos as well as eros. And all that lies in between.

"Vampire Hermeneutics"

Half naked in the airport bathroom at Alice Springs in Australia, I found myself staring down in horror at my private parts, where, it seemed the Black Death was erupting out of my skin. It seemed like an unfortunate place to die without the specialized medical treatment I would surely need; I was a long way from home. I inspected the black streaks of the emerging scourge more closely. You will appreciate that I would have given almost anything to be able to substitute shame at being consumed by the gaze of Derrida's cat. At least the cat was over there, witnessing at a distance, perhaps carnivorous in Derrida's extended sense, and yet not literally devouring me. But the alien force that had invaded me here in this bathroom did not seem to brook a negotiated settlement.

Here are some facts about leeches. Leeches are hermaphrodites, so each leech is both male and female, though they need each other to reproduce. Only a few species of leeches feed on blood. They all have thirty-four body segments with a sucker at the front, surrounding the mouth, and another at the rear end, and many tiny eyes, which help them find food. Blood-sucking leeches can ingest several times their empty body weight at a sitting, and live on a single meal for several months. I had been swimming in one of the pools in the otherwise arid Kings Canyon, situated in Watarrka National Park. Two of these little guys had found their summer lunch, and it was me.

So it was not Black Death breaking out of my body, but a couple of black leeches who had become quite attached to me. Derrida writes that the only responsible decision requires that we go through the undecidable. Fortunately he added that it did not mean that we necessarily had time to kill before deciding. Sometimes one needs to decide straight away, ideally yesterday. I did not hesitate. The leeches peeled off quite easily, and very responsibly, leaving a pink footprint similar in color to Georgia O'Keeffe's calla lilies, where they had gently dissolved the skin to get a better grip.

Being touched is not always welcome. We speak of inappropriate touching, a touch of evil, of the weak-minded being "touched," perhaps by the devil; we avoid the touch of the leper, or the untouchable. Touché, we say in fencing or disputation, for a successful hit or wound. The bite of a vampire takes the kiss a touch too far. In comparison, the mini-vampire leech is more of an irritant than a threat. And if, as I suspect, what Von Uexkhull says about ticks[13] is equally true of leeches—that their behavior is governed by something like three basic sensors: blood temperature, butyric acid from the skin, and finding a hairless site—the opportunities for a sophisticated hermeneutics of such a touch are limited. But what may be true biologically is far from true symbolically and culturally. There are very few more potent personal or political slurs than blood-sucker, the parasite that drinks our vital fluids. And although the leech is rivaled in this respect by the wound-cleansing maggot, its well-known medical uses are overshadowed by our anxiety at its insouciant disregard for the integrity of our bodily boundaries. To Derrida's shame at being looked at by his cat, we would counterpose disgust, horror, and alarm. This is only compounded by ticks that bury their heads in our skin, snakes that inject their venom, and worms that live coiled in the gut. These creatures all move beyond surface touch to penetration, the gentle enabling of anti-coagulants to help blood flow, toxins that paralyze and so on. They seem to know what they're getting into from the start; they know us from the inside. These creatures touch us, but the hermeneutics begins with the reversal in which we reflect on the experience of being ourselves more than touched.

What for Merleau-Ponty is a chiasm of touching, primarily in the literal sense, is here being thought of as a broader possibility of reversal, in which each and every passivity can be the subject of a reflexive receptivity, either as a new complex experience or as an ongoing process of transformation.

These experiences of violent touch can of course be replicated in the human world, with rape, torture, and violence of all sorts, not to mention the slings and arrows of outrageous fortune, with hurricanes, disease, where it is our material exposure that is at issue, an exposure constitutive of our being. Here is perhaps one of the richest sites of a carnal hermeneutics—experiences of joyful explosion of boundaries, and of the anxious defense of such boundaries. Some of these boundaries are, as we say, real, and others merely constructed, perhaps manufactured, the better to manipulate us. Touchings of all sorts do not merely disclose such boundaries, they open them to scrutiny, transformation, renegotiation.[14] A critical carnal hermeneutics would reflect on the emancipatory possibilities latent in the maintenance and the overcoming of the various boundaries that constitute both our identity, and our delight.

Umbilicus

Toward a Hermeneutics of Generational Difference

ANNE O'BYRNE

> Grammatology must pursue and consolidate whatever, in scientific practice, has always already begun to exceed the logocentric closure.
> —Jacques Derrida, *Positions* 36

If we think of bodies, as Descartes did, as entities that cannot occupy the same place at the same time, we find ourselves thinking of solid forms—cones, cubes, spheres—that occupy space to the exclusion of others. Each geometrical shape is clear and distinct, so that when we imagine them as concrete forms their edges are sharp, their surfaces hard and their internal solidity unbroken by gaps or splits or emptinesses. We imagine solid bodies—steel balls, wooden cubes, glass prisms—that abut, touch one another, lie side by side, bump into each other, but cannot be in the same space. Then, when we hear the word *body* as *my body, animal body, human body, warm body, your body, anybody*, the edges curve and blur, the surface puckers and wrinkles, hair sprouts, gaps open, hearts beat, and the body is in a constant process of inhaling and exhaling, ingestion and elimination, including and excluding.

Fortunately, the *logos* of life is ready to hand, already equipped with the authority to teach us how to see our bodies. All the internal spaces have been explored to the microscopic level, and biology continues to generate ever more detailed images of the living world from the minutest components of living cells to the forms of ecosystems. It has made possible the spectacular medical technologies that led to the elimination of smallpox and is working now to treat and cure cancers. So, with health as the common value and imaging technology as its rhetorical device, it naturally takes the lead in showing us our bodies. Given such knowledge and guidance, what purpose could a hermeneutics of the body serve? After all, a mature science is not captured in a caricature nor exhausted by its accompanying technologies, and biology is already a multi-faceted mode of interpreting the living world. When the biologist engages in basic research and when she is alert to the aporias in her models, she is already approaching a biohermeneutics. What can carnal hermeneutics add?

The carnal problem is the problem of how to *think* about flesh. Biology already *knows* flesh, but the question is how we are to do justice to it immanently?[1] How are we to think of flesh in a fleshy way? According to one tradition of interpretation, this is indistinguishable from the problem of how to find the *meaning* of the flesh: Of what whole is it a part? Of which universal is it an instance? Toward which end does it reach? Basic research and moments of self-reflection notwithstanding, in biology the question itself remains largely obscured by the demands of utility and the epistemologies of the natural attitude. A hermeneutics of the flesh, unlike a *logos*, displaces the categories of use, knowledge, and meaning in favor of carnal sense. We cannot determine in advance what this will be—we need a hermeneutics of the flesh to get to work on it—but just as Heidegger embarked on his existential analytic with the assertion that the Being of what is to be studied is "each time mine," we can get onto the circle of interpretation just behind him with the assertion that the flesh to be studied is each time my flesh.[2]

Our living bodies appear and announce themselves in motion: the movement by which they differentiate themselves from one another is a movement of coming to be and passing away, growth and decay, going from one place to another. This is not a matter of universal flux, since each body is distinct in the time and place of its coming to be and skin is the semipermeable membrane that distinguishes inside from outside. Nor is it a matter of these bodies being distinct but interchangeable, mere tokens of a type. Geometry supplies the type of which each solid, cone-shaped object is a token, and each object approaches or falls short of the perfection of the geometrical form. Biology indicates the laws with the body and its components must obey and offers paradigms that this or that body may match. Yet the living body has no perfection; it approximates nothing but itself, and this is true at every stage of life. What can we grasp as *all of life* or *the whole body*? Healthy growth is not an approach to wholeness; fruitful maturity is not fulfillment; decrepit aging is not imperfection. Instead, our bodies are finite and are thus subject to the condition of *in*finitude. That is to say, our bodies' limitedness means that they are always unfinished, not because we are too young or too old and not because of the accidents of being in the world. We are ready to die as soon as we are born, but it is also true that we each die without having completed what was started with our birth. We are constitutively unfinished.[3] The wrinkles, blotches, and scars accumulated on our skin as we age are not signs of the fall from pristine newness, since we are never pristine. Our coming into the world involves being marked by the wound of birth. We share with all humans and almost all mammals the umbilical scar it leaves—our first scar, the mother of all scars.

Apart from being unfinished, our bodies are not hermetic, and their ways of being permeable and penetrable have occasionally emerged not just in biology but also in the philosophical conversation, sometimes in the service of philosophical argument, sometimes as a source of somatic wisdom to either complement or disrupt philosophy's abstractions. Philosophy is full of eyes that see; the fact that light enters our eyes is the classical starting point of philosophies of perception. Aesthetics, for its part, is attuned to sensation but has largely adhered to the custom of privileging sight. Yet if we take seriously the thought that aesthetics is the philosophy of taste we must think of bodies as more than eyes and ears. The mouth opens and the tongue begins to feature not as the tool of and metaphor for language but as the organ of taste and the site where the metabolic transformations of consumption begin. Saliva begins that work of dismantling and digestion. A solid body cannot absorb other substances; it has none of the internal differentiation and none of the hollows and tubes that make it possible to incorporate the materials that our bodies must take in if we are to live. Those bodies are packed full of organs that slip against one another, held together by the strings and tubes of sinew and vein. Moreover, while there is no place in a solid body for other bodies, the innards of a living being must have room for the essential microscopic fauna that inhabit us, occupying the gaps and spaces inside us.

These beings—we—who eat and excrete and breathe are also beings who kiss and have sex, who bring into play other orifices and openings, other modes of bodies' being in the same place at the same time. Our skin keeps us apart, marking the limit of the mass of matter we each think of as our own, but—particularly in our sexual and sexualized being—this means we are utterly exposed to one another, ex-*peau*-sed, in Jean-Luc Nancy's term, in the most generalized sort of openness, that is, to the touch of others. While Merleau-Ponty led us to the importance of touch as perception, Nancy leads us to consider skin as an existential condition, and touch as what always puts us in touch with the world. This turn to touch is not just a shift in emphasis, an attempt to give an undervalued sense organ its due. In the context of Nancy's renovation of the Heideggerian thought of *Mitsein*, and his insistence on our existential ex-*peau*-sition, it turns out to be a radical reworking of our practices of interpretation that turns us toward the flesh and eventually displace meaning in favor of sense.

Hermeneutics already guarantees that the point of embarkation is not determinative and is itself radically underdetermined, but it is not trivial. So when Heidegger begins his existential analytic with the statement that the Being of the entity under consideration is "each time mine," he opens mineness as a question of belonging and being: Does my being belong to me? Am I my being? Much of what follows in *Being and Time* is a struggle to unfold these questions. Now, embarking as an embodied being with the fact of embodiment in mind, the questions shift and expand: Am I flesh? What is the carnal sense of being? Is this flesh mine? Does it belong to me? What is the carnal sense of belonging? The body that is mine is inevitably a navel-scarred body, so this means starting with the flesh understood as wholly mine *and* wholly entwined with another.

I propose here a circle of carnal interpretation that is an umbilical circle. The navel marks the flesh that is most mine as also once belonging—and in certain ways still belonging—to another. It marks us as vulnerable and disrupted from the beginning, and as generated and generational. It suggests our beginning in sexual difference but its universality offers the commonness of origin rather than the difference of phallus and vulva. It directs us to the phenomenon of gestation, apparently well-known by medicine in the age of medical imaging but still impossible to produce technologically, and still surprisingly mysterious to biology and obstetrics. It leads our thinking toward what has been famously unthinkable in our individual psychic histories.

Philosophical approaches to umbilical bodies fall easily into taxonomy, into a habit of moving from perception to breathing to sex, as if each orifice, opening, and organ had to be assigned to one category and only one, as if seeing, breathing, eating, and love-making were all discrete events or activities or ways of being. Skin and touch ruin these attempts at categorization and Nancy's response is often to eschew taxonomies in favor of lyrical, fluid lists. In *Corpus* he writes: "Ego forever articulating itself—*hoc, et hoc, et hic, et illic* . . . —the coming and going of bodies: voice, food, excrement, sex, child, air, water, sound, color, hardness, odor, heat, weight, sting, caress, consciousness, memory, swoon, look, appearing—all *touches* infinitely multiplied, all *tones* finally proliferating."[4]

After all, skin is complicated, in the sense of *complico*, to fold together. It is not simple and sometimes it will take lyrical convolution to do it justice. It does not mark the inside from the outside with one smooth surface, like the shell of an egg. It is turned and folded where our joints move and where our eyes open; it gives way to nails at the fingertips, and to wet tissue on the other side of the lips; it folds over cartilage on the ears. It is a barrier, but a permeable one, and one that can be penetrated and wounded but that also heals and scars. So, as we live, as our soft, vulnerable bodies knock around a world of sharp edges, our skin accumulates its own idiocyncratic scars and folds from exposure to the walls and trees of our childhood, the surgeon's knife, the machines we get caught in, the weapons wielded against us, the sun. Our common scar, the circular fold of skin at the center of us, is the place where the hermeneutic circle makes a Mobius twist and interpretation turns inside out. We all have navels because we were attached before we were anything else; an umbilical hermeneutics thus allows us—obliges us—to resist singular reductive interpretations and to approach by a circuitous route.

The Circuitous Route

Is carnal hermeneutics then a sort of navel-gazing? Is it merely self-referential and detached from the world? No, since hermeneutic practice necessarily demonstrates that attachment to the world comes in many forms beyond the reductive responses of technology. But it shares something with the fourteenth century navel-gazers—*omphaloskopoi*—of Mount Athos, who were practitioners of hesychasm, a style of meditation that required turning inward and using a combination of prayer and breathing, a psychophysical technique developed to open the meditator to the light of Christ. Although always reaching for an experience of the divine, the practice was intensely embodied in ways that lead to deep confusion on the part of the monks as they tried to translate their experience into recognizable and orthodox terms. They offered accounts "of miraculous separations and reunions of the spirit and the soul, of the traffic which demons have with the soul, of the difference between red lights and white lights, of the entry and departure of the intelligence through the nostrils with the breath, of the shields that gather together around the navel, and finally of the union of Our Lord with the soul, which takes place in the full and sensible certitude of the heart within the navel."[5] If the teachings spoke of the mind descending to the heart, was what the meditator experienced the movement of the mind to the physical, beating heart? What was the nature of those lights? Were they perceived with the eyes? At least, the doctrinaire Barlaam of Calabria saw the exercise as confused at best and its related doctrines as heterodox at worst. It was he who gave the practice its nickname. Carnal hermeneutics is not a meditative practice or a dogma, but hesychasm, understood as a set of somatic exercises paired with repetitive incantation, engaged the problems of a Christian Platonist tradition in ways that were both embodied and interpretive. Carnal hermeneutics is not navel-gazing, but what was ridiculed as *omphaloskepsis* was surely a carnal hermeneutics *avant la lettre*.

Far deeper in the past of our Greek-Christian-Jewish traditions, Plato himself offered a distinctly un-Platonic history of the navel or *omphalos*. In Aristophanes's speech in the *Symposium* the navel is the wound left by Apollo when he split those mythical and monstrous circle people in two:

> [Zeus] bade Apollo turn its face and half-neck to the section side, in order that every one might be made more orderly by the sight of the knife's work upon him; this done, the god was to heal them up. Then Apollo turned their faces about, and pulled their skin together from the edges over what is now called the belly, just like purses which you draw close with a string; the little opening he tied up in the middle of the belly, so making what we know as the navel. For the rest, he smoothed away most of the puckers and figured out the breast with some such instrument as shoemakers use in smoothing the wrinkles of leather on the last; though he left there a few which we have just about the belly and navel, to remind us of our early fall (190d–191a).

The circle people were cut in two because they launched an attack on the gods, so Zeus felt compelled to cut them down to size. The navel is the reminder of that punishment, the scar of separation. In this story it precedes even sex; only later, when the half-people start dying off because they spend all their time clinging to each other, does Apollo pull their genitals around to the front so they can at least have sex and then get on with things. The umbilical scar they bear is the sign not of a lost *together-ness* but a lost *oneness* that can never be reclaimed. We may have a certain temporary access to it in the ecstatic union of sex, or we may achieve an attenuated version of it in the generation of children, but that original unity is irretrievable.

Still earlier, in another myth of Zeus, the navel takes on a sacred function.[6] Zeus wanted to figure out the exact center of the flat, round earth, so two eagles were released from opposite ends of the earth. They met at Delphi, which Zeus then marked as the Omphalos, the navel of the world, setting in place there an egg-shaped stone. According to Jane Ellen Harrison's research into the origins of Greek religion, the myth marked the accession of the Apollo cult at Delphi, displacing the cult of the matrilineal gods and taking over the sacred stone that had been placed there long before in the service of an older ritual. Henceforth the priestesses who inhaled the vapors from the cleft in the rock would be priestesses of Apollo. By the time of Aeschylus the cult is thoroughly ensconced, but the opening scene of *Eumenides* nevertheless gives us pause. The oracle of Apollo inspired Orestes to murder his mother and now we see him, stained with the blood of Clytemnestra, at the altar in the innermost sanctum at Delphi; if we now know that this altar was the *omphalos*, and if we see him depicted in many vase-paintings draped over or clinging to the white cone- or dome-shaped stone, we have an intimation of what lay beneath Apollo's triumph and what survived and exceeded it.[7]

Luce Irigaray places Clytemnestra at the center of an umbilical psychoanalysis, arguing that just as the killing of the father in Freud's *Totem and Taboo* obscures the possession of the mother, Oedipus's defining difficulty is not his ambivalence towards his father but the power he does not have over his mother. His own blinding madness is a reactualizing of the madness Orestes undergoes in the aftermath of his own matricide. Psychoanalysis allows us to shy away from the maternal body, fearing it as the darkest continent and failing—as does the culture at large—to provide an image of the placenta and womb that surrounded us as our first home. Instead it empowers us to loathe that body as silent and ensnaring. Such obscure power as it holds must be tapped and appropriated by the phallus. She writes:

> The genital drive is theoretically that drive by which the phallic penis captures the mother's power to give birth, nourish, inhabit, center. Doesn't the phallic erection occur at the place where the umbilical cord once was? The phallus becomes the organizer of the world through the man-father at the very place where the umbilical cord, that primal link to the mother, once gave birth to man and woman.[8]

Once we understand its place, the phallic erection becomes the masculine version of the umbilical cord.[9]

In another omphalic reading of Sophocles, Elizabeth Bronfen concentrates on the events that immediately succeed Oedipus's moment of recognition.[10] He rushes offstage, into the polluted sanctum of his house, and when he appears again he is blind. But what has driven him to this? Is it the realization that he is his father's killer? Is this an Oedipal moment (in all the received senses of the word) or does it instead belong to Jocasta? Like Irigaray, Bronfen suggests that Oedipus's blinding has less to do with his father's murder and more with his mother, specifically the opportunity he is denied to kill his mother/wife. His mother's moment of recognition precedes his own, allowing her to flee into the house before him and take her own life before he can do it. When he turns into the room, at last knowing everything, he finds Jocasta already dead on their marriage bed, leaving him facing his own fate and his own powerlessness to expunge his guilt. If Freud's Oedipus complex is the fantasy of patricide and possession of the mother, the Jocasta complex is the fantasy of matricide that is frustrated precisely by the mother's self-possession.

Hermeneutics lends us tools for the interpretation of symptoms as well as scripts and, at its origin as a tool for the understanding of sacred texts, it deployed the categories of literal, moral, allegorical, and anagogical levels of interpretation. Plato's words, spoken by the character Aristophanes, make up a comic speech that engages us on many levels at once, though the literal version would be hardly compelling. The myth of the *omphalos* at Delphi could likewise be approached literally, but why would anyone want to? The drama *Oedipus Rex* wholly resists literal understanding. Yet when it comes to reading socially contested sacred texts, the literal approach takes its place among others and, in certain circles maintains primacy. Thus, in the history of Christian Bible studies, the navels of Adam and Eve would occasionally become a lively problem. After all, since the first two people had no parents—specifically, no mother—and were not born but created, why do we imagine them with navels?[11] Indeed, when artists depict them with navels, are they confounding the divine act of creation with a posterior natural fact of birth, as Thomas Browne argued in the seventeenth century when he wrote of "that tortuosity or complicated nodosity we usually call the Navel"?[12] In the Middle Ages, Adam and Eve were sometimes depicted with navels and sometimes without, but by the Renaissance, and certainly after Michelangelo, navels were the norm. Indeed, it is hard to imagine artists of the era, preoccupied by human anatomy, sacrificing the navels of their nudes. Leonardo puts the navel of Vetruvian man at the center of the circle, the circumference of which is touched by the figure's fingertips. We can imagine humans—humanoids or primates—who look quite different from us in many ways, and still think of them as our relatives, but we stumble at the image of an an-umbilical human. We may be able to grasp, on some level of abstraction, what it would be to be descended from someone who was in turn descended from no-one, but the thinking of it runs aground on the image. We all came from flesh, unavoidably.

Epistemology of the Flesh

The moment we decide that the question of Adam and Eve's navels is *not* relevant is the moment we shift away from words or bodies as bearers of literal meaning to other levels of understanding. This is where we find ourselves reaching for and needing to theorize on other hermeneutic planes. It is a shift biology does not often feel a compulsion to make, which is why carnal hermeneutics would have us remember other modes of addressing the umbilicus in order to secure for biology a place *among* the ways of encountering and knowing the truths of the body. It will have much to tell us about the navel, but will tell us most when its authority comes under pressure from a difficulty of its own making, for example, in the case of the dominant model of immunity and autoimmunity, and its inability to explain the survival of the fetus in the maternal body.

The navel is the vestige of the umbilical tube that linked our bodies to the bodies of our mothers, specifically, to the placenta on the inner wall of her womb. At least, by the time we were ready to be born our bodies were sufficiently formed to have a link to another body whereas, in the earliest days and weeks after the zygote attached to the womb wall, the clump of cells that would become a baby was scarcely discernable. The umbilical cord develops along with the fetus. Moreover, it is the conduit through which all the material needed for that development comes. The DNA that will govern so much about our bodies is in place from the moment of conception, but the material needed for producing cell after cell, putting our skin, bones, and organs in place, all comes through the umbilical cord. Given that the maternal body has a distinctive immune system, primed to declare war (according to the dominant immunological paradigm) on foreign elements, and given that the umbilical cord carries two arteries and a vein, sending blood coursing back and forth between the fetus and the gestating body, how is it that the maternal body does not declare war on this half-foreign fetus? Why, instead, do the resources of the body immediately set to work putting in place each part of the new body?

In the words of one researcher:

> The maternal/fetal was a good idea, but we just didn't have the techniques, just didn't have the way of approaching the question. It's something that a lot of people have got into for a short time, and then got out of—the immunological aspects of nature's most successful foreign graft—how the fetus actually survives inside the immunologically hostile mother.[13]

What is significant for hermeneutics is that biology's response to this (technical) gap has typically been to tweak the immunological paradigm, adding some epicycles, but then "get out." Yet National Institutes of Health researcher Polly Matzinger is one of those immunology researchers who chose not to get out. She was bothered by the maternal/fetal question, as well as the question of why we don't have an immune reaction to food or semen or saliva, and choose to pursue them. She went so far as to reject not just the language of violence that is built into the dominant immuno-logical model but also the model of self and nonself which is assumed by the choice between friend and enemy. Self and nonself are not the relevant criteria, she argues.

Matzinger describes her alternative Danger Model in a newspaper interview in terms of community policing rather than armies at war:

> Imagine a community in which the police accept anyone they met during elementary school and kill any new migrant. That's the Self/Nonself Model. In the Danger Model, tourists and immigrants are accepted, until they start breaking windows. Only then, do the police move to eliminate them. In fact, it doesn't matter if the window breaker is a foreigner or a member of the community. That kind of behavior is considered unacceptable, and the destructive individual is removed. The community police are the white blood cells of the immune system. The Self/Nonself Model says that they kill anything that enters the body after an early training period in which "self" is learned. In the Danger Model, the police wander around, waiting for an alarm signaling that something is doing damage. If an immigrant enters without doing damage, the white cells simply continue to wander, and after a while, the harmless immigrant becomes part of the community.[14]

As a researcher in the service of medical science, she is expected to answer what the implications of a change of model are for medicine. Matzinger has a response—it opens up possibilities for vaccinating very young babies—but, as a theorist, she has a broader conception of the value of her model. It is more successful than the Self/Nonself Model since it explains things that the old model could not account for, including the maternal body's immune response to the fetus. The fetus does not cause an immune reaction because it causes no damage (at least on the level of immunity).[15] But it also calls the entire thinking of immunity, auto-immunity, self, other, inside, and outside into question, and at this point Matzinger's thinking brushes up against the limits of the discipline. Or, if the term *discipline* threatens to get in the way of thinking by forcing it back into its place, we can see the *logos* of life giving way at biology's boundary to a living hermeneutics.

Umbilical Hermeneutics

Ricoeur reminds us to ask which problem any given hermeneutic endeavor helps us to work on. What ways of thinking does it give rise to?[16] He also reminds us of the historical awareness that cannot be excised from the practice.[17] A hermeneutics of the umbilicus begins innocently, with the fold of skin on our bellies that signifies nothing or whose significance is already merely known. The umbilicus is not the problem. But when the hermeneutics takes an umbilical turn, acknowledging its circling journey as a journey undertaken in the flesh, by embodied beings, each of whom came from the body of a woman, each of whom bears the mark of that relation, it gives rise to unfamiliar thought, some of it retrieved from the past, some of it arising now, some of it addressing old problems, some of it creating problems where we saw none before. The accumulation of authority to one mode of thinking about bodies—biology—is a problem when we see it naturalized and allowed to slip beyond the deepest questioning. The accumulation of authority to another mode of thinking about who we are—the Cartesian conception of the autonomous individual—becomes a problem in the same way. If the fold at the center of us is the memory of our beginning in another body, autonomy was never a given but an achievement. We were brought into the world; we did not come of our own accord; it took action by others to sustain us before we were even aware of self or world.

Thus an umbilical hermeneutics opens itself to a set of questions that can be gathered under the heading *generational difference*. Dilthey writes of the stream of historical generations arising enigmatically out of the lap of creating nature.[18] We encounter that nature in the person of parents and grandparents—not to mention branching lines of impersonal, immemorial ancestors—who made us come to be, even though none of us asked to be born. What do we owe them, the living and the dead? What is it to us that we were born to them? Then? There? What is the significance of our starting life dependent and vulnerable? Why will we be thrown into a category with the others born around the same time and called "the younger generation," and expected to know what that means, and expected to know what is required of us when the older generations age and die? What injunction do these expectations place on us? How are we to keep interpreting a set of generational relationships that constantly shift and develop? Does being born mean that we owe the world a death? More life? Another generation?

Just as it reminds us of our generational difference *from* our parents, the umbilicus gives us oblique access to the questions of sexual difference by pointing to the sexual difference *between* them, the very difference that drives generation. The navels of all of us, men and women, are vestiges of the material connection between each of us and our mother, a woman who came to be a mother in the context of her (at least) material relation to a man. We are confronted with sexual difference—the question that Irigaray has long pointed to as *the* philosophical question of our time—in the origin of each of us. Our umbilical relation is to a woman, but the condition for its possibility was the coupling of a man and a woman, or, at a minimum, the joining of a sperm from a man and an egg from a woman.

We undergo generation, but if we approach the experience with the hermeneutic method as we have known it, that is, with a hermeneutics that is not yet carnal, generation acquires meaning as history. This was the project set out by Dilthey. On the one hand, there is everything to suggest that this would give rise to sophisticated and valuable thinking. We come to be in a world that already belongs to older generations and it somehow becomes our world just as their history is incorporated into ours. Hermeneutics can claim to be historical thinking *par excellence*, not least on the basis of its near constant attention to its own history, which led Ricoeur to describe it as more aware of its history than any other form of philosophy.[19] That very awareness goes hand in glove with an attunement to the repercussions of contingency and finitude in historical life, and leaves it committed to radical nonmastery and non-self-transparency in relation to its own projects.[20] (Indeed, it is precisely this commitment that makes it too modest to claim surpassing excellence at all.) The meaning of generation is certainly richly historical.

Yet, on the other hand, must hermeneutics insist on meaning? More to the point, will carnal, umbilical hermeneutics insist on it? While hermeneutics's constant self-examination means that the role of meaning develops and changes, there is still a worry that clings to the term, an anxiety that what really matters is not here but elsewhere. Rather than approaching bodies with the interpretive apparatus of sense and explanation, reference and interpretation,[21] might carnal hermeneutics choose to disburden itself of those anxieties? In the search for an immanent, carnal version of *meaning*, *sense* is a promising candidate, and Nancy undertakes the work of unfolding it in *The Sense of the World*.[22] He writes:

> The sense of the word *sense* traverses the five senses, the sense of direction, common sense, semantic sense, divinatory sense, sentiment, moral sense, practical sense, aesthetic sense, all the way to that which makes possible all these senses and all these senses of "sense," their community and their disparity. . . . *The ideality of sense is indissociable from its materiality.*[23]

For Nancy, sense happens in the touch of bodies. *Meaning* lends itself to the thought of hidden meaning, a plan to be discerned if only we have the right eyes for it or if only we apply the right tools. In contrast, sense cannot be given in advance but comes to be in the worldliest way, between us. "Nothing is lacking in our being," he writes. "The lack of given sense is, rather, precisely what completes our being."[24]

The umbilicus gives us the image and the carnal experience of that completeness in lack, our in-finitude. We already *know* that the sort of beings we are come to be in our mothers' bodies, quickened into being in her flesh. Even if, for each of us, it is an immemorial coming to be, the convolution at the very center of our bodies reminds us that what cannot be called to mind can nonetheless be shown on the body. We just have not learned to make sense of it yet.

Getting in Touch

Aristotelian Diagnostics

EMMANUEL ALLOA

Constituting the Corpus, Disregarding the Body

If we look at its history, hermeneutics never was anything but diacritical. In his seminal essay on the origins of hermeneutics ("Die Geburt der Hermeneutik," 1900), Wilhelm Dilthey argued that hermeneutics was born in Alexandria, in the Hellenistic period. Although according to Dilthey the art of *hermēneia* (interpretation) was already practiced in classical Greece, it is only with the post-classical Alexandrian school of philology that hermeneutics became a self-standing discipline. As it were, the problem of the correct understanding becomes all the more insistent as the object of interpretation is far away: from the perspective of the Alexandrian philologists, the ancient Greek world that Homer or Hesiod talked about no longer had much to do with their own. The question which concerned the Alexandrian philologists was whether any criteria could be established in order to corroborate any reading of such remote sources and avoid arbitrary projections. The problem which the Alexandrians first formulated, Dilthey states, is that of hermeneutics as such, and thus "to preserve the general validity of interpretation against the inroads of romantic caprice and skeptical subjectivity, and to give a theoretical justification for such validity, upon which all the certainty of historical knowledge is founded."[1] For the task of securing the legitimate interpretations, the diacritical method was developed, which was both a method for establishing the right reading and also a means of making sure that the right reading would not fall into oblivion.

What then is the diacritical method in hermeneutics? It begins by establishing the textual basis, eliminating inauthentic versions, cleaning corrupted manuscripts, amending ambiguous passages. The Alexandrian philologists, says Dilthey, were the inventors of "criticism," because they developed the art of critical distinction, which eventually allowed for establishing the textual *canon*. For the first time, the entire knowledge of the ancient world was being gathered in huge libraries, but this also meant that several versions of the same source were now competing, requiring decisions on which to keep: "Reviews of texts were prepared, and critical results were inscribed therein through an ingenious system of critical notation. Inauthentic texts were removed, and inventories of all the remaining ones made. Philology had now established itself as the art of textual verification based on intimate linguistic knowledge, higher criticism, exegesis, and evaluation."[2]

A crucial instrument in this "rise of criticism" was the introduction of the so-called diacritical signs. One of the first and foremost urges had been to establish the correct pronunciation for old and foreign texts. Even Aristotle had already underscored this problem: in the classical Greek scripture, it was unclear whether the letters ΟΡΟΣ meant "limit" (*horos*) or "hill" (*oros*). "In written language a word is the same when it is written with the same letters and in the same manner . . . but the words when spoken are not the same"[3] Aristotle also remarks that at his time already, "people put in additional signs."[4] These first diacritical signs (which in this context are referred to by Aristotle as *parasêma*, "signs beneath the signs") are meant to regulate the breath—they were later called *spiritus*—and to indicate whether the vowels were to be pronounced with a rough or a smooth breathing. But given that for a long time, texts were written in continued script (*scriptura continua*) without spacings, another important task of the diacritical signs was to specify how to differentiate words while reading.

The problem took some time to be solved. In the first century AD, Pliny the Elder speaks with bewilderment of a mysterious creature called the "sea-mouse" (*mus marinus*), which, although a marine animal living in the water, goes ashore in order to lay its eggs in a hole which it then covers with sand. Pliny's source for this curious account can easily be identified: it is Aristotle. In his *History of Animals*, Aristotle describes the life-cycle of the tortoise, starting his description with "and the tortoise" (ἡ δ' ἐμὺς, *hê d'emus*).[5] Pliny, who was clearly reading a version of the treatise without diacritical signs, misread the text and understood ἡ δὲ μῦς, *hê de mus*, "and the mouse." As all of the behaviors of the animal were evidently very different from a common land mouse, Pliny added the epithet *marinus*, "sea-mouse."[6]

What was already identified as a problem by Aristotle became all the more urgent in a time when readers had to refer to texts that had become cryptic due to the temporal distance. Whence the introduction, by the school of the Alexandrian critics, of new signs, allowing one not only to regulate how a word was to be pronounced, but more fundamentally even—for an audience which spoke only vernacular *koinē* Greek—how to identify it at all and distinguish it from the next. After the accents, it was then apostrophes ('), hyphens (-) and so-called *hypodiastolē* (') that were introduced, all indicating where words began and ended, and thus ultimately rhythmicizing the text. The correct use of diacritical signs, according to the oldest surviving grammar (commonly attributed to Dionysus the Thracian who taught towards the end of the second century BC), is the first task for the good reader.[7]

If this is the case, then the art of the *kritikos*, the critical interpreter, sets in belatedly, as it were. Belatedly in a first sense, as it emerged in later times, once the "classical" period had ended, and one was required to determine what the "classics" were. But belatedly in a second sense also, because the "correct use of diacritics," which Dionysius the Thracian demanded of the good reader, required in turn that the text on which the diacritics were to be applied be previously established. The hermeneutics which the Alexandrian critics initiated always already takes place *within the world of the text*, selecting, discarding, collating among several possible texts (this is what would permit the determination of which words were deemed worthy of selection: the *enkrithentes*, or the "admitted"), but then also *within a single text*, how to correctly read a given canonical or "classical" text, as the Latins would later say (from *classicis*, or *primae classis*, "first class" authors).[8] The constitution of the corpus of classical texts thus takes place on textual grounds; the hermeneutic exercise is to distinguish the right text among texts, to establish the right actual meaning among competing potential meanings (it is no accident that the God watching over the destinies of hermeneutics—Hermes, the messenger god—was credited, among other things, for providing humans with the technology of writing).

What already holds true for the pagan world, is even more relevant for early Christian hermeneutics. In his attack on the Valentinian heretics, Irenaeus of Lyon accuses them of falsifying the "body of truth" (*sōma tēs alētheias*) by deliberately adding inauthentic parts and forged texts to the Holy Scriptures.[9] In addition, says Irenaeus, even in those cases when they dispose of the right text, they don't read it adequately, because they lack both the "rule of truth" (*kanōn tēs alētheias*) as well as the "rule of faith" (*kanōn tēs pisteōs*). These two rules are fundamental in order to address the problem of the distance between the reader and the original instance of revelation. In his *Confessions*, Augustine is lamenting the fact that he is not in a position to ask Moses to explain his account of what happened during the Creation (hence foreshadowing what Hans-Georg Gadamer will later call the hermeneutical "problem of historical distance," *das hermeneutische Problem des historischen Abstands*).[10] Establishing criteria for distinguishing between authentic and apocryphal versions and setting the correct rules for reading will be a central concern for the early Christian authors. In this process, the scriptures will often be referred to as the *corpus veritatis*, the "body of truth."

In classical Latin, *corpus* metaphorically referred to a collection of books, in expressions like the *corpus iuris*, the collection of the reference texts in law. The church fathers, both Greek and Latin, gave this metonymic transferal from the physical body to a systematized ensemble of texts (which was already partially present in the Platonic tradition[11]) a new consistency. Origen, for instance, considers that the constitution of a cohesive Christianity requires first and foremost the unification of a "body of doctrine" and that this in turn means establishing the correct textual basis of the scriptures.[12] It is in the context of Alexandrian theology that the expression "the body of the text" becomes a recognized trope;[13] though later, there seems to be a need to neatly distinguish the dimension of organic unity which the notion of "corpus" yields from its *bodily* connotations: Irenaeus says the corpus of the true scriptures is composed of limbs that are not made of flesh, but consist of the letters of the Greek alphabet.[14]

What are we to make of these observations? The sources seem to point to the fact that the historical constitution of hermeneutics occurred through the establishment of a textual reference corpus which both implied the simultaneous recuperation of the body metaphor and the exclusion of its fleshly stratum. Moreover, in a number of authors, the distinction between body and soul is reproduced *within* the text: Philo of Alexandria, for instance, says within the textual corpus, a purely bodily, "literal" reading should be separated from a spiritual, "allegorical" reading, while Origen considers that the first immediate take of the text is just the "bodily" level of understanding, which needs to be transcended towards a psychological and then intellectual understanding. It is as if the constitution of the corpus had gone hand in hand with a denigration of the body, or at least with an association of the textual corpus with unity as opposed to the physical body as confusion.

But whatever one is to make of this early history of hermeneutics, and whatever its relevance to so-called scientific hermeneutics, inaugurated by Schleiermacher and Dilthey in the nineteenth century and continued by Gadamer and Ricoeur in the twentieth, another aspect is perhaps of even greater importance. Hermeneutics, it seems, is the project of a critical revision of older sources, deriving its legitimacy from the pre-existence of texts. *The condition for hermeneutics*—one could venture to surmise—*is the presupposition of a textual corpus.* Whatever the operation of amending, glossing, editing, and commenting, the existence of the pre-text is taken for granted. As a result, the meaning of the diacritical operation will be that of an operation *on* signs, specifying them, qualifying them, in terms of a *parasêma*, as signs placed above, beneath or next to other already existing signs which are deemed to be significant, albeit not yet transparent in their full meaning.

"Reading What Was Never Written": Diacritics and Diagnostics

The historical consolidation of the *kritikê technê*—the "art of distinguishing"—into a discipline of textual scrutiny is a later phenomenon which by no means exhausts the potentialities of what the *kritikê* could mean. The trope of the "Book of Nature" that humanity supposedly needs to decipher is itself a retrospective projection made when the paradigm of the Book was generalized onto all types of reading. In his essay "On the Mimetic Faculty," Walter Benjamin curtly questions this reduction of reading to the reading of a canonical *corpus*, asking what it could mean "to read what was never written" (*Was nie geschrieben wurde, lesen*).[15] "Such reading," says Benjamin, "is the most ancient: reading prior to all languages, from entrails, the stars or dances." Only later, he adds, "the mediating link of a new kind of reading, of runes and hieroglyphs, came into use."[16]

What kind of reading is the reading that analyses the movement of a dance, interprets the entrails of animals or finds meaning in the position of the stars? One thing is sure: the language it reads has no alphabet and no predetermined vocabulary. It comes closer to the reading of involuntary mimics and instinctive gestures, of body language in general, which is a language that one speaks without ever learning it. Reading letters on a page, Alberto Manguel once beautifully stated,[17] is only one of its many guises: the hunter reading the spoor of an animal in the forest, the farmer reading the weather in the sky or the fisherman reading the ocean currents by plunging a hand into the water are but a few cases of the infinitely larger number of techniques of reading, a kind of hermeneutics without text, a scriptless interrogation of sorts (let's remember that *hermeneuō* derives from *eirō*, "I ask"[18]).

What connects all these different cases of nontextual reading is the fact that, unlike the reading in a book, these events are strongly context-dependent and their content more resistant to decontextualization: the newly discovered trace of the animal in the woods cannot be infinitely reread, nor can the freshly opened liver of the Babylonian soothsayer or the flight of the birds by the Roman augur. While in the case of a text, the signs to be read already stand out against a meaningless ground, in the case of the nontextual reading, what is to be established first is whether there are any meaningful signs at all, and where to draw the distinction between significance and insignificance (in the case of the Roman augur, with a wand, a demarcation called *templum* was first marked, indicating the space above which the birds' flight was to be considered meaningful). As a result, the nontextual reading tends to be more demanding and to potentially engage more of the reader's sensory and practical capacities—it requires an experiential *knowing-how* which can't be fully and adequately translated into a propositional *knowing-that*.

A good instance of this nontextual interpretation is the physician's reading of the patient. In the ancient tradition of medical symptomatology, the body was considered telling, provided one was able to interpret it. In the Galenic school, a bruise, a knot, a rash, or a sore throat were all considered "signs" (*sēmeia*) that converged into what later came to be known as a "syndrome" (from *syn-dromos*, "running together"). Just as there is a prehistory of nontextual hermeneutics, there is a prehistory of semiotics: In the fifth century BC, Hippocrates established "semiotics" (*sēmeiōtikē*) as one of the branches of medicine, and up until the early twentieth century, students of medicine had to register for "semiotics" as one of their foundation courses. Bodily symptoms become revealing "clues" or "signs" to the trained physician's eyes, who combines them into the "picture" of the illness (it is noteworthy that the expression used in the earliest extant texts on medicine is that of *eidos*, which led Eric Voegelin to claim that Plato's conceptual use of the expression was but a metaphysical transferal from an otherwise rather practical and everyday word[19]).

The art of reading a body is thus an "art of discernment," as Hippocrates puts it, a discipline which has to do with the right *krinein* or discerning, which then allows the full picture to emerge—the *eidos*—and eventually this will lead to a decision about the general state of the patient. Now, as Reinhart Koselleck has convincingly shown, *krisis* stands for a number of different things here: firstly for the observable condition, secondly for the turning point in the development in the course of a sickness, and thirdly for the possibility for the physician to make a judgment about its further evolution: "In the case of illness, crisis refers both to the observable condition and to the judgment (*judicium*) about the course of the illness. At such a time, it will be determined whether the patient will live or die."[20] The diacritical operation of discerning the symptoms and the critical judgment about the future both prepare the *krisis* and draw conclusions from it, this special moment or turning point being generalized to other domains too (for instance Augustine, in his *Confessions*, talks of this "dangerous state which the physicians call 'critical'"; *quam criticam medici vocant*[21]).

What is important, in the context of our analysis, is that the critical value (and hence the possibility of judgment) is grounded, first of all, in practical diagnostics. Hippocrates asserts that "crises, and the other things that give us knowledge, [are known] by the eyes, ears, nose, hand."[22] The doctor needs *aisthesis*, says Hippocrates, and if we are to follow Werner Jaeger's discussion of the medical tradition in Aristotle's time, *aisthesis* should not be translated as the "sense of perception" in general, but rather the doctor's well-pondered sensitivity, or simply a fine-grained "tactfulness" (*ein feines Taktgefühl*)[23]

In order to know properly, it is important to know the ways by which one knows (as in *diagnosis*, from *dia* + *gignoskein*, "knowing-through"). In the Renaissance treatises on medicine, the textual basis for medical knowledge is rejected and physicians are required to use their eyes and hands. In his *Liber introductorius Anatomiae*, published in 1536 in Venice, Niccolò Massa attacks those who have tried writing about things they have never seen with their own eyes nor touched with their own hands (*neque oculis viderint neque manibus tetigerint*).[24] Accordingly, *doctrina* is to be replaced with experiential autopsy (from *aut-opsia*, "seeing with one's own eyes") whereas the surgeon needs to start working with his own hands. Paradoxically, the rejection of written doctrine for the benefit of embodied experimentation is made in the name of textuality. In his *Theatrum anatomicum*, published in 1592, the anatomist Caspar Bauhin presents dissection as a means to finally turn nature into a readable book: into the *liber naturae*, the "book of nature."[25]

But what about the importance of touch in this process? Are seeing with one's one eyes and touching with one's own hands one and the same thing? Does every doctor need to be a surgeon, a *cheirourgos*—literally: a handworker (from *cheir*, "hand" and *ourgos* "worker")—and put hands on what he treats? As far as the ancient Greek physicians were concerned, we regularly find praise of touching in their writings. In his treatise *On the Usefulness of Body Parts*, Galen celebrates the creator for having so wisely formed the palm of the human hand in order to respond to the slightest stimulus and the most subtle change. The hand, he says, is "the most char-acteristic of mankind" and a person's temperament can be distinguished by feeling the palm of the hand.[26] Centuries later, a Renaissance anatomist like Andreas Vesalius states that the hand must be vindicated, as it has been wrongly disavowed (*manus neglecta*): the sense of touch is, he claims, the *primarium instrumentum* of the physician.[27] The praise of the hand traverses the history of medical symptomatology, and reaches even puri-tan Victorian England. In 1759, the English surgeon Henry Thompson claimed that "wounds are distinguished by Sight-Touch-Smell."[28]

Now one could rightly argue that the importance granted to the organ of touch within medicine is rather an exception, caused by its inevitably practical nature, while in the general perspective of a history of the senses there has been—as Richard Kearney suggests in his introductory essay—an overall devaluation of touching in mainstream Western metaphysics. Is carnal hermeneutics the necessary enlargement of text-centered herme-neutics to other forms of understanding? Does any being that "can be understood" take on the form of "language," as Gadamer holds (*Sein, das verstanden warden kann, ist Sprache*)?[29]

But even if language were not the only medium of understanding, it is not certain either whether all forms of sensorial orientation in the world need automatically to take up the form of *understanding*, as both Ricoeur's and Gadamer's definition of hermeneutics holds. I shall forego this ques-tion here as it leads into yet another argument. What I would like to dis-cuss, however, is the suggestion that touch has a capacity for being a means of discrimination and discernment. If this is the case, then one needs to ask whether this is a novel idea, peculiar to late modernity and its more haptic devices, or whether we can find such an idea of the *diacritical capacity of touch* in the tradition too. In other words, we must first establish whether there has indeed been a denigration of carnal touching in the history of Western accounts of sensoriality.

Manus neglecta: Has There Been a Denigration of Touch?

While the structuring of the perceptual faculty into five senses has been remarkably stable since classical antiquity until the Modern Age, these five senses have seldom been treated on an equal footing. Discussing the senses, as it seems, almost inevitably leads to a hierarchization of their powers, ar-ranging them on an ascending or descending ladder. Almost undisputed was the primacy of sight, as the most noble and theoretical of all senses. "We prefer sight to all other senses" so the opening lines of Aristotle's *Metaphysics* read. "The reason for this is that [sight], most of all the senses, makes us know and brings to light many differences between things."[30] Aristotle hence seems inextricably linked to the establishment of vision as the sense of utmost discrimination, where *theoria* is both the sharpest sense and the highest form of ("contemplative") life. Aristotle's account of sight as the most accurate means for grasping the *eidos* or "essence" of things echoes Plato's famous description of thought as the "soul's eye," resulting in what Jacques Derrida called the "heliocentric" pattern of Western metaphysics. When Leonardo da Vinci, centuries later, speaks of the eye as the "window of the soul," this seeming inversion only yet confirms the strict correlation between sight and insight, making vision the highest of all senses, a correlation which Hans Jonas has discussed as the paradigm of the "nobility of sight."[31]

Needless to say, the praise of that sense associated with distance and impassibility had consequences on the other senses too. While to some extent the ear could claim similar qualities as the eye, the further senses became known as the "lower" or "secondary" senses. Smell and taste are, by virtue of their supposed immediacy, less prone to be controlled, while touch is often thought to be the most "passive" sense of all, given that unlike seeing (which allows one to see without being seen) touching something always implies being touched in return. The Renaissance confirms the privilege of vision and the downplay of the lower, tactile senses. Commenting on Plato's *Symposium* and the Platonic notion of "eros," Marsilio Ficino explains why true love "is very foreign to the commerce with the body": beauty, Ficino asserts, concerns only contemplation with the mind, or at best with the eye and the ear, but not the despicable lower senses.[32] Smell, taste, but, above all, touch seize a man's soul, driving him into "lust and madness": the libido of touch (*la libidine del toccare*) is not part of love nor the lover's work, but a kind of dangerous lechery (*lascivia*) and discomposure (*perturbazione*) of the servile man. Only such men yielding to touch "can be seized by the senses and lust, as though by police and a tyrant (*quasi come da birri e tyranno*)."[33]

The idea of touch as a passively suffered experience, placing the experiencing subject in a subaltern position, is also taken up by some thinkers of the Enlightenment. Even Schiller repeats the argument in a comparable fashion, when affirming that the lower, tactile senses are characteristic of a lower form of development in mankind, while the progressive emancipation from their grip allows for aesthetic and intellectual freedom. The object of touch is a violence we suffer (*Der Gegenstand des Takts ist eine Gewalt, die wir erleiden*), while in contrast, "in sight and hearing, the object is a form we create" (*der Gegenstand des Auges und des Ohrs ist eine Form, die wir erzeugen*). As soon as man learns "to enjoy through a sight, vision has an independent value, he is aesthetically free, and the instinct of play [*Spieltrieb*] is developed."[34]

The connection made by both Ficino and Schiller between intellectual knowledge and aesthetic insight, which gives a double reason, as it were, to denigrate touch, is to be found in many authors. The lower senses—asserts Thomas Aquinas among others—are not capable of aesthetic flights of fancy. After all, "we do not speak of beautiful tastes and beautiful odours."[35] Hegel, in turn, asserted in his *Aesthetics* that "the sensuous aspect of art is related only to the two theoretical senses of sight and hearing, while smell, taste and touch remain excluded from the enjoyment of art."[36] Before Hegel, and in a more laconic way, Robert Boyle had dubbed touch to be "the most dull of the five senses."[37]

In Modernity, the presumed disavowal of touch in Western tradition has become somewhat of a *topos* and, in many contexts, authors, poets, and thinkers advocated for the need of getting touch into the overall account of sensorial knowledge. Nietzsche already complains about Kant's dismissive analysis of touch which, according to Nietzsche, was worthy of the "naïveté of a country parson" (*landpfarrermäßiger Naivität*).[38] But can the claim about a general denigration of the haptic dimension of perception ultimately be upheld? What needs to be said is that, roughly in the same period when Schiller defends the superiority of sight, Herder writes his essay *On Sculpture* ("Plastik"), which is, through and through, a vindication of the only true sense according to Herder: touch. Sight, he says, is but a derived impression, "an abbreviated form of touch. . . . Sight gives us *dreams*, touch gives us *truth*."[39]

No doubt hence that a more attentive look at different strands and traditions presents a more multifaceted picture. To be sure, one could easily write a counterhistory of an anticontemplative praise of touch, beginning with Democritus or Lucretius (the latter considered that the nature of the intellect and of the soul must be considered bodily: given that the body knows above all through touch and that touch requires materiality, the soul must have something material[40]), through late Medieval or early Modern positions such as François Rabelais, Michael Drayton (touch is "the King of senses!"), Etienne Bonnot de Condillac, Berkeley, Denis Diderot ("I found touch the most profound and philosophical"[41]), Julien Offray de La Mettrie, Tardy de Montravel ("touch is the most perfect of the five senses"[42]) or Maine de Biran up until Maurice Merleau-Ponty, Henri Maldiney, Gilles Deleuze or even Didier Anzieu and his concept of *Le moi-peau* ("*The Skin Ego*").[43] (In this history, the influence of Alois Riegl's conceptual pair of the "optic" and the "haptic" still needs to be fully pondered.[44])

Given the overwhelming evidence for the importance currently granted to touch—and accordingly to the hand and to skin (the results from evolutionary biology tend to show that the entire nervous system and the brain arise from the ectoderm of the embryo)—one may ask whether this line of thought (if it may be called such) should be considered a subversion of the "heliocentric" valorizing of vision. Would the insistence on carnal ways of exploration be some way of rebuking the impassive, theoretical approach from afar, a way of stressing the internal qualities against the external ones and the synthetic, holistic approach over an analytic one? This was at least Jacques Derrida's suggestion, when in opposition to his own notion of "heliocentric" or "optocentric" metaphysics he spoke, much later, of what he detected to be a "haptocentric" tradition. From antiquity to the seventeenth century and from the seventeenth century to the twentieth there has been, he asserts, "a conspiracy, a philosophical intrigue of touch":[45] Ultimately, haptocentric metaphysics—Derrida maintained in *On Touching—Jean-Luc Nancy*—can be recognize by its privileging identity over difference, immediacy over mediacy, continuity over disruption.[46]

However, Derrida adds a further specification to this haptocentric paradigm: touch is the sense *par excellence* of auto-affection. Wherever there is flesh, Derrida seems to imply, there is auto-affection. The "sensible haptology" deployed by those authors Derrida lists in the philosophical "intrigue" finally results in a "phenomenology of carnal auto-affection."[47] Just as in *The Voice and the Phenomenon* three decades earlier, Derrida had outlined why Husserl's notion of the voice led to auto-affection ("speaking is hearing oneself speak"), in *On Touching—Jean-Luc Nancy*, carnal auto-affection of touch completes the picture ("touching is touching oneself").

As a matter of fact, it can't be denied that in the list of authors associated by Derrida with "haptocentric metaphysics," touch is very often celebrated for the sake of its importance for a self-reflective subjectivity. When the hand is praised, for instance, it is generally for being the utmost subjective expression of man, giving everything it touches its so-called "hand-print." The privileged position of the hand seems to have changed over time. For Aristotle, the hand is the *organon organōn*, the "organ of organs": most malleable, it can adapt to virtually any form.[48] In early modernity, the hand progressively takes up the function of signaling subjectivity. "I am . . . immediately in my finger-tip," says Kant (hence proving Nietzsche's judgment about Kant's supposed dismissal of touch to be too harsh),[49] while in Hegel's *Phenomenology of Spirit*, handwriting (*Handschrift*) is seen as the "expression of interiority" (*Ausdruck des Innern*).[50] As for Heidegger, having a "hand" is intimately tied to humanity (Derrida coined the expression *humainité*, from *humanité*, "humanity," and *main*, "hand"): "No animal has a hand, and a hand never originates from a paw or claw or talon," man however "acts [*handelt*] through the hand [*Hand*]."[51]

Touch: From the Vital to the Interior Sense

There is some reason to hypothesize that where touch was extoled, it was to a large extent associated with the subjectivity of the self, as a kind of means to assure the self of its own existence and peculiarity. Before being an experience of self-affection, touch appears more broadly as a means for self-referentiality, a way to grasp the self (and for the self to grasp *itself*): to think for oneself can be thought of as a way of getting in touch with oneself, *taceo ergo sum*. Even in a slightly less metaphysical context, the reappraisal of touch corresponds only seldom to the vindication of a single, supposedly disregarded sense and more often to a general sense of self-awareness. When in the nineteenth century the anatomist Charles Bell highlights the importance of the "muscular sense," he does not mean a specific sense, but proprioception by and large.[52] Whence the legitimate question whether there has really been, as Derrida claims, some kind of countertradition to the dominance of the eye and of the ear, or whether haptocentric approaches were not, albeit differently, cementing the notion of a perceiving subject mastering his own perceptions.

For sure, one should be wary of too hurriedly considering the traditional hierarchy of senses subverted every time prominence is granted to touch. Thomas Aquinas for instance, commenting Aristotle, acknowledges that touch is "the first sense, root and ground, as it were, of the other senses, the one which entitles a living thing to be called sensitive"[53] The purportedly lowest sense—*tactus*—thus receives a new status: it is the lowest by virtue of being the *radix fontalis*, itself laying the ground to all the others: "touch is the basis of sensitivity as a whole; for obviously the organ of touch pervades the whole body, so that the organ of each of the other senses is also an organ of touch, and the sense of touch by itself constitutes a being as sensitive."[54]

Touch would thus represent the most vital sense, or rather: the symptom of vitality. Only what is capable of touch—and of being touched—can be considered to be alive. (Correspondingly, Heidegger will say that touch is what constitutes the living: although it is commonly said that a stone lying on the ground "touches" the earth, this is a misleading way of speaking.[55]) Probably the earliest trace of this idea is to be found—hardly surprising—in Aristotle. Touch, he explains in *On the Soul*, is the *vital sense* by and large; an animal possess touch for its "being" (*zēn*). The other senses, when given, add up to the animal's "well-being" *(eu zēn)*.[56]

Over the course of time, this conception of touch as *vital sense* seems to have been shifting towards becoming touch as an *interior sense*. In Diderot's entry on faculties in the *Encyclopédie*, we find the notion of the "vital sense" (*sens vital*), which according to Diderot should be deeper than the senses controlled by the will. This last sense is a "sort of touch," capable of transmitting what the other senses yield to a central, inner *sensorium*.[57] A long tradition has prepared this internalization of the vital sense. In a way, Aquinas already provides a testimony of this internalization, when, in his commentary on Aristotle, he says that if touch is the most basic sense of all, conferring sensitivity to the living being, that is because it "lies nearest to the root of them all, the *sensus communis* itself."[58]

Now it has to be said that the notion of a *sensus communis* is indeed to be found in Aristotle himself, with his concept *koinē aisthēsis*. The later commentators, however, found the notion somewhat enigmatic, and much literature has been devoted to defining its possible meaning. Augustine, for instance, acknowledged Aristotle's concept, which he referred to as *sensus communis*, but preferred talking of a *sensus interior*, an internal sense. Daniel Heller-Roazen has retraced the long history of this progressive internalization of the vital sense in his book *The Inner Sense of Touch*, showing how the internal sense, initially associated with the *vis sentiendi*, progressively shifts to being the central organ of understanding or *vis intelligendi*.[59] Gregory the Great speaks of a *sensus cerebri* which "presides within," Scotus Eriugena equals the *sensus interior* with thinking, which rules over the external senses, while Avicenna considers that the internal sense culminates in the *vis cogitativa*, the intellectual faculty.[60] Angels have a *sensus interior* too, and even the purest of all—no need to have a body for self-knowledge: touch is internalized and spiritualized, as that feeling by means of which a being may know of itself, without any distorting intermediary.

Now how is it that within the faculties of the soul, the functional position granted to the allegedly lowest sense—touch—is suddenly occupied by the intellect? Were we not told, according to the optocentric-heliotropic reading, that it was sight which traditionally directly led to the highest intellectual activities? The suspicion we would like to raise here is the following: could it be that touch supposedly yields a quality which is not even conferred on sight, a quality which supposedly is that of thinking? Aristotle is invoked once again with his account of the thinking soul as *noēsis noēseōs*: there is no difference between the thinking soul and its object, as to think is to assimilate a thought. Only "once the intellect has become each of its objects . . . can it think itself."[61] Is the reason for the continuity—or should we say the *contiguity*?—between touch and thinking that both are supposedly without any intermediaries and that they grasp their object in an immediate way? In the following and last section, I aim to show why, at least as far as Aristotle is concerned, and against a certain dominant interpretative strand, *there are no unmediated senses*—including touch.

Why All Senses Require a Medium: Aristotle's Take on Touch

"Is then the perception of all things," Aristotle asks in his treatise *On the Soul*, "one only, or is it different of different things, just as it is now generally supposed that taste and touch both act by contact [*haptomenon*], but that the other senses act at a distance [*apothen*]?"[62] In this passage, Aristotle seems to consider two alternatives: (1) *All* senses are structured in a similar fashion. According to Aristotle, this was the dominant opinion among the Pre-Socratic philosophers. Such unified conception of perception, as it were, means reducing all senses to a kind of touch. (In *De sensu*, Aristotle complains about the fact that all "natural philosophers" have taken touch to be the prototype of all the other senses.[63]) (2) There are *certain* senses which are based on a haptic, immediate contact while *others* occur at distance, in a mediated way. Elsewhere, he explains that what is related to "touch occurs by direct contact with its objects, and that is why it has its name. The other sense organs perceive by contact too, but through a medium; touch alone seems to perceive immediately."[64] According to such an opinion, one would need to distinguish between senses which operate "by themselves" (*di'autēs*) and senses which operate indirectly, "through something else" (*di'heterou*).

What must be questioned here is whether the opinion "now generally supposed" (*kathaper nun dokei*) is endorsed by Aristotle or not. Some prominent readers were convinced of the former. According to one of the most widely recognized scholars of Aristotelianism Enrico Berti, "Aristotle demonstrates that some senses require a medium situated between the sensorium and the sensible object, for sight and hearing for instance, while others don't require any medium."[65] What needs to be said, however, is that if this were the case, Aristotle would only be reformulating in a somewhat modified way an older idea which we find in Plato and which concerns an internal division of the senses.[66]

In the *Philebus*, the five senses are divided into two main categories: on the one hand, the immediate senses such as touch and taste, held impure when related to basic needs, and on the other hand the noble but uninterested senses such as smell, hearing, and sight.[67] Such a conception clearly opposes the older conception of senses as all being molded on touch: it is now vision which offers the prototype of perception, as a way of elevating the soul above the realm of needs and towards contemplation. In an early text, the *Protrepticus*, which was purportedly written during his early period at Plato's Academy, Aristotle stresses explicitly such connection between vision and *theoria*: "The activity of reason is thinking, and thinking is visual perception of intelligible things, just as perception of visible things is the activity of sight."[68] Such an association of seeing with knowing can be found in the famous beginning of the first book of *Metaphysics*, which is generally held to stem from the same period at the Academy. (Yet even in a later text such as *On Generation and Corruption*, we find the claim that "sight is preeminent [*proteron*] over touch."[69])

Should this be taken as evidence that Aristotle adopted Plato's intellectualism, hence establishing detachment as a general criterion for the validity of sense? If this were the case, Aristotle would indeed be cementing the hierarchy of the senses, organized around the two poles (*viz.* touch and vision), as respectively immediate and distanced senses: just as vision, hearing equally requires distance, and as a consequence it is admitted, in the first book of the *Metaphysics*, as the source of knowledge allowing for learning.[70] Such an epistemological criterion—the primacy of the distanced *vis-à-vis* the immediate—is then arguably turned into a moral one which would explain the polarization of the two regimes of sensoriality. The two inferior senses (touch and taste) are those by means of which man is closest to the animal, as they are subject to potential depravation and slavishness, while there can't be any excess, Aristotle claims, in sight, hearing, or smell. (Smell itself, however, seems to be a shaky candidate: while taking over Plato's division, which places smell in the noble senses by virtue of its operating at a distance—we would not call intemperate "those who enjoy the smell of apples, roses, or incense"[71]—Aristotle also opens up the possibility of a depravity of smell which happens when man behaves bestially and hence reduces smell to a contact sense.[72] On the other hand, taste can rise to being a higher sense when used as a means for discrimination, such as in the case of the cupbearer.[73])

Let's now return to the question as to which of the two options presented —is there a *single* modality of perception or are there *two kinds of perception* (*immediate and mediate*)—is the one favored by Aristotle himself.

If, as the first option holds, perception were one, and all perceptible objects reduced to tangible things, this would contradict the idea presented earlier that every specific sensorial capacity corresponds to a *specific* object of sensation: to the capacity of seeing (*opsis*) corresponds the visible (*hōraton*), namely, the color (*chrōma*); to hearing (*akoē*) corresponds the audible (*psophētikon*), namely, the sound (*psophon*); to tasting (*geusis*) a specific taste (*chumos*); to smelling (*osphrēsis*) the tasteable (*osphranton*); and to touch (*hapsis*) the touchable (*hapton*).[74]

If the second option were true, this would contradict the other basic idea of Aristotle's theory of sensation, i.e., that the specific object of sensation (*idion aisthēton*) is connected to the sense organ (*aisthētērion*) through a medium (*metaxy*). As Aristotle puts it: *anagkaion ti einai metaxy*—"there must necessarily be a medium."[75] If touch and taste are immediate and don't require any medium of sensation, the general claim about the fact that every sense has a specific medium collapses. The Peripatetic commentator, Themistius, had well perceived the requirement of consistency here: "If all perceptions happen through a medium, then touch likewise."[76]

There are good reasons, therefore, to consider that neither option can be held to be Aristotle's own opinion. But how could a contact sense such as touch possibly function as a mediated sense? Let's go back for a moment to Aristotle's argument for the necessity of a sensorial medium. The most extended argumentation is laid out in the analysis of vision: seeing happens—in both the local and operative sense—*through* a medium which Aristotle calls "the diaphanous" (from *dia-phainesthai*, "appearing through"). Without the medium of visibility, there can't be any vision at all ("for if one puts that which has color right up to the eye, it will not be visible"[77]). The point here is to rebuke Democritus's conception of the void: "Democritus is mistaken in thinking that if the *metaxy* were empty, even an ant in the sky would be clearly visible; for this is impossible."[78] Were the medium empty, "not merely would accurate vision be impossible, but nothing would be seen at all."[79]

Granted that this analysis is exemplary for all other senses at distance, is this also true for proximal senses such as taste and touch? While all ancient commentators have considered it self-evident that all "upper" senses had their own medium (even introducing names where Aristotle had not given them any: *diechēs* for the medium of hearing and *diosmōs* for the medium of smelling), opinion diverged on the proximal senses. Now one could raise the question as to why proximity should be an argument for mediation: after all, is not smell a sense of proximity too? But the real puzzle lies elsewhere: how could there be a medium between the touching organ and the touched object?

As I have tried to show elsewhere,[80] Aristotle seems to have evolved within his own thinking in order to accommodate the idea of a medium of touch. As often, some decisive clues can be found in the more empirical texts, in this case in the treatise on *Parts of Animals*. In the first, more general part, touch is related to flesh (*sarx*) as its organ. The subsequent sections seem to modify this picture, as Aristotle takes his empirical studies on animal physiology into account. At some point, the situation is presented as doubtful: flesh might suddenly be not only the organ, but also the medium of touch, "comparable to the pupil *plus* the whole of the diaphanous in the case of sight."[81] A little later, this moment of indecision is overcome and Aristotle makes a statement: "the primary sense-organ of touch is not the flesh or a corresponding part, but something internal."[82] We find an echo of this statement in *On the Soul*, where it is said that the organ of sense is *entos*, "within."[83] By such a decision of internalizing the organ and locating it next to the heart (where, this said in passing, it is also next to the "common sense," the *koinē aisthēsis*), flesh (*sarx*) can receive a new function: from now on, it can act as a medium.

While influent commentators, from Alexander of Aphrodisias to Enrico Berti (or, more recently Johansen[84]), have maintained that flesh was the organ of touch and that touch was immediate, one should recall that there was also a long parallel tradition which epitomized why flesh was described by Aristotle as a medium, and not as an organ. Themistius makes that argument, after him Averroes[85] and, in the Latin Middle Ages, several such positions can be mentioned (in the fourteenth century, Nicolas d'Oresme affirms that *caro non est organum in tacto, sed est medium*[86] and even Suárez still recalls this conception in the early seventeenth century: *caro non est organum, sed medium*[87]).

What about taste then? Unlike the discussion of flesh and touch, it has to be said that the *Corpus aristotelicum* which has been handed down to us is less explicit on this matter. Does Aristotle claim that, among all senses, taste is the only immediate sense? In *On the Soul*, we find the following remark "But the perception does not arise for us through a medium. . . . Therefore there is no medium [sc. in taste]."[88] Although the statement was formulated in an irrevocable way, commentators sought to explain it, as Aristotle didn't seem to have good arguments here. According to Aquinas, the reason is simply that taste is a kind of touch and as a "kind of touch, the tasteable is not perceived through any extraneous medium."[89] But what if touch itself were not immediate either? What kind of consequences has this on taste? Could there be a medium of taste, just as there is a medium of touch? Aristotle hints at this possibility.

Taste, he says, does not arise through a (external?) medium "but by the flavour's being mixed with moisture, just as in the case of a drink."[90] In his *Long Commentary* on Aristotle's treatise *On the Soul*, Averroes elaborates at length on the importance of saliva for taste: "nothing receives the sensation of flavor, which is called taste, unless the flavor is in a liquid and the liquid is in what is flavorful either in act or in potency, for instance, salt, which is in proximate potency to being wet since it is dissolved quickly and it dissolves liquids which are on the tongue."[91] Avicenna, in turn, who already knew about the nervous system, states that the organ of taste consists in the nerves in the tongue, while he credits the saliva for being the medium. While he wants to take a middle ground between the argument of either the tongue or the heart as the organ of taste, Albertus Magnus instead sides with Avicenna when he also reiterates that the medium of taste is saliva.[92]

There is some ground to the conclusion then that, while in proximal senses such as taste or touch, the medium cannot be separated from the organ, this fact does not annul the functional distinction between both. Rather, there seems to be a concrescence between the medium and the organ: they are *sumphuēs*, "grown onto each other," just as the air is to the ear.[93] Among the most notable details of Aristotle's analysis of the perceptual medium is the fact that he does not distinguish between natural and artificial media: mention is made of cases such as pressure applied to a membrane wrapped around our skin, or blows to a shield which the soldier holds in front of him. The transmission of the movement is instantaneous and the soldier feels "at once" (*hama*).[94] As we can easily see, however, the point here is that *sensation, though instantaneous, is not immediate*: although it would be absurd to consider these accoutrements as part of ourselves, they nevertheless react just in the way our flesh does—or rather, our flesh acts the way such an accoutrement would.

It has been observed that "contemporary scientists have criticized the Aristotelian picture of touch as a contact sense" and that many examples taken from ethology show that many animals actually feel through hair follicles, whiskers, and antenna.[95] I hope to have shown that Aristotle does not think of touch as an immediate sense, but at best as a proximal sense (*egguthen*). And indeed, proximity is not immediacy; just as to show that touch involves a sense of proximity is to show that it involves a sense of distance.[96] Moreover, I hope to have made clear that not only the higher but *all* the senses are means of critical distinctions. As already mentioned, it is Aristotle himself who stresses the connection between thinking and touch: unlike some of his commentators, however, this connection is not made in the name of some purported immediacy common to thinking and touch.

In *On the Soul*, Aristotle sets up a criterion for the anthropological difference which is far less known than the famous *zōon logon echon*. Man is lacking behind many animals, he says, and his perception is less precise, but there is one sense by which he differs from all other animals: touch. In touch, man "is much more discriminating than the other animals. This is why he is of all living creatures the most intelligent."[97] Not content to affirm such a thesis, Aristotle also justifies it: "Proof of this lies in the fact that among the human race men are well or poorly endowed with intelligence in proportion to their sense of touch, and no other sense; for men of hard skin and flesh are poorly, and men of soft flesh well endowed with intelligence."[98] Aristotle wrote the earliest extant treatise on understanding—the *Peri hermeneia*—but in his theory of perception, he showed how there can be a kind of discernment which precedes the codified tradition, a corporeal knowledge which precedes the knowledge of the *corpus*, an art of *diakritikē* which does without diacritical signs.

From here, two ways open up: the first consists in a broadening of hermeneutics beyond what was outlined in the first section "Constituting the Corpus, Disregarding the Body" as the textual bias of hermeneutics towards what was epitomized in the second section as the "reading of what was never written." Certainly eyes are not the only organs of reading a text—fingertips can fulfil, that task almost with equal precision, as the Braille script proves. But the textual bias remains, albeit in a disguised form: beyond the already scripted text, one can think of the hand as a means of reading bodies as symptoms or auspices of a hidden meaning (just as psychoanalysis reads the symptoms referring to an unconscious "structured like a language"—as Lacan famously claimed).

But what if that desperate search for a hidden message preceding the act of interpretation were not only vain, but even counterproductive? That was the creeping suspicion that befell Schleiermacher, when he eventually began questioning the "rage of understanding" underlying the old hermeneutic project. Could it be that this "rage of understanding" (*Wut des Verstehens*) even impedes "sense to arise"?[99]

Reconnecting with Aristotelian diagnostics—merely sketched here—may show us an alternative route: that of sense as a means of *orientation* rather than of *understanding*. Whether we still want to call this kind of diacritical thinking "hermeneutics" or not is possibly of secondary importance. In any event, to reconnect with Aristotle's account of diacritical orientation in the phenomenal world does not amount to giving away the notion of sense altogether, but rather to giving it a new orientation, a new *sense*, and displaying how much sense owes to those bodily senses in which it is (not only etymologically) rooted and to those sensorial milieus in which we evolve.

Between Vision and Touch

From Husserl to Merleau-Ponty

DERMOT MORAN

> No phenomenology of life, of body and the flesh, can be constituted without basing itself on a phenomenology of touch.
> —Jean-Louis Chrétien, The Call and the Response[1]

> The characterization of the human being as a rational animal is already present in the form and organization of his *hand*, his *fingers*, and his *fingertips*; partly through their structure, partly through their sensitive feeling. By this means nature has made the human being not suited for one way of manipulating things but undetermined [*unbestimmt*] for every way, consequently suited for the use of reason; and thereby has indicated the technical predisposition, or the predisposition of skill, of his species as a *rational animal.*
> —**Immanuel Kant, *Anthropology from a Pragmatic Point of View*, 1798**[2]

It is commonly recognized that Maurice Merleau-Ponty's phenomenology of embodiment depends heavily on Edmund Husserl's analyses of *Leiblichkeit* as found in the latter's unpublished *Ideen* II.[3] In this paper[4] I shall argue that Merleau-Ponty, especially in his posthumously published *Le Visible et l'invisible*,[5] significantly reinterprets and transforms the phenomenon of the "double sensation" (*Doppelempfindung*), i.e., one hand touching the other,[6] discussed by Husserl. Husserl claims the double sensation belongs exclusively to touch and indicates a priority of touch over sight in the composition of the living organic body (*Leib*). In contrast, Merleau-Ponty rejects both of Husserl's theses. For him, reversibility and doubling of sensation are characteristic of all five sensory modalities. Moreover, precisely because of this intertwining of the senses, he maintains—

contra Husserl—that there is no priority of touch over sight. Indeed the double sensation precisely illustrates what Merleau-Ponty variously calls the "chiasm,"[7] "interlacing,"[8] "overlapping,"[9] "blending,"[10] "coiling over," "inversion," and even the "metamorphosis,"[11] of the "flesh" (*la chair*—a term which Merleau-Ponty sometimes uses as equivalent to Husserl's *Leib*) and of the activity of "sensing" of all the senses. For Merleau-Ponty, this "duplicity" and "reflexivity of the sensible,"[12] has ontological significance and expresses the ambiguous character of human embodied being-in-the-world, expressed in his late conception of the "flesh of the world"[13] or "flesh of things."[14]

Merleau-Ponty's conception of this reflexivity is radical: reflexivity is characteristic of *all* the senses; indeed it prefigures and founds the reflexivity of thought. Merleau-Ponty—citing the testimony of painters (André Marchand and Paul Klee)—evocatively expresses this intertwining as it is found in sight, such that just as the seer *sees* the visible so too the visible in a sense *sees* the seer.[15] In *Visible and Invisible* he writes:

> As many painters have said, I feel myself looked at by the things [*je me sens regardé par les choses*], my activity is equally passivity—which is the second and more profound sense of the narcissism: not to see in the outside [*dans le dehors*], as the others see it, the contour of a body one inhabits, but especially to be seen by the outside, to exist within it, to emigrate into it, to be seduced, captivated, alienated by the phantom, so that the seer and the visible reciprocate one another [*se réciproquent*] and we no longer know which sees and which is seen.[16]

The very flesh of the external world, embodied in sensuousness, mirrors the embodied subject's own flesh: "it is already the flesh of things that speaks to us of our own flesh."[17] There is not just a remarkable correlation between the world's availability to perception and human perceptual systems, but the human subject is itself part of this world and is also the perceived.

Merleau-Ponty's departure from Husserl on the priority of touch over sight and on the universality of the reflexivity of the senses needs to be more carefully charted, including the study of important intermediaries who point the way for Merleau-Ponty, among them Husserl's own former student and colleague at Göttingen, David Katz (1884–1953),[18] who went on to become perhaps the most innovative psychologist of color and touch of the twentieth century. Although the limits of space do not permit me a thorough accounting of Katz's work—which explored in great empirical detail the parallels and differences between the senses of sight and touch—I will offer some preliminary connections between Katz's work and Merleau-Ponty's work, especially the early discussion of spatial perception in the *Phénoménologie de la perception* (1945).[19]

Touch and Sight in the History of Philosophy

The topics of the primacy of touch and the interrelationship between sight and touch have been discussed since Aristotle's *De anima*.[20] In modernity, George Berkeley's groundbreaking *New Theory of Vision*[21] argued for the *heterogeneity* of the objects of touch and sight such that touch and sight deliver different ideas of space that may subsequently become intermingled or confused by the perceiver. For Berkeley, touch fixes the size of objects that get smaller or larger to vision as they move away or approach the viewer. The idea of according a certain primacy to touch is already found in John Locke's *Essay Concerning Human Understanding* Book II chapter IX § 8, as well as in Étienne Bonnot de Condillac's *Traité des sensations*.[22] According to Condillac, who agrees with Berkeley and is critical of Locke's acceptance of innate powers of the mind, touch assists the eyes in the assessment of distance, size, and figure.[23]

During the early decades of the twentieth century, Husserl's phenomenology at Göttingen was closely associated with the then current empirical psychological explorations of perception, especially the senses of vision and touch[24] and the constitution of space.[25] Indeed, phenomenology appears to have anticipated and even influenced some of the later findings of Gestalt psychology.[26] Erich R. Jaensch,[27] Heinrich Hofmann,[28] Wilhelm Schapp,[29] Jean Hering,[30] and David Katz,[31] among others, studied perception both from the view of psychology and phenomenology with Husserl in Göttingen, often taking part as subjects in the laboratory experiments of Husserl's colleague, the Göttingen psychologist Georg Elias Müller.[32]

Of course, the discussion of what is immediately given in perception (the "proper sensibles") had a longer tradition in empiricism, including Berkeley, Hume and Reid, and in the Kantian tradition (relating to his account of the matter and form of sensuous intuition), but Husserl appears to strike out on his own path, with groundbreaking results. Husserl is fascinated by the fact that the senses convey the sense of a single, seamlessly unified sensuous world, with touch and vision combining to give rise to one single shared space. But how is this possible? This is both Berkeley's and Husserl's question.

Husserl's answer in his *Ding und Raum* lectures[33] is that spatiality is constituted by objectivated sensory experiences (i.e., sensory experienced contents that are somehow interpreted as properties of objects) combined with interpreted sensations of bodily self-movement:

> A body is constituted as a sensuous schema by the sense of touch and the sense of sight, and every sense is a sense through an apperceptive conjunction of the corresponding sense-data with kinaesthetic data.[34]

According to this account, the presented sensuous content (i.e., experiences of colors, shadings, light, darkness, in the case of sight) is coordinated with a complex of kinaesthetic sensuous experiences to yield the "sensuous schema" (not yet the full object, because temporality, causation, etc., have still to be considered).[35] Husserl is, of course, not claiming in Berkeleyan fashion that the so called external, material object is formed exclusively from our *ideas* of it such that there is no external material world, but rather that the object as experienced is assembled out of our experiences (color, shape, etc.) and certain correlated bodily movements (eyes, neck, head, sweeping movements of the fingers, and so on). Indeed, this approach corresponds with Berkeley's approach in his *New Theory of Vision*.

Also similar to Berkeley, Husserl claims in his 1907 *Ding und Raum* lectures that the ocular visual field, taken strictly on its own, is actually experienced as a two-dimensional field, at least if we attend only to the visual image or "phantom" as Husserl calls it (i.e., the purely sensibly apprehended thing as it appears minus its full causal interconnectedness with other things):[36] "The visual field, as a strictly ordered system of two 'dimensions,' has its fixed orientations, and so does, accordingly, the oculomotor field as well."[37] Both the visual and oculomotor fields in themselves are two-dimensional[38] and what they present are "phantoms" in Husserl's sense. Merleau-Ponty agrees. In *The Visible and the Invisible* he writes:

> The binocular perception is not made up of two monocular perceptions surmounted; it is of another order. The monocular images *are* not in the same sense that the thing perceived with both eyes is. They are phantoms and it is the real; they are pre-things and it is the thing.[39]

Husserl wants to preserve the phenomenological intuition that we can actually *see* space (and do not just apply it in some Kantian manner to structure our sensuous intuiting), including empty space. Furthermore he believes, and Merleau-Ponty follows him here, that it is the animate body's *movements* (approaching, receding, turning, focusing, reaching, grasping) that allow us to penetrate "into" the visual field as it were, that yields up the experiences of depth and distance.[40] There can be no sensory experience without bodily movement (even the eyes must saccade in the act of seeing, never mind the blinking of the eyelids). As Merleau-Ponty will later insist: "*Wahrnehmen* and *sich bewegen* are synonymous."[41]

It is important to emphasize that, for Husserl, in *Ding und Raum*, the "field of vision" (*Sehfeld*) or "visual field" (*das visuelle Feld*), understood as a two-dimensional continuous spread of colored images and shapes, is not yet what Husserl calls "empirical," i.e., experiential, space in the full sense. The visual field as such must not be conceived as a "surface in objective space."[42] In fact Husserl employs the term "pre-empirical" (*präempirisch*) to refer to this layered stratum of images and their associated contents that make up visual space as experienced.[43] At this level, every "image" is coordinated with a specific and predelineated set of kinaesthetic sensations (which may include movements of the eye, head, neck, torso, and so on). Moreover, to complicate matters, each kinaesthetic sensation pertaining to ocular experience can in principle be coordinated with *any* visual image ("every [kinaesthetic] sensation is compatible with every image"[44]). A series of eye movements or a series of head movements can each reveal the same visual scene and the particular series of movements are neutral with respect to what they convey, i.e., the movements do not predelineate what range of visual sensations will be uncovered by them (this may not be true of the other senses). Husserl also recognizes that, depending on the circumstances, one sensory modality can stand in for or correct another,[45] as touch does for someone with poor sight or sight must do for the tactile feel of objects that are out of reach (i.e., that ceiling looks smooth). Let us take first consider what Husserl was trying to do.

The Roles of Touch and Vision in Constituting Spatiality

In *Thing and Space* Section 46 Husserl focuses on the constitution of space insofar as this is achieved through vision and touch.[46] In a quite Berkeleyan manner, he discusses visual and touch sensations separately as to whether they underpin different "spaces." Is visual space essentially different from tactile space? For Husserl both sets of sensations (tactile and visual) are marked off from the other sensory faculties (olfactory, auditory) because they cohere together into a "field of sensations" (*Empfindungsfeld*). This concept of a "field" is crucial,[47] and is explicated by Husserl as a "pre-empirical expanse" (*präempirische Ausdehnung*) with determinate fillings. For Husserl, among the senses, one can genuinely speak only of visual and tactile sensations as being organized into "fields."[48] While Husserl acknowledges that olfactory, auditory and thermal sensations may also be said to belong to "fields" in some looser sense, he denies that they contain in themselves "primordial pre-empirical extension" (*ursprünglicher präempirischer Extension*).[49] Smell and taste on their own lack this "pre-empirical expanse" and hence do not underpin extension. Color, however, has a character of being a particular shade with a certain amount of "brilliance and saturation," all of which require expanse and filling: "the red-moment, with such and such brilliance and saturation (*Helligkeit und Sättigung*) is what it is only as the fullness of a certain extension; the red-moment expands."[50] Husserl sees that the quality of visual experience is copresented with a certain not yet fully "objective" extension.[51] There are specific aspects of the quality in a narrow sense—its brightness, saturatedness, and so on. Extension can be experienced with different degrees of "filling." The visual field is continuous, with no gaps, although it has limits. It also has a center which has sharp definition, as well as a fading off. Although it appears two-dimensional, it nonetheless has a horizon that is indeterminately far away. In contrast to vision that is oriented away from the body into the distance, embodiment does not allow us to withdraw from ourselves: "we cannot approach or recede from ourselves at will."[52]

Husserl also discusses the sensations that give the sense of movement (*self-movement* as opposed to the sensation of *being moved*).[53] He employs two terms: "sensations of movement" or "kinetic sensations" (*Bewegungsempfindungen*) and "kinaesthetic sensations" (*kinästhetische Empfindungen*). He expresses a preference for the term "kinaesthetic" and regards the former term as "unusable" since it is, for him, overly charged with psychological meaning.[54] Moreover, sensations of movement as such (e.g., the landscape going by as I sit in the train) are different from experiences of my own body willfully moving.

Kinaesthetic sensations (*kinästhetische Empfindungen*),[55] for Husserl, strictly speaking, are those sensations of movement which occur when I move myself, i.e., "sensations" by which I am aware of movements on and in my body.[56] This term was frequently employed by German, British, and American psychologists of the day.[57] Husserl does not clearly indicate if kinaesthetic sensations include all forms of proprioceptive experience, muscle sensations, experiences of effort, force, balance, and so on.[58] A kinaesthetic sensation, for Husserl, must have its "locus" or "position" (*Stellung*) in a particular part of the body, must be under voluntary control, or as Husserl puts it, have the character of "I can" (*Ich kann*) such that it can be controlled through "practice" (*Übung*).[59] Not all body sensations are kinaesthetic sensations. Furthermore, it is not clear if Husserl considers *all* kinaesthetic sensations to belong essentially to touch (i.e., if I extend my leg out under the table, is this sense of the limb extending communicated through touch?). It does seem that he considers the experiences of walking, sitting, and so on, as primarily constituted out of touch sensations.[60]

Husserl's view is that there is an "extensional moment" (*das extensionale Moment*) in both vision and touch but that these "pre-empirical" experiences of spatiality are not yet sufficient to produce the experience of empirical spatiality. The sensation of *movement* (and specifically *self-movement*) is also necessary. Movement sensations always have position but do not necessarily add to the "projection" (*Projektion*) of a thing (I suspect that Husserl means here that the moving of the visual field when I walk, for instance, is not attributed to the objects themselves which I am passing). Movement sensations are quite different from those of vision and touch and do not primarily constitute the body in terms of its own characteristics. At times, Husserl speaks as if movement sensations have no "matter" (he makes a similar claim about time-sensations in his *Lectures on Time Consciousness*),[61] that is, they do not contain a determinate sensory qualitative content (feelings of *willing* are similar in this respect). This is a very interesting phenomenological observation.

In *Thing and Space* § 47, as elsewhere, Husserl claims that the "ego-body" (*Ichleib*) is a kind of physical body (*Körper*)—subject to causal laws—that is yet different from other physical objects because of its animateness, which means it is subject to voluntary control.[62] Husserl's first point is that visual experiences are not experienced as "localized" in the body in contradistinction to the way in which I locate touch sensations in specific parts of my body. Vision, although it does issue "from the head," in an experienced way, is not conspicuously a bodily performance.[63] All visual experiences, colors, and so on, take place *at a distance from me* and not on my surface. Similarly, Merleau-Ponty writes: "to see is to have at a distance" (*voir c'est avoir à distance*).[64] The opposite is the case with touch which requires contact with its object, although interestingly Merleau-Ponty will emphasize that there is still a "gap" or *écart* in the case of touch, since touching and touched never merge into one.

In *Thing and Space* section 47, Husserl goes on to discuss the phenomenon according to which, when I touch the smoothness or roughness of the object, I also have a sense of that smoothness "on or in the appearing finger tips."[65] He writes:

> If with my left hand I touch my right, then along with the touch sensations and the kinaesthetic sensations there is constituted, reciprocally, the appearance of the left and right hands, the one moving over the other in such and such a manner. At the same time,

however, i.e., with a reversal of the apprehension (*bei Wechsel der Auffassung*), the self-moving appears in an other sense, which applies only to the body, and in general the same group of sensations which have an objectivating function are apprehended, through a reversal of the attention and apprehension, as subjectivating and specifically as something which members of the body, those that appear in the objectivating function, "have" as localized within themselves.[66]

For Husserl, if we limit ourselves solely to the visual experience of space and to kinaestheses, the body cannot be constituted as *my* body. The body has a special relation to visual space in that it is invariant with regard to its position, always "here" as opposed to objects that are over "there." But it is not yet experienced as *my* body since seeing as a subjective experience does not include a reference to the organ that does the seeing. As Husserl points out, we never have a pure sensation of light just as it is experienced that is not at the same time the communication of the presentation of the colored visual thing.[67] The eye cannot perceive itself by its visual sensations but knows of its existence by its being able to move and be touched. In other words, movement and touch sensations found our sense of the "object" *eye*.

The experience of tactile space, on the other hand, allows us to call the body "mine" by virtue of the "double-sensation" (*Doppelempfindung*) that characterizes it through the exercise of the organ of touch. When I touch my own body (and not merely look at it), for example, when my hand touches my leg, I am aware of a "positional-givenness" (*Stellungsdatum*) in my hand because my hand organizes the spatiality of my tactile consciousness. I also apprehend a "profile" of my leg and grasp my leg as mine (through the *being-touched* sensations occurring at the same time in my leg). But this could be reversed and the leg could be the perceiver: I could touch my leg against my hand. Through experiencing the body as self-touch it is constituted as *mine* in tactile space alone. Interestingly, Condillac makes the same point in his *Traité des sensations* in his discussion of the hypothetical statue at the point where it has only touch-sensations. When I touch myself, I have the experience of "I and again I." Condillac writes:

> It is accordingly through this sensation that the body, spatial objects begin for the statue, through which it recognizes what belongs to it. It learns to know its body and to know itself in all the parts which compose it, because, as soon as it places his hand on one [of these parts], the same sentient being responds to itself in some way from one to the other: "it is I." As it continues to touch itself, throughout

the sensation of solidity will place resistance between the manners of being, and everywhere also the same sentient being will answer itself: "it is I; it is again I."[68]

According to Condillac's thought experiment, the statue learns to say "I" as a result of discovering the same sentience in each of the touched parts of the body. The hand runs itself smoothly along the surface of its body and discovers only itself. For Condillac, this tactile contact with the body also includes the sensory experiences of resistance and solidity. It is through experiencing these sensations (in fact in discovering its own body) that it comes to have a sensation (later "idea") of *external* material body.

This phenomenon of the "double sensation" of the hand that can touch a part of its own body or itself became a recurrent theme in nineteenth-century German psychology.[69] Indeed, recognition of the peculiarity of touch can be traced back to Aristotle in *De anima*. Aristotle even discusses a "touch illusion" whereby one crosses the fingers of one hand and touches an object with the outside of the fingers and has the sense of touching two distinct objects. Aristotle's illusion is taken up and discussed by the German psychophysicist E. H. Weber in his groundbreaking studies of touch published in 1834 and 1846.[70] In *Der Tastsinn*, Weber claimed that perception combined touch and sight but that sight is more accurate than touch for localization:

> The touch organs, like the visual organs, have a localization sense, but to a far less developed degree: we therefore owe our accurate perception of spatial relationships to both senses.[71]

Weber also discusses the issue of whether two sensations arise when sensitive areas touch each other. He claims (and Merleau-Ponty will develop this idea) that the two sensations do not simply merge into one so as to lose their separate identities: a cold limb touching a warm limb reveals both heat and cold; or a hand touching the forehead.[72] Weber is concerned with which body part feels like the subject touching and which the object being touched. In one hand touching the other (palm touch the back of the hand), he opts for a physiological explanation and suggests that the "object" is that skin which has the thinner epidermis.

It is possible that Husserl learned of the concept of "double sensation" from the Göttingen psychologists, possibly from the students he shared with Georg Elias Müller who ran the Göttingen Psychological Institute. Müller himself remained quite aloof from Husserl and disapproved of him. But Husserl explicitly employs the term "double sensation" (*Doppelemp-*

findung), common in the psychological literature, in *Ideas* II.[73] Here he regards it as unique to touch as opposed to sight.

In *Ideas* II Husserl claims to be interested precisely in the "intertwining" or "interweaving" (*Verflechtung*[74]) between ego-body and object. He sees the sensations as having an objectivating function of allowing the object (smooth surface) to appear, as well as the body touching it (fingertips) and the sensation of the body as a "bearer of sensations" (*Träger der Empfindungen*). Husserl's analysis of the double sensation is very complex and is discussed primarily in *Ding und Raum* and in *Ideen* II. He denies that "kinaesthetic sensations" have any "matter" but they permit an apprehension that transforms them in a more determinate way. Kinaesthetic sensations and their flow motivate the apprehension of new presentations (turning my head opens up a new angle of vision on the object). Furthermore, Husserl believes sequences of kinaesthetic sensations themselves (such that those of the eyes are similar to those of the head) are "phenomenologically related" (*phänomenologisch verwandt*)[75] while remaining separate and not "passing over into each other."[76] There is much to explore here. Does Husserl mean that head movements *feel* more or less the same as shoulder movements in terms of the pure quality of the experience or that they can stand in for one another in revealing the same perceptual scene? Other psychologists had explored whether different regions of the body or skin yielded different tactile sensations. I think Husserl does not come to a decision on these points. The main issue for him is that kinaesthetic sensations combine with their related visual sensations to provide a foundation for the constitution of the physical thing in perception. Secondly, he thinks that series of kinaesthetic sequences can stand in for one another (instead of moving my eyes left, I can turn my head left and reveal the same visual scene):

> Our body (*Leib*) contains several systems of movement (*Bewegungssysteme*), which, however, can stand for one another vicariously (*für einander vikariieren können*) and thereby do not have, relative to each other, a different constitutive significance for the constitution of space.[77]

In relation to the purely visual perception of "pre-empirical" depth, Husserl maintains it cannot at all be analogous to the perception of a straight line spread out on a two-dimensional plane. Indeed, Merleau-Ponty will make the same point in criticizing both empiricist (Berkeleyan) and intellectualist accounts of the perception of depth: "In both cases depth is tacitly equated with *breadth seen from the side*, and this is what makes it invisible."[78] Breadth and depth are as distinct from one another as are temporal and spatial distance.[79] This pre-empirical "sensation of depth" (not yet true "objective" depth) is borne out of the experience of color with extension and a certain "relief" (*Relief*) between colors.[80] This "relief" is the pre-empirical correlate of depth. It has a "near-far" structure inside the "up-down" and "left-right" structure of the visual field. Husserl emphasizes that the concept of a two-dimensional plane does not underlie or found the concept of three-dimensional bodily space; it is precisely the other way round.[81] Only *because* there is genuine three-dimensional space do two-dimensional planes make sense.[82]

In agreement with Condillac in his *Traité des sensations*, Husserl characterizes touch as an omnipresent but dispersed sensation. We can attend to elements of it at will (I can now attend to and notice my toes in my shoes or the back of my legs against the chair which were not salient before my attention lit them up), but there is a continuous sense of the body being present to itself, through something like an inner sensation of touch.

Touch and Vision in Husserl's *Ideas* II

Husserl's *Ideas* II develops an ever more layered account of the constitution of material, animate, and spiritual natures in the world. The aim of Part II of the book is to determine the manner in which physical objects (including embodied persons) are constituted. Again, Husserl wants to explore all the "strata" and "layers" as given in sensory experience (especially touch and vision). Their psychic being (in contrast to the material object which in principle can remain unchanged) is one of constant flux.[83] Similarly, it has no parts; unlike a material body, it is not separable into pieces. Material things are not conditioned by their past, unlike psychic animate beings.[84] Moreover, as grasped *in the personalistic attitude*, "in immediate spiritual apprehension"[85] the human being is experienced as a human *person* (about which a great deal more needs to be said).

In *Ideas* II § 36, as part of a general investigation of the manner in which the body is apprehended in our animate living, Husserl is interested in the manner in which the lived-body (*Leib*) is constituted as a "bearer of localized sensations." "Localization" means, for Husserl, as for the psychological tradition of that time, both that the sensations are somehow distinguished with regard to a certain place in the body and are recognized as belonging phenomenally to it.[86] Ernst Mach, for instance, characterizes emotions as not well localized sensations, and William James speaks of self-consciousness as largely localized in the head. These "localized sensations"—also calls "sensings"[87]—are not directly sensed in our sensory awareness but can be brought to attention by a shift of apprehension.

In *Ideas* II Husserl begins his analysis by acknowledging several features that apply to touch and not to vision. There are parts of the body that can be both touched and seen, parts that can be touched but not seen (e.g., lower back, back of the head), but there is also a very particular difference between visual and tactile appearings. In *Ideas* II § 36, Husserl introduces the example of the right hand touching the left. The touching hand has to make movements in order to feel the smoothness and softness texture of the touched hand. This touching gives rise to sensations which Husserl calls "indicational sensations of movement" (*die anzeigenden Bewegungs-empfindungen*) and with them come the "representational" (*repräsentieren-den*) sensations or "appearances" of smoothness. These representational sensations of smoothness in fact belong to the touching right hand but they are "objectivated" or localized in the touched left hand. But Husserl goes on to say that, in the touched left hand also, I have sensations that are active and "localized" within it. In other words, I am aware of the left hand *as sensitive to being touched* and this sensitivity possesses its own peculiar kind of sensation complex. Both touching and touched hands have their respective "touch sensations":

> If I speak of the *physical* thing, "left hand," then I am abstracting from these sensations. . . . If I do include them, then it is not that the physical thing is now richer, instead *it becomes Body, it senses* [*es wird Leib, es empfindet*]. "Touch"-sensations belong to every appearing objective spatial position on the touched hand, when it is touched precisely at those place. The hand that is touching . . . likewise has its touch sensations at the place on its corporeal surface where it touches (or is touched by the other).[88]

As with Sartre, to grasp the hand as an objective hand is to abstract from or, as Sartre would put it, "surpass" this field of sensory experiences and objectify the hand as a distinct object on its own independent of the sensations. If I apprehend the hand with its sensings, Husserl continues, then I am apprehending it as my living body (*Leib*). The hand can be touched, pressed, stroked, pinched, etc. by the other hand or other bodies. In this context, Husserl speaks of the sensation being "*doubled*"[89] when one hand touches or pinches the other. There is doubling but no identity.[90]

Furthermore, Husserl (followed by Katz and Merleau-Ponty) notes that the sensations can linger after the touching is completed and the hand or fingers have been removed.[91] There are great complexities involving the sensation of touch. I can sense my fingers moving and touch not just surfaces but things beneath the surface (I can press on the bone beneath my skin). Touch yields different sensations: I can feel not just coldness, smoothness, and softness, but also heaviness, immobility, and so on (indeed, Weber made a detailed study of perception of weight). These specific kinds of experiences (of motion, weight, etc.) Husserl calls, employing a neologism, "sensings" (*Empfindnisse*).[92]

Husserl distinguishes between "indicational or presentational" sensations,[93] i.e., sensations that are interpreted as properties of the object, and the sensings themselves, which he speaks of as "touch-effects" of the thing. I press my finger on the surface and apprehend the table's solidity and also that that *solidity* is causing the sensation of pressure in my finger. These are apprehended by "different directions of attention." Husserl says we can thus feel the surface as cold and my finger touching it as "cold." These are two experiences of cold in the one experience.

Husserl says one hand touching the other is an even more complicated scenario. Husserl claims that each hand experiences this "double sensation" and each is apprehended in a two-fold way. Each hand has a sensing and a sensed and both occur simultaneously. There is a double constitution of the body with both "positional-givenness" (*Stellungsdatum*) and "aspect givenness" (*Aspektdatum*). As Husserl will elaborate in a Supplement to *Ideas* II, the body is both *ichlich* and *ichfremd* at the same time.[94]

Most importantly for our purposes in this paper, Husserl claims in *Ideas* II § 37 that this "double sensation" (*Doppelempfindung*) or "double apprehension" (*Doppelauffassung*) belongs exclusively to touch and *not* to vision. He declares: "in the case of an *object constituted purely visually* we have *nothing* comparable."[95] Although the eye in one sense "touches" the object it sees (alights on it), the eye itself does not appear as a component in its own vision. Likewise, we see colors but there is no comparable localized sensing of the experiencing of color or of the eyes that are doing the seeing. Moreover, one eye cannot *see* the other eye directly (and as an active sensing organ) as one hand can *touch* the other. I do not constitute my eye as an external object in the same way I constitute the touching hand as an object over and against a second touched object. All Husserl will allow is that the eye can itself be a field of localization, in that it can be a center for touch sensations (the eyeball can be touched, we can feel the localized movement of the eye in the eye socket, through "eye muscle sensations," and so on). In general, for Husserl: "I do not see myself, my body (*Leib*), the way I touch myself"[96] and he concludes, "The role of the visual sensations in the correlative constitution of the body and external things is thus different from that of the sensations of touch."[97]

Touchability, for Husserl, is something that pertains to all visible things (at least in principle—one cannot touch the sky, for instance), but not all touchable things are visible. Crucially, Husserl maintains that the sense of touch has primacy with regard to localization and someone without the sense of touch could not at all have an appearing body.[98] Someone who simply *saw* his body (e.g., as Sartre describes looking at his hand as an alien object resting on the table) would have no experience of it as one with his living body since it lacks kinaesthetic character. The hand is mine because it is animated through my sensation and touched by me. All the other senses are, then, subordinate to touch, in regard to their role in constituting *Leib* as *Leib*.[99]

Merleau-Ponty's Synaesthesia of the Senses in *Phenomenology of Perception*

As is well known, Merleau-Ponty's *Phenomenology of Perception* draws heavily on various resources, including phenomenological analyses of perception (found especially in Husserl, Stein, Schapp, Katz, Linke, and Fink), as well as the then current Gestalt accounts (Gelb, Goldstein, Köhler, Koffka, Wertheimer, Gurwitsch, etc.) and those of clinical psychologists (most notably Marius Von Senden[100]). From Schapp, for instance, Merleau-Ponty takes the claim (also found in Husserl) that we see the surfaces of things as revealing something of their internal natures: "The brilliance of gold palpably holds out to us its homogeneous composition, and the dull colour of wood its heterogeneous make-up."[101]

Merleau-Ponty's general aim in his *The Phenomenology of Perception* is to argue for a sentient subject prior to intellection that has his or her own way of experiencing the world. The life of hands, eyes, and ears are "so many natural selves."[102] His target is both empiricist and intellectualist accounts of sensation. In his chapter on "Sense Experience," Merleau-Ponty relies heavily on David Katz's studies of color.[103] Similarly in his chapter on "The Thing and the Natural World," he discusses, in relation to constancy phenomena, touch invoking Katz's study.[104] In relation to color, Merleau-Ponty follows Katz's account of the distinction between "surface colors" and "color areas." Surface colors are properties of objects, whereas colored areas (such as the sky) are more complex: located at a distance, on a parallel frontal plane, flat. He also draws on Katz's discussion of our manner of experiencing lighting and illumination, the "logic of lighting."[105]

Merleau-Ponty discusses touch in relation to the feeling of constancy of weight. He remarks, with a footnote to Katz: "Thus analysis of the perception of weight elucidates the whole of tactile perception: the movement of one's own body is to touch what lighting is to vision."[106] He goes on to distinguish between active (the "knowing touch") and passive touch (passive touch is mostly the inner feeling of being touched in an area without that area itself engaging in a corresponding reciprocal probing, e.g., when the inside of the ear is touched). Movement is necessary for touch—certain tactile qualities (roughness, smoothness) disappear if movement is eliminated. He draws on Katz's *World of Touch* to support the claim that temporality is an integral aspect of touching. Not only must the fingers be moved over a surface in objective time, but the temporal extension of the touch sensation is an important feature in our sense of the spatial continuity of the surface. For Merleau-Ponty, "smoothness is not a collection of similar pressures, but the way in which a surface utilizes the time occupied by our tactile exploration or modulates the movement of my hand."[107] And again: "Movement and time are not only an objective condition of knowing touch, but a phenomenal component of tactile data (*des donnés tactiles*)."[108] Merleau-Ponty is making the general claim that human action assumes a "global bodily knowledge" (*un savoir global du corps*) that systematically embraces all parts of the body.[109]

In his study, Katz particularly emphasized the role of the hand and the range and complexity of its various modalities of touching, stroking, grasping, poking, rubbing, and so on. Indeed, he is Merleau-Ponty's source for the supposed Kantian claim that "the hand is an outer brain."[110] Katz also distinguished between the sense of something vibrating and the sense of pressure. Merleau-Ponty, following Katz, also emphasizes the hand as a tool for exploring space. However, as Merleau-Ponty says, it is not, strictly speaking, the hand that touches; the whole body touches. At the same time, Merleau-Ponty reiterates a point Husserl and Edith Stein also both make, namely, that I keep the sense of touch *at an unspecified distance* from myself: "It is not I who touch, it is my body."[111] I feel a part of my body being touched, e.g., the table touches my leg.

In contrast to Husserl, Merleau-Ponty emphasizes the deep parallels and continuities between touch and vision, faculties that are more usually contrasted in regard to constituting the sense of materiality and spatiality. For instance, it is often thought that the sense of touch disappears when one lifts one's hand off one kind of surface before touching another surface. Merleau-Ponty, on the contrary, thinks a kind of indefinite sense of touch remains. It is not, Merleau-Ponty says, "a tactile nothingness" but "a tactile space devoid of matter, a tactile background."[112] Similarly, for both Katz and Merleau-Ponty, there is a kind of tactile *memory* akin to a visual after-image. When I touch the surface of a material (e.g., silk or fur), I have a sense of what that surface feels like and I will expect that sense in future contacts with the material. There is a kind of "memory" in my body for what it feels like to lean against a wall, to have my back touching the chair, and so on. Through this memory I gain a sense of the "constancy" of the object.[113]

Katz distinguishes between the subjective (I feel my finger being pricked) and the objective (I am touching something sharp) dimensions of touch (and sight), and believes this varies in different experiences. Normally, one is oriented to the objective but, in case of pain for instance, the subjective side predominates. Touching a surface with gloved fingers still gives an impression of a surface on the other side of the glove. In *Phenomenology of Perception* Merleau-Ponty emphasizes the manner in which touch brings body and world literally into contact with one another, unlike the situation of sight (which gives me the sense that I am "everywhere and nowhere"):

> Tactile experience, on the other hand, adheres to the surface of the body; we cannot unfold it before us and it never quite becomes an object. Correspondingly, as the subject of touch, I cannot flatter myself that I am everywhere and nowhere; I cannot forget in this case that it is through my body that I go to the world.[114]

Merleau-Ponty thinks that the experience of "lived" depth (not simply the putative assumption that it is breadth seen from the side, seen by another) reveals the world as it is formed by us prior to the imposition of science,[115] as "grasped from within,"[116] not due to the assumptions of some "natural geometry." There is need to rediscover the undeniable experience of depth before it is objectified. Perception is "initiation into the world"[117] and Merleau-Ponty speaks of a "primordial depth."[118] There is a "depth" to colors prior to them being attributed to things. I press my pen through the white to write on the paper. For Merleau-Ponty, prior to geometrical three-dimensionality, there is the "existential" experience of depth as "the link between the subject and space."[119]

Merleau-Ponty's overall claim is that it is the body as a whole and the whole system of sensory experiences that give us our sense of objects in the world. There is not just a "reality-for-sight" (*une réalité-pour-la-vue*) and a "reality-for-touch" (*une réalité-pour-le-toucher*) but one "absolute reality" based on "my full co-existence (*ma pleine coexistence*) with the phenomenon."[120] He goes on to say that "the brittleness, hardness, transparency, and crystal ring of a glass all translate a single manner of being."[121] This is, for Merleau-Ponty, what Husserl means by the presence of something "in person," "in the flesh."[122] There is not the sense of different sensory streams but of the one sensible world.

The Reversibility of Flesh in the Late Merleau-Ponty

Some fifteen years after the *Phenomenology of Perception*, in his much discussed chapter on "The Intertwining—The Chiasm" in the unfinished *The Visible and the Invisible*, Merleau-Ponty tries to articulate that phenomenological sense in which we find ourselves as perceivers in a world of the visible which envelops us and which, as it were, mirrors us as seers:

> The visible about us seems to rest in itself. It is as though our vision were formed in the heart of the visible, or as though there were between it and us an intimacy as between the sea and the strand.[123]

The seer does not disappear into the visible or vice versa but the seer forms part of the visible and is in communication with it. We don't have any sense that we create the visible, rather we ourselves are visible within this sphere of visibility: "my seeing body subtends my visible body, and all the visibles with it. There is a reciprocal insertion and intertwining (*entrelacs*) of one with the other."[124]

In this text, Merleau-Ponty attempts to express this "intertwining" of visible and vision, of "sensed body" (*corps senti*) and sensing body (*corps sentant*), which is for him at the heart of his ontological monism of *flesh*. He speaks of our vision "palpating" (literally touching) the visible[125] and of the seer as "incorporated" into the visible in what is a genuine incarnation. Similarly, with regard to touch, there is also an intertwining: my hand, felt from within, is "also accessible from without."[126] There is an internal "synergy" in the senses such that I can, for instance, feel myself touching and being touched at the same time.[127] It is as though there is a "pre-established" harmony between seer and the visible. It is "flesh offered to flesh."[128] Flesh (*la chair*) is, for Merleau-Ponty, an "ultimate notion . . . not the union or compound of two substances but thinkable in itself."[129] Flesh, moreover, is essentially characterized by reversibility, and in this regard Merleau-Ponty takes up the exemplary case of one hand touching the other (and fingers touching) to confirm reversibility as an essential characteristic not just of touch but of sensibility as such. For Merleau-Ponty there is a circle or circuit of touching and touched; and similarly there is a circle of seeing and the visible.[130] There is, furthermore, an intertwining between the senses, an "inscription of touching in the visible, of the seeing in the tangible—and the converse."[131] Merleau-Ponty writes:

> When one of my hands touches the other, the world of each opens upon that of the other because the operation is reversible at will, be-

cause they both belong (as we say) to one sole space of consciousness, because one sole man touches one sole thing through both hands.[132]

Merleau-Ponty claims the unity of the experience of both hands is akin to the unity of both eyes. Our consciousness is sustained by the prereflective, preobjective unity of my body.[133] Moreover, what unifies my body is also that which opens my body to the experience of others' bodies. Two human subjects' bodies touch each other in a handshake[134] and this reversibility is already prefigured in the single subject. The world is actually an "intercorporeal being"; my body "couples" with the "flesh of the world."[135] Merleau-Ponty finds this embodiment and reversibility in other areas, especially, in the coupling of vocalization and being heard. I can hear my own voice; I can listen to myself speaking. He takes reversibility to be indicative of human being-in-the-world. This reversibility has within it a certain distantiation. I cannot ever completely coincide with my self in the act of self-touching, rather I have a presence to myself which at the same time indicates the absence of self ("*une presence à Soi qui est absence de soi*").

In the late Merleau-Ponty, "intercorporeality,"[136] with its flesh-touching-flesh scenario, is part of a new ontology that replaces traditional subject-object dualism. Merleau-Ponty speaks of this reversibility as always "imminent" and never in fact consummated or "realized in fact."[137] When one hand touches the other, there is never complete coincidence; the experiences do not completely overlap. There is a "hiatus" between the touching hand and the touched. For Merleau-Ponty, there is a "chiasm," an intertwining, between touch and sight, such that neither is prior to the other (except, perhaps, when one of them is dysfunctional).

For Merleau-Ponty, the reversibility that for Husserl constitutes the essence of touch also characterizes seeing and visibility and indeed sensuous incorporation in general (including the incorporation of the voice). As Merleau-Ponty puts it, the relation between the seeing and the seen is a "remarkable variant" of that between the touching and the touched. According to Merleau-Ponty, the eye is as "close to" the visible as the hand is to the tangible, so close that, like the hand, it virtually palpates things within its own medium of light, shadow, and distance. The focusing of the eye reaches out as it were to embrace light, to touch the light that touches it, the light that envelops the visible things. Merleau-Ponty writes:

There is a relation of my body to itself which makes it the vinculum of the self and things. When my right hand touches my left, I am aware of it as a "physical thing." But at the same moment, if I wish, an extraordinary event takes place: here is my left hand as well starting to perceive my right, *es wird Leib, es empfindet*. The physical thing becomes animate. Or, more precisely, it remains what it was (the event does not enrich it), but an exploratory power comes to rest upon or dwell in it. Thus I touch myself touching: my body accomplishes "a sort of reflection." In it, through it, there is not just the unidirectional relationship of the one who perceives to what he perceives. The relationship is reversed, the touched hand becomes the touching hand, and I am obliged to say that the sense of touch here is diffused into the body—that the body is a "perceiving thing," a "subject-object."[138]

Note that in this passage Merleau-Ponty is directly quoting Husserl's *Ideas* II: *es wird Leib, es empfindet*[139]—in relation to body (*Körper*) *becoming animate* (*Leib*), and also in recognizing that the doubling and reflexivity of the senses is already a "kind of reflexion" (*eine Art von Reflexion*).[140]

In his 1961 essay "Eye and Mind," Merleau-Ponty emphasizes the "interlacing" (*l'interlacs*) between seer in the seen and vice-versa.[141] There is an essential "undividedness" (*l'indivision*)[142] between sensing and sensed (and, as Merleau-Ponty will suggest, between thinking and self-reflection). Without a body that can reflect itself in touching and seeing "there would be no humanity." The double sensation has now become a cipher for the reflexivity of consciousness and an essential trait of humanity itself.

Conclusion

Husserl's remarkably detailed and innovative accounts of sensuous perception and specifically of the nature of touch and its priority for embodiment (*Leiblichkeit*) provided the ground for Merleau-Ponty's more speculative metaphysical elaboration of the flesh. For Husserl, touch and vision combine to form the unified field of perception, but the kinaesthetic field, itself belonging primarily to touch, gives touch a certain "primacy." Furthermore, Husserl presents the phenomenon of the "double sensation" as unique to touch and as highlighting the role of touch in the constitution of the body as *Leib*. His Göttingen student David Katz expanded in great empirical detail on the senses of touch and vision and the parallels between them, and his charting of the relations between touch and sight had a deep effect on Merleau-Ponty especially when he was writing *Phenomenology of Perception*. Whereas Sartre, in *Being and Nothingness* (1943), rejects the double sensation as a merely contingent feature of our embodiment,[143] Merleau-Ponty gives the double sensation ontological significance in his late works, including "The Philosopher and His Shadow" (1959), "Eye and Mind" (1961), in the chapters of the posthumously published *Visible and Invisible* (1964), and the associated *Working Notes* (1959–1961). For Merleau-Ponty, this phenomenon of "intertwining" and "reversibility" introduces a new ontological paradigm of flesh, overcoming Cartesian dualism of mind and body, and expresses the condition he calls "intercorporeity" (*l'intercorporéité*).[144]

The phenomenology of touch and of intertwining continues to be a topic of discussion in Jean-Luc Nancy, Jacques Derrida, Luce Irigaray, and others.[145] Irigaray, for instance, implausibly in my view, accuses Merleau-Ponty of absorbing touch into sight,[146] whereas in fact he takes the reversibility that Husserl finds peculiar to flesh to apply to all aspects of incorporation. It is absolutely not a question of giving priority to the visible. Rather Merleau-Ponty is focusing on vision to show that the intertwining occurs there also and not just in touch: "my body sees only because it is a part of the visible";[147] "the visible takes hold of the look."[148] Indeed, Merleau-Ponty is trying to reconceive vision as a kind of touch; he is precisely *not* prioritizing vision over touch. Merleau-Ponty complained that everything "we say and think about vision has to make a thought of it."[149] In one of his late *Notes de travail*, commenting on Descartes's *Dioptrics*, he especially criticizes Descartes for tracing back seeing into the mind so that all that remains is the *thought* of seeing,[150] "contracted into a metaphysical point." The opposite is the case, Merleau-Ponty writes:

> For finally we know no vision but that by a composite substance (*substance composée*), and it is this subtilized vision (*cette vision subtilisée*) that we call thought—if being is to disclose itself, it will do so before a transcendence, and not before an intentionality, it will be the engulfed brute being that returns to itself (*l'être brut enlisé qui revient à lui-même*), it will be the sensible that hollows itself out (*le sensible qui se creuse*).[151]

It is this "hollowing out" of the sensible in its incorporated self-reflexive intertwining with its unity and distantiation (*l'écart*) that truly characterizes human being-in-the-world as flesh, and which is better captured, according to Merleau-Ponty, by painting rather than technicized science.

Husserl's careful prying apart of the layers of sense-constitution at the level of prereflective embodied sensibility needs to be revisited. In particular, his account of the role of kinaesthetic sensations in the constitution of the perceived object needs a considerable amount of elaboration and updating. An especially challenging issue is whether the sense of touch has profiles, horizons, and backgrounds, in the same manner as vision. It may very well be that further exploration will continue to confirm and enrich Husserl's original breakthrough. What is undeniable is that, through the elaborations of Katz and the transformations of Merleau-Ponty, Husserl's phenomenology of embodied perception had a remarkable influence on twentieth-century studies of vision, touch, and incorporation in general.

Biodiversity and the Diacritics of Life

TED TOADVINE

Contestation over the line between life and death is perhaps the defining problem of contemporary philosophy no less than of today's politics. From chemical weapons to drones to climate change, we confront negotiations over what counts as life as well as over the right, or the authority, to end it, if not also the responsibility to preserve it. The stakes are real in these efforts to mark off a singular line between life and death, the living and the nonliving, what will live and what will die, what is living within us and what is not. Yet as Derrida reminds us, with particular attention to a privileged site of this contestation, the putative limit between Man and Animal, there is always a "heterogeneous multiplicity" of the living, a "multiplicity of the organizations of relations between living and dead, relations of organization or lack of organization among realms that are more and more difficult to dissociate by means of the figures of the organic and inorganic, of life and/or death." No singular line divides the living from the dead because these very terms are simultaneously "intimate and abyssal," nonobjectifiable, irreducible to simple exteriority.[1] To this insight, that the relations between life and death are never a simple exteriority of terms, we must also add Agamben's recognition that our humanity is itself a production of these negotiations between life and death, that *homo sapiens* is in fact a machine for producing the human through a set of mirrors by which we recognize a reflection of ourselves in the animal that we are not and thereby constitute ourselves as human through its exclusion.[2] This is why the phenomenology of animality, from Husserl through Heidegger to Merleau-Ponty, has always focused on and delimited the animal dimension *of the human being*, attending to *our own* share of "bare life," rather than to an investigation of the lives of nonhuman others on their own terms.[3]

This complication of the problem of life destabilizes phenomenology itself, since phenomenology can only begin from a certain differentiation between experience and objective events, the intentional and the merely causal, or between sense and non-sense. As Derrida again has shown us, phenomenology always begins from and assumes a certain auto-affection, a certain self-presence, to the exclusion of whatever exceeds or refuses such presencing. And perhaps the consequence of this is a certain silencing of phenomenology. Yet this silencing may not be the opposite of speaking, and perhaps the auto-affection of phenomenology does not exclude a certain hetero-affection, an encounter with what can only be presented excessively and in its very refusal of our terms.[4] If this is so, a phenomenology that can express the heterogeneous relations between life and death in their carnal manifestation may provide a distinctive opportunity, and bear a singular responsibility, in the effort to renegotiate our sense of animality, humanity, and life.

This question of how to think life without thereby setting it up as the opposite of nonlife, of recognizing its auto-affection without refusing hetero-affection, is at stake in the ubiquitous charge to preserve "biodiversity." Since its introduction in the mid-1980s, the concept of biodiversity has dominated public perceptions of the value of nature as well as conservation research and policy on an international scale, with endorsements that span from Pope John Paul II to the World Wildlife Fund.[5] The international influence and reach of the concept is exemplified by the 1992 United Nations Convention on Biological Diversity, which specifies the "conservation of biological diversity" as a primary goal, and the UN's declaration of 2011–2020 as the Decade on Biodiversity, which embraces the strategic aim of integrating biodiversity values into all levels of government decision-making and "mainstreaming" biodiversity across government, society, and economy. In a matter of decades, biodiversity has become the leading buzzword for environmentalism. This popular success is very much in keeping with the intentions of those scientists and conservationists who first introduced the concept for propaganda purposes. As David Takacs notes in his interviews with many of those involved, "Scientists who love the natural world forged the term *biodiversity* as a weapon to be wielded" in the battle over public opinion about natural resources.[6] The success of their efforts is reflected in the immense investment of resources into the biological study and management application of biodiversity in the intervening decades, so much so that ecological research since the late 1980s may well be described, in David Tilman's words, as the "biodiversity revolution."[7]

Yet despite biodiversity's resonance within the public imaginary, it is far from obvious that this concept can live up to its reputation.[8] In the scientific context, biodiversity is currently defined as the diversity or variability of life at all levels, in a broadly inclusive sense.[9] But there is a growing consensus among scientists and environmental philosophers that biodiversity in this broad sense is not empirically tractable in a way that could be applied in specific management contexts.[10] Furthermore, the long-standing assumptions about the relationship between biodiversity and different kinds of ecosystem functioning, such as the diversity-stability hypothesis (that greater diversity leads to greater ecosystem stability), have not been borne out by the scientific research. Although to date at least 400 studies have attempted to link biodiversity and ecosystem function, these studies are very limited in scope. Nearly all focus on just one component of biodiversity (species richness), they tend to work with species assemblages that are easy to manipulate experimentally (e.g., terrestrial annual plants), and most have been conducted at very small scales of space and time (relative to the scale of ecosystems). Furthermore, many of these studies have been fraught with experimental design problems. Consequently, empirical evidence for a clear, consistent and general relationship between biodiversity and any aspect of ecosystem functioning is very thin, leading biological ecologists Diane Srivastava and Mark Vellend to conclude that studies of the relationship between biodiversity and ecosystem function have "little to offer in the way of practical advice for conservation managers."[11]

More importantly, the popular justifications for attributing ethical value to biodiversity have been shown to suffer serious flaws. In *What's So Good about Biodiversity?*, Donald Maier examines what he takes to be the most promising of these arguments and finds them "mostly so fragile that they crumble before modest scrutiny."[12] In fact, he reports being stunned that he could not find "a single argument that does not have serious logical flaws, crippling qualifications, or indefensible assumptions."[13] The self-described aim of his book, then, is to "declare the Emperor naked" in the hopes of saving what is truly valuable in nature from the harms to which it is increasingly subjected through the application of this misguided concept.[14]

Such critiques of the received concept of biodiversity raise the question of whether we do, in fact, value life for its diversity per se. This is a distinct question from whether we value particular species, however rare, or particular ecosystems, whatever their characteristics. The question is rather whether we value—for its own sake—the *differences between* the countless manifestations of life on all scales. There are numerous well-known arguments for the normative force of biodiversity that have tried to make the case that we do or should value life's differences, and it is just such arguments that Maier has catalogued and critiqued. Under his descriptions, the biodiversity project begins to look suspiciously like the reduction of nature to a "catalog of biota and biota-related entities" that have been "sliced and diced in strategic and tractable ways" for the purposes of scientific investigation and, perhaps ultimately, for economic evaluation.[15] But in rejecting this biotic inventory approach, Maier also sets aside anything like a value for the difference or variability of life as such. So the question remains: Why do the *differences* within and between forms of life matter? An answer to this question depends, first of all, on how we understand these differences—that is, on whether there is an alternative conception of the variability of life to the slice-and-dice model rejected by Maier. I propose such an alternative here under the rubric of "biodiacritics," inspired in part by the "diacritical hermeneutics" advanced by Richard Kearney. Hermeneutics, for Kearney, concerns the "practice of discerning indirect, tacit or allusive meanings, of sensing another sense beyond or beneath apparent sense."[16] And Kearney already notes that hermeneutics in this sense involves "interpreting plural meaning in response to the polysemy of language *and life*."[17] There are many senses of "diacritical" at play here for Kearney, but a significant one hearkens back to the medical practice of diagnosing bodily symptoms, that is, of *dia-krinein* as "reading the body," reading its differences as they negotiate the lines between life and death. For Kearney, such diacritical reading culminates in a "carnal hermeneutics" that definitively carries us beyond the human, extending, he claims, to "diacritical readings of different kinds of Others—human, animal or divine. All with skins on."[18]

My aim is to explore here in more detail what form such a diacritical hermeneutics of life, a biodiacritics, might take. To do so, I turn to a source that I share with Kearney, namely, the diacritical account of language, perception, and ontology that Merleau-Ponty developed, starting in the 1950s, on the basis of his readings of Saussure and Valéry. For Merleau-Ponty, the key insight of diacritical difference is that it describes a system consisting only of differences without positive terms. He presents this notion of the diacritical with respect to language in the opening lines of his 1952 essay, "Indirect Language and the Voices of Silence":

> What we have learned from Saussure is that, taken singly, signs do not signify anything, and that each one of them does not so much express a meaning as mark a divergence of meaning between itself and other signs. Since the same can be said for all other signs, we

may conclude that language is made of differences without terms; or more exactly, that the terms of language are engendered only by the differences which appear among them."[19]

Language is a system of differences without terms, but it hangs together as a system nonetheless, embodying what Merleau-Ponty calls a "unity of coexistence, like that of the sections of an arch which shoulder one another."[20] Merleau-Ponty increasingly comes to recognize that this notion of diacritical difference as a unity without positive terms applies not only to language but equally to perception and ultimately to ontology as such. As Emmanuel Alloa has argued, the famous ontology of flesh that Merleau-Ponty proposes in his final works can be understood as the culmination of this extension of the concept of the diacritical.[21] Starting from some hints in Merleau-Ponty's own remarks about life, I suggest that the diacritical perspective captures a certain phenomenological insight into the experience of life as difference—not only, that is, as variability between a ready-made catalog of tractable units, but difference all the way down. Far from eliminating any sense of life's unity, though, a diacritical notion of life articulates our sense that life hangs together, that it has a "unity of coexistence"—like the sections of an arch—without this unity requiring anything like the Clementsian harmony of nature that has been so roundly rejected. From here, we can also then explore the specifically hermeneutical task of biodiacritics, that is, its attention to the other sense "beyond or beneath apparent sense." Most importantly, such a hermeneutics reveals the immemorial temporal dimension of our relationship to diacritical life. It is precisely insofar as life, in its diacritical structure, institutes an evolving history or even a figured memory—a memory that embraces us as living creatures—that it commands our respect and hospitality.

To understand what is at stake in "biodiacritics," we begin with the diacritical account of language, perception, and ontology advanced by Merleau-Ponty, who introduces the phrase "diacritical difference" to name the Saussurian insight that language consists only of differences without positive terms. Already at the level of language, this has interesting implications. First, it implies a reversal in our usual way of thinking about the relation between identity and difference, which is that we begin by identifying relevant subsisting units—sentences, words, phonemes—and on this basis determine their differential relations.[22] Merleau-Ponty's reversal suggests that differences do not presuppose identities; rather, difference precedes and constitutes identity.[23] As he admits, "this is a difficult idea," even a paradox comparable to those of Zeno, since it seems that we would already need to know a language in order to learn it.[24] But it is this paradoxical circle that properly defines language as an instance of diacritical difference, since language, "in the presence of those who are learning it, precedes itself, teaches itself, and suggests its own deciphering."[25] It can do so only through its internal distribution of differences, which is what the child enters into through the process of babbling, or what the reader encounters when learning the experimental grammar and vocabulary of, say, a modernist novel. Language is "far less a table of statements which satisfy well-formed thoughts than a swarm of gestures all occupied with differentiating themselves from one another and blending again."[26] This means that we can only learn a language by immersing ourselves in it and allowing its self-differentiation to play through us, through our bodily gestures, including the gestures of the vocal cords. It is through our corporeal mimicry of a language's style, its manner of segregation and precipitation, that a new register is opened for expression. One cannot learn a language piecemeal, then, but only by a total immersion into the play of differences that constitutes its expressive capacity.

Second, even though language is a swarm of differences, it maintains an effective unity precisely because it functions to express, to say something. And it is because language succeeds in expressing, that is, because we do speak and understand one another, that we know that its paradoxical circularity is only a theoretical problem. This unity of coexistence is possible precisely because language is not a collection of pre-existing units but a whole that differentiates itself, such that each node within this web consists fundamentally of its references to the rest. "It is the whole that possesses meaning, not each part,"[27] as Merleau-Ponty says, and yet there is an "immanence of the whole in the parts"[28] defined by each moment's reflection of its divergence in relation to all others. Furthermore, this system is in a constant ferment that incorporates semantic slippages and contingencies of all sorts, putting them into play to enrich its own expressive possibilities, and thereby converting the accidental into the meaningful and the rational.[29] Merleau-Ponty calls this creative ferment "originary" or "primary" differentiation, an "inexhaustible power of differentiating" that leaves in its trail the sedimentations that we call words, syllables, and letters.[30]

We must nevertheless resist the temptation to think of this system as a thing, or as an assemblage of things, which is a temptation born of language's own tendency to cover its tracks as it leads us toward what it expresses. The meaning is in the whole, but it is not localizable, and certainly not in the sounds you hear or in the words on the page, which are only the traces that the process of differentiation has left in its wake. The meaning of an expression is not contained in the words but rather at their intersections and in the intervals between them, in their absences and folds.[31]

Meaning requires these interruptions and intervals, just as the words on the page require space between them, or as the phrases that we utter require the punctuations of silence. We typically overlook the intervals, as well as the words, in favor of what we are speaking about, just as we see without ever giving notice to our eyes or to vision's regular interruption by their blinking. The third interesting consequence of the diacritical perspective, then, is that language is essentially indirect and allusive, precisely because its meaning rests in the intervals of difference. Merleau-Ponty goes so far as to say that all language is fundamentally silence.[32] He is speaking here not of the sedimented words that populate dictionaries, which have perhaps become sufficiently fossilized to be affixed with a label, but rather of the event of expression as originary differentiation, where a "lateral or oblique" meaning begins to form among and between the jostling edges of words.[33] It is when language is at its most expressive that it most keeps silent. And this returns us to Kearney's definition of hermeneutics as the practice of "discerning indirect, tacit or allusive meanings, of sensing another sense beyond or beneath apparent sense." Rather than reading or listening past the silences, such a hermeneutics cultivates a listening-between; it gives an ear to the silent call between the words.

Thus far, we have only considered the diacritics of language, but for Merleau-Ponty this account will also apply, in its own fashion, to the sensible world and the sensing body. In a note titled "Perception and Language" from October 1959, he writes:

> I describe perception as a diacritical, relative, oppositional system—the primordial space as topological (that is, cut out in a total voluminosity which surrounds me, in which I am, which is behind me as well as before me . . .). . . . But there is all the same this difference between perception and language, that I *see* the perceived things and that the significations on the contrary are invisible. . . . [T]he only thing finally that is seen in the full sense is the totality wherein the sensibles are cut out.[34]

As this note already intimates, the sensible and language, or the visible and the invisible, turn out to be the primary axes of Merleau-Ponty's later ontology, the ontology of flesh. And Merleau-Ponty arrives at this ontology by following through the implications of diacritical difference that he first describes in the linguistic field.

This development is already at work in the recently published lectures from his 1953 course, *Le Monde sensible et le monde de l'expression*, where we find the following note: "Consider sensation itself, the act of sensing, as the intervention of a figure on a ground. Modulation. As a sound modulates silence. As a color modulates an open space by varying it. Every sign is diacritical."[35] The reference here to sensation as always involving a figure on a ground should remind us of Merleau-Ponty's earlier descriptions of perception as always having a gestalt structure. What I see, hear, or smell must stand out against a background; it must differentiate itself from a level that is taken as the norm. And we should also notice that this figure-ground structure is essentially differential: the figure can only be determined in relation to a ground *that it is not*, and it becomes a figure only by differentiating itself from the ground. If a figure-on-a-ground is the simplest moment of perception, then perception can have no positive or self-identical terms. The ontology of gestalts that Merleau-Ponty had proposed in his very first book, *The Structure of Behavior*, is already, then, an ontology of difference. But, with diacritics, we move beyond a nested hierarchy of figure-ground structures to recognize that each node or each fold within the system echoes the modulations of all the others, and that such foldings incessantly institute new levels and dissolve old ones, pell-mell, entangled, baroque. And this is precisely the insight of the diacritical system to which Merleau-Ponty will, in the end, give the name "flesh." As he writes in a note from December 1959,

> Replace the notions of concept, idea, mind, representation with the notions of dimensions, articulation, level, hinges, pivots, configuration—The point of departure = the critique of the usual conception of the *thing* and its *properties* . . . critique of *positive* signification (differences between significations), signification as a gap . . . founded on this diacritical conception.[36]

As we can begin to see here, diacritical difference institutes its own internality, its own immanence; it has a kind of "for itself," which would not be that of consciousness as it is classically understood in terms of auto-affection—that is, as pure presence to itself—but would instead be a "for itself" through auto-divergence, though a kind of incessant differentiation and deferral.

One way to think about Merleau-Ponty's aim here, as David Morris has compellingly argued, is as the effort to avoid confusing being with determinate being. For Morris, "[Merleau-Ponty's] concepts of structure, expression, the invisible of the visible, and écart variously seek to avoid this error by conceptualizing being as engendering determinacy—yet not from any already determinate sense."[37] And Morris is attentive to the way that this releasing of being from determinacy will demand a new thinking of the biological, since (in his words), "the presumption [of determinate being] is repeated in current views that determinate organisms must have already determinate developmental causes or 'programs,' or the deeper, typical view that even an evolutionary cosmology at bottom turns on already determinate information, matter, law, etc."[38] The diacritical perspective avoids such determinacy precisely because it is differentiation and deferral all the way down, precisely because it is primordially the emergence and dissolution of intervals and spacings. And this is arguably why Merleau-Ponty insists that fundamental ontology can only proceed indirectly or negatively. As his much-cited note from February 1959 puts it, "*One cannot make a direct ontology.* My 'indirect' method (being in the beings) is alone conformed with being—'negative philosophy' like 'negative theology.'"[39]

Let us return, then, to the specific question of what this means for a possible biodiacritics, that is, for a diacritical conception of life. For a start, recall Heidegger's lesson that life is not a discovery of biology, but rather something that biology—to the extent that life is its subject matter—must always presuppose. Heidegger explains the matter as follows in the third volume of his lectures on Nietzsche:

> As a science, all biology already presupposes a more or less explicitly drawn essential delimitation of appearances that constitute its realm of objects. This realm . . . is that of living beings. Underlying the delimitation of this realm there is again a preconception of what distinguishes and sets apart living beings as such, namely, life. The essential realm in which biology moves can itself never be posited and grounded by biology as a science, but can always only be presupposed, adopted, confirmed.[40]

Now, whether it remains true that the science of biology today in its varied interdisciplinary forms—for instance, molecular biology or biogeochemistry—presuppose any sense of "life" as their focal realm is open to debate. But Heidegger's point is that a pre-theoretical experience of life, life as a phenomena, precedes any biological investigation of living things and cannot be derived from it. And, whether or not contemporary biology addresses itself to "life," human beings certainly continue to do so, particularly insofar as life challenges us to respond to it with a proper hospitality.

Our suggestion, then, is that this pre-theoretical understanding of life is fundamentally diacritical, not unlike our pre-theoretical immersion into the sensible and the linguistic fields. And although his remarks concerning the diacritics of life are brief and condensed, we can already locate a proposal along these lines in the notes for Merleau-Ponty's 1959–1960 course on the concept of nature, where we find the following:

Life is not a separable thing, but an investment, a singular point, a hollow in Being, an invariant ontological relief . . . the establishment of a level around which the divergences begin forming, a kind of being that functions like an arch. . . . But life is not negativity: it is a pattern of negations, a system of opposition that means that what is not this, is that.[41]

It is probably unnecessary to recall that it is precisely this example of the arch, the stones that hold each other up without any external support, by which Merleau-Ponty first characterizes the diacritical difference of language years earlier. Now, as we have already mentioned, this figure of the arch suggests a kind of "hanging together," a sort of unity of interdependence, or what Merleau-Ponty himself calls a "unity of coexistence." And this seems comparable to the hanging together typically associated, at least in the popular mind, with ecology. For instance, deep ecologist Arne Naess writes that "The study of ecology indicates an approach, a methodology which can be suggested by the simple maxim 'all things hang together.'"[42] This "hanging together" may sound dangerously close to the organicist conception of ecology put forward at the beginning of the twentieth century by Henry Cowles and Frederic Clements, which would later inspire the popularized notion of ecology as a science of interdependence, balance, and harmony. When A.G. Tansley proposed the concept of "ecosystem" in the 1930s, it was with the explicit intention of replacing such organicism with a model of biotic and abiotic interactions purely in terms of the material exchange of energy and nutrients.[43] One virtue of biodiacritics is that it makes room for the hanging-together of life while avoiding both the finalism of the Clementsian superorganism and the reductionism of Tansley's ecosystem. On the diacritical view, what joins the different nodes and folds of life is nothing more than the intervals or gaps that constitute them; each implies the whole and therefore hangs together with the whole insofar as its own identity is the determinate negation of every other moment within that whole. Just as a gestalt joins figure with ground precisely insofar as it differentiates them, so biodiacritics connects every level and aspect of life as moments of its own dehiscence. And there is nothing metaphysically mysterious about this sense of hanging-together through difference rather than identity, since it is what we rely upon constantly in the case of language and perception. More generally, the superorganism and the ecosystem are both models for thinking life that start from determinate being, which makes them incapable of grasping the emergence of determinacy from the primordially indeterminate process of differentiation itself. What escapes them both, in other words, is that life's self-differentiation is a process of *expression*, that is, of the auto-production of sense.[44] It is because this auto-production of sense has no transcendent guide or invisible hand that it can incorporate into its movement, just as does language, all manner of accidents, and historical contingencies.

Evolutionary biologist George Williams compellingly makes this case in relation to the eye, that favorite of intelligent design theorists from William Paley to the present. The vertebrate eye achieves its function quite marvelously, but rather than offering an example of intelligent design, Williams argues, it is actually rather stupidly designed, given the functionally arbitrary and even downright maladaptive features that it must overcome, such as the inversion of the retina, which requires light to pass through the nerves and blood cells before reaching the rods and cones, and the placement of the optic nerve on the wrong side of the sensing layer, so that it must pass through a hole in the retina to reach the brain. This hole in the retina is the cause for our so-called "blind spot."[45] Now, there are many examples of such "maladaptive historical legac[ies]," according to Williams, and every organism manifests features that are functionally arbitrary or maladaptive. But the point is that, just as language converts contingency into meaning by orienting itself toward the task of expressing, so evolution transmutes the lead of historical contingency into the gold of a functioning organism—into an eye that, despite its inherited blind spot, serves to see.

Neo-Darwinists will, of course, emphasize natural selection as the primary mechanism for this transmutation, and certainly fitness operates as a negative constraint; it weeds out what is not sufficiently adapted to survive. But as Williams's own examples show, life involves a productivity in excess of mere utility. As Merleau-Ponty puts it, "Life is not only an organization for survival; there is in life a prodigious flourishing of forms, the utility of which is only rarely attested to and that sometimes even constitutes a danger for the animal."[46] It is this "prodigious flourishing" of sense, as the auto-production of meanings generated through difference, that biodiacritics brings into focus. Quoting Merleau-Ponty again, "life is not uniquely submitted to the principle of utility, and there is a morphogenesis that has expression as its purpose."[47] Expression is the key term here, and this is what finds no place in the Neo-Darwinian account. On this point, biodiacritics rejoins the recent work of Elizabeth Grosz, who argues that "art and nature, art in nature, share a common structure: that of excessive and useless production—production for its own sake, production for the sake of profusion and differentiation."[48] Life evolves, elaborating and articulating itself, only because, like language, it creates its own conditions for fermentation, only because it too is fundamentally a primordial principle of differentiation. Grosz focuses in particular on the excessiveness introduced by sexual difference and the selections to which it gives rise, selections that precisely reward what can stand out and be noticed, what appeals and attracts, so that for her sexual selection's production of the pleasurable cuts across the grain of natural selection's bias toward utility. Sexuality is not primarily about reproduction but instead "a fundamentally dynamic, awkward, mal-adaptation that enables the production of the frivolous, the unnecessary, the pleasing, the sensory for their own sake."[49] While Grosz seems correct to emphasize the new dimensions of expression that sexual difference opens, we must also account for the expressive productivity that makes the institution of sexual difference itself possible. What I have termed biodiacritics is precisely the primordial, expressive ferment that produces all such differences, sexual difference included.

Our description so far should help us to measure the distance between biodiacritics and the received concept of biodiversity. The word biodiversity typically inspires us to imagine a natural setting populated with visually obvious variation, the maximally diverse grouping of species that we can picture together. Voila, biodiversity! But this particular place, with these particular species, is not equivalent to their diversity. To arrive at their diversity, we must first determine our level of analysis—genetic, taxonomic, ecosystemic—and within that level the composition, structure, or function under consideration. In short, we need to identify units and then measure how many we have and how different they are from each other. But notice that, once we have shifted to a consideration of the differences as such—to the biodiversity as such—we are no longer concerned with these particular individuals, or even these particular genes, species, or ecosystems. Indeed, we could swap out one for another and maintain the same level of diversity; we might even increase the diversity if the one that we swap in is more different from the others than the one removed. So, the first point is that biodiversity, as the differences between the units under consideration, is not to be confused with the units themselves; and preserving a certain degree of biodiversity does not guarantee preserving any particular species, or gene, or ecosystem.[50] In fact, the loss of any one species in particular, from the perspective of biodiversity in general, across its many levels and categories, is relatively insignificant.

While biodiversity is a measure of difference, the difference at stake here is not comparable to what we have been calling diacritical difference, as the example of swapping out one unit for another makes clear. This is because biodiversity presupposes the identity of the units in question; it treats this identity as independent of the differences that these units have from each other or the whole. In other words, the measurement of diversity presupposes determinate being. But the point of diacritical difference is that difference precedes identity, that the play of indeterminate difference is generative of determinacy. On this understanding, each node in the web of difference—each gene, each species, each ecosystem—is what it is only in terms of its immanently articulated difference from all of the others. Its differing from each of them in specific and concrete ways is what makes it salient as the particular node or fold within the whole that it instantiates. Each moment emerges like a figure from the complex ground of life as a whole, and so its identity bears a nonsubstitutable reference to this whole and to its situation within it. And so, from a diacritical perspective, the substitution of a single unit is a transformation of the whole and of all of the differential relations of which it is composed.

To put this another way, when biodiversity aims to measure difference, it inevitably obscures the intervals, the deferrals, the gaps by which biodiacritics is defined, since it takes determinate identities as its starting point. But as we have said, the expressive moment of differentiation is located precisely in such intervals. Life is located not in its units, but in the productive and expressive self-generation of the whole. And if we have some hesitations about the substitutability of any particular life for another, this may be because our pretheoretical intuitions about life reveal to us this manner of its hanging together. If we can adjust our sensibilities to consider the interval itself, to practice a hermeneutics of the "sense beyond or beneath apparent sense," we will see that the intervals are not merely spatial gaps, like blank spaces on a page, but that they are also temporal; they are, in fact, a form of memory. From the perspective of biodiversity, it is easy to forget one species in favor of another, since their differences are of a common coin. But, for biodiacritics, there can be no such forgetting.

Let me clarify this point by returning, first, to George Williams's account of evolutionary maladaptations. For Williams, the example of the eye illustrates the historicity of the evolutionary process, the fact that a particular historical legacy is written into the bodies of all living things. He offers us an evocative description of our own sense of loss when such an historical legacy vanishes from the earth:

The generation of diversity by cladogenesis [that is, by the differentiation of the phylogenetic tree] furnishes every population with a unique set of historical legacies. In this sense, an organism is a living record of its own history. . . . The loss of the Stellar sea cow and the Adam-and-Eve orchid were the same kind of loss to historical scholarship as the burning of the library at Alexandria. The current wholesale extinction of organisms is especially tragic and ironic because we are only now learning to read history in molecular struc-ture, where the writing may well prove clearer and more detailed than in morphology and other phenotypic end states.[51]

Williams's insight here is even more profound than he manages to articu-late. Each organism is a record of its own history because it embodies this history as a kind of corporeal memory, as a folding accumulation within it of the diacritical differences through which its ancestors became what they were, and through which it becomes what it is. This rejoins a similar insight from Elizabeth Grosz, drawing on Henri Bergson, when she writes that "life, even the simplest organic cell, carries its past with its present as no material object does."[52] Certainly Williams is correct that the vanishing of such memory is a great loss to knowledge. But more than this, since we are ourselves nodes within the diacritical structure of life, every such loss diminishes us as well; it reconfigures our own differential identities. The memory of *all* of life figures into the identity of *every moment* of life. It is precisely this kind of memory and loss that biodiversity indexes cannot measure. And it is this sense of loss that guides our intuitions about the irreplaceability of each form of life that is vanishing from the world.

If our account of biodiacritics is correct, then it is precisely in the folds of life, in its gaps and spacings, that the immemorial dimensions of its evolutionary and cosmic history are lodged.

Rather than compare each species to a book, or even to a library, it would be more appropriate to compare it with a language, since each species carries within it a unique reservoir of expressive possibilities that, although they exist as nothing more than virtual differences, embody a unique memory that is the dynamic legacy of their becoming. We know that, when a language is lost to the world and its last speakers fall forever silent, an entire cultural memory vanishes along with it, a whole world forever closes, and this loss is a diminishment of us all.[53] When a language vanishes, we lose not only something within the world, but the world it-self, the very opening up of the world. The same must be said about each living thing, which embodies in the folds of difference that constitute it an immemorial history that distinguishes its life from ours even as it com-pletes us. Extinction is therefore the loss of our own past, the redrawing of the differences that compose our own identity, not only in the present or the future, but in a prehistory to which our identities remain liable. What will we have become, what will life have become, when the prehistory that makes our very time possible is rewritten, when life's relationship with death is renegotiated immemorially? At stake in such renegotiation is not only the loss of a species but the very end of the world.

Divine Bodies

The Passion According to Teresa of Avila

JULIA KRISTEVA

Teresa of Avila (1515–1582) experienced and wrote about what we call mysticism at a time when Spain's glory and power—that of the Conquistadors and the Golden Age—began its decline. Erasmus and Luther were shaking up traditional beliefs; new Catholics such as the Alumbrados attracted Jews and women; the Inquisition banned books in Castilian; and trials to determine the "*limieza de sangre*" multiplied. The daughter of a "*christiana vieja*" and a "*converso*," Teresa, in her childhood, witnessed the case brought against her father's family in which they had to prove they were truly Christian and not Jewish. Teresa's own "case" as a nun practicing orison, the mental prayer of amorous fusion with God through which she experienced ecstasy, would be investigated by the Inquisition. But this was before the Counter Reformation discovered the extraordinary complexity of her experience as well as its usefulness to the Church, which sought to marry asceticism (demanded by the Protestants) to the intensity of the supernatural (propitious to popular faith). Teresa de Cepeda y Ahumada was beatified in 1614 (thirty-two years after her death), canonized in 1622 (a "saint" forty years after her death), and would become in 1970, in the wake of Vatican II, the first woman Doctor of the church, alongside Catherine of Sienna.

The Mystic and the Christian Faith

I will begin my account of her mystic experience by presenting two lines of thought of a more general, philosophical, and political nature.

The Catholic mystic—in its two apogees: first, in the twelfth century with the mystic Rhineland and second, following the Council of Trent and the Counter Reformation with, in particular, the Spanish saints, Teresa of Avila and her friend John of the Cross—is situated in *internal exclusion* to Catholicism: in its margins and yet at its heart. In this paradoxical position, the mystic is a bearer of in-depth anthropological knowledge, which a psychoanalytical reading can transform into clinical and semiological truth (by which I mean relative to sexual and linguistic economy). I shall focus on three elements of this knowledge-ignorance, which Teresa's experience pushes to a paroxysm and a clarity never before reached.

Intrinsic to Christianity is an unshakable faith in the existence of an Ideal Father and an absolute love for this loving Father, who would be, simply put, the foundation of the speaking subject. In turn, the speaking subject is none other than the subject of amorous discourse. This is the Father of *Agape* and *Amor*, but who is not *Eros*. "I love because I am loved, therefore I am" could be the syllogism of the believer, which Teresa acts out in her visions and ecstasies. Freud is far from rejecting the existence of this "loving father." He alludes to him in "The Ego and the Id" when he discovers the "primary identification" with the "father of individual prehistory" (not to be confused with the father of the collective prehistory of the "primal horde"); he possesses the qualities of "both parents" and identification with him is "*direkte und unmittelbare*" (direct and immediate). For the psychoanalyst this is but a variant of the "Oedipal father." On the other hand, in its ignorance of the Oedipus complex, the Christian faith only retains a de-eroticized love of and for the Father, as the foundation for the possibility of speaking, which exists if and only if the words spoken are words of love. We can go back to the "Song of Songs," as Teresa and other mystics did, to find the source of this copresence of word/love.

Nevertheless, this extreme idealization is only maintained in its pure state, and with an injunction to repression, by the Church's exoteric message. On the contrary, in her position of internal exclusion, the mystic constantly resexualizes idealization. Freud sheds light on this logic of alternation in the economy of drives: when the processes and excitation go over certain quantitative limits, they are eroticized or de-eroticized. Mystics, especially Teresa, experience this reversal; some, and our saint more than others, are actually able to name it. From here on the alternation between idealization/desexualization/resexualization and vice-versa transforms love for the Ideal Father into the nonstop frenzy of drives, a *passion for the Father, which turns out to be a sadomasochistic father-version*, a "*père-version*." Drastic fasting, penance, flagellation—often using bouquets of nettle on open wounds, convulsions even to the point of epileptic comas, which take advantage of vulnerable neuronal and hormonal states—these are just a few of the sadomasochistic extravagances that mark these ongoing "exiles of the self" in Him (to borrow one of Teresa's expressions) or this transference toward the Other (to use my terms). More than the "beaten child," and beyond him or her, it is the "beaten Father" that Christianity venerates in the Christ-like Passion with which the believer identifies. And, in an extreme manner, it similarly venerates the mystic in prayer. It is a gratifying way, if such a thing is possible, to support suffering humanity as well as the passive femininity in both sexes, and even sadomasochistic violence. Dostoevsky's remark "It's too idealistic and because of this, cruel" (cf. *Humiliated and Offended*) could sum up the mystical father-version/"*père-version*" and Teresa's own experience.

However, this incitement to suffering is appeased in Christianity by oral gratification: *the Eucharist* reconciles the believer with the beaten Father and, furthermore, it even attributes qualities of the good mother to the body of this Man of pain: "I" become myself by swallowing the Other. In the Middle Ages, numerous melancholics and anorexics flocked to the church to eat a sliver of the bleeding, mistreated body of the Man-God, which allowed them to subsist many years in a state of exaltation, in spite of their hunger, through oral *and* symbolic satisfaction. For having *made idealization-resexualization oral*, Christianity simultaneously made *the word* itself the ultimate object of desire and love: "Nothing entering a man from the outside can defile him but the things that come out of a man render the person unclean" (Matt. 15:11 and Mk 7:15). Teresa is not only conscious of this essential orality of her love for the Husband, endowed with maternal attributes, but she forcefully claims it, and with disarming ingenuity takes the plunge that leads from this God with breasts to the pleasure of saying, from the pleasure of nursing to verbal sublimation: "The soul said that it savored the milk flowing from God's breast," wrote the saint in her *Thoughts on God's Love*.[1] In the same breath she comments on the famous verse of the *Song of Songs* "May he kiss me with kisses of his lips," before punctuating: "These words can be understood in many ways . . . but the soul is not concerned with that. What it wants is to *pronounce it*" (*el alma no quiere ninguno, sine decir estas palabras*).[2] From the pleasure of nursing at the breast to the pleasure of saying: what is the difference? Is it not the same *jouissance*? Teresa is on her way to becoming a psychoanalyst. Consequently genitality disappears from her fantasies, for it is displaced and becomes the pleasure of rebirth through orality. This rebirth is doubly assured: by the cannibalistic identification with the beaten Father on the one hand and, on the other, the regaining of Time as a form of eternity of the word, which becomes the original object of desire (object "*a*"), a narration open to the infinite search for necessarily subjective meaning.

Teresa's Visions

These three aspects of the Christian faith that the mystic highlights—first, an ideal Father exists, Faith is the love of and for this father; second, this idealization resexualizes itself: the Father is a beaten father and I take pleasure alongside him in his castration and death; and third, I also identify with Him through the orality of the Eucharist and the word, a veritable creator of parthenogenesis, of a self-engendering of the Ego which opens Time and sublimation for me—provide a subtle and highly efficient device. One that at once provokes, accompanies, and modulates the accidents incurred by the untangling of drives, which is to say the dissociation of the erotic drive and the death instinct: somatization, perversion, sublimation.

One understands that in a libidinal system thus constituted, the feminine and the maternal are absorbed in the subject of sublimation's permanent gaining back of its demanding singularity. Duns Scotus's emphasis on the *ecceitas* was to formulate this culmination of Christian faith in truth, understood as singular and boundless. The experiences favored by this fulfillment will necessarily be *writing* (as a clarification of the experience) and *foundation* (political act which innovates institutional space and communal temporality). Teresa takes on the reform of her order as a shoeless Carmelite a short time after having begun the writing of *The Book of My Life* (1562). She continues to write while founding seventeen monasteries over a span of twenty years. In doing so, she shows herself to be "the most virile of monks"—"I am not a woman, I am hard-hearted," she wrote—while at the same time fervently defending feminine specificity: she held, for example, that women are more fit than men for practicing the spiritual exercise of prayer. She also fought against the Church's hierarchy and the royalty as an advocate of female monasticism. You can see that it is not "sexual difference" (a modern problem), but Teresa's very particular economy of sublimation, which is nevertheless dependent on the Catholic faith, which interests me here. As an introduction to Teresa's singular experience, I shall examine several aspects of her writing and visions.

The only girl in a family of seven boys (before the birth of the last two children, a girl and a boy), she was very attached to her mother and father, her brother Rodrigo, her uncle Pedro, and her cousin, the son of her other paternal uncle, Francisco, in a family with incestuous overtones. The family was well-to-do but eventually hit hard times. Teresa lost her mother at the age of thirteen. When she decided to become a Carmelite and donned the habit of the Convent of the Incarnation on November 2, 1536, she was twenty-one and her body was a battleground. She was caught between her *guilty desires*, which she only mentions in her *Life*, specifying that her confessors prohibited her from speaking about it and *idealizing exaltation* as shown by her intense devotion to Mary (Virgin Mother) and Joseph (symbolic father). With marvelous lucidity, she confides in her biography how these torments drove her to convulsions and a loss of consciousness sometimes followed by comas that lasted up to four days. The French epileptologist, Dr Pierre Vercelletto, like the Spaniard, E. Garcia-Albea diagnosed this as "temporal epilepsy."

These fits were accompanied by "visions" which the cloistered nun described as "auras"—not "sights" by the "eyes of the body," but which I would willingly call "incarnated fantasies"—in which all the senses perceive the enveloping, reassuring presence of the loving Husband. The ideal Father who persecutes her by making her hurt to the bone, is transformed into a loving father: Teresa succeeds where Shreber fails. God no longer judges her, or at least less and less, because he loves her.

The "visions" translate this saving alchemy. First of all, the "vision" is only a "severe face" disapproving of its overly offhand "visitors"; then it even becomes a "toad" that fattens without stop (perhaps an hallucination about the sex of the visitor?). Finally, it turns out to be the Man of Pain himself, such as the nun saw him in the statue of Christ in the convent's courtyard: a martyred man whose sufferings she delightfully identifies with.

Delighted is the word: Teresa is at last united with "Christ as man" (*Cristo como hombre*) and she appropriates him, "certain that the Lord was inside me" (*dentro de mi*). "I could not then doubt that he was in me or that I was myself lost in him" (*yo todo engolfada en el*).[3] The senses thus exalted end up canceling themselves out: the soul is incapable of "work," of anything but "abandon," an exquisite passivation in bliss: "One doesn't feel anything, we take pleasure without knowing what we're taking pleasure in";[4] "deprived even of feeling,"[5] "a kind of delirium."[6] It is a matter of the positive and negative, of *jouissance* and extreme pain, always the two together or alternating. The body is crushed and exiled in a fainting fit where the psyche is in turn shattered outside of the self, before the soul is able to begin the narration of this state of "loss." Teresa first tried out this narrative on her panicked and/or charmed confessors before writing it down and before they, Dominicans or Jesuits, authorized her to write. Later they insisted that she do so. The acme of these "visions" in which all the senses fuse and participate is found in the description of the Transfixion, depicted in marble by Bernini (1646) and which Lacan delighted in. I will cite it here:

> Oh, how often, when in this state, do I remember that verse of David: *Quemadmodum desiderat cervus ad fontes aquarum*, which I seem to see fulfilled literally in myself! . . . When these impulses are not very strong they appear to calm down a little, or, at any rate, the soul seeks some relief from them because it knows not what to do. . . . At other times the impulses are so strong that the soul is unable to do either this or anything else. The entire body contracts and neither arm nor foot can be moved. If the subject is on his feet, he remains as though transported and cannot even breathe: all he does is to moan—not aloud, for that is impossible, but inwardly, out of pain. It pleased the Lord that I should sometimes see the following vision. I would see beside me, on my left hand, an angel in bodily form. . . . He was not tall, but short, and very beautiful, his face so aflame that he appeared to be one of the highest types of angel who seem to be all afire. They must be those who are called cherubim. . . . In his hands I saw a long golden spear and at the end of the iron tip I seemed to see a point of fire. With this he seemed to pierce my heart several times so that it penetrated to my entrails. When he drew it out, I thought he was drawing them out with it and he left me completely afire with a great love for God. The pain was so sharp that it made me utter several moans; and so excessive was the sweetness caused me by this intense pain that one can never wish to lose it, nor will one's soul be content with anything less than God. It is not bodily pain, but spiritual, though the body has a share in it—indeed, a great share. But, when this pain of which I am now speaking begins, the Lord seems to transport the soul and to send it into an ecstasy, so that it cannot possibly suffer or have any pain because it immediately begins to experience fruition.[7]

Her "torture" is "bliss," and this amalgam of pleasure and auto-erotic pain unites in a spiritual *jouissance* or "fruition" as she says, a kind of massive masturbation well aware of the "corporal form" with lips hemmed in the ideals of the Bible and the Gospels. In this era radiating with the likes of Erasmus, the "Illuminated," and converted Jews and numerous women called "*alumbrados*," the *humanity of Christ* was in the air. Teresa's ecstasies are composed of words, images, physical sensations, mind and body, body and mind, all without distinction: "the body has a share in it: indeed, a great share." The experience is also dual: "object" of her transports, the Carmelite mystic is no less a "subject" as well, her "graces" and "raptures" are rendered with astonishing lucidity. Lost and found again, inside and out, and vice versa, Teresa is a fluid, a constant streaming of water, which is her element: "I have a particular attraction to this element and I have observed it with close attention." Her thought as well takes the form of a flowing metaphor.

The enigma of Teresa is less in her raptures than in the narrative she makes of them: do the raptures only exist in these narratives? Regardless of whether they were in fact bouts of epilepsy, what interests us is the filtering of shock, of the release of drives, through the sieve of Catholic code, in Teresa's Castilian language. It was this that both allowed for her biological survival and secured her place in our cultural memory. She is completely conscious of this. The Carmelite wrote of "making this fiction (*hacer esta fiction*) to be given for understanding."[8]

Teresa's "Fiction"

Regarding Teresa's "fiction," I will first examine the state her religion called ecstatic, which I would qualify as a *regression* to what Winnicott referred to as the "psyche-soma." I will then look at her use of the water metaphor, which I will explain is not a metaphor but a metamorphosis. Lastly, I will comment on her identification with the Divine she finds at the heart of her *Interior Castle*, in the seventh chamber. Thus I shall get to the heart of Teresa's paradox of a God that can only be found in the depths of the writer's soul.

Regression to the Psyche-Soma

Teresa began her "search" by a "suspension of powers" (as at the time, understanding, memory, and volition were called) to attain what must be referred to as a state of *regression* where the thinking individual loses the contours of her identity, and below the threshold of consciousness, becomes what could be called a "psyche-soma."[9] In this state—which for the psychoanalyst goes back to the archaic states of osmosis between the newborn, even the embryo, and its mother—the relation to self and other are fleetingly maintained by an elaborate infra-linguistic sensibility whose intensity is in direct proportion to the loss of the faculty for abstract judgment. Another kind of "thought" results from this, a non-thought, an underwater dive which the term "mind" does not convey as well as "sensorial representation" or the "psyche-soma": as if the reasoning "mind" went from *being in the world* to an "imaginary elaboration" inhabiting the entire body, to *touching-feeling the outside and the inside*, both its own physiological functions and the outside world, without the protection of "intellectual work" or the help of a judging conscience. D. W. Winnicott was surprised that we locate the "mind" in the brain while certain regressive states of his patients attested, he believed, to the fact that all the senses and organs participate in both self-perception and the perception of the world: that the psyche is body (soma) and the body (soma) is psyche.

How does one speak of the psyche-soma's self-perception in emotive states, as in the case of Teresa, Jesus's wife, or that of an intense transference with borderline personalities?

The Teresian style is continuously anchored in *images*, themselves meant to transmit *visions* which do not call on sight (or at least not sight alone), but inhabit the body-and-mind entirely, the psyche-soma. Firstly and essentially, such "visions" can only lend themselves to *touch*, *taste*, and *hearing* before transiting through *sight*. Let us say, therefore, that a *sensitive imaginary*,[10] rather than "imagery"—"imagination" or "images" in the scopic sense of the word—convokes *words* in Teresa's writings so that they become the equivalent of what Teresa *felt*. In turn, they put into play what is felt by her addressees: the confessors who demanded and encouraged these texts, her sisters who glorified her, and readers present and to come.

Metaphors, comparisons, or metamorphoses? How did Teresa appropriate the Castilian language to make it say that the love relation between a cloistered nun and her object of desire, *the other being*—inside the self and/or outside the self—is a *sensitive relation*? How does one speak in a contagious way of this otherness that separation in love makes her feel, but which can also fulfill her through love? This alterity is neither an abstract law, nor a spiritual vocation, nor a metaphysical worry, but is inevitably a call-and-answer, reciprocal and asymmetrical, between two living bodies in desirous contact? A bond between two contagious desires? Would it be an intimate illumination, or a resurgence of the evangelical theme of baptism? Or an act of loyalty to the spiritual alphabet of the "*alumbrado*" Francisco de Osuna who guides Teresa's mental prayers and whose *Third Spiritual Alphabet* abounds with images of water and oil to evoke the state of abandon (*dexamiento*), dear to the enlightened (*los Alumbrados*), and which this author readily likens to the newborn nursed by its mother? All these at once, no doubt, not to mention the more or less unconscious regression of the lover in love with her ideal Lord in an embryonic state, touched/bathed/nourished by amniotic fluid. The fact remains that the "image" of *water* comes straight away to Teresa's pen: "water is my element,"[11] she says.

At the same time she takes refuge in her *condition as a woman* by using it as an excuse for her ineptitude with "spiritual language" and for the "recreation" of resorting to "comparisons." Thus justified, she distinguishes between four types of prayer which she describes as "four waters" that water the garden of the person praying: the well, the water-wheel, the river, and rain.[12]

The Water Metaphor

From her writings, I gather that, for the cloistered nun, water signifies the link between the soul and the divine: an amorous relation that unites the dry earth of the Teresian garden with Jesus. Springing from the outside or the inside, active and passive, neither one nor the other and without confusing itself with the gardener's labor, water transcends the earth that I am and makes it other: a garden. I only become a garden through the touch of a vivifying medium: water. I am not water, because I am earth; but nor is water God, for he is the Creator. In our encounter, water is the fiction, the sensitive representation: it represents the space and time of body-to-body contact, the copresence and copenetration which makes being *living being*. For the fiction of water joins me to God without identifying me. It maintains the tension between us and, while filling me with the divine, it spares me the folly of confusing myself with it: water is my living protection, my vital element. Representing the reciprocating contact of God and His creature, water dethrones God of his suprasensitive status and brings him down, if not to the role of gardener, then at least to that of the cosmic element that I taste and that nourishes me, which touches me and that I touch.

Husserl said that "fiction constitutes the vital element of phenomenology as it does for all eidetic sciences."[13] From this we can gather that fiction "fertilizes" abstractions by using rich and exact sensorial elements transposed into clear images. Never perhaps has this value of fiction as a "vital element" for the "understanding of eternal truths" been as justified as in Teresa's use of water when putting her prayer states into words on paper. Hers is a telling example of this quest for sublimation through words aspiring to resexualize, by merging with, the experience of regression-amorous exaltation.

To put it differently, the word "water" not only represents the encounter of the "Earthwoman" saint with her heaven, but in the state of prayer, Teresa immerses herself above the barrier of word-signs in the psyche-soma. It's through her fiction (better and differently than with her epilepsy) that she escapes the "powers" (understanding, memory, imagination). Thus, that which remains "words" is no longer a "signifier-signified" separated from "referent-things," as is customary with "words-signs" in an exterior reality. On the contrary, prayer, which amalgamates the ego and the Other, also amalgamates the word and the thing: the speaking subject undergoes, or nearly undergoes a catastrophic mutism, the self "loses itself," "liquefies," "becomes delirious." Halfway between these two extremes, a thin membrane rather than a bar separates the word from the thing: they contaminate each other and alternately dissociate. The self loses itself and finds itself again, devastated and jubilant, between two waters. Collapse on one side, rapture on the other: the fluidity of the aquatic touch accurately translates this alternation.

Teresa plunges into her maternal language as if it were a *bath* consubstantial with the experience of engendering a new self nestled in the Other, a self who loves the Other. This self absorbs the Other who in turn absorbs the self. Water imposes itself as the absolute, inevitable fiction of the amorous touch: I am touched by the touch of someone else who touches me and whom I touch. Water: fiction of the decanting between the being that is other and unspeakable intimacy, between Heaven and the vagina, the exterior and the internal organ.

Here water is neither a comparison nor a metaphor but both at once, with one playing off the other like symmetrical opposites. There is even a canceling out of water with fire, and vice-versa, in a stack-up of contradictory images, losing the stream of logic these multiple inversions and cancellations in order to create, after all is said and done, a perceptible *fluidity of meaning* itself. But also to contaminate us with the psychic, physical, cosmic, and stylistic dynamic of its own metamorphoses, in the sense of Baudelaire who refused "the poet's brain" "comparing himself to a tree." He claimed "to make [it] a reality."

Paradis artificiels. Not to be *like* the other but to *be the other*. "Water is not like divine love, water is divine love and vice-versa. And I am made of it, we are made of it, me, you and God Himself." Such is the meaning of Teresa's image of water which moves us away from stylistics to confront us with the work of the psyche-soma which the writer tries to convey.

To the incredulous skeptics of the twenty-first century that we are, Teresa splits her intellectual/physical/psychic identity in and through the amorous transference with the Being who is All Other: God, the paternal figure of our childhood dreams, the elusive spouse of the *Song of Songs*. By this deadly and pleasurable metamorphosis, which appeases the melancholic pain of being inconsolably abandoned and separate, she appropriates the Other Being in an infra-cognitive, psycho-somatic contact. This in turn leads her to a dangerous and delicious regression outlined with masochistic pleasure. It's not rhetoric that helps us read her, but Aristotle's brilliant revelation in *On the Soul* and *Metaphysics*, which posits *touch* as the most fundamental and universal of all the senses. If, in fact, every living body is a tactile body, the sense of touch functions so that "that with which I enter into contact, enters into contact with me."[14] Initially and through her fiction of water, Teresa, who sees herself bathed by the Other, occults the mediation and fantasizes that she and her Husband are submerged in one another. But at the same time, by diffracting the water between God, the gardener, and the four ways to make the source flow, she implicitly critiques this immediacy; she distances herself from it and tries to unleash her painful yet jubilant auto-eroticism in an accumulation of physical, psychic, and logical acts. Not water but the fiction of water diffuses the fiction of an absolute touch in a series of auxiliary parables (*noria*, well, water, gardener); she couples it with its contrary (fire), makes it provoke contradictory states, before looking for other images, then altogether losing interest in images, words, writing, and withdrawing from exchange and love. Would water, consequently, be as much a fiction of the divine's sensorial impact on Teresa as it would a critique—unconscious, implicit, ironic—of this impact of the divine itself? Leading to the dissolution of the Ideal Father, of the Other in the praying nun, the writer?

The Interior Castle

If water is the emblem of the relation between Teresa and the Ideal, we can understand that her *Interior Castle* (which is in reality the "metapsychology" of Teresa, the voyage through the different stages of the psyche to its truth) is not a fortress but a puzzle of "chambers" (*moradas*) with permeable walls. *This is to say that transcendence according to Teresa turns out to be immanent*: the Lord is not above but in her! Needless to say, this didn't exactly put her in good stead with the Inquisition, and her confessors and editors hastened to tone down her claim.

But it was not without consequences.

Might the first one be an irony that borders on atheism? In a page not included in her *Way of Perfection*, Teresa advises her sisters to play chess in the nunnery even if this is not allowed, in order to "put the Lord in checkmate."[15] This impertinence resonates with the famous saying by Master Eckart: "I ask God to leave me free of God."

The second is formulated by Leibniz. He writes in a letter to Morell, on December 10, 1696: "As for Saint Teresa, you are right to regard her work highly; in it I found this wonderful thought that the soul must proceed as if there was only itself and God in the world. This opens up a considerable realm of philosophical speculation which I successfully put to use in one of my hypotheses." Is Teresa the inspiration behind Leibnitzian monads, always already containing infinity? Might she be the precursor of infinitesimal calculus?

The sublimatory passion of Teresa is sublime in its risks, in its *jouissances*, in its lucidity and, of course, in its masochism. We modern thinkers claim to be freed of this: but can we be so sure? And if so, at what price?

—Translated by Anne Marsella

Refiguring Wounds in the Afterlife (of Trauma)

SHELLY RAMBO

> For these stories of trauma cannot be limited to the catastrophes they name, and the theory of catastrophic history may ultimately be written in a language that already lingers, in these texts, after the end, in a time that comes to us from another shore, from the other side of the disaster.
> —Cathy Caruth, *Literature in the Ashes of History*[1]

Introduction

As trauma theory narrated shattering endings, it turns, in a new century, to imagine impossible beginnings. How do we figure life? The task of carnal hermeneutics, as described by Richard Kearney, is to read between text and body, to think with multiple senses about the meaning of (embodied) life. How might carnal hermeneutics, as it draws on multiple senses, participate in the work of refiguring traumatic wounds? The essays in this volume note the privileging of the visual as the dominant sense in Western philosophy. The study of trauma, largely a Western enterprise, is often referred to through the image of invisible wounds; thus, the work of trauma healing is to bring these wounds to the surface—to make visible what is invisible. Might the "working through" of traumatic wounds draw on multiple senses, placing visibility alongside the senses without a sole reliance on the gaze? I want to show here how reading carnally might not only open up to other senses but also rewrite the central parable of trauma—the parable of Tancred and Clorinda—and the wound as the central image for trauma. The route that I take in doing so is through a rereading of an ancient scar story in the Christian tradition. The scar emerges as a site of touch in which wounds are transfigured, providing new insights for theorizing three wounds: traumatic wounds, gendered wounds, and Christian wounds.

The Afterlife of Trauma Theory

> As we contemplate the future of trauma studies and the changing nature of violence and power, this volume inspires us to construct new parables beyond Tancred and Clorinda.
>
> Gert Buelen, Samuel Durrant, and Robert Eaglestone,
> *The Future of Trauma Theory: Contemporary
> Literary and Cultural Criticism*[2]

In the preface to *The Future of Trauma Theory*, Michael Rothberg calls for the construction of "new parables" for the twenty-first century study of trauma. He writes, "Trauma today is probably not the trauma of twenty years ago and certainly not the trauma of the early twentieth century."[3] He grounds this call in a reference to the "parable of trauma" that Cathy Caruth identified in her 1995 work, *Unclaimed Experience*—the parable of Tancred and Clorinda.[4] Tancred, the warring crusader, kills his lover, Clorinda, who is disguised as an enemy knight. Yet the tragedy lies in the fact that he slays her a second time, as his sword pierces a tree in which her soul is held captive. Clorinda's cry resounds. Sigmund Freud had briefly invoked this wounding scene in his early observations of WWI combat veterans. Caruth designated this as a parable because it depicts the problem at the heart of trauma—the "unwitting" return of an experience that was *not known* in its first instance. This unwilled second wounding is what makes trauma distinct from other experiences of violence; what is not known and not integrated returns as if to "possess" the person in the aftermath. The wound, in essence, does not close.

Trauma, literally translated "wound" from the Greek, expanded into a discourse of suffering that attested to the violence of the twentieth century and its aftermath. As the diagnoses of PTSD pervaded the clinical world and the public consciousness, questions about the extent of harm that humans can both wield and endure surfaced. Diagnosing and healing traumatic wounds involved sight and sound. Freud noted that physical wounds could be addressed because they could be seen; but psychic wounds lodged within persons were invisible and thus more difficult to heal. Dori Laub, psychoanalyst and Holocaust survivor, presented the challenge of listening to the testimonies of survivors. He writes, "The listener to the narrative of extreme human pain, of massive psychic trauma, faces a unique situation. . . . He or she must *listen to and hear the silence*, speaking mutely in silence and in speech, both from behind and from within the speech."[5] The vocabulary of trauma circled around seeing and hearing; thus, laying out the challenges of trauma healing—of making visible what is invisible and of listening to what cannot be spoken.

Caruth and Laub's insights inaugurated what has been referred to as trauma theory. The analysis of the Holocaust and its aftermath brought together scholars across academic disciplines, gathering them around the enigma of suffering. Previously held assumptions about language and the nature of human experience were in question. Shoshana Felman and Dori Laub's book, *Testimony: Crisis of Witnessing in Literature, Psychoanalysis, and History*, captured a significant moment at Yale University in the early 1990s.[6] As the influence of Jacques Derrida's thought spread in the United States, the English department was wrestling with the legacy of Paul de Man's wartime journalism and his sympathies with the anti-Semitic policies of the German Third Reich. The ethics of interpretation and literary criticism were in question. These convergences were fertile soil for an "ethical call" in literary criticism, in which the problems of language and representation reflected the enigma of wounded experience and its historical transmission.[7]

The challenge of interpretation was conveyed in the figure of the wound. In a tribute essay to Hans-Georg Gadamer, Jacques Derrida reframes the misunderstandings between them using the vocabulary of trauma. He explained the rift between himself and Gadamer as a wound that might be healed by the mutual admiration they shared for the poetry of Paul Celan, the poet whose haunting expressions of Holocaust witness brought the quandary of survival to the forefront of literature.[8] For Derrida, the practices of reading, writing, translation, and interpretation each involve wounding, a description of literature resonant in the post-Holocaust context.[9] Thus, trauma theory casts hermeneutics as a wounded enterprise; the work of writing and translation was newly understood as a complex process of receiving and handing over not what is simply known but, rather, what is unknown. Interpretation becomes bound up in the ethical task of witness to unspeakable events in history.[10]

The question of whether, and to what degree, traumatic wounds can be healed is at the heart of trauma studies. Can literary criticism, thus, also enact a "working through" of the wounds of history?[11] Trauma theory provided a testimony to the aftermath of violence; but as it turns into a new century, Rothberg and others are asking about its future. While Caruth so adeptly developed the landscape of the *aftermath* two decades ago, she gestures in her newest work toward what I will call the *afterlife* of trauma. She figured this afterlife in Clorinda's cry from the site of the wound, which signaled the possibility of witness and, thus, an ethical response to traumatic suffering. Yet her newest work carries this forward even more explicitly. In her long-awaited second book, *Literature in the Ashes of History*, she opens with an essay titled "Parting Words: Trauma, Silence, and Survival." Interestingly, Caruth wrote a version of this essay shortly after publishing *Unclaimed Experience*; but it was largely overlooked, overshadowed perhaps by the reception of the larger volume.[12] Placing it at the beginning of this new volume, the essay frames the other essays by presenting the notion of life as a departure from death, from the site of ashes; it is a beginning distinct from the notion of survival that was so well developed in early trauma theory. She asks: "What is the nature of a life that continues beyond trauma?"[13] Perhaps this essay's eclipse in scholarly reception and its delayed reception can be explained via the dynamics of trauma that Caruth outlined two decades earlier.

This "departure" is important, because it marks the need to refigure wounds in the afterlife. Trauma is often conceived of as an event of death and an impossible survival. If we conceive of trauma as a "death" involving a multisensory shattering of meaning, then its afterlife will require a multi-sensory reconstitution of life. While trauma is figured as wound, its afterlife might be figured as scar, as a textured surface that serves as a critical crossing between death and life, interior and exterior, hidden and revealed. Moving between wounds and scars requires theorizing the textured surface of skin. This shift to the afterlife expands the featured senses of "classical trauma theory"—sight and sound.[14] While Caruth's work was indebted to the "linguistic turn," carnal hermeneutics enacts another important turn—or turning—between text and body that is vital to the future of trauma studies. Theorizing matter is especially important given the somatic realities of trauma. Thus investigating the senses upon which trauma theory rests is important. This means conceiving of the work of "working through wounds" more broadly than through the senses of sight and sound. What if "working through" was a matter of touch?

Wounds in the Afterlife

Within the Christian tradition, it is impossible to escape wounds. Wounds stand at the center of the Christian story. And interpretations of truth pour from these wounds—theories of redemption, salvation, sacred stories of creation and recreation. Trauma theory presses this narrative in particular ways, foremost by providing pause to the claims of resurrection, of triumphant life arising from death. Instead, trauma theory prompts rereadings of death and life.[15] What if the transmission of the crucifixion event is an unintegrated event of suffering that underlies Christianity? Prompted by

Caruth's work, religion scholars revisited the sacred texts, reading through the double structure of trauma.[16] In the liturgical life of Christians, the wound(ing) is repeated as the stories are told, passed on, and performed in the Eucharist; crucifixion wounds are, thus, continually open, continually bleeding. Yet, in shifting to questions of the *afterlife* in trauma theory, I am ushered into another moment in this Christian narrative, an encounter with wounds on the other side of death—the wounds of resurrection. The stories of the risen Christ appearing to the disciples, displaying his wounds, are featured in the Gospel of John. Here, the figure of Christ returns. But in his postresurrection appearances, he appears with wounds on his body. I want to suggest that these resurrection marks might tell a different story about wounds.

Let me narrate this by way of the most famous depiction of resurrection wounds, Caravaggio's depiction of the disciple Thomas, as he encounters the resurrected Christ.[17] The painting provides an interpretation of the gospel account. Thomas, one of the twelve disciples of Jesus, is not present when Jesus first appears to the disciples in the Upper Room. In this first scene, the gospel writers tell us that a group of disciples is gathered; Jesus appears (ghostly entrance), offers them words of peace, shows them his hands and side, and offers them the gift of the Holy Spirit. Thomas, not present with the others, hears them talking about this miraculous resurrection. He responds to them: "Unless I see the mark of the nails in his hands, and put my finger in the mark of the nails and my hand in his side, I will not believe" (John 20:25). Jesus appears again, this time, engaging Thomas directly. The reading that this artist presents is a reading of an open wound and a plunging finger. Not only is the wound *open*; Thomas enters the wound. In the account in the Johannine gospel, the figure of Jesus appears to Thomas and invites him to thrust his finger into his side. The text never tells us if Thomas does touch; it is implied. But Caravaggio has Thomas plunging his finger in. The traditional reading of this text is that Thomas's doubt obstructs him from believing in the risen Jesus and that Jesus appears to him, offering him proof that he is who he says he is. He is, indeed, the one who rose from the dead. This is the story of the triumph of Christian faith. This reading has so powerfully captivated the Western imagination in that it also translates into the context of modernity, in which Thomas's doubt comes to represent modern man—the man of science, the skeptic.[18] A lot of interpretive weight is placed on a certain reading of this encounter. This resurrection account is tied to the *afterlife* in its religious sense, the promise of life after death. The resurrected Jesus links Christians to a future—salvation, the promise of life to come, and the most curious and tangled claim that Christian bodies will be resurrected after death. Thomas's profession of belief via this encounter secures a future for Christians.

But could we read it *otherwise*? Could a rereading of the Thomas story yield a *new parable* for the future of trauma theory? As the figure of Christ bears the marks of death, I want to suggest that they are not simply marks of past suffering. But what kinds of marks are they? Are they marks of life that perpetually refer back to death? Has the Christian imagination continually opened this wound, and thereby located the promise of life in a violent death? Philosopher of religion, Grace Jantzen, critiqued the necrophilia of the Western Christian tradition.[19] This continual return to the death wound has, in her reading, patriarchal underpinnings. In turn, many feminist and womanist theologians turned away from making meaning of crucifixion wounds.[20] Little has been done, however, around these marks. Is this wound on the other side of life simply a repetition, taking us back to the event of suffering; or is there a significant "departure" signaled in the resurrection wound?

In a recent article titled "Writing Trauma: Narrative Catharsis in Homer, Shakespeare, and Joyce," philosopher Richard Kearney distinguishes between wounds and scars.[21] Resonant with the "material turn" in affect studies, Kearney is attempting to correct a nonmateriality within continental philosophy.[22] Rethinking hermeneutics, as such, has moved Kearney into the arena of trauma. He is reengaging one of the central questions of trauma theory: can trauma be "worked through"? For Kearney, narrative is cathartic, stories are told and can have a healing effect. His work in Northern Ireland is grounded in his commitment to storytelling as a practice of healing. Trauma studies has pushed Kearney to the limits of narrative, to ask if there are some experiences that *cannot* be "worked through."

In his reading of three epic texts—Homer's *Odyssey*, Joyce's *Ulysses*, and Shakespeare's *Hamlet*—Kearney examines transgenerational wounding between fathers and sons. In his reading of Homer, he turns to the scene in which Odysseus reappears to his son Telemachus, wounded from his journey and appearing before his son as a beggar. Telemachus does not see the "scar" on his father's body. Euryclea, Odysseus's nursemaid from youth, recognizes him by touching his scar. In turn, Argos, his boyhood dog, recognizes him by way of smell. For Kearney, healing requires recognition; wounds must be recognized in order to be healed. But they are recognized by way of scars that appear on the surface of the skin. And unlike much of Western philosophy that identifies recognition with sight, Kearney points to the other senses operating in these texts.

Kearney turns to these scenes in search of a "writing cure." These texts, in their writing and transmission, not only "hand over" stories of wounding, they, via the storying, work through the wounds. When Joyce writes the "father-son idea" in *Hamlet* into *Ulysses*, this is, in Kearney's view, Joyce's attempt to work through the trauma (although "unwittingly"?). For Kearney, these wounding episodes within the epics operate like parables—they narrate the journey, might we say, of "wounded" existence. Here, he distinguishes between wounds and scars. He writes, "While the wound is timeless, the scar appears in time: it is a carnal trace which can change and alter over time though it never disappears." According to Kearney, scars are connected to the practice of writing—writing on the body, an inscription on flesh. "Put simply: while the wounds remain timeless and unrepresentable, scars are marks left on the flesh to be seen, touched, told and read."[23] Inscriptions on flesh, scars figure wounds, but they do so productively; they are sites, might we say, of testimony to unrepresentable wounds. We see inflections of "classical trauma theory" in his writings; traumatic wounds are inaccessible and fall outside of representation. Scars then bring these wounds to the surface; they "work them through" by storying them.

He uses the strikingly religious language for "working through"—scars transfigure wounds. If trauma has traditionally been figured in the wound, might we think about the afterlife of trauma via another figure—*the figure of the scar*? This distinction of scars and wounds is a helpful one for several reasons. First, the scar is not an open wound; it is closed. Yet the wound is marked/remembered by the pattern it forms on the skin. The wound is not erased, but it is also not perpetually open. In trauma terminology, there is no repetition compulsion. Second, the site of the scar marks a boundary between person and society, individual body and the social body, psyche and matter. It marks a pivotal crossing between interior and exterior. Third, the scar is a creative site of witness and potential healing. It is also a social site.

The Christian story is the paradigmatic Father-Son wounding story. Could we place this story alongside the other epic stories and characters—reading it, as Kearney does, for what it reveals about wounds and scars? Might the wound on the other side of death, this resurrection wound in the Thomas story be, in fact, a scar that marks the past suffering *yet* departs from it? Of course, Caravaggio offers it to us as a gaping wound; the Greek text moves from Thomas's request to touch the *tupon* (prints/type) on the side to the invitation to Thomas to thrust his hand into the *pleuron* (the pleural cavity). In Kearney's vision of carnal hermeneutics, body and text are both represented in this encounter between Thomas and Christ. Is it a wound? A scar? Or as Kearney presents it, does this vision of the afterlife narrate a journey (akin to Homer's *Odyssey*) of "traversing wounds on the way to healing"?[24] The journey that Kearney presents is a journey of fathers and sons. In exploring scars in the afterlife, I want to introduce a mother-daughter story. What does the scar reveal?

Macrina's Scar

At the end of Gregory of Nyssa's fourth-century hagiography (*Vita*) of his holy sister Macrina, there is an extended episode that is often referred to as the "scar scene."[25] Early Christian scholar Virginia Burrus drew attention to it more recently in a short essay titled "Macrina's Tattoo."[26] Macrina is a curious figure in Gregory's writings. Her identity is clearly inscribed by Gregory, but Francine Cardman notes that there are moments in which Macrina disrupts Gregory's authorial control.[27] She takes the scar scene to be one such moment. One of the earliest articulators of Christian ortho-doxy, Gregory defers to his sister Macrina on matters of the afterlife. In *On the Soul and Resurrection*, Macrina guides Gregory in Christian teachings about death and the afterlife.[28] Macrina is aligned with the heroes, the martyrs, the philosophers (Socrates, Diotima, Thekla, Odysseus), tutoring Gregory in what I will call "critical passages" between death and life. The scar scene in the text occurs after Macrina has died. There is no doubt that Gregory not only reads her as one who has lived a life in imitation of the Christ; she is one who becomes, by the end of the *Vita*, the Christ. She is transfigured as the Christ. Thus, the connection between the postdeath burial scene here and in the gospel account is clear. I want to read this scene more closely, and begin to think of it as a new parable for trauma and its afterlife.

Gregory draws us to her bedside. It is evening and the lamp is brought in, as Macrina says her "nocturnal prayers" breathing her last. After hear-ing the news of her death, they can hear the sounds of weeping virgins just outside the door. "The lamp of our life has been extinguished," they cry. "The light that directed the path of our souls has been taken away." Inside, the women begin to prepare Macrina's body for burial. Two women are in charge of the preparations—Vetiana (widow) and Lampadium (deacon-ess). It is clear that they are not only maidservants; they are disciples of Macrina's. Macrina had insisted that Gregory assist in the burial prepara-tions. This places Gregory in the midst of the women. It also places him in contact with her body, a body that, throughout the *Vita*, he has praised for its covering—the ideal ascetic.

They begin "the great assignment," by discussing the type of linens that they should use to prepare the body.[29] As Macrina had eschewed adorn-ment during her life, the maids discuss whether it is appropriate to clothe her in fine linens, to prepare her, like a bride, to meet her divine Bridegroom. It is important to note how much of this scene is dominated by two objects: lamps and clothing. Gregory is emphasizing how difficult it is to see; the lamps are brought in, but it is still difficult to find your way in the dark. Robes, garments, and clothing also play a critical role. This is fitting for a burial preparation scene, but Gregory is also playing in this account with the covering over and concealment of the body, which tie not only to the asceticism of Macrina but to his notion of "garments of skin" prominent in his reading of human nature and sin. There is a continual play in this account between seeing and not seeing, between concealing and revealing; any unveiling is coupled with a veiling.

But then Vetiana pulls the lamp close to Macrina's body and pulls back part of Macrina's robe (she "laid bare part—*meros*—of the breast"). "Do not pass over the greatest of the miracles of the saint," she says. She reveals a small, almost imperceptible mark on Macrina's skin. She asks Gregory, "Do you see this faint (*lepton*—τὸ λεπτὸν) sign/mark (σημεῖον) hidden below the skin?" It resembles a scar (στίγματι) left by a small (λεπτῆς) needle. The problem of seeing is front and center here. Do you see what is faint, small, hidden, covered? Vetiana proceeds to tell Gregory the story of the scar. Macrina developed a mass or growth (τὸν ὄγκον) that was spreading and moving toward her heart. If left unattended, it would threaten her life. Her mother, Emmelia, pleaded with her to go to the doctors, but Macrina resisted—not wanting to "lay bare" her body to the eyes of men. Instead, she went to the sanctuary and prayed all night, with tears flowing, she cried out to God for healing. The tears poured to the ground, and the tears mixed with soil, produced mud that Macrina used as a *pharmakon*, a medicine, rubbing it over the surface of the mass. When she returns home, Emmelia implores her again to seek help, but Macrina invites her mother to reach inside her robe, and to make the sign of the cross over the site. Immediately, the mass disappeared. The mother's fingers trace skin, as if to *work* in the mud—the balm—created through prayer-filled tears.

The mass disappears, but a mark remains. Vetiana assigns meaning to it; she indicates that the mark remains as a reminder of divine consideration, as a memorial of a divine visitation. The discussions of adornment resume. Following Lampadium's instructions, they settle on covering Macrina with Emmelia's dark robe. Note that with her name, the lamps reappear.[30] The robe is pulled over the body—the compounding of darkness—the dark night and the dark robe. But light begins to shine through the covering; Macrina's body begins to glow through the robes. Gregory returns in first person here: "But even in the dark, the body glowed, the divine power adding such grace to her body that, as in the vision of my dream, rays seemed to be shining forth from her loveliness."[31] The luminous transfigured body reminds Gregory of an earlier dream in which he was holding the relics of the martyrs in his hands; the relics (the parts) glowed. The implication is that Macrina's part (*meros*) glows; here, she joins the ranks of the martyrs.[32] The scene closes with the sounds of women outside the door, weeping, singing, and mourning the loss of their leader. The stories of Macrina's other healings begin to be shared, as Gregory closes out his account. His *vita* ends much like the Johannine gospel, spurring testimonies that exceed the container of the text: "All the books in the world could not contain everything that Jesus did . . . [everything that Macrina did—the healer, the Christ]" (John 21:25).

Scars in the Afterlife

I want to highlight three aspects of this scar scene that rewrite our conception of wounds and their afterlife. First, Gregory's account features the problem of vision throughout, and the account does not follow a clear movement from invisibility to visibility. The scar is not the surfacing of the wound but, instead, a distinctive mark linked to suffering but not straightforwardly so. The scar is not simply a mark of past suffering but a departure from it. Touch marks this departure, interrupting the path from invisibility to visibility, not to displace vision but to place it alongside other senses. The concealment and problems of recognition in this story are resonant with the vocabulary of trauma. The wound is hidden and witnessed only by way of moving through layers of misrecognition. The crisis of witness is also represented here. But the important element of this parable is that this wound on the other side of death is *transfigured*. It is transfigured by the work of healing, enacted through a mother's touch. The scar does not turn us back into the wound but, instead, focuses the work of healing on the surface. The gaze is disrupted and the scene is focused on other senses; here, on the touch between daughter and mother. The scar marks the site differently, departing from the wound and thus, renaming, remarking it.

Macrina's scar is unique in that it not a direct product of an earlier wound. The mark remains on the body as a sign of healing; it is a mark produced not by an internal wound but by its exterior witness. This gap between Macrina's disease and the scar is significant. Not subject to the diagnostic gaze, we know little about the nature of her "wound." Translated as sore, disease, and tumor, it is not clear whether the growth was visible on her skin. Georgia Frank implies that the sore was not a visible wound on the body; instead, the sore was internal. She writes, "Untouched by scalpel or nails, she bears a scar where none belongs."[33] Thus, the mark not inscribed on a previous sore but marked healing of an internal sore that was never visible. We tend to think of a scar as a product of a wound, as evidence of its closure. Yet Macrina's scar is different. In Vetiana's account, the scar is the work of divine visitation, marking "divine consideration." In one reading, the invisible wound is made visible in the scar. This is a wound brought to the surface of the skin. This is the unisensory reading via "classical trauma theory." Yet, reading carnally, touch (the work of Macrina's fingers and her mother's touch) highlights the work of healing and points to the possibility of marking life differently. The mark is a multisensory production, featuring touch rather than vision.

This aligns, in interesting ways, with Cathy Caruth's "departure" into life. Although *Unclaimed Experience* introduces Caruth's claim that trauma involves an awakening to the inaccessibility of an event, her reading of the awakening in "Parting Words" might extend beyond Clorinda's cry to a synesthesia of witnessing. This might attest to transfiguration *in life*, in which the mark of wounds remain but are altered by the presence of witnesses. While the scar is revealed (to Gregory) after her death, Macrina bore this scar *in life*. In Virginia Burrus's account, she connects Macrina's ancient tattoo to her own tattoo, noting that the artist's ink marks a departure into a new identity without erasing the memories of wounds that have marked her body. Tattoos, in modern practice, are the artistry on skin that often narrates a story of wounds that cannot be told, at least not directly. We are thus turned back to life differently, to envision in the scar what Burrus refers to as "the scarred joy of life (of a Life)."[34]

Second, Gregory is situated in the company of women. The primary actors here are Macrina, Emmelia, and the maidservants. While Gregory is the author of the account, there is a question as to what extent he is in control of his pen. Late ancient Christian scholars have offered helpful insights about the scar, particularly in respect to gender. Cardman raises the question, "Is she ever available to the reader apart from Gregory's representations of her?" Is Macrina perpetually pinned under the pen of her theological brother? Cardman turns to this scar scene, suggesting that it signals some resistance to Gregory's authorial control.[35] The use of lamps and clothing alone could convey that Gregory, as narrator, is "in the dark" as well as slightly disturbed by the "laying bare" of his sister's body to the human eye. He is, in his words, "disquieted"—not simply by the fact of her death but by the demonstrative mourning of the nuns, whom he chastises for their excessive gestures of grief.[36] The point that I am making here, is that Gregory, as author, as brother, is displaced in this mother-daughter-maidservants scene. This is not the "good death" as he envisions it.

The problems of representation and narrative are at the center of trauma studies. Can trauma be "worked through"? Carnal hermeneutics insists that this "working through" is work between text and body, requiring multiple senses. This is not just a question of a survivor bringing the story to light; it is the broader question of the politics of storying truths. While the scar is disclosed to Gregory, this parable repeatedly witnesses to the covering over, the difficulty of seeing. Gregory, as author, is caught off guard in his writing; the account started off, he tells his reader, as one thing, and then it grew to something that he cannot quite name. As much as Macrina's scar writes wounds anew on the surface of the skin, the degree of visibility of the scar itself is continually in question. In terms of trauma, this politics on the surface of the skin propelled Judith Herman's publication of *Trauma and Recovery*.[37] By linking the male war experience and the female experience of sexual abuse, Herman was aware of the gendered stakes of bringing wounds into the public gaze. Herman's work featured the problem of visibility, linking it to gender. Herman notes that there are certain moments when trauma rises into public consciousness; then it recedes. The student of trauma must track this disappearance, this covering over, because there are political reasons for keeping trauma invisible. The Macrina postdeath scene connects to the history of trauma via psychoanalysis and to the famous 1887 painting, *Une Leçon Clinique à la Salpêtrière* (A Clinical Lesson at the Salpêtrière) by Andre Brouillet, which positions the woman's "hysterical" body as an object of the gaze of the men of science.[38]

The gaze is problematized. This is the searing force behind Judith Butler's dual works on war and torture—*Precarious Life* and *Frames of War*—in which Butler calls attention to the lens through which the media makes the suffering of some visible and others invisible.[39] Macrina's scar brings to the surface, albeit in fourth century mode, these politics. Macrina refuses to be the subject of study, "*une leçon*" laid bare before the eyes of men, and thus subject to the diagnostic gaze. She refuses to be diagnosed—stigmatized. Can she be marked/identified otherwise? These are questions that encircle the interpretations of women in early Christian texts, but they are questions that are strangely relevant to trauma. This call to multiple senses, and sense-making, is important because vision is also bound up in politics.

The politics of trauma and recognition turn us to see that the concealment of wounds might be deliberate, thus bringing the necessity and urgency of witness out of a clinical framework alone into a broader arena of political and social analysis. This is what I mean by highlighting the texture of the scar, as I emphasize both its resistance to being "smoothed" over and the layers on the surface that compound suffering. If the layers of gender and race are accounted for in the study of trauma, the scar could mark unmarked existence, and, in Butler's terms, mark lives that are not counted as lives.[40]

Yet interpreting the mother-daughter story in terms of scarred flesh raises concerns. Amy Hollywood writes, "When in contemporary feminist discourse, identity is defined primarily (if not solely) in terms of traumatic suffering, there is the danger that "woman" will signify only victim and that feminist politics will be reduced to reactionary forms of *ressentiment*.[41] Hollywood's assessment is a response to the writings of Luce Irigaray. In "When Gods Are Born," Irigaray imagines the coming of flesh in contrast to the dominant Christian story in which incarnation is always supplanted by crucifixion. Resurrection after death is the paradigmatic Father-Son story of salvation. New life emerges from the crucifixion wounds. Irigaray provides a vision of pure flesh, unmarked by pain: "The deepest depths of the flesh, touched, birthed, and without a wound."[42] She reflects a flight away from reinscription of Father-Son wounding in its various incarnations in Western thought. She crafts a vision of resurrection and rebirth that will not return us to the site of wounds for our healing. There is no Thomas scene following Irigaray's resurrection.

Catherine Keller responds to Luce Irigaray's erasure of wounds on the body of the resurrected woman, the vision of the pure flesh of becoming.

> I wonder, though, if we need to think this body as quite so pure, so new-born as Irigaray's woundless utopia of the flesh. I suspect rather that the deep flesh, even in its resurrection, will carry the scars.[43]

Working within the Christian textual tradition, she can trace the problematic inheritance of glorified wounds for women. To attribute significance to wounds has been problematic (redemptive suffering), but to erase them is a failure to "work through" these wounds. Amy Hollywood expresses something similar: "Although I embrace Irigaray's desire to bring pleasure, possibility, and natality into philosophy and psychoanalysis, I think there is a danger in refusing to think, *at the same time*, the realities of loss and limitation."[44] While celebrating the joys of existence, does Irigaray fail to acknowledge the ambiguities of embodied existence?

Macrina's scar may offer another way of interpreting resurrection via scars. Garments play a major role in this scene and in Gregory of Nyssa's overall theology, and it is impossible to account for it fully here. Garments have broader implications for how Gregory understands human nature; he uses the image of cloth to narrate the journey of creation, fall, and redemption. While naked, and thus blameless, at creation (Edenic origins), humans must robe after they have violated God's command. They are given garments of skin, signs of their creaturely, and fallen, nature. The progression of a holy life involves a shedding of the sinful nature— the garments of skin—and eventually the putting on of a new garment, a glorious garment in which one stands before God, righteous in God's sight. This scar scene represents a critical juncture—between disrobing and robing. As the women gather around Macrina, a new garment is being sewn.[45] Gregory is referring, in this scene, to resurrection flesh. In Gregory's broader theology, resurrection flesh would be a newly woven garment, placed over the believer when the garment of flesh was shed. But Macrina's account presents a crossing in Gregory's thought.[46] Cameron Partridge makes this link, noting: "What he can say is that humans will be transfigured, their bodies rewoven like new cloaks. Macrina's body is emblematic of this change, the subtlety of her scar like the first thread of her heavenly garment."[47] Emmelia's touch on the surface of the skin may be likened to the puncture of a needle that begins to weave new cloth. But the challenge, in navigating Gregory's account is not to trade in flesh for a glorious garment, but to witness both *at the same time*.[48] The scar marks a site of transfiguration, and might we say, a glimpse of shared flesh in a different iteration than what Irigaray provides. What is important to remember is that this "miracle" did not happen after she died; the resurrection flesh was already threading. The smallest needle thread just below the surface and circles over, providing a vision of flesh that figures the complex layering of life, in all of its ambiguities.

What I am reaching for, as are Hollywood and Keller, is a way of affirming scars not as a reinforcement or reinscription of wounding (making them definitive for women's identity), but as a way of marking and illuminating the complex textures of life—both joys and pain, pleasures and agonies. Theologians Mayra Rivera Rivera and Sharon Betcher are attentive to refiguring flesh and parts (*meros*) without subscribing to the necrophilic repetitions of the Father-Son story.[49] This will require a tricky use of the pen, Hollywood notes, and may be what she is referring to when she states, "feminists need to *use* these ambiguities politically and metaphysically."[50] This texturing work, this artistry, writes *between* text and body, pointing to the "writing cure" that Kearney seeks and yet begs questions of gendered writing.

Third, Macrina's scar offers a way of rereading Christian notions of resurrection. In Christian thought, disciples gather around the central Father-Son story. Here, disciples gather around a mother-daughter healing story. I want to point us to back to the Thomas account, to reflect on what happens to this scene when we read it via Macrina's scar. The figures start to move around in our Caravaggio scene. As I noted, the connection between Macrina and the risen Jesus is evident. We could then position Gregory as Thomas, approaching the body of Macrina to witness the "miracle."[51] The maidservants (the disciples) gathered around would fill out this scene. But that is not quite right, if we stay close to the account. In Gregory's "unwitting" rewriting of the Thomas story, Gregory is not so clearly the figure of Thomas. He is displaced from this position, becoming part of the crowd of disciples witnessing the miracle. Instead, Emmelia, the mother, *is* Thomas, who approaches the wounds of Macrina with doubt—pleading with Macrina to consult with the experts in order to be healed. Macrina's refusal leads to a Gethsemane-like experience, as she pleads for healing. She then invites her mother to reach inside the robe and touch. We have something very different here from the plunging finger of Thomas who is invited by the risen Christ to reach into the pleural cavity. Instead, we have a mother-daughter healing scene; the mother touches the skin, as if to smooth the *pharmakon* into her daughter's skin. She touches rather than penetrates—a counterpoint to the plunging finger of the traditional Thomas. And here she offers a different way of reading this text, emphasizing not the play between belief and doubt but, instead, the healing that comes by way of touch. This strikes me as profound. What is the "truth" narrated here? As I noted before, this gospel account is often presented as representing the triumph of Christian faith; Jesus's invitation to Thomas prompts this profession—"My Lord and my God."

What is not developed, in Freud or Caruth, is the religious dimension of the Tancred and Clorinda tale. In this "romantic epic," Tancred is a Christian crusader who has fallen in love with Clorinda, a Moslem warrior-maiden who, upon her deathbed, converts to Christianity. The battle setting is the First Crusades, and the title of Tasso's epic poem "Jerusalem Delivered" declares the triumph of Christianity over Islam. Is this also the parable of religious violence and its repetition in history, the tale of a gaping wound and continual bloodshed? If so, new parables must be envisioned. Could the mother-daughter parable of healing touch point us to a different interpretation of this passage, interpreting resurrection not as a triumphing claim that garners the *unique* truth of Christianity but that links those within this tradition to the vision of healing so central to the narrative of Jesus's life? The plunging finger of Thomas that seeks to secure belief is transfigured into the healing finger—changing the "truth" that emerges from a reading of this scene. As the continually open wound turns the tradition inward to secure the truth of Christian faith, the work of the scar, on the surface of skin, might birth a political theology rooted in a vision of healing.

Conclusion

If hermeneutics begins in the flesh, this beginning, via trauma, will have to be imagined with marked flesh on the other side of death. The paradigmatic Christian story of wounds yields more than meets the eye. Perhaps resurrection is not the miracle that come to us from an otherworldly shore, but the "greatest miracle" of flesh reconstituting on this shore through a synesthesia of witness.[52] The scar, Vetiana tells us, is a mark of divine consideration, a marking that reaches down to the earth and, by swirling mud and tears, mixes a healing salve, a marking created by a finger, prompted by a daughter's call to mark her body otherwise. Gregory did not intend to write this account in this way; Olympius, its recipient, had urged him to write "an artless and simple narrative."[53] Given that Gregory's account has gone on too long, he tells his readers that he will not be able to tell everything in its proper order.[54] Macrina's death, and the disquieting sounds of the disciples' mourning, take the pen in another direction.

This Is My Body

Contribution to a Philosophy of the Eucharist

EMMANUEL FALQUE

"Blessed are those who are invited to *the marriage supper of the lamb*. . . . Let us rejoice and exult and give him glory, for the marriage of the Lamb has come, and his bride has made herself ready; to her it has been granted to be clothed with fine linen, bright and pure . . . Come, gather for the great *supper of God*" (Rev. 19:9, 7–8, 17; NRSV). [1] John's call in Revelation is an invitation to the banquet. A "lamb" is standing there, sacrificed, ready to be viewed, worshiped, but also eaten. In a well-known controversial Flemish altar piece in St. Bavon cathedral (Ghent), the Eyck brothers drew its features in "The Adoration of the Lamb" (1432). Shortly before the execution of this work, the reformers John Wycliffe and Jan Hus maintained that "Christ is not identical to or really in the sacrament on the altar in his own physical person" (John Wycliffe), yet the Eyck brothers demonstrated realism and substantiality by displaying Christ openly on the altar as a lamb. This reality of presence surprises us and remains to be claimed as a "real presence" waiting for us.

In Pope John XXIII's opening remarks at the Second Vatican Council (1962), he called Catholic thinkers to explain doctrine "in such a way that it responds to the requirements of our age," and to do so "by following the research methods and the presentation employed by modern thought." [2] It goes without saying that it is not a question of rejecting the tradition, quite the opposite. One only finds the new by relying on the old, renewing interpretation more successfully by being firmly grounded on dogma and its oldest formulations. The statement *"hoc est corpum meum"* ("this is my body") is certainly first a question of faith and hence of personal conviction. Yet it also points to "a matter of culture" (according to Jean-Luc Nancy), making the terms of a "credible" and not merely "believable" Christianity all the more urgent. Christianity harbors in itself the cultural and conceptual resources for reaching the very core of the human and for transforming it from the inside. Apologetics is neither first of all about conversion nor solely a matter of reason. Most fundamentally it comes down to "touching deeply," to realizing that nothing human will be "transformed" if it is not first of all assumed by the Son of Man: "what has not been *assumed* has not been *redeemed*," Gregory Nazianzus reminds us, "and only what is *united to God* is saved" (Letter to Cledonius). It is therefore advisable to question the entirety of human experience, everything involved in the Eucharist, in order to be transformed by God: *animality* (Eucharistic heritage [the figure of the lamb]), *the body* (Eucharistic content [this is my body]), *eros* (Eucharistic modality [a body given]), and finally *abiding* (Eucharistic aim [remain in me and I in you]).

The act of "eating, even of chewing, the flesh" and of "drinking, even gulping down, the blood"—"whoever eats of my flesh and drinks my blood" (John 6:56)—certainly caused scandal at the time. We should not forget it today, especially when coming forward to commune. "Worse than having a perverted soul," Charles Péguy reminds us, "is to have a soul of [mere] habit."[3] Philosophy, theology, phenomenology, or the sacramental domain, are not merely a matter of words. They imply an "experience" that would disappear if it could not be expressed (intuition without concept) and would be emptied if it did not have to be lived (concept without intuition). What is valid for other modalities of existence in translating Good Friday or Easter *philosophically* is even more valid for Maundy Thursday, because the viaticum and hence the daily nature of our being here below is also involved. To the *philosophical triptych*—suffering, birth, body—responds a *theological triduum*: passion, resurrection, Eucharist. By holding onto human unity, its radical assumption and transformation by the divine is revealed. Human experience and the mystery of God so closely overlap in the figure of the God-man, that any desire to separate them would be deluded.[4]

Philosophy at the Limit

To enter into the theological mystery of the Eucharist paradoxically comes down to questioning the limits of philosophy, or rather of a certain kind of phenomenology. Although the analyses of suffering (Lévinas), death (Heidegger), flesh (Henry), gift (Marion), or of birth (Romano), might illuminate what there is of passion or resurrection in them, nothing ensures that they are sufficient in themselves for expressing what in them belongs to the "body" as such, and hence also to the Eucharist. A "reverse shock" is produced, this time from theology onto phenomenology, as soon as it is a question of the "Eucharistic mystery," and hence also of the "organic body." The current phenomenological practice actually amounts to illuminating the given of the revealed (prayer [Jean-Louis Chrétien], incarnation [Michel Henry], the gift [Jean-Luc Marion], liturgy [Jean-Yves Lacoste], etc.), while hardly ever questioning the effectiveness of their instruments for identifying what in this belongs to theology—so that theology itself becomes, at times, completely phenomenological.

One should nevertheless wonder, less about the relevance of these tools than about their possibility of expressing *the entirety* of human and hence also of divine experience. Theology itself shows phenomenology its "limits," here including phenomenology's hegemonic conceit of mistakenly rejecting any other form of thought (especially "metaphysical"). This is what happens in an exemplary fashion with an authentic and anti-Gnostic interpretation of Tertullian, discrediting any attempt that would link him phenomenologically to the "flesh" or to the "lived body" (*Leib*), rather than to the "body" or the "materiality of the extended thing" (*Körper*). Christ "was looked on as a man for no other reason whatsoever than because he existed *in the corporeal substance* of a man," Tertullian specifies, "of the *muscles* as clods; of the *bones* as stones; the *mammillary glands* as a kind of pebbles . . . the close *junctions of the nerves* as propagations of roots, and the *branching courses of the veins* as winding rivulets, and the *down* (which covers us) as moss, and the *hair* as grass, and the very treasures of the *marrow* within our bones as ores of flesh."[5] Far from remaining a simple "flesh without body," especially in the case of Tertullian or Irenaeus (Henry), the body of the incarnate Son is given *also* as "body without flesh" in the sense of a truly incarnate humanity or an "incorporated" humanity, in terms of the "world" and "materiality." The human is not first of all made "flesh" (*Leib*), but also "body" (*Körper*). Rather, by a surprising inversion of the German terms in sacramental theology—*der Leib Christi. Amen.* ("The body of Christ. Amen")—the term "body" expresses less the simple lived experience of a flesh than Christ as really present, given to be eaten and drunk, even if his organicity here is not solely identified with his simple historicity.[6]

Theology's reverse shock onto phenomenology, of the weight of the body as "incorporation" (*Verkörperung*) on its lived experience as "incarnation" (*Verleiblichung*), questions the limit of philosophy. This questioning arises from Christ's substantial incarnation, which raises doubts about the phenomenologist's choice to privilege the "body proper" (*corps propre,*

Leib) over the "material body" (*corps matière, Körper*), the lived experience of the body over the organicity of the body. Yet, one cannot reduce the substantiality of any human corporeality to its pure and simple materiality. Between the "extended body" (Descartes) and the "lived body" (Husserl), I contend there is the "spread body" (*corps épandu*). Its organic reality in no way succumbs either to extension of matter into "length, largeness, depth" (objective body), or to the lived experience of a flesh in the mode of self-affection or of appropriation (subjective body). Consisting of "fluttering, of sniffling, and gurgling," as there are also "digestion, secretion, cicatrization, or respiration" (the unconscious aspect of the body in Nietzsche), the "*spread body*" demarcates a kind of border zone, or an intermediary body, between the *extended body* (simple materiality) and the *lived body* (pure subjectivity).

Spread out on a bed on the verge of falling asleep, on an operating table just anaesthetized, or even on the cross to the point of dying, this body does not stop being human. It still signifies a differentiated alterity, possessing traits that mark its specificity: two legs, fineness of skin, delicacy of touch, sexuality, which, if not proof of its humanity, at least serve as its "sign."[7] Yet it possesses simultaneously a "portion of animality," which it could not repudiate entirely: "Nothing is given to us as real besides our world of *appetites* and *passions*," Nietzsche says, "as a kind of *instinctive life* in which all *organic functions* are still synthetically intertwined along with self-regulation, assimilation, nutrition, elimination, exchanges, as a *performance of life*."[8] Following the "leading thread of the body," and in order to recover "the primitive text, the coarse text, the natural human," we meet up with our humanity's *Abyss*, its *Chaos* never entirely overcome. Through this a real content (fleshly, human, even cosmic or animal) is given to Christianity's claim that "this is my body." Consequently, for Nietzsche, as maybe also for Christianity, it is first of all "the body that philosophizes"— *der Leib philosophiert.*[9]

The Pascha of Animality

In becoming incarnate God certainly did not become an animal. The Council of Trullo (692) required that the Savior's human image be substituted for that of the lamb, so as to withdraw the incarnate Word from animal paganism and from the purely Jewish sense of the sacrificed lamb.[10] Nevertheless, God cannot remain indifferent to this internal chaos, this abyss of our passions and impulses, which a certain type of contemporary phenomenology has largely spiritualized or even denied (Merleau-Ponty probably excepted). "Body without consciousness" defines animals; "consciousness without body" delineates angels. The second (angelism) should be envied no more than the first (animality). Pascal's saying is well known: "The human being is neither angel nor beast" (L678/B358) and it is "much more miserable if one has fallen from higher up" (L122/B416).

The silence about *animality*, especially when it comes from theologians who at times seem to have eliminated the question (with notable exceptions like John Scotus Erigena or Francis of Assisi), surprises the philosopher who has treated it continually for more than a century (Husserl, from Uexküll onward, Heidegger, Derrida, Deleuze, Henry, etc.). It goes without saying that speaking *philosophically* of "animality" is not to speak of "animals" or even of a straightforward difference between human and animal. Animality instead provides a "mode of access" to our corporeality. Philosophy and theology both must rediscover this. Animals matter little; what matters is this chaos of passions and impulses that God came to assume, in a Eucharistic body-to-body (*corps-à-corps*),[11] waiting to convert *everything*, including the "realm of which one can no longer say anything" (Heidegger about Nietzsche), the "mix of sensations," absolutely resistant to any subsumption (Kant).[12]

The fear of *animality* comes most frequently from its confusion with *bestiality*. As the animal remains the bedrock of the human via incarnation or incorporation, the beast marks what is possible for the human below the level of animality. It is as if the human had the sad privilege of falling to a depth the animal itself would be unable to reach (prostitution, pornography, gluttony, etc.) The "beast crouches to lust after you," tempting Cain (Gen. 4:7). Similarly, Revelation speaks of the "scarlet Beast full of blasphemous names" (Rev. 17:3). Yet bestiality, that is, the body's fall into sin, in no way disqualifies animality, whether the animal world (cosmology) or our own animality (anthropology). Being incarnate neither in animality nor in bestiality, God no less takes responsibility for the entirety of "our" humanity. Because nothing human is foreign to him (Terence), he comes to assume all in order to save all—our animality to turn it into humanity (salvation by solidarity) and our bestiality to purify it fully (salvation by redemption). Here is "the lamb of God who takes away the sins of the world" (John 1:29, 36). Animality in the *figure of the lamb* and bestiality in the *lamb sacrificed* for our sins, belong fully to salvation history, the former because it assumes our integral being (passions, impulses, interior chaos), the latter because it joins and converts all of our being gone astray (vices, sins, lusts, etc.). The integral being hence designates first the incarnate human being, but not independently of the organic dimension by which it is also constituted. It does so to the point of animality, even of bestiality, of which we could not easily rid ourselves.

"This is my body" is hence first a phrase capable of bearing all: humanity, animality, and bestiality. Indeed, the Eucharist not only intends to deify us, through a participation in the mystery of divinity, which is certainly essential but would make us abandon the limits of our created being. While it moves us from humanity to divinity (divinization), the act of communion calls us first to transition from our animality to humanity (humanization), into the implied filiation (Trinity). Only integration into the Trinitarian mystery will be able to save us (Col. 1:16). Son in the son, and not in the guise of quaternity (Fourth Lateran Council, 1215), the human being remains human entirely, in a bodily incarnation to its accomplishment in glory. Divinizing the human while never surpassing it—those are the stakes of the Eucharist as gift of the organic to the organic. If the human "should aspire to be *pure spirit* and to reject the flesh as pertaining to his animal nature alone," recalls Benedict XVI in *Deus est caritas*, "then spirit and body would both lose their dignity."[13]

This Is My Body

The phenomenological description of the "flesh" (*Leib*) led me in my prior work to reflection on the resurrection. Raised in his living body, the Resurrected Christ shows the *kind of being* of his incarnate body. The reference to the ghost that has "neither flesh nor bones" means *that it is really him* who suffered and is raised: "*It is really myself.* Touch me and see; for a ghost does not have flesh and bones, as you see that I have" (Luke 24:39). Appearing at the lakeshore, his disciples recognize him by his "eating" (John 21:1–14); disguised as a gardener, Mary Magdalene identifies him by his "voice" (John 20:11–18). He shows Thomas his wounds, allowing faith to recognize the sign rather than reason searching for a proof (John 20:24–29). "Coming out of the tomb" (John 5:29), bodies boast less of their organicity than of the assumption of the totality of what they were even before being raised. Aquinas insists that "even if one does not use them, all of these kinds of organs (limbs, intestines, genital organs, etc.) will be there in order to restore the integrity (*integritatem*) of the natural body."[14] The organs matter less for themselves than for what they signify—that is, this lived experience by which we express ourselves.

The essential question remains: How does the Eucharist meet up with our viaticum and our "being on the way"? What does it have of *materiality*—of Christ's body but also of ours—as soon as the resurrection consecrates its expressiveness? By privileging the self-affectivity of the flesh in philosophy (*Leib*) or the expressiveness of lived experience in theology (symbolism) too much, have we not omitted a fundamental dimension of the body's organicity in philosophy (*Körper*) or of its depth and its "realism" in theology? This is far from denying the validity of the lived experience of the body or the manifestation of the flesh for expressing what belongs to the resurrected body: "There is one glory of the sun, and another glory of the moon, and another glory of the stars . . . so it is with the resurrection of the dead" (1 Cor. 15:41–42). How will this self-affectivity join up with the reality and substantiality of this incarnate body? The move from death to resurrection points from (suffering) "body" to (resurrected) "flesh" and transfers it from resurrection to Eucharist, from (resurrected) flesh to (given) body. Born in a "body" in Bethlehem, the Son of man, like any human being, is called to become "flesh" in his resurrection, but only by going through a "body-to-body" in the narratives of the passion, consecrating the "flesh" as what always bears the traces of his "body" (via the stigmata). Suffering and death show the "body" about to putrefy, the resurrection signifies the "flesh" or the rebirth of what is traversed, and the Eucharist takes on the "organicity" without which the Son of Man never would have been truly incarnate.

The scandal of the Eucharist is born precisely from the justifiable lack of understanding in those for whom it was first meant: "The Jews then disputed among themselves, saying: 'How can this man give us his flesh to eat'?" (John 6:52). Nevertheless there is no dearth of strategies of avoidance for "habituating" oneself to the strangeness of the Eucharistic table: exegetical, theological, or pastoral. First, *exegesis* insists correctly on the Hebraic origin of the "flesh" as a designation for "the entire human being" and on "blood" as marking our participation in the life of God (like the aroma of the sacrificed lamb rising all the way to the divine nostrils). The argument may well be true, but does justice neither to the Jews' initial surprise nor to the need for reading the Eucharistic sacrament today within a tradition that is Greek (*soma*) or Latin (*corpus*) and not originally Hebraic (*basar*). One should not read the Scriptures outside of their translation and transmission within the tradition, especially when moving from the Semitic to the Hellenic. Second, from the *theological* point of view one often appeals to the "symbolic" to justify the Eucharistic sacrament. Certainly, the sensible can be linked to the intelligible and the bread to nourishment or the wine to life. Yet, symbolism often becomes an argument for justifying the reconciliation of the sensible and the intelligible, of the human and the divine, and thereby reducing the raw depth of created being. Even so, in philosophy the "symbol" is not only what unifies, but what repels in its sensory depth and sends us back to what we are ourselves—what theology also reaches when interrogated: "If symbol is a wall," Maurice Blanchot underlines, "then it is like a wall that, far from opening wide, not only becomes more opaque, but with a density, a thickness, and a reality so powerful and so exorbitant that it transforms us."[15] The Eucharistic symbol sends us back first to the depth of Christ's body, or even to the question of its and our organicity, rather than toward "the swerve of the flesh," which philosophy and theology have a constant tendency to perform. Finally, in the category of the *pastoral*, the symbol of the "meal" still has to be recovered, thereby allowing us to recognize that "we are" *also* the shared bread. The congregation, however, understood in the Catholic sense, refers not only to the assembled people but finds on the Eucharistic table also the "real" presence. The meal is not only composed of the guests, but also of what is given to "drink" and to "eat." We have forgotten too much as we have progressively turned away from the central reason of our Christian life: "this is my body."

Even today we do not stop being surprised by this "body" offered on a banquet table. What yesterday caused scandal in a Jewish culture (John 6:56), remains so also in the Latin context. Augustine reminds us of "that seeming *insanity* (*furor*) and constant madness (*insania*)" of giving people flesh to eat and blood to drink. Is it not "the same insanity and sober inebriety" "when the Lord said, 'Except a man eat my flesh and drink my blood, he shall have no life in him' (John 6:53)?"[16] Thus, a kind of "quarrel of the flesh" innervates Eucharistic philosophy, from the painter Francis Bacon seeing, not without reason, "crucifixions at the butcher's" (*Logic of Sensation* [Deleuze]), to the state of the problem as it was articulated and then solved by Charles the Bald in the ninth century: "What the mouth of the faithful receives in church, is it *in mystery* or *in truth*?" "In mystery" (*in mysterio*), the body of Christ will immediately be symbolized (Ratramnus, Béranger). Only the interior disposition of the communicant matters, not the consistency of what is given to eat. "In truth" (*in veritate*), following Radbert (Paschasius Radbertus, Abbot of Corbie) and Lanfranc, it is fully and completely reified. Simply a "veil" for Christ's body and blood, the species of bread and wine remain such only to the extent that their absence could repel us. Aquinas claims it is in order not to "scare us" by transforming the bread into body and the wine into blood and "so as not to seem stupid around the pagans," that the species of bread and wine remain such after they are consecrated and that they are not immediately given to contemplate or to digest, the body (flesh [*viande*]) and the (hemoglobin) blood of the Savior.[17]

One will certainly recall other reasons for holding onto the permanence of the species. Only the progressive distinction between the "true body" (*corpus verus*) and the "truly body" (*corpus vere*) will resolve what the quarrel so far only highlighted: from the "true body" (*corpus verus*) as historical body of the crucified Jesus that one certainly could not eat, to the risk of declining into a stupid and intolerable cannibalism. Yet, in order not to lose the "pathic" marks of his incarnate being, communion concerns the "truly body" (*corpus vere*) of the resurrected Christ. The threefold body of Amalarius of Metz, brought to light by Henri de Lubac in *Corpus mysticum*—the "immaculate body joined to the blood" (host in the chalice), the "wandering body resurrected and eaten" (bread of the faithful), and the "resurrected and preserved body" (Eucharistic reserve, adoration, tabernacle)—are joined in a sole body in order to form the "total Christ" (*Christum totum*). This is a solution of continuity not satisfied with the consuming of flesh.[18]

Eucharistic symbolism hence still awaits its counterpoint in realism. By insisting too much on the subject's consciousness at communion, another version of the "shared meal," one probably loses the meaning and the consistency of what is eaten and given to adore. Far from rejecting "transubstantiation," or rebaptizing it as "transsignification" or "transfinalization," it would regain the depth for which it was originally introduced: "By the consecration of the bread and wine a change takes place in which *the entire substance* of the bread is changed into the *substance* of the Body of Christ our Lord, and *the entire substance* of the wine into the *substance* of His Blood. This change the Holy Catholic Church fittingly and properly calls 'transubstantiation.'"[19]

The Force of the Body

What is the potential of this for the "force of the body" or for the possibility of speaking about this "body-to-body," namely of the gift of the organic to the organic and of its erotic modality? One need never have lived either the "Eucharistic meal" (*Cène Eucharistique*) or the "erotic scene" (*scène érotique*)—although one should guard against making too much of this play on words—to see that the erotic scene also enlightens the Eucharistic meal, even if it cannot be reduced to it. As I will discuss below, neither equivocity (Nygren) nor univocity (Marion) between eros and agape are sufficient for telling us everything about eroticized love, if it is not at the same time converted into charity: "Yet eros and agape—ascending love and descending love—can never be completely separated," underlines the encyclical *Deus est caritas*. "*The element of agape* thus enters into this love, for otherwise eros is impoverished and even loses its own nature" (§7); but "Eros is thus supremely ennobled, yet at the same time *it is so purified* as to become one with agape" (§10). If there is transubstantiation, this would mean also the transformation of the human into the divine, at the same time as it consecrates the bread to make it "body" and the wine to turn it into "blood."

"Transubstantiation" certainly does contain "substance" and with it obviously false accusations of presence (Heidegger, Derrida). Yet in order to understand substance correctly, one should know that it goes back to the "act of being" in Aquinas, and to the "acting force" and the "substantial link" in Leibniz.[20] A reversal takes place, which makes "transubstantiating" not the result of an operation on a body, but the principle of a *force* able to "embody." For the naive principle that "the body gives the force," one should substitute the Spinozist discovery that "the force produces the body." The *conatus* or "the effort to persevere in one's being" not only makes an effort to survive, as one usually falsely believes, but above all an effort to diversify, to adapt, or even to create. We do not know "what the body is able to do" as long as we do not allow the body its "proper power" (Spinoza). The force of life makes the living being, not the reverse. One becomes an herbivore by nourishing oneself from herbs and a carnivore by feeding on one's prey. Far from denying our nature or the created world, such a vision helps us see how much our body also participates in the "acting force" of Him who has desired us.[21]

If a "primacy of the flesh over the body" grounds contemporary philosophy's "swerve," a different primacy of "weakness over strength" also remains unquestioned today. Certainly the welcome of the other, the face and counterintentionality, have challenged the total exercise of mastery and authentic Dasein's power to control everything. Yet due to this "passivity," one forgets "activity." Insisting too much on the benefits of weakness and vulnerability neglects the virtues of activity and power. Unlike the overman called to surpass everything, the Christian remains no less "strong" by Him who comes to give himself to us and confers on us his own "power" at Pentecost: "You will receive *power* (*dynamis*) when the Holy Spirit has come upon you," Christ tells his disciples, "and you will be my witnesses" (Acts 1:8). Paul explains: "You were also raised with him through faith in the power of God, who raised him from the dead" (Col. 2:12).

The "body-to-body" of the Eucharistic sacrament does not remain indifferent to such a "sharing of forces." This is true of Eucharistic agape as for conjugal eros—the second really gaining its meaning fully only from the first. The bodily union is no more fusion in the erotic than it is a simple unification in the Eucharistic. Becoming "a single flesh" (Gen. 2:24) does not deny that one still remains "two bodies." Love is not born from difference in order then to suppress it; it "*is* differentiation of two beings who nevertheless are not absolutely different one from the other."[22] In other words, the strength of one does not disappear in and by the force of the other. To the contrary, it is rein*force*d; it finds in difference the dimension of its alterity and the necessity of its identity. The union of the man to the woman "masculinizes" him via the force which is suitable to him, while the union of the woman to the man "feminizes" her via the resistance that she can put up against him. The union of the flesh is not accomplished without the difference of bodies. Rather this difference supports it. What is true of alterity in carnal eros is even more true of differentiation in Eucharistic agape: *Ego do corpus meum—Accipio* ("I give you my body—I accept it"), according to a marriage ritual in fifteenth century Avignon, as if anticipating in the erotic union of bodies the *hoc est corpus meum* of the Eucharistic sacrament.[23]

The Eucharistic Eros

Paradoxically, Christ places the sixth day on the first day, switching the "creation of man and woman" in Christianity with the "creation of heaven and earth" in Judaism. The Pharisees question Jesus in order to "put him to the test": "Is it lawful for a man to divorce his wife for any cause?" (Matt. 19:3) "according to what Moses' law commands" (Mark 10:3–4). Christ responds: "Have you not read that the one who made them at the beginning, made them male and female" (Matt. 19:4) or that "from the beginning of the creation, God made them male and female" (Mark 10:6). Short of a serious hermeneutic error, highly unlikely (at least intentionally), a real reversal takes place between second and first testament. While Genesis says that "in the beginning" (*bereshit*) "God created the heavens and the earth" (Gen. 1:1), and that only on the sixth day he "created humankind in his image, in the image of God he created them, male and female he created them" (Gen. 1:27), the synoptic Gospels put sexual difference "in the beginning" (*in arche*), as if the *sixth day* had in Christianity become *the first day*, such that "the masculine and the feminine are revealed as being *ontologically* part of creation, and hence destined to exist beyond the present, obviously in a transformed fashion."[24]

This inversion in the hebdomary calendar, regulated by the six days of creation, confers on sexual difference in Christianity a role not to be minimized. The "difference of origin" holds from the origin. To confuse the real intention of eros and agape, means not paying attention to this difference. (1) To demand the "sense of the limit" as principal dimension of our created being, (2) to show the "human meaning of the tension of desire," and (3) to allow the word (*la parole*) to say itself in the "weaknesses of the flesh," all justify how such a sexed alterity is at work within them—in the sense of an eros that is not without consequence for Eucharistic agape.

(1) In the fusion of the flesh the difference of bodies is reinforced. Everything flows from and depends upon the reality of the "limit" that God gives to Adam, also to teach him to love himself in the difference, namely from the creation of Eve and from sexual difference as such: "In this *limitation* [Adam] had his life," underlines Bonhoeffer, "but he could still not really love this life in its limitation." Therefore God "out of this mercy . . . created a companion for man who must be at once the embodiment of Adam's limit and the object of his love. . . . The other person is the *limit* placed upon me by God. I love this *limit* and I shall not transgress it because of my love."[25] Far from confusing the "limit" with the "unlimited," which properly speaking constitutes sin, the limit constitutes my created being and hence must be wanted and desired. This poses the risk of neither seeing nor understanding that nothing must be feared more than to cross the boundaries that God has established. Thus, the man will love his wife as his most proper and most immediate limit ("this is bone of my bones and flesh of my flesh" [Gen. 2:23]), and the wife also will love her husband as one engendered of her and not only the origin from which she has been drawn: "just as woman came from man, so man comes through woman, but all things come from God" (1 Cor. 11:12).

This also applies to the Eucharist. Its point is not to merge but above all "to unite by differentiating," that is to say, to love. A paradoxical "love at the limit" invites us to communion. The point of the priest's words,[26] according to which "by the mystery of this water and wine we come to share in the divinity of Christ who humbled himself to share in our humanity,"[27] is neither to get beyond nor to forget the common human condition. Instead, it reinforces it and even takes it on, including the chaos of the world and of our humanity, of our animality. "Phenomenological finitude" returns to what remains in it of the "theological limit." The limit is observed from one side as finitude in Heidegger, while it is desired by the other side as the creation of the human as a being commensurate with his state by Aquinas. We should recall Aquinas's statement about limited proportion, according to which "all that has participation in anything *is* in this thing in the mode of what participates, because *nothing can be received beyond its measure.*"[28]

Far from the viewpoint of the revealed or the unlimited, which contemporary phenomenology often employs in an unquestioned manner, the love of the limit therefore becomes that toward which we summon erotic conjugality and Eucharistic agape. The man becomes more of a "man" or "masculinized" when he meets his wife, just as the woman becomes more of a "woman" or "feminized" when she is united to her husband. The same is true in a paradigmatic fashion for Eucharistic communion. Those who approach the "Table of the Lord" live their humanity more fully as they take up their created being, to the extent that God deepens and measures the gap between his own "unlimited" being and our own "limit," in order to better send us back to it. Love *is* differentiation, which makes "communion," in all senses of the word. One does not assimilate God into oneself, but one is in some way "incorporated into him," following the example of the priest by way of a "consumed human" (Abbot Chatrier).

(2) In the approach of the meal (*Cène*) (scene), "desire" hence refers not only to the "passion," at least in the passive sense of the "pathos" of suffering and of abandonment to death. It also means "passion," in the active sense of strain, or even of the search for union, as in the case of eros the lover goes in search of the beloved in order to be better unified but also to be differentiated: "I have eagerly desired to eat this Passover with you before I suffer" (Luke 22:15). The active passion of "desire" on Maundy Thursday chronologically precedes the passive reception of "suffering" on Good Friday. A doubling of desire here renders it "anthropogenic," to use Hegel's terminology in the *Phenomenology of Spirit*. As Alexandre Kojève explains, "Desire is *anthropogenic* (or humanity's generator) and thus differs from animal 'desire,' by the fact that desire is not aimed at our real, positive, and given object, but at a *different Desire*. In this way, in *the relationship between man and woman*, for example, Desire is only *human* if one desires *not the body* but the *Desire of the other*, if one wants to 'possess' or 'assimilate' the *Desire as Desire* . . . : human history is the history of *desired Desire*."[29]

What is true of the differentiation between man and woman (desire of the other rather than the need to consume or to destroy the other), is hence even truer of the difference between human and divine. The "*desire* of a great *desire*" (doubling of desire) to eat the Passover with his disciples on Maundy Thursday shows a desire, in Christ and his Eucharistic agape, which is in some way "theogenic": to give himself up to humans, as is also expressed in the eros of an "anthropogenic desire," that of giving oneself to the other. Through Desire rightly understood, one becomes oneself: the man as "man" vis-à-vis his "wife" (and vice versa), and God as "God" vis-à-vis creation in general (and vice versa). The structure between eros and agape is not only one of parallelism or even of analogy, but of "incorporation," in this instance of human love into divine love. The excess of Desire in Eucharistic communion does not transpose the erotic for the liturgical, according to ecstatic transfers. On the contrary, it sweeps it along and incorporates it into itself, in their respective differences, in such a way that the united lovers are held in "the hand of God," like Rodin's sculpture by the same name, where the "spouses embrace each other as contained in Him who clasps them."[30]

(3) Thus, the word would not finally be exempt from the erotic or the Eucharistic act. Certainly a "promise" concludes the union of the spouses in order to allow them to unite conjugally. Yet the contract, concluded or set via the "oath," is not enough to nourish faithfulness, if it relies not at the same time on a "faithfulness of the flesh," which alone can make it last. A "consummated marriage" (*matrimonium consummatum*) must correspond to a "concluded marriage" (*matrimonium ratum*) in order for it to be valid, at least in the Church. What is true on the day of the spousal union must hence also be true on a daily basis, at the risk of holding onto a "yes" relying only on its contract, but not on its accomplishment in corporeality. John Paul II explains the Canon as follows: "The coming into being of marriage is distinguished from its consummation, to the extent that *without this consummation* the marriage is not yet constituted in its *full reality*. The fact that a marriage is *juridically contracted* but *not consummated* (*ratum—non consummatum*) corresponds to the fact that it has not been *fully constituted* as a marriage."[31]

The word is hence not given only *before* the erotic act or the Eucharistic agape. It is certainly a performative statement, in which the "spoken yes" of consent seals the spousal union, just as is the case in the consecration "this is my body" for the Eucharistic conversion. Yet the linguistic act also plays its role *afterwards*, indeed *at the same time*, as the act of corporeality, inasmuch as the speaking also allows to "say" what the sexed eros or Eucharistic agape does not know how to express. If it is phenomenologically a "happy fall of the flesh" to the extent to which I could never "sense what the other senses or what he feels" (enigma of the touching-touched in Husserl or Merleau-Ponty), then the meaning of "speaking" becomes integrated into this "flaw," namely as the necessity of *saying* and of *expressing* to the other what my body and the other's body would never alone be able to signify. Having in oneself "the feelings of Christ Jesus" (Phil. 2:5), or "marrying the conditions of Christ to the sacrament of the altar in the Eucharist," precisely comes down to entering this new dimension of a language directly united to corporeality. Thus speaking is never disconnected from our incarnate being and from its pathos.[32]

Abiding

I have shown how current phenomenology is marked by a triple hypertrophy, so that borrowing from it to speak of the Eucharist is not sufficient for descending to the depths of our "abyss": The phenomenological excess of "sense over non-sense" (the always present primacy of intentionality), the increase of "flesh over body" (speaking of lived experience, but without measuring the weight of organicity ["unconsciousness of the Nietzschean body"]), and the eulogy of "weakness in the forgetting of force" (derived from the welcome of the other so systematized as to have become instrumentalized). It was useful to develop the following three traits of the viaticum as a joining in the union of bodies and in Eucharistic communion: our *interior chaos* made up of passions and impulses (Eucharistic heritage [animality]), the *power of the body* also to be able to transform everything (Eucharistic content [corporeality]), and *the harmony of hearts* to the extent they can be given (Eucharistic modality [eros]). What remains now is only its finality, which is what in the final analysis gives it meaning: "Those who eat my flesh and drink my blood abide in me, and I in them" (John 6:56).

"Remaining," abiding (*la manence*), in no way amounts only to "permanence" or the accusation of "presentifying." "Real" presence is not real because it is turned into a thing, but because it is given and ready to be consumed or, better, desired. It is in the distance of the desired, by God, that the tabernacle gains meaning, as the awaiting of the Eucharistic body in order to be adored and eaten. "Love makes the body" more than "the body makes love." Accordingly one will expect that the beloved will always desire and watch for us. The meaning of "the *gift* of his presence" must first be heard in this way, as it is unendingly continued and always waits to summon us. One must say with Marion that "in the *eucharistic present*, all presence is deduced from *the charity of the gift*; all the rest in it becomes appearance for a gaze without charity: the perceptible species, the metaphysical conception of time, the reduction to consciousness, all are degraded to one figure (or caricature) of charity."[33]

To learn to "live," both the world and myself by the other, such is the Eucharistic and the erotic ambition. Far from fleeing beyond my humanity (angelism) or to fall below its imposed limit (bestiality), a "Eucharistic *enthusiasm*," etymologically innervates the act of communion, in the sense that I am fully incorporated into God. In this my animality, my corporeality, and my act of desire take on meaning and are converted. The "abiding" of the human body is in a Christian sense that of the "body of God," in the sense that during the ascension, according to Romano Guardini, "Christianity has dared to place the (human) body into the most hidden depths of God."[34] What is true of the eschatological is by anticipation also true of the Eucharistic, prefigured in the erotic spousal union and fully accomplished in the Eucharistic viaticum. The nuptial blessing underlines this magnificently: "Brothers, ask of God to bless the new spouses who *have just received together the body and the blood of the Lord,* and for that *in giving themselves one to the other* they become *a single flesh and a single spirit*: give them *the body of your Son* by whom will be realized *their unity.*"[35]

—*Translated by Christina M. Gschwandtner*

Original Breath

KARMEN MACKENDRICK

> The paths to God are as numerous as the breaths of the creatures.
> —**Ibn al-'Arabi, quoting a Sufi saying, in William Chittick,**
> *The Sufi Path of Knowledge: Ibn al'Arabi's Metaphysics of Imagination*

Let There Be

> . . . articulation before the letter, apparition of something where there
> was nothing or something else.
>
> **Maurice Merleau-Ponty, *The Visible and the Invisible***

In the beginning, God speaks.[1]

It is not clear that this marks a very promising start for a carnal herme-neutics. If we could somehow take a text by itself, out of its context and history, it might. But, of course, this story of Genesis enters into the long history of the Abrahamic faiths. There it encounters in subsequent millen-nia an insistence on a God who is beyond and outside all time and place. That already makes speaking very strange, and it becomes stranger still with the insistence that creation must be *ex nihilo*, that before this speak-ing creator there is *nothing*, not even the matter out of which a world can be formed—and that the speaker is likewise immaterial, a God thoroughly disincarnate. Without a material body to form the words or air to carry the vibrations, "speaking" here becomes something odd indeed. And language in general follows it, rendered disincarnate in its meanings. If this is where we begin to read, if this is the genesis of meaning, is hermeneutics destined against incarnation from the start?

If creation is the work *ex nihilo* of a creator whose eternity is utterly separate from time, then the creational speaking can at best be a rather stretched metaphor; the "voice" is disembodied, speaking at no time from nowhere to no one. But Genesis, it turns out, does not give us very firm ground for these disincarnating claims. "In the beginning, when God created the heavens and the earth" (Gen 1:1),[2] we cannot, admittedly, have the heavens and the earth already in place and formed: that leaves no room at all for creative activity or beginning, and so the story goes nowhere. But that does not mean that we cannot have them at all. Rather, "the earth was a formless wasteland, and darkness covered the abyss, while a mighty wind swept over the waters" (Gen. 1:1–2).[3] *There is*, though in a way that, as formless, cannot quite be specified except by negations—of shape, of fertility, of light. That *there is* gives us a new possibility for reading the voice, as something still strange and wonderful, but closer to and more resonant with voice as we know it, voice with which we speak, voice as vibration given meaning in flesh.

The first things spoken in the story are well known: "Let there be light" (Gen. 1:3), God says; "Let the water under the sky be gathered into a single basin" (Gen. 1:9), and so on. God seems to speak in a kingly fashion, commanding; and if we were understanding creation as *ex nihilo*, then we would see those commands as sufficient to bring about results even if there were no one (indeed, before the light, no thing) to follow them. But if there is *not* no thing, then it is the earth and the water, and the darkness and the light, that follow God's commands—or, more promisingly, that *respond* to God's speaking in their very movements and formations. If they respond, then that speaking is something different from the disembodied voice of the ultimate ruler, something more promising for the materiality of words, and indeed of the sense of the world.[4] This sense is divine, but the divine must be infinitely relational, an infinite conversation.

Such a possibility arises not only in the unformed earth, but in the ambiguity of that which blows over the waters. I have used the New American Bible translation here, and it declares that "a mighty wind swept over the waters" (Gen. 1:2). Most often, however, English versions render the phrase *ruach elohim* not as "mighty wind," but as "Spirit of God." Sometimes this spirit "moves" upon the waters, or "sweeps" over them. Often it more vaguely "hovers."[5] Both words in the translated phrase are ambiguous— breath (which here as in many languages bears the implication of spirit), or wind; god, or divine, or mighty.[6] As is usual with translations, this presents a problem of choice. If, however, we choose not to choose—or rather, if we choose the ambiguity of divine breath *as* a mighty wind blowing over the abyssal and unformed—then we hear an intriguing voice beginning to sound, not just in the blowing of the wind, but in the creation of the world.

Attending to the phenomenology of word-making, we realize that the resoundings of that voice echo in bodily speech. All of our speaking is modulations of breath, raw material shaped and stretched and cut by our body's movements, from our diaphragms to our lips, made into sound, breathed out on our own small wind. The divine breath in Genesis's first beginning moves upon the abyssal waters and the dark sky and the formless earth; they move responsively. Again, we might read them as responding to command, and although the God in this story is not the omnipotent divinity of later theologies, gods do tend to be in charge. But imagine this as something more intimate, a breath given form by matter and matter its meaning by breath: a voice, a speaking (or, as Hildegard of Bingen beautifully argues, a singing)[7] in which chaos moves into the shape and the song of a continuously emerging world. God says, and light moves, and water, and earth, and it is good. In this sense even this first word is breathed, there on the waters when God began creating, and a wind moves upon the waters. World is both divine word given voice by the earth, and the earth's form shaped by divine breath, bearing that trace of its own brush with divinity.

That God writes twice, once in creation and once in scripture, is a commonplace of late ancient and medieval commentary that allows the possibility of reading divinity in the world and the enticing complexities of reading the world within scripture. If we take creation as breath moving matter—that is, as voice speaking—then this inscribing is also a voicing. The world becomes a strange sort of book that is its own coauthor and reads itself aloud, a song that composes itself in the singing.

Promising though it might be, this forming is not the end of the Genesis stories of making. Once formed, the world is filled, and as this happens, divine speaking becomes more self-evidently a matter of address. First there are plants, and then the animals, who are urged to "be fertile, multiply . . ." (Gen. 1:22). The animals do not speak words back to their creator, but, like primally chaotic matter, they respond, giving the speaking its meaning within the world, embodying it in their very movements. Their actions, their very ways of being, speak in harmony with the request given to them, and with the matter of the world in which they tend to find themselves rather more at home than humans do.[8]

It is only then that God, having spoken among Godself (Gen. 1:26), creates human beings to whom it likewise speaks, giving them the same commandment as the other animals. Like the others, humans do not appear to have words to answer the divine commandment. They are, however, given a special place: in common with other animals, they are commanded to multiply and they are given plants for food (Gen. 1:29), but uniquely, they are given dominion over the earth and its living species (Gen. 1:26, 1:28)—an infamous moment that has been used to justify human disregard for the rest of the planet as something simply placed at our disposal. After this, God rests.

All this would be complex enough. But famously, it is here that Genesis takes a deep breath and begins again, as an older story is imperfectly tacked onto the first. In the second beginning, we do not learn of the response between matter and breath/wind, nor hear of divine creative voice. All that is condensed into a preliminary statement: "At the time when the Lord God made the earth and the heavens—while as yet there was no field shrub on earth and no grass of the field had sprouted . . ." (Gen. 2:4–5). But we do read of a first human, shaped out of the matter of that earth, as the animals were in the previous version (Gen. 2:7). Once more, breath moves: having molded a man from earth, God "blew into his nostrils the breath of life, and so man became a living being" (Gen. 2:7). With that divine breath, the man lives—but there is nowhere to put him.

So, once again, we read that God makes plants, as a paradisiacal garden is quickly put together for this created human. The garden supplies all of the man's physical needs, including the aesthetic (Gen. 2:8–9). The man (this time minus the co-created woman of the first story) is told "to cultivate and care for" the land (Gen. 2:15), rather than to dominate it. In a move the first story is missing, he is warned against eating from the tree of knowledge of good and bad (Gen. 2:17), a warning that will become significant in the story's next chapter.

Speaking, With and Over

> A word, so long as it's not absorbed without remainder to a sense, remains essentially extended between other words, stretching to touch them, though not merging with them: and that's language as body.

> **Jean-Luc Nancy, *Corpus***

No longer homeless, the first man is nonetheless lonely, or at least alone—and God feels that this is not good for him (Gen. 2:18), a truth that must be self-evident, as we are not told why (even God, though, has an "us" to whom to speak, both in the first story [Gen. 1:26] and in this second [Gen. 3:22]). The first man is a single word, meaningless until he is put into place, as if into a sentence—but he still needs others with whom he can speak so that the sentence may have meaning. So from the same earth, God makes the animals, which he then sends before the human.

The interaction here is intriguing: "So the Lord God formed out of the ground various wild animals and various birds of the air, and he brought them to the man to see what he would call them; whatever the man called each of them would be its name. The man gave names to all the cattle, all the birds of the air, and all the wild animals. . . ." (Gen. 2:19–20).

So what sort of relation is language making here, when the man calls the animals by their names? Patricia Cox Miller, in "Adam, Eve, and the Elephants," warns us of an often overlooked conflation in a widespread answer to that query. The scene of

> Adam naming the animals in Gen. 2:19–20 is understood, by an intertextual sleight of hand, in concert with Gen. 1:26, the passage in which God gives humankind dominion over the fish, the birds, and the domestic and wild animals. . . . Such a view of the dominical Adam separates the human from the animal rather than placing the human in a continuum with the flesh-and-bones materiality of the natural world.[9]

With this conflation, we can ignore the breath that moves over and forms the unformed world and moves into and animates the living animals, and declare that only breathed into human nostrils is divine breath anything special: divinity speaks to, and through, us alone.

This interpretation, Miller notes, justifies the further claim, popular in Patristic commentary, that human speech is driven by reason, and both exemplifies and justifies our dominance over all other species.[10] The tradition carries over well into medieval interpretation too, across the Abrahamic traditions.[11]

But then something odd happens. For Dante in his *De vulgari eloquentia* (ca. 1302–1305), human language moves uniquely between our unusual neediness (we lack both the natural instincts that allow animals to communicate and the spiritually reflective capacity of the angels) and our vaunted rationality.[12] Language is firmly linked to reason, but it cannot be disembodied. Despite his "rational" emendations of scriptural texts, Dante seems to remember that meaning in Genesis must move in the world of matter.

This remembrance struggles against centuries of interpretation insisting that the first man is distinguished by his perfect mind, thereby set above all other animals, who are carnal alone; and that mind displays itself in the unique capacity for language, which no longer emerges in the world as a whole. Meaning may be divine—there is a strong theological component to most premodern semiotics—but like the divine, it seems to have been tidily discorporated. This is not a world in song. Can our saying, then, serve to do anything other than rule? Can we remember how to mean in matter, to harmonize with the flesh of the world?

Even in these same sources, there is evidence that we can. Despite his turn to the reasonableness of language, Dante sees the first word, a word that will become the source of all language, as something else—a cry of joy. "As to what was pronounced by the voice of the first speaker . . . I have no doubt that it was the name of God, or *El* . . . [I]t is reasonable that he who existed before [the Fall] would have begun with a cry of joy; and, since there is no joy outside God, but all joy is in God, and since God Himself is joy itself, it follows that the first man to speak should first and before all have said 'God.'"[13] The breath breathed into the first man's nostrils is exhaled in the very joy that it names.

Breath is drawn in as life and breathed out as joyfulness. I have wondered elsewhere if every cry of joy might not harbor some trace of divine delight.[14] I am still inclined to see the first human speaking as the address to the animals, but I don't see why there should not have been some delight in it, too—perhaps even, from the lonely and singular human, a cry of joy, or of hope.

Whatever the first word may be, there is another naming to come. Returning to the Genesis story, we find that the call to the animals has not quite assuaged the first man's loneliness. Not that the man doesn't like the animals, so far as we are told, but they aren't of his kind, and so are not quite able to satisfy his need for companionship—as, we must realize, God also was not, so we should hesitate to assume that this is a sign of animal inferiority. One more act of creation takes place, this time out of the man's own living matter, making a second human. How does he respond? Just as he did to the animals: he calls, he names, the woman thus created ("This one shall be called 'woman'" [Gen. 2:23]). But this call is differently heard, as communication within a species generally is, and the woman stays with him as one who is suitably companionate and helpful.

We could read this with feminist indignation, and sometimes I find myself tempted to do so (turning in preference toward the dual creation of the first story), and we might not even be wrong: maybe the woman is just another animal under the dominion of the man (who will even rename her, later on, as Eve [Gen. 3:20]). But there are other readings of this combination of namings, and perhaps we might more hopefully say that the gift of companionship is rightly met when we call by name, when we acknowledge what the other is, human or not; that there is a special companionship among our own species, those materially most like us, but that this does not exclude the possibility of calling across to others.

The realization that we need not conflate the stories of naming and dominion can allow us to reread the former, against the insistence on a natural domination granted by rationality; this, in turn, will allow us to reincarnate language, to read once more the word made flesh. We have to go back to the point that in Genesis God *does not know* the names in advance, and this suggests that the animals are genuinely unnamed until the man encounters them—sees them, at least; undoubtedly smells them; hears those who make sounds, pets those who invite touch. Adam does not *know* the names and get them right; either he makes them up, or he recognizes them in the animals themselves. There is no indication that the names preexist the calling. The God of Genesis does not instruct Adam to designate the animals so that a proper typology may be formed, or to enhance their use value, or to know which among them might be suited for food (in fact, the human beings in this story seem to be contentedly vegetarian or maybe vegan; it will only be after the Fall that God clothes them in leather [3:21]). Rather, God sends the animals and *waits* to see—to hear—how Adam calls them (2:19). God appears to be a little bit curious, interested in hearing how the animals are called, how the man will respond to their presence. The man in turn is not simply identifying, but calling; not simply designating, but naming, so that each animal may be called by name. And God does not *instruct* the man to label the animals (though the stories of competition with the angels read Genesis thus), but sends the animals before him on the assumption that the man *will* respond to their presence by calling them: not just directing meaning to matter, but responding as one body to another in meaningful voice, voice that gives meaning as sound, sound born on breath to move the world. God is not exercising dominion over this first human, nor giving him subjects for domination of his own, but offering him possible companions, so that he will not be lonely; and the man is not exercising dominion over the animals, but responding to their presence, forming his breath into sounds among theirs. That he will still need a companion of his own species suggests a limit to this friendly possibility, its need for a supplement, but not an exclusion of it.

In his beautiful, angry, and elegiac text, *The Animal Side*, Jean-Louis Bailly views our own naming of animals, an echo of this first human naming, as itself something akin to divine act. The divinity, however, is not so much in our possession as in the language in which we are immersed (in, to turn from Bailly back to Genesis, the ever-speaking, word-made material world), and so does not at all grant superiority. Bailly reads naming poetically and Neoplatonically: "[T]he rain of the One, dispersed by language, drop by drop, is an infinite dissemination, and . . . with fingers pointed and names brandished, tentatively, as with the images we create, we lag behind and beneath all language, beneath its every modulation, its every utterance . . . ."[15] Humanity, following this first human speaking, points by hand toward the animals and calls them by name, in a paradigmatic dispersal of language. But the pointing is *tentative*, awaiting and depending upon the response that will let us know if we have named rightly, the response that is the very meaning of right naming. The finger beckons as much as it indicates. In Genesis, God's own self acknowledges the rightness of the call as it emerges into this relation. Indeed, for Dante, Thomas, and Moses Maimonides, prelapsarian human language is *perfect*. But what does that perfection mean when this first man talks to the animals?

Speaking Flesh

> [T]he question is . . . whether every relation between me and Being, even vision, even speech, is not a carnal relation, with the flesh of the world.
>
> **Maurice Merleau-Ponty, *The Visible and the Invisible***

With or without the presumption of rational dominance, linguists, semioticians, poets, and theologians have long turned to Genesis in what Umberto Eco calls "the search for the perfect language," a dream of utterly perfect and transparent communication—a dream we have already seen at work here. *The* perfect language precedes division. The episode of naming seems to bear this perfection; the names that Adam calls are so rightly the names of the animals that God accepts them without hesitation; perhaps the animals do as well. This is the language that falls apart after the Fall itself. But what was the nature of its holding together, when time was good?

By now the world's speaking is quite polyphonic. To review quickly, God speaks: to the formlessness and abyssal, to the animals, to the humans, to the multiplicity of itself. The world, the animals, the humans, and the self of God respond, in their widely varied fashions. The man speaks: to the animals, to the woman, to God. The woman speaks: to the serpent, to the man, to God. The serpent speaks, generating millennia of argument. Commentators have been somewhat invested in assuring us that whatever the serpent is up to here (and who or whatever speaks through him), the animals, generally, are speechless.

Even in the service of reading the creation stories for the possibility of speaking and song, I am not quite prepared to claim that the animals are word makers, any more than I would claim this of the world formed of matter and breath. But let us look at an equally intriguing possibility. Not one of animals making words, but one of a meaningful, significant appearance, a movement that is also a phrasing—like that of grammar or music, a speaking with the world in which humans are included.

On the notion of meaningful animal phrasings, Bailly quotes Maurice Merleau-Ponty:

> "A field of space-time has been opened: there is the beast there," [Merleau-Ponty] writes, and the whole animal realm is for him like the nonclosed sum of those fields of singularity, or like a grammar— in other words, a nonfinite possibility of phrasings. . . . Merleau-Ponty can say that "the form of the animal is not the manifestation of a finality, but rather of an existential value of manifestation, of presentation," that is, an appearance to be understood entirely as a language.[16]

For the animals, Bailly argues, that appearance is not other than reality or truth. Oddly to the human mind, there is no representation superadded to animal movement. Before they are represented, before the word becomes a sign used for designation, the animal world is a space for a curious presentation. The animals in their own spaces are

> profoundly inscribed in the writing of their lives and in their material surroundings. . . . The expanse that is present, that responds "present," as it can do by leaving the scene, and by taking its leave, as it can do in Africa, with something tense and nonchalant at the same time, a sort of perfect harmony in the wake of a giraffe ambling along and living before our eyes in the other world of the film that it is making in slow motion . . .
>
> The giraffe, for example, but also all the others, and each one in a unique film developed differently every day, a film whose scenario . . . has in any case no need for us in order to write itself . . .[17]

There is no separate representation here, no language animals have *about* what appears, what they are, what they do. Their film is not something they are thinking up and preserving for a later view. No book *about* the world, no song *about* creation: only the world in which the animal tracks and motions, like our own, inscribe sense and vibrate with divine breath; the book and the song and the speaking that *there is*, that is both matter and life. Theirs is *an appearance to be understood entirely as a language*. When in Genesis the animals appear before the man, and he calls them by name, he exhibits his understanding of the appearance-language in the form of words, words that God likewise understands: he responds to the appearance understood as a language with words understood as names. He and the animals are matter with the breath of life, immersed in the same breath-blown world. "[T]heir form, like our own, is finite. . . . What surrounds it, welcomes it, threatens it, is infinite"[18]—their appearance in what is (like) a language, like our own emergence in(to) words, can never be narrowed down to those in it, but must consider the space as well, a space mutually made with those who move there. The hermeneutics of such a language, the ways by which it means and it can be read, must be carnal throughout.

Animals and humans share the breath of life, the divine breath that as wind blows the world into habitable form. In the very unfolding of their present and presence, animals enact their own "texts," as if the division we must make between presentation and representation did not exist. As if, that is, their language were a correspondence so pure that the very idea, the very distance necessary for one thing to correspond to (or with) another, ceased to be. As if *theirs* were the perfect language, the primal identity that Adam voiced, or echoed in vocalizing, when he first called them all by name, so rightly that the call belonged immediately to each of them—as if God saw, and heard, that this too was good. With the placement of the animals in the world, four different modes of meaning interact harmoni-ously: those of God, matter, human, animal. The goodness of language has to belong to, has to be breathed and sung by, all of them. Only the postlapsarian world brings dissonance and incomprehension. Language approaches perfection not in domination, but in harmony.

Miller raises the possibility of reading Adam among the animals, in this Edenic perfection, as something other than a force of domination: "Does [Adam], like animals, exist in the world 'like water in water,' as Georges Bataille suggested? That is, is Adam's intimacy with the world so profound that there is a natural continuity between the human and the animal?"[19] On such an Orphic reading, language is made not to dominate, but to call, from the beginning in which matter and breath are given to one another. Adam is brought those animals not to show who is in charge, but because it is not good for him to be alone. In language, our own finite form reaches beyond itself. If there is a right name for the animals in the story, it can-not belong solely to humans. It must be right for the animals, too, and for God, who hears and acknowledges it; it must move rightly in the world. It must somehow belong to, somehow harmonize with, the animal phrasing; it must in sound be resonant with what appears, must ripple within it. And the movement must matter as much as the mind.

If we read in each of the creation stories that of which it speaks in most detail—in the first, the speaking creation of the world that will be inhab-ited by the humans who come last in it; in the second, the creation and speaking-with of those humans in the world created around them—then a divine carnality of meaning does, in a particular fashion, keep emerging. This is not simply a creation *by* voice, however allegorical its form. Creation *becomes* voice, the interaction of matter and breath. The world's movements continue the speaking, or even the song. And it is breath too that moves in, and moves, all animals (humans too), breath by with we live—but by which and as which we can only live as material.

Despite the tendency to rejoice in human dominance and "natural" superiority, the hagiographic and ascetic traditions, Miller notes, sometimes give us richer options for human-animal interaction. She describes the story of the anchorite Theon, "with the face of an angel giving joy to his visitors by his gaze and abounding with much grace." The tracks of animals could be seen near his cell, and "They say he used to go out of his cell at night and keep company with wild animals, giving them to drink from the water that he had." Miller speculates that "[P]erhaps . . . like Adam, Theon existed with the animals in the world like water in water, in an intimacy so profound that the animal and the angel were one."[20]

In such an intimacy, the joyful cry of "*El!*" and the calling of names to the animals are equally instances of perfect speech. Neither call creates fusion; the man, like the animals, will need another of his own species (though this pairing will not necessarily turn out all that well, and perhaps Adam leaving Paradise considers that he should have taken the dog). But they are harmonious in the world not yet out of tune with itself. A perfect language breathes in harmony with matter, with flesh and its meanings.

Language must be as much polyphonic song as useful tool. And perhaps, in this world, the human not only exists, but speaks, like an animal and an angel: with a speech as world-suited as the animals to whom it calls, a speech as able to call the divine as the angels are, because that calling is in the very matter of the world (suitability to the world and to God are not so disharmonious after all). We call from body to body, breath to breath, to each other, to animals, to divinity, to the world.

Again, I have no wish to conflate animal inscription with human speaking, nor, as one who has been in love with words since before my first memories, to claim that there is nothing special about the latter. But, like others who share that love, I cannot help thinking of a perfect language. And when I look where others have looked, what I see is not perfect control of or through words ("the question" of "which is to be master, that's all"),[21] but the sense of language transfigured, even when written, to the motility of speaking; of a body that breathes song, of divine animality, of continuous carnal creation, the breath of each body speaking its part in making the meaning of the world.

On the Flesh of the Word

Incarnational Hermeneutics

JOHN PANTELEIMON MANOUSSAKIS

We have to begin by reminding ourselves of this simple truth: that "the Word became flesh"—it was not the flesh that became word, it was not the carnal that became spiritual or must become spiritual. Contrary to the usual accusations brought against Christianity, to spiritualize the flesh and its affectations would simply amount to getting Christianity backwards—it would mean to undo Christianity and worse "in its name." Finally, it would mean to unravel Christianity's absolutely nonnegotiable claim, the claim by which Christianity stands or falls, that "the Word became flesh."

I do not mean to dismiss or ignore the long and various Christian traditions that seek to do precisely this and, what is worse, from within the Church. But this was because already from the beginning the enemy, so to speak, was within the Church's citadel. In fact, that very citadel was erected by some of the best—after all they are still standing—material: namely, and I am about to point fingers now, Plato's sublation and incorporation of cultic and mythic religion to a new absolute system, though the best of Platonists would be rightly offended by the word "system" here, which, to the extent it incorporated religion—"orgiastic religion" Patočka says[1]— became a higher, subtler, more sophisticated form of religion that most of you might recognize even today in Christianity.[2]

The question is of course quite old; it goes back to Luther's indignation with reason ("a whore") and even further back to Tertullian's famous question: "what does Jerusalem have to do with Athens?" Yet, what we have here, what these initial remarks open for us, is more than a question, it is a fascinating history of readings and appropriations, or rather, of *mis*readings and *mis*appropriations.

We have forgotten that the task we were given was not to turn the flesh into spirit, the sensible into suprasensible—that, after all, has proven to be the easy part and, as we have already mentioned, others were better at it—rather, the task we were given was the far more difficult operation of incarnating the spiritual, rendering the suprasensible sensible, which is the sensible thing to do, and, scandal of all scandals, which Kierkegaard never tired of reminding us, of particularizing the abstract and universal.

The very practice of hermeneutics—ἑρμηνεύειν—retains some of the ambiguity discerned here. To be a hermeneut could mean to take Hermes as your guide, to function in place of Hermes, that is, like the god of translation. I use this term in the broadest possible sense: to move from one place to another, to transfer, *meta-pherein* (the metaphoric is an indispensable part of the hermeneutic operation), to render the one by means of the other, ἄλλως ἀγορεύειν, thus the allegorical, and so on. But from where and to where? Hermes, again, provides us with a clue: Hermes was better known as ψυχοπομπός—the guide of the souls—literally the one who leads the souls from their carnal dwellings, their somatic tombs, to the place of the spirits, to the spiritual (and invisible, thus, to Hades).

Hermeneutics, therefore, has a share in the blame for disincarnate abstraction. In the most literal sense, the process in question is that of textual interpretation, transferring and translating the flesh of the letter into the sense of the spirit: to its *meaning*. Thus, all too often the hermeneut can become blind to the visible, to the word as written sign. And then, the incarnation of sound and thought must be reversed: what the hermeneut sees is what cannot be seen, the invisible or the spiritual. Hermeneuts would read between the lines, behind the words, outside the text (*hors texte*) but never the sign—or, more precisely, what they take to be only a signifier that one must pass over in a hurry, for a higher place (*anagoge*), a different place (*allegory*), throwing the written word aside (*parable*), carrying ceaselessly this process of spiritualization, textual rumination, chewing the text but refusing to incorporate it. Hermeneutics can become the reverse of digestion, a process of excretion, spitting out, throwing up.

On the other hand, "take, eat, this is my body." The Word who became flesh said these words, which appropriately became text—and I would like to remind us that the first theological method, since this is what St. John the Theologian does, is not to *read* the text but to *eat* it.

So I went to the angel and said to him, "Give me the little book." And he said to me, "Take and eat it; and it will make your stomach bitter, but it will be as sweet as honey in your mouth." Then I took the little book out of the angel's hand and ate it, and it was as sweet as honey in my mouth. But when I had eaten it, my stomach became bitter. And he said to me, "You must prophesy again about many peoples, nations, tongues, and kings." (Rev. 19:9–11)

"Take, eat." I'd return to this phrase and to the image of eating, digestion, and incorporation.

Now we have seen, briefly, that at least one endemic processes of hermeneutics as such is a movement from the concrete and the particular to the universal—to turn the body of the text into a *theoria*. It is no accident that the great Christian hermeneuts were also the great ascetics. Think of the father of Christian hermeneutics, the one who systematized the allegorical interpretation of the Scriptures, the great Origen. That Origen has also a deficient Christology is extremely telling, but that is perhaps of interest only for the theologians. For now I will call attention to the connection between monasticism and the spiritual reading of the Scriptures, which, at the same time, allows us to add a third common characteristic, their distance from the Eucharistic site.

A reference to some radical tendencies within the Reformed Churches is here unavoidable: the privilege of the Word of God (*sola scriptura*) over the Eucharistic presence of the Risen One, which becomes only a memorial, is an example of the connection we seek to establish. Perhaps even more pertinent (but I am afraid more obscure as well) would be the example of Hesychasm, an example of Orthodox spirituality's radicalization, where the Eucharist becomes sometimes entirely secondary, overtaken by the priority given to the efforts in achieving inner purification and illumination by means that are individual (individual prayer, fasting, practicing certain bodily postures, etc.) and thus lie outside the Eucharistic site of the ecclesial community. The privilege of *hesychia* (stillness, silence), fundamentally gnostic in its provenance, forgets that "in the beginning" was not silence but "the Word," the Λόγος, whose eternal utterance creates the world in all its noisiness. Let no one, then, despise the noise of the World lest he despise the Word that resounds through it.

Language (and ultimately the *Logos*) is the background to any silence. Giving priority (chronological or otherwise) to silence is to fall prey to the Gnostic/Origenistic/Neoplatonic temptation. Could silence even have been perceived (to make now a phenomenological observation) without the anterior experience of language/music/noise? Or to put it otherwise: what comes first—movement (language) or rest (silence)? Here, I think, the allegiance between Neoplatonic *stasis* (rest) and Gnostic *sige* (silence) is quite telling, and decisive for this discussion.[3] Buddhism culminates in silence (e.g., the silence of Vimalakirti). Given the disembodying tendencies of Buddhism,[4] this is all the more reason to be suspicious of any emphasis on silence. Similarly, we are not surprised by the priority given to silence in Heidegger's analysis of Dasein (itself one of the most disembodied philosophical constructions out there), since, for Heidegger, not only is silence prior to discourse, indeed its possibility, but also higher than language, insofar as conscience "speaks solely and constantly in the mode of silence."[5] Yet, does not Psalm 46:10 ("Be still, and know that I am God") instruct us to be still or silent? The stillness to which this Psalm refers to is an epistemological stillness ("and know . . ."), that is, only the stillness of man, so that he may be able to perceive ever more acutely the Logos of God.

The Spirituality of the Body

I will use an example from a classic of Christian spirituality, St. Augustine's *Confessions*, in which, even a reader as astute as von Balthasar[6] is not exempted from seeing a process of mystical ascent, ultimately not much different than Plotinus's, instead of an exemplary case of carnal hermeutics on which the language of the text so stubbornly insists.

In employing the language of the Scriptural parable of the prodigal son in almost every turn of his narrative, St. Augustine not only Christianizes the Neoplatonic structure of descent (*katastrophe*) and ascent (*epistrophe*), around which the *Confessions* as a text is organized, but also alters it in a way that is decisive for incarnational hermeneutics. In our reading, we should be able to discern St. Augustine's criticism of the hegemonic primacy of vision and, as a result of that critique, the emergence of the alternative process of incarnating the spiritual. Thus, we will add to the two conversions around which conventional readings of the *Confessions* usually structured themselves—that is, the conversion of the mind (in Book VII) and the conversion of the heart (in Book VIII)—a third one, that has remained undetected so far, namely *the conversion of the flesh*, or better yet, the conversion *to* the flesh. Thus, I offer this reading as an example of what Richard Kearney has recently called a "carnal hermeneutics."[7] St. Augustine's narrative suggests such a descent into the bodily in two main cases: 1. by the reversal of the traditional hierarchy of the senses, whereby he places vision at the lowest end and gives priority to touch, as vision's very opposite, insofar as tactile intimacy necessitates the annihilation of distance on which vision operated;[8] and 2. by the consistent and constant employment of the parable of the prodigal son that would allow him to place a newly discovered emphasis on the flesh.

The episodic and fragmented nature of Augustine's past life must be rhapsodized into a unity—a unity, however, that can only come from a unified self. How is the self unified? By its return to the one God. What prompts or enables that return? Certainly not space. Thus, he writes:

> Not with our feet or by traversing great distances do we journey away from you or find our way back. That younger son of yours in the gospel did not hire horses or carriages, nor did he board ships, nor take wing in any visible sense nor put one foot before the other when he journeyed to that far country where he could squander at will the wealth you, his gentle father, had given him at his departure.[9]

Yet, not by the turning of the mind either, unless it is a mind affected by the after (*meta-noia*). We recall again that monstrosity which Augustine so aptly describes in Book VIII: "The mind commands the body and is instantly obeyed; the mind commands itself, and meets with resistance."[10] Can we reverse this chain of command? Can we say that the body could perhaps command the mind and that mind would obey? The prodigal's *metanoia* that set him upon the journey back to the paternal house was not a mental, spiritual, or psychological affectation, but physical, as physical and visceral as hunger can be. The task in the *Confessions* is not to spiritualize the flesh, but to incarnate the spirit, and in this regard the verticality of the Greek schema (Platonic and Neo-Platonic) of ascents and descents has to be abandoned for the sake of a communion between exteriority and interiority. Yet, as long as hunger is only "interior," that is, spiritual, it is not even perceived as hunger at all. "I was inwardly starved of that food which is yourself, O my God. Yet this inner famine created no pangs of hunger in me."[11] Spiritual hunger remains ineffective. Let us return to the Lucan parable:

> After he had spent everything, there was a severe famine in that whole country, and he began to be in need [ὑστερεῖσθαι/egere]. So he went and hired himself out to a citizen of that country, who sent him to his fields to feed pigs. He longed to fill his stomach with the pods that the pigs were eating, but no one gave him anything (Luke 15:14–16).

Notice that from all the images that the Gospel could use in order to convey the state of human misery, the evangelist chose that of *hunger*. Eating is not only a way of recognizing our dependency to each other and to the world—so much for the prodigal son's claim to independence!—but by eating we assimilate the world into ourselves, we turn that which is outside inside. Think of this passing from outside to inside and you will discover that this opposition is nothing else than the exemplification of distance and fragmentation. Ultimately, distance comes down to this opposition between an inside (that I identify with myself) and everything else that is outside me. In eating, however, this wall of separation collapses—when I am hungry I am really hungry for the Other (following Sartre and Levinas)—and eating is one of the ways we have of overcoming the isolation that is the result of being scattered beings. Eating declares—willingly or not, and contrary to all our illusionary attempts to self-mastery and independence—my dependence on the world, on the cows which provide me with their meat, but also on the grass that fed the cows, on the water that fertilized the soil on which that grass grew, and so on. "But eating, by contrast, is peaceful and simple; it fully realizes its sincere intention: 'The man who is eating is the most just of men.'"[12] A referential totality is presented in every meal whereby the entire world is eaten. *When I eat, I eat the world.* But even more than the world, I eat the labor and the effort, the care and the artistry of the people who cultivated, prepared, and cooked my food. No meal is ever solitary—even if I eat alone in the seclusion of my room—every meal is a public and communal event. A community established and referred to by every bite.

It is also a way that can take place only by means of and thanks to our bodies. Obviously only an embodied being can be hungry and only an embodied being can eat. Contrary to what one might believe, our best chance to overcome the fragmentation that human nature imposes on us is through our bodies. It is our body that abridges the distance that keeps separating us from others, but it is our body that allows us to be united with God—it is not accidental that we *eat* the Eucharist and that that the liturgy takes the form of a meal, such as the meal that the Father offers in celebration for the return of the lost son: "Bring the fattened calf and kill it. Let's have a feast and celebrate" (Lk. 15:23). As it is not an accident that we have these gifts on account of the body that Christ took upon Himself in His kenotic effort to traverse the land of distance that separated us from Him. In Christ, God is not any more a god who sees (*theos*) but a god who touches and can be touched even to the folly of being-eaten. In eating, I make the world my flesh and my blood, *not* my spirit, but I incarnate or rather I incorporate—the original and literal meaning of incorporation—the world that, otherwise, would have remained an abstraction in spite of its cows, its grass, and its soil. Spiritualization posits a real danger that seeks to cancel out both the incarnation as well the transubstantiation of the Eucharist. Every time one partakes of communion he or she does not change the host into their body but it changes them—in an inverse digestion indicative and exemplary of inverse intentionality—into His body. As

Augustine was told: "I am the food of the mature; grow then, and you will eat me. You will not change me into yourself like bodily food: you will be changed into me."[13] The Church is turning the world into Christ a mass at a time. There is no room here for the "spirituality" of Gnosis. It is for this reason that the Church could not compromise with any of the versions of immortality that classical thought had made available to her—neither the immortality of the soul alone, nor reincarnation—but insisted upon the scandalous and paradoxical notion of the resurrection of the bodies. Without a physical body, our experience of the distance that separates us from each other becomes permanent. It is in this sense that we read in the parable of the rich man and the poor Lazarus that: "between us and you a great chasm has been set in place, so that those who want to go from here to you cannot, nor can anyone cross over from there to us" (Lk. 16:26). For it is only as hell that a human being can experience the absence of communion with other beings.

Speaking of hell, it is only the devil who despises the body and everything bodily, because he despises the *communion* which the human body can effect. His greatest disadvantage is precisely the fact that he is a spirit. He does not need to fast for he abstains from food entirely, nor does he need to resist the temptations of fornication for he cannot engage in any sexual act at all—yet this is precisely the impediment to his repentance: without a body that can feel the effect of hunger, the want that reveals one's dependency and restores one's humility, the devil cannot repent.

This, I believe, explains the systematic and, at times, elaborate employment of the language of hungering, eating, and feasting in the *Confessions* that begins in Book I and extends through Book X, where memory is compared to the stomach of the mind.[14] It also sheds some light on a broader operation of incarnation set in motion in the *Confessions*, best exemplified perhaps by the assignment of the same key adjective, "restless" (*inquietum/inquieta*) in describing both the spiritual longing of the heart[15] and the physical manifestation of his sexual desire in his youthful erections.[16] The desire for God is not independent from the desire for the other human; nor is the desire for rest promised in God's kingdom contrary to the satisfaction that the body seeks. One who has not felt the latter would rarely and only with difficulty seek the former.

Finally, hunger entails a temporal element. Despite satisfying my hunger, in the course of time, I will become hungry *again*. Hunger and its satisfaction by eating demarcates the before and after of the body's time. Before repentance's after-thought (*meta-noia*) there is the after-body (*meta-somoia*): a body that becomes hungry is a body affected by time. The proof is again in the Scriptural parable of the prodigal son:

After he had spent everything, there was a severe famine in that whole country, and he began to be in need [ὑστερεῖσθαι] (Lk. 15:14).

The Greek verb employed here to denote a need that is most physical, namely hunger, means primarily "to come late," "to be too late." Ὑστερέω implies a lack or want first and foremost in terms of lateness (ὕστερος).[17] The prodigal son was, like Augustine, late ("Late have I loved you . . ."[18]). This ethical lateness is first inscribed and awakened in the body.

Our desires were given to us by God as a pedagogical exercise in learning how to seek that which is other than ourselves and beyond ourselves; the flesh as a bait, one may say, that, in catching us, might drive us outside our spiritual selves. In the words of Richard Kearney, "the most alimentary is the most elementary."[19]

Desire and the Eucharist

The confessional opening of the *Confessions* (where, by confession, one understands primarily praise and prayer) draws attention to the other alternative, an alternative that is almost destined to fail with regards to God, namely, language. The problematic of language is introduced by Augustine's emphasis on the literal meaning of infancy, as his "unspeaking stage" in life.[20] Language comes as a remedy to a fundamental experience of a primordial separation, a separation that manifests itself first in the distinction within/without, inside/outside: "I was frustrated in this, because my desires were inside me, while other people were outside and could by no effort of understanding enter my mind" (quia illae [voluntates] *intus* erat, *foris* autem illi).[21] The first experience of fallenness (trauma) is the separation from others, in terms of a distance in space.[22] Language here, as in Freud's celebrated example of the child's game while uttering alternatively the words "fort/da," becomes the means to cope with and remedy a painful absence. To this one, immediately, Augustine adds a second one: the separation from oneself, in terms of a distance in time. "My infancy has been so long dead now, whereas I am alive,"[23] he begins in his attempt to remember what cannot be recalled. "For what is it that I am trying to say, Lord, except that I do not know whence I came into this life that is but a dying . . . I do not know where I came from."[24] The mystery of memory, as it will be fully developed in Book X, is first disclosed through forgetfulness. "So I have been told, and I believe it on the strength of what we see other babies doing, for I do not remember doing it myself."[25]

Both experiences, separation from others, namely space, and separation from oneself, namely time, are, for Augustine, but two aspects of the same condition, namely of the *diastemic* nature of the fallen creation. Language, then, is grounded in such a condition and it is itself regulated by it. In Book X language is a privileged example of time, for to speak takes time and one cannot speak but in time. But language also "takes" space: the meaning of a word is determined by its position in a sentence. And even though one can use language to communicate with another, not every other speaks my language, as young Augustine learns from his painful attempts to master Greek.[26] Even among speakers of the same language, language can be the source of misconceptions and misunderstandings, thereby my separation from the Other is emphasized once more. Thus, "the very birth of language" is organized by the spatial and temporal interplay between presence and absence—the need to make present, if only in symbolic form, what is absent.[27]

Phenomenology's original contribution, however, consisted precisely in the recovery of the absence of the absent, by refusing to substitute it with a quasi-presence (e.g., the image "in" the mind in the absence of the thing itself, etc.) and by drawing attention to the role that absences play in the intentional life of the consciousness, where every aspect is always given together with a prospect and a retrospect, every presence is surrounded by absences. In short, if consciousness is not limited to the presence of the present—something that would have been consciousness's death—if it is able to intend what is absent, it is by virtue of an absence or an absencing. Thus, we can say, together with Ricoeur, that what language is for the psychoanalyst, intentionality is for the phenomenologist.[28]

The similarity extends further. As in every act of speech there is always an unspoken remainder, so every act of intentionality remains fundamentally partial and incomplete. Its partiality is twofold and has to do with the mutual embodiment of the thing given and of the intending consciousness. For by no act of perception could I ever see a thing in all its aspects and from all its angles; and, similarly, there could be no consciousness that is not embodied and thus, by its very embodiment, limited.

The incompleteness of intentionality is so crucial that in Husserl's writings it becomes the criterion of distinguishing between the unreflective and reflective consciousness:

> A veritable abyss yawns between consciousness and reality. Here, an adumbrated being, not capable of ever becoming given absolutely, merely accidental and relative; there, a necessary and absolute being, essentially incapable of becoming given by virtue of adumbration and appearance.[29]

We could say now without further delay that what makes the difference between reflective and unreflective consciousness, between the consciousness of itself, and the consciousness of the world and its manifestations, is nothing else than the body. Yet, we would be equally right in saying that what makes the difference between reflective and unreflective consciousness is nothing else than time. For if the presentation of phenomena is necessarily adumbrated this is because they cannot give themselves all *at once*, but rather only through the unfolding of time—a time that is ultimately grounded in the consciousness itself.[30] How are we to think of this homology between the bodily and the temporal with which phenomenology presents us? We spoke above about the body's time but it would not be accurate to speak of the body's own time; rather, the time is the body's, even before it is the mind's (internal time) or the world's (objective time). And it is, in fact, through that time that the mind's affliction of self-deception and self-division can be overcome.

We will leave aside for now Merleau-Ponty's insight that the body in its ambiguous state (neither consciousness nor a thing of the world) is phenomenology's closest approximation to the Freudian unconscious.[31] It is the body, Ricoeur notes, in its capacity for sex (and for eating, I would add) that enables us to exist "with no distance between us and ourself, in an experience of completeness exactly contrary to the incompleteness of perception and spoken communication."[32]

Such acts of embodiment as having sex or eating become the moment of truth—"from the start the question of pleasure is the question of truth"[33]—insofar as the self-deception enabled precisely by the opening between the reflected and the unreflected, the saying and the said, is eliminated by the closing of that very distance of self from itself by the descent to the bodily. Nevertheless, this descent remains always something desired but never completely achieved—the impossibility of desire, the impossibility of "existing as body, and nothing but body"[34] is due to the inescapable fact that desire itself is always articulated. That is, desire is fundamentally a demand on the Other, for it is never simply the desire *for* the Other but the desire for the Other's desire, the demand "Desire me!" Only for him who becomes fully and entirely flesh (John 1:14) and who is one with the utterance "this is my body,"[35] only from him who is this body and nothing but his body, can the descent to the bodily not only become possible but actual in a desire that is no longer desired but lived.

Notes

Introduction: Carnal Hermeneutics from Head to Foot
Richard Kearney and Brian Treanor

1. See Richard Kearney, "What Is Diacritical Hermeneutics?" in *The Journal of Applied Hermeneutics*, vol. 1, no. 1, ed. Nancy Moules (University of Calgary, 2011); "Eros, Diacritical Hermeneutics, and the Maybe" in *Philosophical Thresholds: Philosophy Today*, vol. 55, eds. Cynthia Willett and Leonard Lawlor (2001); and "Diacritical Hermeneutics" in *Hermeneutic Rationality/La rationalité herméneutique*, eds. Andrew Wiercinski et al. (Munster: LIT Verlag, 2011).

2. See Anne Davenport's "Translator's Note" in the endnotes to Chrétien's "From the Limbs of the Heart to the Soul's Organs," in this volume.

3. See Christina M. Gschwandtner's "Translator's Note" in the endnotes to Falque's "This Is My Body," in this volume.

The Wager of Carnal Hermeneutics
Richard Kearney

1. See our hermeneutic analysis of the other as alien, stranger and foreigner in our Introduction to *Phenomenologies of the Stranger*, eds. Richard Kearney and Kascha Semonovitch (New York: Fordham University Press, 2011) and *Hosting the Stranger*, eds. Richard Kearney and James Taylor (New York: Continuum Press, 2011).

2. See Richard Kearney, "What Is Diacritical Hermeneutics?" in *The Journal of Applied Hermeneutics*, vol. 1, no. 1, especially notes 5 and 6. See also Paul Ricoeur's hermeneutic analysis of Homeric recognition in *The Course of Recognition* (Cambridge, MA: Harvard University Press, 2005).

3. See Chapter 1, "In the Moment: The Uninvited Guest" in Richard Kearney, *Anatheism* (New York: Columbia University Press, 2010). One might also mention here Jesus' curing of the blind man where the senses of sight and touch are synesthetically crossed as well as his repeated post-resurrection acts of sharing food with his disciples, at Emmaus, at lake Galilee and Jerusalem, where his risen identity is revealed through "tasting and touching." For a fuller treatment of the many literary and artistic renditions of Biblical and Gospel scenes of touching and tasting, see Jean-Luc Nancy, *Noli me Tangere* (New York: Fordham University Press, 2006) and Richard Kearney, *Flesh: Recovering our Senses in an Age of Excarnation* (forthcoming).

4. I am grateful to my brother Michael Kearney, for bringing this scene to my attention and the Buddhist image of the "co-arising of body and mind" like "two sheaves of reeds." See also Joanna Macy, in *Mutual Causality in Buddhism and General Systems Theory: The Dharma of Natural Systems* (Albany, NY: SUNY, 1991).

5. Aristotle, *De Anima* 2, 423. This references, as well as further citations of *De Anima* refer to the translation by J.A. Smith which is available both in print (London: Clarendon, 1931), and on the Internet Classics Archive, http://classics.mit.edu/Aristotle/soul.html. Citations include the book number (e.g., 2) and Bekker number (e.g., 423).

6. Aristotle, *De Anima* 2, 421.

7. Aristotle, *De Anima* 2, 418.

8. Aristotle, *De Anima* 2, 428.

9. See Jean-Louis Chrétien's illuminating commentary on Aristotle's claim that touch is the most universal of all the senses in an essay entitled "Body and Touch" in *The Call and the Response* (New York: Fordham University Press, 2004), 92–94. I am deeply indebted to Chrétien's brilliant hermeneutic retrieval of Aristotle's reading of the senses in *De Anima*, Book II, ch. 11, and also to John Panteleimon Manoussakis and Emmanuel Alloa for their recent innovative retrievals, both represented in this volume (see references in notes 10 and 21 below).

10. See commentary by Chrétien, "Body and Touch," 95–96 and the fascinating reading by John Panteleimon Manoussakis of these same passages in the *De Anima* in "Touching," part 3 of *God after Metaphysics: A Theological Aesthetic* (Bloomington: Indiana University Press, 2007). Aristotle notes that the fact that we perceive through the medium of touch—namely flesh—"escapes us" (Aristotle, *De Anima* 2, 423b) and this gives rise to various metaphorical readings of the flesh—as an air-envelope, membrane, watery second skin, etc. And, we might add, its very enigmatic character has provoked countless different philosophical readings including those cited and featured in this volume (see essays by Chrétien, Alloa, Manoussakis, Nancy, et al.). Given Aristotle's revolutionary claim that "flesh is not the organ but the *medium* of touch" (ibid.), and that all sensing—from top to bottom—is "mediated," we have grounds for claiming that every act of human sensation, no matter how basic, is already an exercise in hermeneutic *Verstehen-Befindlichket* (to borrow Heidegger's language from *Being and Time*).

The hermeneutic as-structure is never absent. There is no escaping hermeneutics, even if one wanted to. Manoussakis develops Aristotle's insight into touch in terms of a threefold distinction between "grasp," "caress," and "kiss" in line with contemporary phenomenological hermeneutics, while Alloa in his essay in this volume—"Getting into Touch"—retraces the genealogical rapport between ancient Alexandrian hermeneutics and Aristotelian diagnostics.

11. Chrétien, "Body and Touch," 85. It is also worth noting here that in a curiously enigmatic passage in the *Metaphysics* Theta, ch. 10, 1051b, 23–25, Aristotle speaks of apprehending the truth of something in terms of "touch" (*thigein*) and of ignorance in terms of a lack of "touch," or as we might say, being out of touch. And he goes on in *Metaphysics*, XII, 7, 1072b, 21, to claim that "It (mind) becomes thought by touching and thinking . . . ." It is important to note that the verb used for touching in the *Metaphysics* is *thingangein* while in the *De Anima*, it is *haphê/haptesthai*. I am grateful to my colleagues Thomas Sheehan, Arthur Madigan, and Erin Stackle for discussion of this passage.

12. Chrétien, "Body and Touch," 87–90.

13. See the very insightful distinction between the infant mouth as *os* or as *bucca* in its first gestures of touching and tasting, Jean-Luc Nancy, *Corpus*, trans. Richard Rand (New York: Fordham University Press, 2008), 2–122. Nancy's phenomenological description of the body's radical exposure to the other from birth is captured in his wonderful neologism "expeausition"—the exposition of skin to skin (ibid., 14 ff.). See also his essays in this volume, "Motion and Emotion" and "Essential Skin" in the chapter "Rethinking Corpus," where he speaks of the most basic epidermal responses of skin being, from the outset, both completely psychological and physiological—two forms of the same thing. It would be interesting to bring Nancy's hermeneutics of "corpus" into dialogue with the recent work of philosophers engaged in more empirical-cognitive research, such as Catherine Malabou, Sean McGrath, and Evan Thompson, or with empirical psychologists like Matthew Fulkerson, *The First Touch: A Philosophical Study of Human Touch* (Cambridge, MA: MIT Press, 2014).

14. Linguistics and psychoanalysis can also provide many interesting insights regarding the original relationship between proto-speech sensibility and speech proper. See in particular Roman Jacobson's intriguing analysis of the transition from infant "babble" to speech (which influenced the hermeneutic phenomenologies of Merleau-Ponty and Alloa) and Freud's famous description of the child's first acquisition of language as a synesthetic game of *fort/da* where the child touches a spool of cotton (pulling and pushing it out of vision) while pronouncing the words, "gone, back again" (see *Beyond the Pleasure Principle*). It might be recalled here that Aristotle had already noted the proto-hermeneutic power of the voice in *De Anima*: "Not every sound made by an animal is voice . . . what produces the impact must have soul in it and must be accompanied by an act of imagination, for voice is a sound *with a meaning*, and is not merely the result of any impact of the breath as in coughing" (220b, 30).

15. Jean-Luc Nancy, "Essential Skin," in this volume.

16. Chrétien, "Body and Touch," 98.

17. Aristotle, *De Anima* 2, 428a.

18. Chrétien, "Body and Touch," 98. On the question of hermeneutically reading scars and wounds (traumata), see also our analysis of Euryclyeia's touching/reading of Odysseus's scar in Richard Kearney, "Writing Trauma: Narrative Catharsis in Joyce, Shakespeare and Homer" in *Giornale di metafisca* 1 (Fall 2013).

19. On the importance of the handshake for the primal turning of hostility into hospitality see Richard Kearney, "Welcoming the Stranger" in *All Changed? Culture and Identity in Contemporary Ireland*, eds. Andrew O'Shea et al. (Dublin: The Duras Press, 2011). Think of the first wager of open hand to open hand in the encounter between the rivals Diomedes and Glaucus in Homer's *Iliad* or in Abraham's greeting of the strangers at Mamre. For some recent pioneering experimental research into the primordial role of the hand, see *The Hand, An Organ of the Mind: What the Manual Tells the Mental*, ed. Zdravko Radman (Cambridge, MA: MIT Press, 2014). The contributors to this volume challenge the dichotomy between thought and touch, promoted by Cartesian dualism, and explore the possibility that the hand possesses its own special "know-how," enabling "enhanded" beings to navigate the natural, social, and cultural world without presupposing propositional thought or preconceived mental plans.

20. Aristotle, *De Anima* 2, 418.

21. Aristotle, *De Anima* 2, 412a. Cited and commented by Chrétien, "Body and Touch," 101–105. "The delicacy of touch has for its horizon the spirit's discernment, and since the spirit is always that of a living being whose life is always exposed, it cannot for a single moment uproot itself from what founds it. Our sensitivity analyses differences at the heart of the world by articulating them to our life, depending on how clear the peril is. The primal and inalienable place of this articulation is touch, which explains why Aristotle attributes primacy to touch . . . The affected being is not thought here as an obstacle to discernment but as the condition of greater discernment" (ibid., 105). See also Emmanuel Alloa's very engaging reinterpretations of Aristotle's notion of mediality to which my own hermeneutic reading in this essay is deeply indebted, "*Metaxu: Figures de la médialite chez Aristote*" in *Revue de Métaphysique et de Morale*, November 2, no. 62 (2009) and "*La Chair comme diacritique Incarné*" in *Chiasmi Inernational* (Paris: Vrin, 2010).

22. Chrétien, "Body and Touch," 108. I am also indebted to Alloa for the Paz quote and would suggest that a hermeneutics of the senses could also benefit from the rich examples of poetic synesthesia to be found in the work of other writers (Gerard Manley Hopkins, Christian Wiman, and Sinead Morrissey (to name but some).

23. Chrétien, "Body and Touch," 110–113. See also Alloa on taste, *op. cit.*

24. For Aristotle's critique of the materialist notion of immediate perception see Alloa, "*Metaxu*," 252–253.

25. Aristotle, *De Anima* 2, 419.

26. Aristotle, *De Anima* 2, 423b. As *metaxu*, flesh has the potentiality to discern hermeneutically between opposites, differences, variations. "What is "in the middle" is fitted to discern; relative to either extreme it can put itself in the place of the other" (Aristotle, *De Anima* 2, 424a).

27. Alloa, "*Metaxu*," 260.

28. See Chrétien's instructive review of medieval philosophical commentaries on Aristotle's theory of touch—especially Bonaventure and Aquinas, *op.cit*, 103–105; and also Alloa's review of the Romantic attempt to revive touch (e.g., Schiller's plea for primacy of touch over sight in his essay "On Sculpture": "sight gives us dreams, touch gives us truth," cited in "Getting In Touch" in this volume).

29. See Heidegger on Augustine: "The remarkable priority of 'seeing' was noticed particularly by Augustine, in connection with his interpretation of *concupiscentia*: 'seeing belongs properly to the eyes. But we even use this word 'seeing' for the other senses when we devote them to cognizing. For we do not say, 'Hear how it glows,' or 'smell how it glistens,' or 'Taste how it shines,' or 'feel how it flashes'; but we say of each 'see' . . . 'see how it sounds,' 'see how it smells,' 'see how it tastes' etc. . . . Therefore the experience of the senses in general is designated as the 'lust of the eyes'; for when the issue is one of knowing something, the other senses, by a certain resemblance, take to themselves the function of seeing—a function in which the eyes have priority." Heidegger is quoting from Augustine's *Confessions*. See *Being and Time*, trans. Macquarrie and Robinson (Malden, MA: Blackwell, 1973), 215–216.

30. Edmund Husserl, *Ideas Pertaining to a Pure Phenomenology and to a Phenomenological Philosophy*, Second Book, trans. R. Rojcewicz and A. Schuwer (Dordrecht: Kluwer, 1989), 153. Hereafter referred to as *Ideas II*.

31. Husserl, *Ideas II*, 152. Husserl makes the distinction between two different ways of experiencing the same sensation, or more accurately the two simultaneous sides of the same act of touching: *Empfindung* as the experience of the touched object (as cold, hard, etc.) and *Emfindnis* as the localized sensing in my touching fingers. So when my hand touches my hand, for example, my touching-touched hand appears as both touched *Körper* with objective physical qualities (that I can see) and also as a touching lived body, *Leib* (that I can feel). The self-touching hand becomes, for Husserl, a reversible auto-affection between skin as sensed object and as sensing subject. (I am indebted here for the insightful comments of Nibras Alchehayed, Andrea Staiti, and most especially Dermot Moran who writes on this subject in great detail in this volume). In section 2 of Supplement XII to *Ideas II*, entitled "sensibility as the Psychic Basis of the Spirit," Husserl goes on to suggest that even the most basic "sensuous data of the instincts," as "primal lived experiences," are already informed by "acts of the spirit" which "direct rays of spiritual regard onto something affecting the subject." These acts of spiritual sensibility range, he says, from the "lowest levels" of sense instinct to the highest acts of "theoretical thinking, artistic creation and ethical-social behavior" (ibid., 346).

32. Husserl, *Ideas II*, 155.

33. Husserl, *Ideas II*, 175–178. In Chapter 4, Husserl explores the "constitution of psychic reality in empathy." In paragraph 46, he talks of the need to go beyond "solipsistic self-experience" declaring that "it is only with empathy and the constant orientation of empirical reflection onto the psychic life which is appresented along with the other's Body and which is continually taken objectively, together with the Body, that the closed unity, man, is constituted, and I transfer this unity subsequently to myself" (ibid., 175). Citing Aristotle's *De Anima*—one of the few citations in his entire analysis in *Ideas II*—Husserl talks of "body and soul forming a genuine experiential unity" (ibid., 176) in time and space, and sharing the "same sensibility" with others through a process of analogizing and "substitution by trading places" (ibid., 177). "The things posited by others are also mine: in empathy I participate in the other's positing . . . from that 'here' my Body is 'there,' just as the other's Body is 'there' from my 'here'" (ibid.). In Supplement XII to *Ideas II*, Husserl adds the following promising note to the possibility of a hermeneutics of carnal empathy: "Where is empathy to be accommodated? The regulation of sensibility is (with respect to the sensibility of sensation and also with respect to the sensibility of feeling and every primal sensibility) an intersubjective one. Account must be taken of this at the appropriate place" (ibid., 347). This account was, arguably left to Husserl's disciples, Max Scheler and Edith Stein (who was working on a transcription of *Ideas II*, as she developed her own ideas for her doctoral dissertation, *On the Problem of Empathy*; see note 46).

34. See Ricoeur's reading of flesh as an umbilical "scar" and pre-natal memory in *Freedom and Nature: The Voluntary and the Involuntary*, trans. Erazim Kohák (Evanston, IL: Northwestern University Press, 1966), 439–443. Jean-Luc Marion has also contributed rigorous phenomenological analyses of the role of flesh as exposure to alterity and saturation in such works as *Being Given* and, more recently, *The Erotic Phenomenon* (Chicago and London: University of Chicago Press, 2007), especially chapter four, "Concerning the Flesh and its Arousal." And one might also mention here the carnal-material phenomenologies of *la chair* developed by Michel Henry and Emmanuel Falque, both featured in this volume.

35. Husserl, *Ideas II*, 151.

36. Husserl, *Ideas II*, 157.

37. Husserl, *Ideas II*, 158.

38. Husserl, *Ideas II*, 159.

39. Husserl, *Ideas II*, 166.

40. Husserl, *Ideas II*, 157.

41. Husserl, *Ideas II*, 160.

42. Husserl, *Ideas II*, 163.

43. See also Husserl: "The Body . . . as a material thing . . . as localization field for sensations and for stirrings of feelings, as phenomenal partner and counterpart of all perceptions of things . . . makes up a fundamental component of the *real givenness* of the soul" (ibid., 165). This phenomenological givenness is linked to the primacy of touch over sight (and even movement) for Husserl: "It cannot be said that this subject *only* sees his Body, for its specific distinctive feature as Body

would be lacking him, and even the free moment of this 'Body,' which goes hand in hand with the freedom of the kinesthetic processes, would not make it a Body" (ibid., 158, my italics).

44. On this Freudian notion of the body as unconscious extension of the psyche, see Nancy, *Corpus*, 21 ff. and Derrida, *On Touching—Jean-Luc Nancy*, trans. Christine Irizarry (Stanford: Stanford University Press, 2005), 11–19.

45. Husserl, *Ideas II*, 168.

46. This Husserlian paradox of presentation-in-appresentation (Husserl, *Ideas II*, 177–178) is at the core of Edith Stein's *On the Problem of Empathy* (Washington: ICS Publications, 1989). It also plays a part in Max Scheler's work on empathy and sympathy as discussed by Dan Zahavi in his recent "Beyond Empathy: Phenomenological Approaches to Intersubjectivity" in *The Journal of Consciousness Studies*, vol. 8, nos. 5–7 (2001), 151–167. Drawing on the work of Scheler, Heidegger, Merleau-Ponty, Husserl and Sartre (and engaging with recent debates in cognitive science), Zahavi presents an overview of some of the diverse approaches to intersubjectivity that can be found in the phenomenological movement which, he rightly argues, involve much more than a "solution" to the "traditional" problem of other minds. Intersubjectivity doesn't merely concern concrete face-to-face encounters between individuals but a whole play of perception, tool use, emotions, drives, and different types of self-awareness. In empathy the three regions "self," "others," and "world" intersect and belong together. For a more critical account of empathy, inspired by Edith Stein's emphasis on the nonprimordial relationship with the other in empathy see Rowan Williams's Tanner Lectures, entitled "The Paradoxes of Empathy" delivered at Harvard University, April, 2014.

47. Husserl, *Ideas II*, 174–177.

48. Jean-Paul Sartre, *Being and Nothingness*, trans. Hazel Barnes (New York: Philosophical Library, 1956), 218.

49. Sartre, *Being and Nothingness*, 304.

50. Sartre, *Being and Nothingness*, 355.

51. Sartre, *Being and Nothingness*, 353.

52. Sartre, *Being and Nothingness*, 263.

53. Sartre, *Being and Nothingness*, 354.

54. Sartre, *Being and Nothingness*, 352.

55. For Sartre this means that we attempt to learn our being through the revelations of language. "Thus there appears a whole system of verbal correspondences by which we cause our body to be designated for us as it is for the Other by utilizing these designations to denote our body as it is for us" (Sartre, *Being and Nothingness*, 354). But this hermeneutic process of linguistic signification is precisely *not* what occurs, for Sartre, in the pre-linguistic carnal caress itself.

56. Sartre, *Being and Nothingness*, 388.

57. Sartre, *Being and Nothingness*, 388–389.

58. Sartre, *Being and Nothingness*, 389.

59. Sartre, *Being and Nothingness*, 389.

60. Sartre, *Being and Nothingness*, 389.

61. Sartre, *Being and Nothingness*, 390.

62. Sartre, *Being and Nothingness*, 393.

63. Sartre, *Being and Nothingness*, 393.

64. Sartre, *Being and Nothingness*, 393. Sartre: "In my desiring perception I discover something like a *flesh* of objects. My shirt rubs against my skin and I feel it. What is ordinarily for me an object most remote becomes immediately sensible; the warmth of the air, the breath of the wind, the rays of sunshine etc.; all are present to me in a certain way, as posited upon me *without distance* [my italics] and revealing my flesh by means of their flesh. From this point of view, desire is not only the clogging of a consciousness by its facticity; it is correlatively the ensnarement of a body by the world. The world is made *ensnaring*; consciousness is engulfed in a body which is engulfed in the world . . . the for-itself [thus] attempts to realize a being-in-the-midst-of-the-world . . . . that is why sensual pleasure is so often linked with death . . . for example, the theme of 'pseudo-death' so abundantly treated in all literatures" (ibid., 392).

65. Emmanuel Levinas, *Totality and Infinity*, trans. Alphonso Lingis (Pittsburgh, PA: Duquesne University Press, 1969), 257.

66. Levinas, *Totality and Infinity*, 257.

67. Levinas, *Totality and Infinity*, 257–258.

68. Levinas, *Totality and Infinity*, 258.

69. Levinas, *Totality and Infinity*, 258.

70. Levinas, *Totality and Infinity*, 258.

71. Levinas, *Totality and Infinity*, 259.

72. Levinas, *Totality and Infinity*, 249.

73. Levinas, *Totality and Infinity*, 260.

74. Levinas, *Totality and Infinity*, 261.

75. Levinas, *Totality and Infinity*, 261.

76. Levinas, *Totality and Infinity*, 262.

77. Levinas, *Totality and Infinity*, 264.

78. Levinas, *Totality and Infinity*, 264.

79. Levinas, *Totality and Infinity*, 263.

80. Levinas, *Totality and Infinity*, 265.

81. Levinas, *Totality and Infinity*, 265–266.

82. See Luce Irigaray's trenchant and timely analysis of Levinas, "The Fecundity of the Caress: A Reading of Levinas's *Totality and Infinity*, 'Phenomenology of Eros'" in *An Ethics of Sexual Difference*, trans. Gillian Gill (Ithaca, NY: Cornell University Press, 1993), and "Questions to Emmanuel Levinas on the Divinity of Love" in *Re-Reading Levinas*, ed. Robert Bernasconi and Simon Critchley (Bloomington: Indiana University Press, 1991).

83. Levinas, *Totality and Infinity*, 262.

84. Levinas, *Totality and Infinity*, 262.

85. Levinas, *Totality and Infinity*, 265.

86. Levinas, *Totality and Infinity*, 266.

87. Levinas, *Totality and Infinity*, 266.

88. Levinas, *Totality and Infinity*, 266.

89. Maurice Merleau-Ponty, *Phenomenology of Perception*, trans. Colin Smith (London: Routledge, 1962), 106.

90. Sartre, *Being and Nothingness*, 304.

91. Maurice Merleau-Ponty, *The Visible and the Invisible*, trans. Alphonso Linguis, (Evanston, IL: Northwestern University Press, 1979), 273.

92. Merleau-Ponty, *The Visible and the Invisible*, 134, 146.

93. Merleau-Ponty, *The Visible and the Invisible*, 155.

94. Merleau-Ponty, *The Visible and the Invisible*, 264.

95. Merleau-Ponty, *The Visible and the Invisible*, 142.

96. See Derrida's critical reading of Merleau-Ponty's phenomenology of touch as a haptocentric intuitionism, in "Tangents III" in *On Touching*, 190 ff.

97. Merleau-Ponty, *The Visible and the Invisible*, 147.

98. Derrida sees Merleau-Ponty's treatment of carnal reversibility and reflexivity as neglectful of radical difference and "non-coincidence" (*op. cit.*, 213 forward). He also suspects Chrétien of a similar haptocentrism of spiritualized flesh, informed by a mystical theology of Christocentric incarnation ("Tangents V," 244 ff.). This modern haptocentric tradition of reversible incarnation is seen, by Derrida, as a successor to the former optocentric tradition of Platonic metaphysics (also termed "heliocentrism" and "phonologocentrism" by Derrida). Both traditions, he argues, share a certain closure vis-à-vis the radical alterity and spacing of *différance*. More generally one may say that Husserl's original phenomenology of touch in *Ideas II* gave rise to two parallel and sometimes opposing readings: the first which stresses the primacy of *Leib*, as symmetrical double sensation (Merleau-Ponty, Henry, Scheler), the second which stresses the asymmetrical pressure exercised by *Körper* as alien body (Sartre, Levinas, Derrida), resisting the haptocentric circularity and reversibility of *Leib*. It seems to me that the hermeneutics of corporality adumbrated in the later work of both Ricoeur and Nancy are attempts to rethink and surpass these two rival readings in a new direction. Most of the essays in this volume, in my opinion, follow this new orientation of carnal hermeneutics and diagnostics, albeit each in a unique way. There is no prefixed agenda.

99. Merleau-Ponty, *Phenomenology of Perception*, 154.

100. Merleau-Ponty, *Phenomenology of Perception*, 156–157.

101. Merleau-Ponty, *Phenomenology of Perception*, 157.

102. Merleau-Ponty, *Phenomenology of Perception*, 159.

103. Merleau-Ponty, *Phenomenology of Perception*, 160.

104. Merleau-Ponty, *Phenomenology of Perception*, 161.

105. Merleau-Ponty, *Phenomenology of Perception*, 163.

106. Merleau-Ponty, *Phenomenology of Perception*, 165.

107. Merleau-Ponty, *Phenomenology of Perception*, 166.

108. Merleau-Ponty, *Phenomenology of Perception*, 166.

109. Merleau-Ponty, *Phenomenology of Perception*, 169.

110. Merleau-Ponty, *Phenomenology of Perception*, 171.

111. Maurice Merleau-Ponty, *Le Monde Sensible et Le monde de l'expression*, ed. Emmanuel de Saint Aubert (Geneva: Metispresses, 2011).

112. Merleau-Ponty, *Le Monde Sensible et Le monde de l'expression*, 203–204.

113. Merleau-Ponty, *Le Monde Sensible et Le monde de l'expression*, 211.

114. Merleau-Ponty, *Le Monde Sensible et Le monde de l'expression*, 204.

115. Merleau-Ponty, *Le Monde Sensible et Le monde de l'expression*, 204.

116. Merleau-Ponty, *Le Monde Sensible et Le monde de l'expression*, 206.

117. Merleau-Ponty, *Le Monde Sensible et Le monde de l'expression*, 204–205.

118. Merleau-Ponty, *Le Monde Sensible et Le monde de l'expression*, 205.

119. Merleau-Ponty, *Le Monde Sensible et Le monde de l'expression*, 205.

120. Merleau-Ponty, *Phenomenology of Perception*, 246.

121. Merleau-Ponty, *Phenomenology of Perception*, 246.

122. Ricoeur, *Freedom and Nature*, 86.

123. Ricoeur, *Freedom and Nature*, 87–88.

124. Ricoeur, *Freedom and Nature*, 91.

125. Ricoeur, *Freedom and Nature*, 91.

126. Ricoeur, *Freedom and Nature*, 93.

127. Ricoeur, *Freedom and Nature*, 93.

128. Ricoeur, *Freedom and Nature*, 94.

129. Ricoeur, *Freedom and Nature*, 99.

130. Ricoeur, *Freedom and Nature*, 122.

131. Paul Ricoeur, *Critique and Conviction* (New York: Columbia University Press, 1998) 39.

132. Paul Ricoeur, "Hommage à Merleau-Ponty" in *Lectures 2: La Contrée des Philosophes* (Paris: Le Seuil, 1962), 163–164. One of the aims of our carnal hermeneutics project is to bring Merleau-Ponty's radical phenomenology of flesh (working forwards to a diacritical hermeneutics with his notion of diacritical perception) with Ricoeur's hermeneutics of the text (working backwards to his early phenomenology of embodiment in light of his later hermeneutic reflections on flesh as paradigm of "oneself as another").

133. Paul Ricoeur, "Wonder, Eroticism and Enigma" in *Sexuality and the Sacred*, eds. James Nelson and Sandra Longfellow (Louisville, KY: John Knox Press, 1994).

134. Ricoeur, "Wonder, Eroticism and Enigma," 141.

135. Ricoeur, "Wonder, Eroticism and Enigma," 141.

136. Ricoeur, "Wonder, Eroticism and Enigma," 140.

137. Ricoeur, "Wonder, Eroticism and Enigma," 141.

138. Ricoeur, "Wonder, Eroticism and Enigma," 141.

139. Ricoeur, "Wonder, Eroticism and Enigma," 141.

140. Paul Ricoeur, *Oneself as Another*, trans. Kathleen Blamey (Chicago: University of Chicago Press, 1992), 318.

141. See Ricoeur's cogent critique of Derek Parfit's "puzzling cases" of consciousness without bodies as well as of technological fictions of disincarnate human identities (Ricoeur, *Oneself as Another*, 150–151). Ricoeur's main literary example

is Robert Musil's *Man without Qualities*, but one could also add more recent sci-fi movies like *Simone* or *Her* where a virtual OS (computer operating system) is divorced from physical touch and taste, with dramatic existential consequences. Ricoeur's basic point is that if one deprives the human of its terrestrial-corporeal anchoring one deprives the self of any perduring lived identity as constancy-in-change (*idem-ipse*). Ricoeur argues that literary fictions, unlike technological fictions, remain imaginative variations on "an invariant, our corporeal condition experienced as the existential mediation between the self and the world" (ibid., 150). This invariant anchoring of lived corporeality testifies to the ontological condition of carnal selfhood in "acting and suffering persons" (ibid., 151).

142. Ricoeur, *Oneself as Another*, 322.

143. Ricoeur, *Oneself as Another*, 322.

144. Ricoeur argues that Heidegger never developed a real ontology of flesh, though he possessed all the ingredients for such a project. His notion of *Befindlichkeit*—affective state of mind expressed in our moods—was particularly promising in this regard (Ricoeur, *Oneself as Another*, 327 and note 34). It is telling that Heidegger acknowledged Aristotle's interpretation of "affects" (*pathe*) as the "first systematic hermeneutic of the everydayness of Being with one another" (Martin Heidegger, *Being and Time*, trans. John Macquarrie and Edward Robinson [New York: Harper, 1962], 178); but he did not, alas, himself push this hermeneutic in the direction of an "ontology of flesh" open to the world of others. In spite of his investigation of Dasein as "thrownness," he did not develop a hermeneutic reading of "the properly passive modalities of our desires and our moods as the sign, the symptom, the indication of the contingent character of our insertion in the world" (Ricoeur, *Oneself as Another*, 327, note 34). In Heidegger a temporality of disincarnate Dasein (transcendental ontology) ultimately trumped a spatiality of incarnate flesh (carnal "ontics"). Ricoeur asks pointedly: Why "did Heidegger not grasp this opportunity to reinterpret the Husserlian notion of flesh (*Leib*), which he could not have been unaware of, in terms of the analytic of Dasein?" Ricoeur's answer: "If the theme of embodiment appears to be stifled, if not repressed in *Being and Time*, this is doubtless because it must have appeared too dependent on the inauthentic forms of care—let us say, of preoccupation—that make us tend to interpret ourselves in terms of the objects of care. We must then wonder if it is not the unfolding of the problem of temporality, triumphant in the second section of *Being and Time*, that prevents an *authentic* phenomenology of spatiality—and along with it, an ontology of the flesh—from being given its chance to develop" (Ricoeur, *Oneself as Another*, 328). Heidegger sought to redress this lacuna somewhat in his *Zollikon Seminars* 1959–1964 (Northwestern University Press, 2001).

145. Ricoeur, *Oneself as Another*, 322.

146. Ricoeur, *Oneself as Another*, 324.

147. Ricoeur, *Oneself as Another*, 324.

148. Ricoeur, *Oneself as Another*, 324. See Didier Franck, *Chair et Corps: Sur la phénoménologie de Husserl* (Paris: Editions de Minuit, 1981), 109–111. Ricoeur relies heavily on Francks's influential commentary for his reading of Husserl. He

adds: "The kind of transgression of the sphere of ownness constituted by appresentation is valid only within the limits of a transfer of *sense*: the sense of ego is transferred to another body, which, as flesh, also contains the sense of ego. Whence the perfectly adequate expression of alter ego in the sense of a 'second flesh' ('*seconde chair propre*')" (Ricoeur, *Oneself as Another*, 334).

149. Ricoeur, *Oneself as Another*, 324.

150. Edmund Husserl, *Cartesian Meditations*, trans. Dorion Cairns (The Hague: Nijhoff, 1969), 97.

151. Ricoeur, *Oneself as Another*, 326.

152. Ricoeur, *Oneself as Another*, 326.

153. In addition to Ricoeur's critical reading of Levinas in this regard, we should note again here Luce Irigaray's pioneering feminist-psychoanalytic critique of Levinas's phallocentric metaphysics as well as the new feminist hermeneutics of the semiotic lived body in such thinkers as Kristeva, O'Byrne, Rambo, and McKendrick, all represented in this volume. Kristeva's new feminism of the body is linked to her project for a new humanism informed, in part, by a retrieval of the deep unconscious resources of the "sensible imaginary" in writers like Colette, Duras, and Teresa of Avilla.

154. Ricoeur, *Oneself as Another*, 333.

155. Ricoeur, *Oneself as Another*, 333.

156. Ricoeur, *Oneself as Another*, 334.

157. Ricoeur, *Oneself as Another*, 335.

158. Ricoeur, *Oneself as Another*, 355.

159. Ricoeur, *Oneself as Another*, 336.

160. See the current development of diacritical hermeneutics and diagnostics by Emmanuel Alloa, Ted Toadvine, and Brian Treanor (all featured in this volume) as well as our own recent publications, Richard Kearney, "What Is Diacritical Hermeneutics?," cited above; "Eros, Diacritical Hermeneutics and the Maybe," *Philosophical Thresholds: Crossings of Life and World, Selected Studies in Phenomenology and Existential Philosophy*, vol. 36, Special SPEP supplement, *Philosophy Today*, vol. 55, ed. Cynthia Willett and Leonard Lawlor, 2001; and "Diacritical Hermeneutics" in *Hermeneutic Rationality/La rationalité herméneutique*, ed. Andrzej Wierciński et al. (Munster: LIT Verlag, 2011).

161. Ricoeur, *Oneself as Another*, 366.

162. Ricoeur, *Oneself as Another*, 337.

163. Ricoeur, *Oneself as Another*, 338.

164. Ricoeur, *Oneself as Another*, 339.

165. Ricoeur, *Oneself as Another*, 399.

166. See Brian Treanor's most recent work in environmental diacritical hermeneutics, "Narrative and Nature: Appreciating and Understanding the Non-Human World" in *Interpreting Nature: The Emerging Field of Environmental Hermeneutics*, eds. Forrest Clingerman, et al., (New York: Fordham University Press, 2013) and "Emplotting Virtue: A Narrative Approach to Environmental Virtue Ethics" (New

York: SUNY, 2014). One should mention here the importance of also bringing such diacritical-carnal hermeneutics into dialogue with recent innovative developments of "life" philosophy by Renaud Barbaras, Gilles Deleuze, and Claude Romano, in the wake of Henri Bergson and Hans Jonas; and, finally, with the interesting work being done in the post-Wittgensteinian philosophies of Stanley Cavell, Stephen Mulhull, Hilary Putnam, Robert Brandom and other proponents of linguistic pragmatism who resist metaphysical dualism and redirect our attention to the richness of ordinary human experience in the flow of life. One does well to recall Wittgenstein's claims in the *Philosophical Investigations*, that "the human body is the best picture of the soul" and that human meaning comes in "forms of life."

167. We are currently preparing a volume on this subject, entitled *Flesh: Recovering our Senses in an Age of Excarnation* (forthcoming). See our piece, "The Age of Excarnation," *New York Times*, Sunday, August 30, 2014.

Mind the Gap: The Challenge of Matter
Brian Treanor

1. Henry David Thoreau, *Walden* (Princeton: Princeton University Press, 1971), 97–98.

2. Antoine de Saint-Exupéry, *Wind, Sand and Stars*, trans. Lewis Galantière (New York: Harcourt Brace, 1992), 218.

3. Plato, "Phaedrus" in *Collected Dialogues*, trans. Edith Hamilton and Huntington Cairns (Princeton: Princeton University Press, 1961), 478 (230a).

4. In previous work, I've focused on the ways in which narrative and imagination can contribute to our flourishing, but always with an explicit proviso that narrative and imagination are only part of a larger picture that includes the carnal body, material place, other beings, and additional entities, the understanding of which might benefit from other, nonnarrative, modes of knowing and understanding (see *Emplotting Virtue* [Albany: SUNY: 2015], especially, for example, 191–196). My current work is developing other parts of this picture, including carnal embodiment and material environment, especially with an eye toward the experience of vitality or joy. In this volume, Karmen MacKendrick, Anne O'Byrne, David Wood, and others address, directly or indirectly, the role of the carnal body in self-understanding and, therefore, in living well.

5. I'd make a similar argument with respect to place and, therefore would suggest that a carnal hermeneutics of the body and an earthy hermeneutics of place would, together, contribute substantially to hermeneutic accounts focused on the text and on other persons.

6. Exceptions to this trend are found in feminism, race theory, and queer theory. Many thinkers in these fields do think of the body in terms of signs, signifiers, and the like—the terms of body-as-construction rather than body-as-carnal-reality. However, in these fields there are also thinkers that attend to materiality to a greater degree than the work found in other fields of philosophy. Thus, feminism,

race theory, and queer theory represent very natural dialogue partners for carnal hermeneutics; and essays in this volume—by Kristeva, O'Byrne, and Rambo—make some progress in this area, at least in terms of feminism.

7. *Material Feminisms*, eds. Stacey Alaimo and Susan Hekman (Bloomington: Indiana University Press, 2008), 1.

8. It is worth noting the curious relationship between the second and third reasons: the former claims we need to rehabilitate an appreciation for the role of carnal and physical materiality in the face of an overwhelming emphasis on linguistic construction, while the latter suggests the need to reaffirm the role of interpretation precisely in response to thinkers seeking to rehabilitate realism, but who overreact in dismissing hermeneutics outright. This tension between reaffirming the carnal and material while insisting on the enduring significance of hermeneutics raises important questions about the relationship between interpretation and reality, between the symbolic and the material, between understanding and explanation, and between thinking and living.

9. Quentin Meillassoux, *After Finitude: An Essay on the Necessity of Contingency*, trans. Ray Brassier (London: Continuum, 2008); Graham Harman, *The Quadruple Object* (London: Zero Books, 2011); *Material Feminisms*, eds. Stacey Alaimo and Susan Hekman (Bloomington: Indiana University Press, 2008); Timothy Morton, *Hyperobjects: Philosophy and Ecology after the End of the World* (Minneapolis: University of Minnesota Press, 2013); Jane Bennett, *Vibrant Matter: A Political Ecology of Things* (Durham, NC: Duke University Press, 2010); Ray Brassier, *Nihil Unbound: Enlightenment and Extinction* (London: Palgrave Macmillan, 2010); Michel Serres, *The Five Senses: A Philosophy of Mingled Bodies*, trans. Margaret Sankey and Peter Crowley (London: Continuum, 2008); Catherine Malabou, *What Should We Do with Our Brain?*, trans. Sebastian Rand (New York: Fordham University Press, 2008); Bruno Latour, *Pandora's Hope: Essays on the Reality of Science Studies* (Cambridge, MA: Harvard University Press, 1999). For the past several years I have been thinking that there is something like a "new realism" or "new materialism" in the air at conferences and in publications. My own engagement with the primary sources began with Meillassoux and Bennett, followed by articles by Morton and Harman. Peter Gratton's book, *Speculative Realism: Problems and Prospects* (London: Bloomsbury, 2014), which he very kindly made available to me in draft form, was helpful to me by providing an overview of many of the thinkers I'm categorizing as "new realists." Of course, my characterizations of these thinkers and the potential for hermeneutic engagement with them remains my own, and objections should be directed accordingly.

10. Peter Gratton, "The Power of Things and the Nature of Politics," in *Speculative Realism: Problems and Prospects* (London: Bloomsbury, 2014), chapter 5 passim. Prof. Gratton graciously provided me with a pre-publication copy of his manuscript. All citations to his book will be by chapter title and the page number of the draft manuscript, which, hopefully, will allow interested readers to find relevant passages from his work.

11. See Gratton, "Object-Oriented Ontology," in *Speculative Realism*, chapter 4. Citing Graham Harman, "The Road to Objects," *Continent* 3.1 (2011): 167, 172.

12. Ray Brassier, "I am a nihilist because I still believe in truth: Ray Brassier interviewed by Marcin Rychter," *Kronos* 4 (March 2011) http://www.kronos.org .pl/index.php?23151,869. Accessed January 13, 2014.

13. Alaimo, *Material Feminisms*, 4.

14. Elizabeth Groz, "Matter, Life, and Other Variations," in *Philosophy Today* 55 (2011): 17.

15. On the Ptolemaic nature of contemporary philosophy see Meillassoux, "Ptolemy's Revenge," in *After Finitude*, passim. On the unfortunate coincidence of correlationism and environmentally destructive behavior, see below (note 23), also Lynn White, "The Historical Roots of Our Ecological Crisis" in *Science*, vol. 155, no. 3767 (March 10, 1967).

16. Meillassoux, *After Finitude*, 5. Meillassoux identifies at least two types of correlationism: weak correlationism and strong correlationism (Meillassoux, *After Finitude*, 30 ff.). Weak correlationism is associated with Kant, since he claims that we cannot have knowledge of the thing-in-itself (the noumenal object), but only the thing-as-we-perceive it. True, we can think the thing-in-itself, know it exists and that it is non-contradictory; but we cannot know it (Meillassoux, *After Finitude*, 35). The result? We do not experience or know the thing itself, which is separated from us by an unbridgeable chasm. Strong correlationism—associated with phenomenology and, implicitly, hermeneutics and deconstruction—goes even farther, and "maintains not only that it is illegitimate to claim that we can know the in-itself, but also that it is illegitimate to claim that we can at least think it" (Meillassoux, *After Finitude*, 35.)

17. Meillassoux, *After Finitude*, 36–37. Meillassoux argues that the correlationist "end of metaphysics" puts philosophy in a position of fideism, returning thinking to a religious or quasi-religious discourse. In this manner, Meillassoux's speculative realism forms an ally of sorts with various critiques of religion, despite the fact that his philosophy leads him to the consideration of a "possible God."

18. Meillassoux, *After Finitude*, 7.

19. Meillassoux, *After Finitude*, 9–10.

20. Quentin Meillassoux, "Time without Becoming," a lecture at Middlesex University, London, May 8, 2008, http://speculativehersey.files.wordpress .com/2008/07/3729-time_without_becoming.pdf. Accessed January 13, 2014.

21. Meillassoux, *After Finitude*, 119.

22. Meillassoux, *After Finitude*, 13, 17.

23. Peter Gratton points out the thought-provoking coincidence of the publication of Kant's *Critique of Pure Reason* (1783), which Meillassoux and others believe ushered in the era of correlationism, and the dawn of the Anthropocene (following the patent and production of the coal-powered steam engine in 1784), the geological age that displaced the Holocene and which is characterized by a shift in which human activity and influence has become the dominant factor shaping environments: a dramatic loss of biodiversity that has exacerbated the Quaternary

extinction event, accelerating the sixth mass extinction; the dispersal of wastes and pollutants (mercury, dioxins, radioactive materials, etc.) to the farthest reaches of the globe; and the actual modification of the environment on a global scale through the disruption of the carbon cycle and the consequent effect of climate change. This omnipresent influence led writer Bill McKibben to announce the "end of nature"—that is, nature as an independent otherness, "untouched" as it were, by human hands—in his 1988 book of the same name (*The End of Nature* [New York: Random House, 1989]).

24. Harman, *The Quadruple Object*, 47.

25. Timothy Morton, "Art in the Age of Asymmetry: Hegel, Objects, Aesthetics," in *Evental Aesthetics* 1.1 (2012): 132. "Emmanuel Levinas's line about cosmic space is appropriate here: how when I look at the stars, I realize that I am sought out by inhabitants of the intersidereal spaces" (Morton, "Art in the Age of Asymmetry," 134). My thanks, again, to Peter Gratton for directing me to this, and the previous, quotation.

26. Levi Bryant, *The Democracy of Objects* (Ann Arbor, MI: Open Humanities Press, 2011), 20.

27. Brassier, *Nihil Unbound*, xi.

28. "Interview with Catherine Malabou," http://groundworkhilosophy.word press.com/2012/02/17/interview-with-catherine-malabou/. Accessed January 13, 2014.

29. Catherine Malabou, *The New Wounded: From Neurosis to Brain Damage*, trans. Steven Miller (New York: Fordham University Press, 2012), 211. Note that Malabou's work on the "new wounded" overlaps work in carnal hermeneutics (by Shelly Rambo, Richard Kearney, et al.).

30. Gratton, "Malabou's Plasticity and the Real," in *Speculative Realism*, chapter 8. See also Catherine Malabou and Noel Vahanian, "A Conversation with Catherine Malabou" in *Journal for Cultural and Religious Theory* 9.1 (2008): 1–13. Note that a "motor scheme" might as well be a model, trope, or metaphor were it not for the fact that Malabou seeks to distance herself from grammatology.

31. "A Conversation with Catherine Malabou," 11.

32. See Brassier, "I am a nihilist because I still believe in truth," and Thomas Metzinger, *Being No One: The Self Model Theory of Subjectivity* (Cambridge, MA: Bradford, 2004).

33. Sellars, "Empiricism and the Philosophy of Mind," §41, http://www.ditext .com/sellars/epm.html. Accessed January 13, 2014.

34. Gratton, "Ray Brassier's Transcendental Realism: Nothing (Else) Matters" in *Speculative Realism*, chapter 6.

35. See Ray Brassier, "The View from Nowhere: Sellars, Habermas, Metzinger," (2011): 24, http://www.zotero.org/nick_srnieck/items/itemKey/IQUIKJN29. Accessed January 13, 2014.

36. For example, compare Harman's account of the body as object to Marcel's distinction between the body we have and the body we are (see, among much relevant work in continental philosophy, Gabriel Marcel, "On the Ontological Mys-

tery" in *The Philosophy of Existentialism*, trans. Manya Harari [New York: Citadel Press, 1995]).

37. "Detour/return is the rhythm of my philosophical respiration" (Paul Ricoeur, *Paul Ricoeur: His Life and His Work*, ed. Charles E. Regan [Chicago: The University of Chicago Press, 1996] 133). See also Boyd Blundell, *Paul Ricoeur between Theology and Philosophy: Detour and Return* (Bloomington: Indiana University Press, 2010).

38. Paul Ricoeur, *Critique and Conviction*, trans. Kathleen Blamey (New York: Columbia University Press, 1998).

39. Paul Ricoeur, *The Symbolism of Evil*, trans. Emerson Buchanan (Boston: Beacon Press, 1967), 347–357.

40. T.S. Elliot, "Little Gidding" in *Four Quartets* (London: Harcourt Brace, 1943), 59.

41. In Ricoeur and his students we see a commitment to exploration, questioning, and critique, with all the risk and uncertainty that entails. Once one commits to the detour, critique, or doubt, the "return" is never guaranteed. Such hermeneutical critiques must, if they are genuine, be open to the possibility that one will abandon the initial conviction, belief, or position rather than return to it in a new way (for a similar argument, see Richard Kearney, *Anatheism: Returning to God after God* [New York: Columbia University Press, 2010]). Nevertheless, the hope is for some form of return, new conviction, or second naïveté—rather than an interminable, unlivable, skeptical limbo—whether or not the second conviction mirrors in some significant way the initial position. And, critically, even the return to a new conviction or second naïveté is only a point on an infinite spiral, which will move inexorably toward another moment of critique, another detour.

42. The conference was held in Naples in May of 1993, and gave rise to a *Festschrift* volume: *Paul Ricoeur: The Hermeneutics of Action*, ed. Richard Kearney (London: Sage, 1996). My own view is that carnal hermeneutics and environmental hermeneutics are two aspects of the sort of broader and more comprehensive hermeneutics I endorse. Such a hermeneutics should take special care to retrieve or establish hermeneutic contact with material reality, and to engage the account of the same offered in the sciences (ecology, physiology, biology, etc.). This is not because the hermeneutics of the text is wrong, or because material reality is the only reality, or because the sciences are the sole key to truth, but rather because hermeneutics, on this model, is structurally open-ended, because more dialogue (and more dialogue partners) helps us to understand better, and because material reality and sciences have been seated at the periphery of the hermeneutic table until now.

43. Michel Serres, *The Five Senses: A Philosophy of Mingled Bodies*, trans. Margaret Sankey and Peter Cowley (London: Continuum, 2008), 102.

44. Michel Serres and Bruno Latour, *Conversations on Science, Culture and Time*, trans. Roxanne Lapidus (Ann Arbor: University of Michigan Press, 1995), 131–132. Serres's assault on language extends (with some equivocation) to even the language of his own texts: "I have lost my Eurydice: I want to create a body here

and now, but I have only pure abstraction, this vocal emission, soft: Eurydice, Eurydice, I wanted so much to give you life and all I could do was write philosophy" (Michel Serres, *Angels: A Modern Myth*, trans. Francis Cowper (New York: Flammarion, 1995), 171; and, *The Five Senses*, 134). In this vein he excoriates Socrates himself, patron saint and founding martyr of philosophy, for his necrophilic desire for death and for filling every moment of his life—right up to the "private, solemn moment" of death—with chatter (see Serres, *The Five Senses*, 90–91 among other instances). He quips elsewhere: "Those who have no talent for life do philosophy" (Serres, *The Five Senses*, 133).

45. See, for a fine exploration of these categories, Steven Connor, "Michel Serres: The Hard and the Soft," http://www.stevenconnor.com/hardsoft/. Accessed January 13, 2014.

46. Serres, *The Five Senses*, 41.

47. In his introduction Steven Connor notes that the highly aggressive language of *The Five Senses*—and especially of "Tables"—is uncharacteristic of Serres's general approach (see Serres, *The Five Senses*, 7–12). However, there are undoubtedly prickly moments between Serres and Latour in their conversations (Serres and Latour, *Conversations on Science, Culture and Time*).

48. Serres, *The Five Senses*, 88.

49. In fact there is some suggestion of an opportunity to rehabilitate or resuscitate language in the wake of its "death" at the hands of *data* (Serres, *The Five Senses*, 327, 332, 333–345). As we move from engaging the world via language to engaging the world through data, language loses some of its power. Data, however, also occludes reality, possibly to a greater degree than language. This opens the possibility of using language in a new manner, one that, if not identical to hard, sensuous reality, is at least less of a "betrayal" of it.

50. See, for example, Michel Serres, *Hermes: Literature, Science, Philosophy*, ed. Josué V. Harari and David F. Bell (Baltimore: Johns Hopkins University Press, 1983), *Angels: A Modern Myth*, trans. Francis Cowper (Paris: Flammarion, 1995), and Michel Serres and Bruno Latour, *Conversations on Science, Culture and Time*, trans. Roxanne Lapidus (Ann Arbor: University of Michigan Press, 1995), 62–66.

51. Serres, *The Five Senses*, 103. Thus, what science studies is not experience. For example, the scientific account of radiation of a certain wavelength entering the eye, striking the rod and cone photoreceptors in the retina, and so on is not an account of the sensuous *experience of seeing*.

52. Serres, *The Five Senses*, 51.

53. Serres, *The Five Senses*, 112.

54. Serres, *The Five Senses*, 114. "I do not despise books. I love them so much that I have devoted my life to them. I love language so much that I have given it all my time, but we cannot bring a culture, a philosophy, to life without feeding it with what it is not [i.e., the hard]. . . . Professors, critics, theoreticians and politicians live on the closed sides [of language], the writer takes up residence on

its outskirts, in the open, facing things that are sometimes hard" (Serres, *The Five Senses*, 333).

55. See Michel Serres, *Angels: A Modern Myth*, trans. Francis Cowper (Paris: Flammarion, 1995).

56. Michel Serres, *Variations on the Body*, trans. Randolph Burks (Minneapolis, MI: Univocal, 2011), 61, 131, 150–151. Serres, *The Five Senses*, 315.

57. See Serres, *The Five Senses*, 173.

58. Serres, *The Five Senses*, 129. "Tacitly, the body understands the softness of meaning, and that one's retinas are never burned out by discourse, one's back not broken, one's skin not flayed. Looking through a window and seeing that tree down there seems as harmless as saying 'tree,' but looking at the sun which illuminates it is a little harder on the eyes; even more than that, staring at that same sun at midday, in the middle of the Sahara, or being surprised by the flash of a thermonuclear explosion, will end your sight for good. . . . Our bodies understand this discrepancy" (Serres, *The Five Senses*, 113).

59. Serres, *The Five Senses*, 146. The body is not the only black box. Serres also describes the house as a black box, insofar as it insulates us from hard sensuous realities. A little reflection will reveal the accuracy of this metaphor. Modern housing means we no longer feel the weather; whether it is cold or hot, wet or dry, inside the black box of the home we recline in perfect comfort, completely detached from the natural world. Artificial light allows us to ignore the rhythm of night and day. Drugs like caffeine and nicotine help us to ignore our own biorhythms. One could expand on Serres's notion here. Globalized capitalism also functions to insulate us from natural rhythms. We enjoy all sorts of produce out of season, since we can have things flown in from the Southern hemisphere. Indeed, the very notion of food has become largely dissociated from the earthy, hard, natural world from which it comes. For the modern American, "meat and potatoes" come from the supermarket or restaurant, not from the carcass of an animal or from the soil.

60. An intriguing proposal for carnal hermeneutics: Frank Wilson draws on data from neurology, anthropology, linguistics, psychology, and other sciences to make the claim that the hand, the brain, and language coevolved, "with the hand enjoying logical primacy" (Tom White, *In Defense of Dolphins: The New Moral Frontier* [Oxford: Wiley-Blackwell, 2007], 170–174). Bipedalism, which freed up the hands for other uses including tools and other forms of technology, shaped the circuitry and organization of the brain: language evolved in a response to the structure and use of the hand. The result? We construct sentences in the same manner that we construct tools and other objects: "evolution has created in the human brain an organ powerfully predisposed to generate rules that treat nouns as if they were stones and verbs as if they were levers or pulleys" (Frank Wilson, *The Hand: How Its Use Shapes the Brain, Language, and Human Culture* [New York: Random House, 1998], 165. Cited in White, *In Defense of Dolphins*, 172). This claim has remarkable implications suggesting, as it does, that all the products of human intelligence—language, culture, tradition, narrative, religion, art, sci-

ence, and technology—are colored by "the logic of the hand" (White, *In Defense of Dolphins*, 173). Our bodies—and therefore our minds and our languages—co-evolved with certain environments in the world and are indelibly marked by that process: "The mind is the way it is because the world is the way it is. The evolved systems organize the mind to mesh with the world" (Robert Ornstein, *Evolution of Consciousness* [New York: Prentice Hall, 1991], 47). Language circumscribes the way in which we experience and understand the world, but language, it seems, is contingently tied to very specific and ultimately random evolutionary adaptations of the body, adaptations that are useful and successful only in certain contexts.

61. Serres does suggest that hardness is "located on the entropic scale" (Serres, *The Five Senses*, 113). But the increase in entropy still seems to be associated with softening: Serres speaks here of "hardness" rather than "the hard," suggesting degrees of hardness/softness, and his account of Orpheus and Eurydice clearly suggests that death and decay (an increase in entropy) is associated with softening.

62. Serres, *The Five Senses*, 133.

63. A description of exquisite detail that concludes, "it took us so long to finish this bottle that we are still talking about it" (Serres, *The Five Senses*, 152).

64. Serres, *The Five Senses*, 165.

65. This, obviously, does nothing about the hard facts flowing from the second law of thermodynamics: disorder, decay, death. To "spit in the face of death" is to spit in the face of its *absolute significance*, not its inevitability.

66. Erazim Kohák, *The Embers and the Stars* (Chicago: The University of Chicago Press, 1984), 103. Emphases mine.

67. Serres, *The Five Senses*, 230.

68. See for example Serres, *The Five Senses*, 242–244. Serres himself is a philosopher of *mixed* bodies—the subtitle to *The Five Senses*—and is concerned, ultimately, with the relationship between the hard and the soft rather than some absolute, pure, Platonic *eidos* of hardness.

69. In this context some previous work has argued for the power and importance of narrative (Brian Treanor, *Emplotting Virtue* [Albany: SUNY, 2014], and "Narrative and Nature" in *Interpreting Nature* [New York: Fordham University Press, 2013]), but always in the context of the way in which narrative and other ways of knowing supplement each other to provide a fuller picture and better understanding. It is not a matter of science being true or narrative being true in an absolute and monolithic sense, but rather how both science and narrative contribute to our understanding of the truth.

70. Although Erazim Kohák, a philosopher deeply influenced by Ricoeur, does walk further along the detour through material place. Kohák's strain of realism is one that might serve as an example of a phenomenological and hermeneutic realism. Lamenting that, "not since the days of Gorgias, at least as Sextus Empiricus reports his views, has Western thought labored under so profound a fear that, even if there were truth and humans could know it, they could never communicate it," Kohák nevertheless writes, "what surrounds and penetrates us is not merely being but, primordially, *meaningful* being. As Paul Ricoeur reminds us, something must

be for something to be said—there must be meaning to which our words point, not as intruders or impositions, but as expressions of . . . meaning that stands out . . ." (Erazim Kohák, *The Embers and the Stars* [Chicago: The University of Chicago Press, 1984], 48. Emphasis mine.).

71. Serres confesses, perhaps surprisingly, ignorance of much contemporary philosophy, which leads, I believe, to a too-narrow caricature of hermeneutics writ large (see, for example, *Conversations on Science, Culture, and Time*, trans. Roxanne Lapidus [Ann Arbor, MI: University of Michigan Press], 38, 130, 134, etc.). I'm not suggesting we can dismiss Serres's thought—which is rich and provocative—on the basis of such offhand comments. However, while it seems fair to say that some of his criticisms would not change dramatically, even with more familiarity, it also seems fair to say that some of his criticisms seem to ignore the difference between styles of hermeneutics (e.g., Ricoeur and Derrida).

72. Paul Ricoeur, *Time and Narrative*, vol.1, trans. Kathleen McLaughlin and David Pellauer (Chicago: University of Chicago Press, 1984), x.

73. In addition to the essays in this volume, see: *Interpreting Nature: The Emerging Field of Environmental Hermeneutics*, eds. Forrest Clingerman, Brian Treanor, Martin Drenthen, and David Wood (New York: Fordham University Press, 2013); *Eco-Phenomenology: Back to the Earth Itself*, eds. Charles S. Brown and Ted Toadvine (Albany: SUNY Press, 2003); Erazim Kohák, *The Embers and the Stars* (Chicago: The University of Chicago Press, 1984); to say nothing of more poetic works, just as committed to carnality and earthiness, by Thoreau, Snyder, Muir, and others.

74. On this point, note the connection in Hebrew between Adam (man) and *adamah* (earth). Adam is, literally, the one formed from the earth. Note as well that *humus* is related to humility and so suggests not just something about the topics of hermeneutics (humans, earth) but also something about the method of hermeneutics (humility).

75. Serres, *The Five Senses*, 44. Most of us have abandoned a naïve belief that our knowledge and understanding progress in a linear fashion from A to B to C and so forth. Even those who believe in progress recognize that its path is not linear; it takes detours, cuts both long and short, and encounters blind alleys and cul-de-sacs. Moreover, in the wake of Thomas Kuhn and others, we can see how messy, mysterious, and revolutionary the progression of knowledge sometimes is. A path might take us from A to B to C, and then back to B before leaping forward to F. And, in the context of this evolution, our understanding—which takes into account objectifying explanation without being fully reducible to it—takes its own helical journey from A_1 to A_2, A_3, . . . A_n. We always come back to our self—where else?—but it is never the self with which we began.

76. Serres, *The Five Senses*, 41.

77. And hermeneutics agrees: "We all know objective truth is not obtainable . . . but we must still believe that objective truth is obtainable; or we must believe that it is 99 percent obtainable; or if we can't believe this we must believe that 43 percent objective truth is better than 41 percent. We must do so because

if we don't we're lost, we fall into beguiling relativity, we value one liar's version as much as another liar's, we throw up our hands at the puzzle of it all, we admit that the victor has the right not just to the spoils but also to the truth" (Richard Kearney, citing Julian Barnes's *History of the World in 10½ Chapters* [New York: Routledge, 2002], 149).

78. Here, again, Kohák is useful. He integrates a genuine appreciation for the significance of material reality with the insight that matter is not all that matters: "Meaningful being, not pure meaning or sheer being, is reality" (Erazim Kohák, *The Embers and the Stars* [Chicago: The University of Chicago Press, 1984], 48). Also see ibid., 197–203.

79. This landscape is given voice beautifully in Gerald Manley Hopkins's poem *Pied Beauty*, which speaks of reality as "dappled," "stippled," and "brinded"; populated by things that are "original, spare, strange . . . fickle, [and] freckled." This image is one of detailed, particular, material reality; but one that ultimately exceeds our full comprehension, one that exhibits a surplus surpassing the particulars. See "Pied Beauty" in *Gerald Manley Hopkins: Poetry and Prose*, ed. Wilford Davies (London: Everyman, 1998), 48.

80. Richard Kearney, *Anatheism* (New York: Columbia University Press, 2010), 46.

81. See *Interpreting Nature: The Emerging Field of Environmental Hermeneutics*, eds. Forrest Clingerman, Brian Treanor, Martin Drenthen, and David Wood (New York: Fordham University Press, 2013).

82. Richard Kearney, "What Is Diacritical Hermeneutics?" in *The Journal of Applied Hermeneutics*, 2011, no. 2, 8. And, to forestall a related objection, I'd note that "we are far from relativism" as well. See my *Emplotting Virtue* (Albany: SUNY, 2014).

Rethinking Corpus
Jean-Luc Nancy

1. *À la recherche du temps perdu, À l'ombre de jeunes filles en fleurs*, Pléiade, vol. 1, 1987: 716.

2. Ibid. "Le temps retrouvé," vol. 3, 1987: 911.

3. Encyclopedia, "philosophy of nature," trans. Fcse Bernard Bourgeois (Paris: Gallimard, 2004), s. 354: 657.

4. This paper was first presented in Vienna in 2010.

5. We need to differentiate further among the various senses. All participate in touch, inasmuch as they all have the possibility for an identity between sensing and that which is sensed. But each one modifies this identity in its own way, and the difference among the modifications is inherent to the sense, which cannot be single or general. If it were, there would only be an abstract "sensible," a concept of the sensible. But in each system a particular sense is given precedence, while the plurality of the senses is also acknowledged—the fact that they interact in differential and inexhaustible ways. Thus one could approach all of them via the model of touch, and differentiate all of them by relating them to one or the other of the

senses. However, to put it briefly, taste and smell have a different way of engaging the relationship inside/outside; for them there is absorption and assimilation, in a very particular way. Furthermore, taste concerns something to be sensed that is either solid or liquid, while smell concerns something evanescent, gaseous, airborne. Each time the relationship is different, according to the extent and movement that are proper to touch. Each time it is a matter of special touches, whose import varies from one body to another (as when we say that someone "has a nose" or "has an ear"). This "has" is a way of touching/being touched.

6. Ascent of Mt. Carmel, Book 3, Chapter 14, 2ff.

7. In French, taken literally, "touche moi" and "tu te touches" are erotic locutions.

From the Limbs of the Heart to the Soul's Organs
Jean-Louis Chrétien

Out of respect for Chrétien's subtle view that scholarship is *ancilla philosophiae* (servant of philosophy), we have left his footnotes relatively informal and unburdened.—Eds.

Jean-Louis Chrétien's aim in *Symbolique du Corps* is to study the body as a veritable language that gives us a voice to probe and describe our spiritual being as well as the nature of community. The body, Chrétien reminds us, is the very place and the very form in which Spirit comes into the world to dwell with us. The body is the Word-bearer through which meaning reaches us and in which "every possible call is answered." If we fail, however, to appreciate our embodiment in light of the Incarnation of the Word, if we isolate the body into a sort of impoverished self-sufficiency, we miss the radical eloquence that it affords us. In the quest of the body's inexhaustible resources of speech for articulating the inner life, Solomon's *Song of Songs* offers a privileged wellspring of insight since it testifies to man's encounter with God through a wounding of love. The explosive language of the Song thus appears indispensable to the renewal of a theology and philosophy of embodiment.—Trans. Anne Davenport

1. Origène, *Commentaire sur le Cantique des Cantiques*, Prologue, 2, 9, and 13, vol. I, 99–100; in *Sources Chrétiennes*, ed. et trad. Brézard et Crouzel (Paris: Éditions du Cerf, 1991–2) 375–376.

2. The English novelist Anthony Trollope did not fail to use it to literary advantage: "This is when Dr. Grantly stood up. . . . When I say that the archdeacon stood up, I mean that the inner man suddenly leapt up, eager to act, since our man, physically speaking, had been standing all the while, his back to the dean's empty hearth." *The Towers of Rochester*, chap. VII.

3. Cf. the classic study by A. Guillaumont, "Le sens des noms du coeur dans l'Antiquité," in *Etudes sur la spiritualité de l'Orient chrétien* (Paris: Bellefontaine, 1996).

4. F. Suarez, *Opera Omnia* (Paris, 1856), II, 232.

5. B. Pascal, *Pensées*, ed. Le Guern (Paris, 1995) Section 101, p. 105.

6. Jr 4:4, Bible de Jérusalem (French Edition).

7. Ep 1:18, Bible de Jérusalem (French Edition).

8. Jr 4:19. The Vulgate puts: *sensus cordis mei.* Church Fathers such as Theodoret of Cyr will appeal to this passage.

9. Philo, *De praemiis et poenis*, 80, trans. Beckaert (Paris: Éditions du cerf, 1961), 83.

10. Philo, *De praemiis et poenis*, 85, trans. Arnaldez (Paris: Éditions du cerf 1972), 93.

11. E.g. *De somnis*, II, 180; *De mutatione nominum*, 238.

12. Philo, *De specialibus legibus*, III, 6, trans. Mosès (Paris, 1970) 59.

13. Cf. A. Guillaumont, "Le sens des noms du coeur," 59, 65, 71–72.

14. Origène, *Entretien avec Héraclide*, 11, 78–81.

15. Origène, *op. cit.*, 16, p. 89.

16. Origène, *op. cit.*, 16–22, pp. 89–101.

17. On Saint Gregory of Nyssa, see the decisive study by J. Daniélou, *Platonisme et théologie mystique* (Paris: Aubier, Éditions Montaigne, 1953), 222–252, on "spiritual senses."

18. Jn 5:19

19. Saint Augustin, *Homélies sur Jean*, XVIII, 7, trans. Berrouard (Paris: Institut d'études augustiniennes, 1977) 137.

20. Ibid., XVIII, 9, p. 145.

21. Ibid., p. 147.

22. Ibid., XVIII, 10, p. 149.

23. Ibid., p. 151, along with Berrouard's footnote with important references, pp. 736–738.

24. *La Cité de Dieu*, XI, 27, trad. Combès (Paris: Etudes Augustiennes, 1959), pp. 119–121.

25. *Confessions*, X, VI, 8, trad. Tréhorel et Bouissou (Paris: Desclée de Brouwer 1962), p. 155.

26. *Sermo*, 159, IV, 4, PL XXXVIII, 869.

27. *Confessions*, IV, XI, 16, p. 437.

28. *Confessions*, I, V, 6, p. 283.

29. Dt 29:3 Bible de Jérusalem (French Edition).

30. *Qu. In Hept.*, V, 50, PL XXXIV, 770–771.

31. Sg 15:15

32. *En. In Ps.*, 134, 24, PL XXXVII, 1754–1755. The reference is to II Cor. II, 15.

33. F. Nietzsche, *Ecce Homo, Sämtliche Werke*, ed. Colli-Montari (Berlin, 1980), t. VI, p. 366.

34. Luther, CC, p. 736 and 738.

35. Cf. Jean-Louis Chrétien, *Saint Augustin et les actes de la parole* (Paris: Presses Universitaires de France, 2002), chap. III, IV and V.

36. *En. In Ps.* 125, 6, PL XXXVII, 1661.

37. Novalis, *Heinrich von Ofterdingen*, II (trad. Delétang-Tardif, *Romantiques allemands*, t. I [Paris, 1963], p. 399.) Luther's maxim clearly applies to this statement.

38. The classic reference here is 1 Cor 3:2 sq.

39. *Confessions*, VI, III, 3, p. 523.

40. *Confessions*, IX, X, 23, p. 117.

41. *Enar. In Ps.*, 141, 1, PL 37, 1833.

42. Cf. Mt V, 6

43. Enarr. In Ps., 70, 12, PL 36, 900

44. Cassiodore, *Explanatio Psalmorum*, 70, 24, p. 369.

45. Saint Augustine, *Enarr. In Ps.*, 30, s. 3, 6, PL 36, 251.

46. *Confessions*, X, VIII, 12, p. 163.

47. Saint Ambroise de Milan, *De virginitate*, § 59.

48. Saint Augustine, *Enarr. In Ps.*, 13, 15, PL 36, 124.

49. Mt 6:21.

50. *Enarr. In Ps.*, 33, 10, PL 36, 313.

51. *Enarr. In Ps.*, 94, 2, PL 37, 1217.

52. Honorius, PL 172, 456, cf. 1129.

53. Ex 32:9 BJ; Dt 10:16; Jr 19:15.

54. Saint Jérôme, *In Hieremiam*, III, 81, ed. Reiter (Turnhout: Brepols, 1960), p. 172.

55. Rabanus Maurus, PL 111, 156.

56. Saint Gregory the Great, *Moralia*, XV, LIV, 61, p. 788.

57. Saint Gregory the Great, *Homélies sur Ezéchiel*, I, XI, 8, t. I, p. 459.

58. Saint Gregory the Great, *Moralia*, XXXI, XLIV, 85, p. 106.

59. Saint Gregory the Great, *Moralia*, IV, XXXII, 65, p. 208.

60. Wolbéron, PL 195, 1097.

61. Ibid., 1179.

62. Ibid., 1243. This "palate" has passed into profane speech. Littré (s. v.) cites an example drawn from d'Alembert. The English novelist George Gissing (*The Old Women*, chap. 8) evokes a silly woman who "had no palate for anything but the suet-pudding of talk" (a heavy and fatty dish).

63. Wolbéron, PL 195, 1203.

64. Ibid., 1189.

65. Ibid., 1229.

66. Ibid., 1245.

67. A. Guillaumont, *op. cit.*, pp. 26–27.

68. C. Péguy, *Oeuvres en prose completes*, ed. Burac (Paris: Gallimard, 1992), t. III, pp. 1321–1322.

69. M. Heidegger, *Vorträge und Aufsätze* (Pfullingen, 1978), pp. 206–207, trad. Préau, *Essais et conferences*, (Paris, 1966), pp. 258–259.

70. J.-P. Sartre, *L'Etre et le néant*, (Paris: Gallimard, 1965), p. 452.

71. Saint Francis of Sales, *CC.*, p. 13–14.

72. Rabanus Maurus, *De universo*, VI, 1, PL 111, 137 sq.

73. Cf. J.-P. Laurant, *Symbolisme et Ecriture. Le cardinal Pitra et la "clef" de Méliton de Sardes*, Paris, 1988, 154–155.

74. Gilbert de Hoyland, CC, 24, 2–3, t. II, pp. 56–57.

75. Claude Hopil, CC, p. 242, p. 244, p. 246.

76. Saint Francis of Sales, CC, p. 25. Shakespeare, in the same time period, speaks of the *stomach of sense* ("You cram these thoughts into mine ears, against / The stomach of my sense"), *The Tempest*, II, 1. Such recapitulations are rare, but are found in Honorius Augustodunensis.

77. Denys "Aréopagite, *Hiérachie céleste*, XV, 3, trad. Gandillac (Paris: Éditions du cerf, 1970), pp. 172–177 (as well as what follows.)

78. Jean Scot Erigène, *Expositions in Ierarchiam Coelestem*, XV, ed. Barbet (Turnhout: Brepols, 1975), p. 198.

79. Hughes de saint Victor, PL 175, 1143–1144.

80. Jean Scot, *op. cit.*, p. 199.

81. Denys l'Aeropagite, *Noms dicvins*, IX, 5, PG 3, 912–913, trad. Gandillac, *Oeuvres completes*, (Paris, 1980), pp. 156–157.

82. Isidore, *Etym.*, t. II, p. 1–21.

83. Isidore, *Etym.*, XI, 1, § 39, 42, 49, pp. 6 and 8.

84. Ibid., § 108–109, p. 15.

85. Rabanus Maurus, PL, 111, 176.

86. Rupert de Deutz, CC, p. 136. This source escaped the scholarly editor.

87. Origène, *Homélies sur les Juges*, II, 3, trad. Borret et al. (Paris: Éditions du cerf, 1993), p. 80. The same "knees of the heart" will be found in Apponius.

A Tragedy and a Dream: Disability Revisited
Julia Kristeva

1. Notably in his description of the most appropriate possibilities as an analytic of finitude, and in the "proximity" of man with "beings," but not in his singularity.

Incarnation and the Problem of Touch
Michael Henry

1. Truly speaking, following the Galilean reduction, modern biology eliminated sensibility, "subjectivity," and "consciousness" from its topic of research. It no longer talks about life: "we no longer inquire into life today in laboratories." Since its purpose has changed entirely, only the anachronistic use of the Greek name of this science enables this confusion. François Jacob, *La Logique du vivant* (Paris: Gallimard, 1970), 320.

2. It is this dual belonging of the body to the world as both seeing and visible—"touching" and "tangible"—that leads the later Merleau-Ponty to say about this body that is situated in the world at the same time as it opens us up to the world that "it is of the world" (See *The Visible and The Invisible*, 178). For a radical critique of these theses, refer to my *Incarnation: A Philosophy of the Flesh*, ch. 21 and 31.

3. See Kierkegaard, *The Concept of Dread*, trans. Walter Lowrie (Princeton, NJ: Princeton University Press, 1944), 40. Translator's note: the Lowrie translation renders this as "the alarming possibility of being able." That said, I have remained

closer to the French text, which reads "*pouvoir pouvoir.*" This connotes possibility, ability, and power, and so I have rendered it "the power to be able" throughout.

4. Irenaeus, *Against the Heresies*, Book V.

5. This is a translation of Chapter VIII from Henry, Michel, *Phénoménologie de la vie I. De la Phénoménologie*, Collection Epiméthée, Presses Universitaires de France, Paris, 2003, Chapitre VIII Le problème du Toucher.

6. Descartes, *Oeuvres philosophiques*, éd. F. Alquié, vol. II, p 792.

7. Ibid.

On the Phenomena of Suffering
Jean-Luc Marion

1. This is not a tautology (although here tautology could actually seem appropriate), but see Acts 17: 28.

2. Once again, the supposedly head-on opposition between Lévinas and Henry seems very fragile. See Rodolphe Calin, *Lévinas et l'exception du soi* (Paris: Presses Universitaires de France, 2005). For the face also cannot be seen: "The face is present in its refusal to be contained . . . neither seen, nor touched" (Emmanuel Lévinas, *Totalité et Infini* [The Hague: Nijhoff, 1961], 168; *Totality and Infinity*, trans. Alphonso Lingis [Pittsburgh: Duquesne University Press, 1969], 194), because it cannot be aimed at: "The trace of a past in a face is not the absence of a yet non-revealed, but the anarchy of what has never been present, of an infinite which commands in the face of the other, and which . . . could not be aimed at" (Lévinas, *Autrement qu'être ou Au-delà de l'essence* [The Hague: Nijhoff, 1974], 124; *Otherwise than Being or Beyond Essence*, trans. Alphonso Lingis [Pittsburgh: Duquesne University Press, 1981], 97).

3. Respectively, Michel Henry, *De la phénoménologie: Phénoménologie de la vie*, vol. I (Paris: Presses Universitaires de France, 2003), 49 and Henry, *L'Essence de la manifestation* (Paris: Presses Universitaires de France, 1963), 549; *The Essence of Manifestation*, trans. Girard Etzkorn (The Hague: Nijhoff, 1973), 438 (title of §50, which the text itself does not take up again). [Henceforth the first page number refers to the French, the second to the English translation.]

4. Henry, *De la phénoménologie*, 79.

5. Ibid.

6. Henry, *The Essence of Manifestation*, §61, 680/543 and 681/544, respectively.

7. Henry, *De la phénoménologie*, 65 (and 200). See also: "No one has ever seen life and no one will ever see it" (ibid., 48).

8. Henry, *The Essence of Manifestation*, §45, 481/382. This analysis can be repeated one more time when dealing with phenomena that belong to life. Hence the paradox of a "painting [that would] assign itself the task of painting the invisible," precisely the "hieroglyphs of the invisible," for example, in what we call abstract painting. Michel Henry, *Voir l'invisible: Sur Kandinsky* (Paris: Bourin-Julliard, 1988), 22 and 244; *Seeing the Invisible: On Kandinsky*, trans. Scott Davidson (London: Continuum, 2009), 9 and 142.

9. Henry, *The Essence of Manifestation*, §50, 552/440.

10. Henry, *Phénoménologie matérielle* (Paris: Presses Universitaires de France, 1990), 122; *Material Phenomenology*, trans. Scott Davidson (New York: Fordham University Press, 2008), 90.

11. Henry, *De la phénoménologie*, 63. (See the same terms, 198–99.)

Memory, History, Oblivion
Paul Ricoeur

In March 2003 Paul Ricoeur attended the conference "Haunted Memories? History in Europe after Authoritarianism," which was held at the Central European University of Budapest, Hungary. He delivered a lecture in English under the title "Memory, History, Oblivion." The text of this lecture has never been published in English before, though it was translated and published in French in *ESPRIT:* "La pensée Ricoeur," 2006. With the permission of the Editorial Committee, we are happy to include here the original English version (Fonds Ricoeur, October 2010).—Eds.

Skin Deep: Bodies Edging into Place
Edward S. Casey

1. Lisa Guenther, *Solitary Confinement: Social Death and Its Afterlives* (Minneapolis: University of Minnesota Press, 2013), xi.

2. "PsySR Open Letter on PFC Bradley Manning's Solitary Confinement," January 3, 2011. This is part of a letter written to Robert Gates as Defense Secretary that argued that PFC Bradley Manning's being held in solitary confinement at Quantico Marine Corps Base for (at the time) over six months constituted "cruel, unusual, and inhumane treatment in violation of U.S. law." "PsySR" refers to Psychologists for Social Responsibility. The letter states that those held in solitary for longer than ten days invariably had very seriously debilitating effects. They conclude that "solitary confinement can have severely deleterious effects on the psychological well-being of those subjected to it" (cited from the same open letter).

3. Jack Henry Abbott, *In the Belly of the Beast: Letters from Prison* (New York: Vintage, 1991), 45 (cited by Guenther, xi).

4. Jeremy Pinson, cited by Guenther, *Solitary Confinement*, xii.

5. Guenther, *Solitary Confinement*, xv.

6. Ibid.

7. Gaston Bachelard, *The Poetics of Space*, trans. M. Jolas (Boston: Beacon Press, 1964): this is the title of chapter eight of this book.

8. Women are not spared solitary confinement by any means; in California prisons women's solitary confinement has seen a dramatic increase in recent years. For documentation and an eloquent plea for being considered along with men, see *The Fire Inside: Newsletter for the California Coalition for Women Prisoners*, Number 49, Fall 2013/Winter 2014. As most prisoners in solitary remain men,

however, I shall employ the masculine pronoun in what follows to refer to *all* such prisoners.

9. Guenther describes her own project as being a "critical phenomenology" of the prisoner's experience. See *Solitary Confinement*, xiii–xv and especially chapter five.

10. Often one does *not* know how long one will be held, even losing track of how long it has been so far; this de-temporalization is another untoward effect of solitary confinement.

11. Maurice Merleau-Ponty, *Phenomenology of Perception*, trans. D. Landes (New York: Routledge, 2012), 295: "Now if the world falls to pieces or is broken apart, this is because one's own body has ceased to be a knowing body."

12. Nelson Mandela, *Long Walk to Freedom* (New York: Little, Brown, 1994), 389. Mandela also observes that "Time slows down in prison; the days seem endless" (ibid.).

13. For more on the up-againstness of border walls, see *Up Against the Wall: Re-Imagining the U.S.–Mexico Border*, co-authored with Mary Watkins, and appearing in Fall 2014 with University of Texas Press.

14. "In fact the situation [of being in a prison cell] by the very meaning of the given (a meaning without which there *would not even be* any given) reflects to the for-itself its freedom. . . . The situation is a *relation of being* between a for-itself and the in-itself which the for-itself nihilates . . . The situation is the subject illuminating things by his very surpassing" (Jean-Paul Sartre, *Being and Nothingness*, trans. Hazel E. Barnes [New York: Washington Square Press, 1984], 702). But the in-itself—e.g., the prison walls, the miserable body of the prisoner in solitary confinement—is nihilated or surpassed only insofar as it yields a meaning which the for-itself or consciousness of the prisoner chooses to endow it with: this is the narrow edge of freedom to which Sartre points. This is an edge that is more a precarious perch than a secure platform.

15. Maurice Merleau-Ponty, *Phenomenology of Perception*, 213.

16. Octavio Paz, *The Labyrinth of Solitude: The Other Mexico*, trans. L. Kemp (New York: Grove Press, 1985).

17. Guenther, *Solitary Confinement*, xii.

18. Edmund Husserl, "The World of the Living Present and the Constitution of the Surrounding World External to the Organism," trans. F. Kersten, in *Husserl, Shorter Works*, ed. P. McCormick & F. Elliston (Notre Dame: University of Notre Dame Press, 1981), 250. The absolute here serves as "the zero point of orientation" (ibid.).

19. Mandela, *Long Walk to Freedom*, 384.

20. On intentional threads, see Merleau-Ponty, *Phenomenology of Perception*, 88, 132, and esp. 74: "the body, [even when] withdrawing from the objective world, will carry with it the intentional threads that unite it to its surroundings." In the case of the solitary prisoner's body, these threads link up most immediately with its cell-place, and only secondarily with the places that are remembered or

fantasied from within the cell. On "operative [vs. act] intentionality," as "the intentionality that establishes the natural and pre-predicative unity of the world and of our life" (see ibid., lxxxii).

Touched by Touching
David Wood

1. Jacques Derrida, *On Touching—Jean-Luc Nancy* (Stanford: Stanford University Press, 2005), 75.

2. Richard Kearney, "Diacritical Hermeneutics," in *Hermeneutic Rationality*, ed. Maria Portocarrero, Luis Umbelino, Andrzej Wiercinski (Berlin: Verlag Dr. W. Hopf, 2012), 177.

3. My attention to chance sentences that land at one's feet as if on scraps of paper blown by the wind finds some resonance with Derrida's fastening onto an inscription on a Paris wall: "Quand nos yeux se touchent, fait-il jour ou fait-il nuit?" / "When our eyes touch is it day or is it night?" (*On Touching*, 4), or, again: "Someone, you or me, comes forward and says: I would like to *learn* to *live* finally" (from the Exordium to Jacques Derrida, *Specters of Marx* [London/New York: Routledge, 1994]). These words come to us. What are we to make of them?

4. The reference here is to Derrida's *The Animal That Therefore I Am* (New York: Fordham University Press, 2008).

5. George Berkeley, *An Essay towards a New Theory of Vision* (1703) §44, Google digital edition, 2008.

6. Friedrich Nietzsche, *Gay Science* (1882), trans. Walter Kaufmann (New York: Random House, 1991), §59.

7. A reproduction of this painting can be found at http://paintingdb .com/s/7252/

8. Martin Heidegger, *Being and Time*, trans. Joan Stambaugh (Albany: SUNY Press, 1996), 129.

9. Roland Barthes's *The Pleasure of the Text* (New York: Hill and Wang, 1975).

10. *The Pleasure of the Text*, vii–viii.

11. Pablo Neruda, *Selected Poems in Translation* (Online edition, A. S. Kline, 2000).

12. Gerard Manley Hopkins, "Pied Beauty," in *Gerard Manley Hopkins: Poems and Prose* (Harmondsworth: Penguin, 1985), 30.

GLORY be to God for dappled things—
    For skies of couple-colour as a brinded cow;
    For rose-moles all in stipple upon trout that swim;
Fresh-firecoal chestnut-falls; finches' wings;
    Landscape plotted and pieced—fold, fallow, and plough;
    And all trades, their gear and tackle and trim.
All things counter, original, spare, strange;
    Whatever is fickle, freckled (who knows how?)
    With swift, slow; sweet, sour; adazzle, dim;

He fathers-forth whose beauty is past change:
  Praise him.

13. In von Uexküll's words, "the whole rich world around the tick shrinks and changes into a scanty framework consisting, in essence, of three receptor cues and three effector cues—her *Umwelt*. But the very poverty of this world guarantees the unfailing certainty of her actions, and security is more important than wealth. By abridging her indulgence in sensual luxuries, nature has ensured the tick as failsafe an existence as the natural world provides. For animals like us, bathed continually in our own set of sensory inputs, only our imaginations allow us entry into the world of such a creature, an entry essential to the ethological perspective" (Jakob von Uexkull, *A Foray into the Worlds of Animals and Humans: With a Theory of Meaning* [Minneapolis: University of Minnesota Press, 2010]).

14. See Derrida, glossing Nancy: "all one ever does touch is a limit. To touch is to touch a limit, a surface, a border, an outline." Derrida, *On Touching*, 103.

Umbilicus: Toward a Hermeneutics of Generational Difference
Anne O'Byrne

1. See Paul Ricoeur, *Hermeneutics*, trans. David Pellauer (Cambridge, UK: Polity, 2013), 99. "Hermeneutics is not an anti-epistemology, but a reflection on the non-epistemological conditions of (first-level) epistemology."

2. "We are ourselves the entities to be analyzed. The Being of any such entity is *in each case mine [je meines]*" (Martin Heidegger, *Being and Time*, trans. John Maquarrie and Edward Robinson [New York: Harper, 1962], 42). Note Heidegger's comment a few pages later: "The existential [ontological] analytic of Dasein comes before any psychology or anthropology, and certainly before any biology" (*Being and Time*, 45).

3. See Jean-Luc Nancy, "The there is of sexual relation" in *Corpus II: Writings on Sexuality*, trans. Anne O'Byrne (New York: Fordham University Press, 2013), 1–22.

4. Jean-Luc Nancy, *Corpus*, trans. Richard Rand (New York: Fordham, 2008), 27.

5. Barlaam of Calabria, quoted in Steven Runciman, *The Great Church in Captivity: A Study of the Patriarchate of Constantinople from the Eve of the Turkish Conquest to the Greek War of Independence* (Cambridge: Cambridge University Press, 1986), 141.

6. See Jane Ellen Harrison, *Epilogomena to the Study of Greek Religion* (Princeton: Princeton University Press, 1991) and *Themis: A Study of the Social Origins of Greek Religion* (Cambridge: Cambridge University Press, 2010), 385–429.

7. This line of inquiry was quite thoroughly pursued by Harrison in *Themis*.

8. Luce Irigaray, "Body against Body: In Relation to the Mother" in *Sexes and Genealogies*, trans. Gillian C. Gill (New York: Columbia University Press, 1993), 14.

9. Irigaray, "Body against Body: In Relation to the Mother," 17.

10. Elisabeth Bronfen, "Vom Omphalos zum Phallus" in Wolfgang Müller-Funk, ed. *Macht, Geschlechter, Differenz* (Vienna: Picus, 1994), 128–151.

11. See Martin Gardner, *Did Adam and Eve Have Navels?* (New York: Norton, 2000), 7–15.

12. Quoted in Gardner, *Did Adam and Eve Have Navels?*, 8.

13. Max Charlesworth, et al., *Life Among the Scientists: An Anthropologial Study of an Australian Scientific Community* (Melbourne: Oxford, 1989), 214. Quoted in David Napier, *The Age of Immunology: Conceiving a Future in an Alienating World* (Chicago: University of Chicago Press, 2003), 220.

14. Claudia Dreifus, "An Interview with Polly Matzinger," *New York Times*, June 16, 1998.

15. At least not immunological damage. For example, even though it is a myth that the fetus leaches calcium from the maternal body causing tooth loss, the hormonal changes in the pregnant body do increase the likelihood of gum disease.

16. Ricoeur, *Hermeneutics*, 99.

17. Ricoeur, *Hermeneutics*, 99–100.

18. Wilhelm Dilthey, "Über das Studium der Geschichte der Wissenschaften vom Menschen, der Gesellschaft und dem Staat" ["On the Study of the History of the Sciences of Humanity, Society, and the State"] (1875), in *Gesammelte Schriften* V (Stuttgart: Tuebner; Göttingen: Vandenhoeck and Ruprecht, 1914–2000), 38.

19. Ricoeur, *Hermeneutics*, 100.

20. Ricoeur, *Hermeneutics*, 99.

21. Ricoeur, *Hermeneutics*, 53.

22. *Immanent* is itself a freighted term and, besides, sense will not be merely immanent. Nancy at one point tries out *transimmanence* as a way of placing sense. See Jean-Luc Nancy, *The Sense of the World* trans. Jeffrey Librett (Minneapolis: University of Minnesota Press, 1997), 55.

23. Nancy, *The Sense of the World*, 35, 58.

24. Nancy, *The Sense of the World*, 152.

Getting in Touch: Aristotelian Diagnostics
Emmanuel Alloa

1. Wilhelm Dilthey, "Die Geburt der Hermeneutik" (The Rise of Hermeneutics), trans. Frederic Jameson, in *The Hermeneutic Tradition. From Ast to Ricoeur*, eds. Gayle L. Ormiston and Alan Schrift (Albany, NY: SUNY, 1990), 114.

2. Ibid., 105.

3. Aristotle, *De sophisticis elenchis* (*Sophistical Refutations*) trans. E. S. Forster (Cambridge: Harvard University Press / Classical Loeb, 1954), 20, 177b4–7.

4. Aristotle, *Sophistical Refutations* 20, 177b6 (trans. E.S. Forster).

5. Aristotle, *Historia animalium* (*The History of Animals*) , trans. A. L. Peck, (Cambridge: Harvard University Press / Classical Loeb, 1965), V, 33; 558a6–11

6. Pliny the Elder, *Naturalis historia* (*Natural history*), trans. H. Rackham, Cambridge: Harvard University Press / Classical Loeb, 1938), vol. III, Book IX, 76, 166.

7. (Ps.) Dionysius Thrax, *Technē grammatikē* I 41 (*La grammaire de Denys le Thrace*), ed. Jean Lallot (Paris: CNRS Éditions), 2003. The term used by (Ps.) Dionysius for referring to the diacritical signs is *prōsodiai*.

8. Rudolf Pfeiffer, *History of Classical Scholarship: From the Beginnings to the End of the Hellenistic Age* (Oxford: Clarendon, 1968), 207qq.

9. Irenaeus, *Adversus Hareses* (*Against Heresies*, Ancient Christian Writers 64, trans. Dominic Unger and Irenaeus M.C. Steenberg (Mahwah: The Newman Press, 2012), I, 8, 1.

10. Augustine, *Confessions* (*Confessions*), trans. Henry Chadwick, (Oxford: Oxford University Press, 1991), 11, 3, 5.

11. David Dawson, "Plato's Soul and the Body of the Text in Philo and Origen," in *Interpretation and Allegory. Antiquity to the Modern Period*, ed. John Whitman (Leiden: Brill, 2000), 89–107.

12. Origen, *De Principiis* (*On First Principles*), trans. G. W. Butterworth (New York: Harper & Row, 1966), preface, 10.

13. On the origin of the expression "body of the text" see Annewies van den Hoek, "The concept of *sōma tōn graphōn* in Alexandrian theology," *Studia patristica* 19, ed. Elizabeth Livingstone (Leuven 1989), 250–254.

14. Irenaeus, *Adversus Haereses*, trans. Unger and Steenberg, I 14, 3

15. Walter Benjamin, "On the Mimetic Faculty," in *Selected Writings*, vol. 2: 1931–1934, ed. Michael W. Jennings, Howard Eiland and Gary Smith (Cambridge and London: Belknap Press, 1999), 722. The sentence is actually a quote from a play by Hugo von Hofmannsthal, *Der Tor und der Tod*.

16. Ibid.

17. Alberto Manguel, *A History of Reading* (London: Penguin, 1996), 6.

18. On this and more, see Hasso Jäger, "Studien zur Frühgeschichte der Hermeneutik," *Archiv für Begriffsgeschichte* 18 (1974), 35–84.

19. Eric Voegelin, *Order and History III: Plato and Aristotle* (Columbia: University of Missouri Press, 2000), 148.

20. Reinhart Koselleck, "Crisis," *Journal of the History of Ideas* 67.2 (2006), 357–400, see in particular p. 360.

21. Augustine, *Confessiones*, VI, 1 (modified translation).

22. Hippocrates, *De morbis popularibus* IV, 42 (Hippocrates, *Works*, Volume 7: *Epidemics*, ed. Wesley Smith, (Harvard: Classical Loeb, 1994), 137.

23. Werner Jaeger, *Diokles von Karistos. Die griechische Medizin und die Schule des Aristoteles* (Berlin: De Gruyter, 1938), 38.

24. Niccoló Massa, *Liber introductorius Anatomiae, sive dissectionis corporis humani* (Venice 1536), 3v and 4r.

25. Caspar Bauhin, *Theatrum anatomicum infinitis locis auctum* (Basel, 1592).

26. Galen, *De usu partium*, III 1, 10–11. See Luis García Ballester, "Galen as a medical practitioner: problems in diagnosis," in *Galen. Problems and prospects*, ed. Vivian Nutton (London: The Wellcome Institute, 1981) 13–46.

27. Andreas Vesalius, *De humani corporis fabrica libri septem*, (Basel, 1543), 2r.

28. Notes on Surgery, taken from the Lectures read by Henry Thompson at the London Hospital, by Gilchrist Stirling, 1759 (Quoted after Susan C. Lawrence, "Educating the Senses. Students, teachers and medical rhetoric in eighteenth-century London," *Medicine and the Five senses*, ed. W. F. Bynum and Roy Porter [Cambridge: Cambridge University Press, 1993], 310).

29. Hans-Georg Gadamer, *Truth and Method*, trans. Joel Weinsheimer and Donald G. Marshall (New York, Crossroad, 1989), 474.

30. Aristotle, *Metaphysics*, ń 1, 980a25–27 (trans. Ross).

31. Hans Jonas, "The Nobility of Sight," in *Philosophy and Phenomenological Research* 14 (1954), 507–519.

32. Marsilio Ficino, *Commentary on Plato's Symposium on Love*, trans. Sears Jayne, (Dallas: Spring Publications, 1985), 41.

33. Ibid., 76.

34. Friedrich Schiller, *On the Aesthetics and Education of Man. Twenty-Sixth Letter*, trans. E.M. Wilkinson and L.A. Willoughby (Oxford: Clarendon 1982), Twenty-Sixth Letter.

35. Thomas Aquinas, *Summa Theologiae*, Ia, q. 27.

36. G. W. F. Hegel, *Ästhetik (Aesthetics: Lectures on Fine Art)*, trans. T. M. Knox (Oxford: Clarendon Press, 1975), vol. I, 38.

37. Robert Boyle, *Of the Strange Subtlety of Effluviums in Works*, ed. Thomas Birch, (London: J. and F. Rivington, 1776), vol. III, 694.

38. Friedrich Nietzsche, *Zur Genealogie der Moral (On the Genealogy of Morality)*, III. 6., ed. Keith Ansell-Pearson, trans. Carol Diethe, (Cambridge: Cambridge University Press 2007), 74.

39. J. G. Herder, *Plastik (On Sculpture)*, trans. Jason Gaiger (Chicago: University of Chicago Press, 2002), 38.

40. Lucretius, *De rerum natura (On The Nature of Things)* III, 161–166, trans. W.D.H. Rouse, rev. M. Smith, (Cambridge: Harvard University Press / Classical Loeb, 1975).

41. Denis Diderot, *Lettre sur les sourds et muets à l'usage de ceux qui entendent et parlent* [1751], *Œuvres complètes*, ed. H. Dieckmann and J. Varloot, (Paris: Hermann, 1978), vol 4: 206–207.

42. Tardy de Montravel, *Essai sur la théorie du somnambulisme magnétique*, (London: [no publisher], 1785), 50: "le toucher nous est le plus parfait des cinq sens. . . . C'est lui qui assure les jugements que font naître en nous les quatre autres; il rectifie les erreurs que ceux-ci nous feraient souvent commettre."

43. Didier Anzieu, *The Skin Ego*, trans. Chris Turner (New Haven: Yale University Press, 1989).

44. See my essay Tactiques de l'optique, postface to Alois Riegl, *L'industrie d'art romaine tardive*, with a preface by C Wood (Paris: Macula, 2014), 402–427.

45. Jacques Derrida, *On Touching. Jean-Luc Nancy*, trans. Christine Irizarry (Stanford: Stanford University Press, 2005), 137.

46. Ibid., 156.

47. Ibid., 247.

48. Aristotle, *De anima* III, 8; 432a1 (*On the Soul*), trans. Hett (Cambridge: Harvard University Press / Classical Loeb, 1957).

49. Immanuel Kant, *Träume ein Geistersehers* [1764], AA II: 32 (*Dreams of a Spirit-Seer*, in *Theoretical Philosophy 1755–1770*, ed. David Walford with Ralf Meerbote [Cambridge: Cambridge University Press, 1992], 312).

50. G.W.F. Hegel, *Phänomenologie des Geistes* §316 (*Phenomenology of the Spirit*, trans. A. V. Miller, with a foreword by J.N. Findlay [Oxford: Oxford University Press, 1977], 189).

51. Martin Heidegger, *Parmenides*, trans. André Schuwer and Richard Rojcewicz, (Bloomington: Indiana University Press, 1998), 80.

52. See Charles Bell, *The Anatomy and Physiology of the Human Body* (London: Logman, 1826).

53. Thomas Aquinas, *Sentencia libri De anima*, 602 (*Commentary on Aristotle's On the Soul*), trans. by Kenelm Foster and Sylvester Humphries, (New Haven: Yale University Press, 1951), 187.

54. Ibid.

55. Martin Heidegger, *Die Grundbegriffe der Metaphysik*, §47 (*The Fundamental Concepts of Metaphysics. World, Finitude, Solitude*), trans. William McNeill and Nicholas Walker (Bloomington: Indiana University Press, 1995), 187.

56. Aristotle, *On the Soul* III, 13; 435b5 and 435b20.

57. Denis Diderot, Jean Le Rond d'Alembert, *Encyclopédie ou dictionnaire raisonné des sciences, des arts et des métiers* (Paris: Briasson et al., 1756), vol. 6: 367–368.

58. Thomas Aquinas, *Sentencia libri De anima*, 602 (*Commentary on Aristotle's On the Soul*), trans. by Kenelm Foster and Sylvester Humphries (New Haven: Yale University Press, 1951), 187.

59. Daniel Heller-Roazen, *The Inner Sense of Touch. Archaeology of a Sensation*, (New York: Zone Books, 2007).

60. H. A. Wolfson, "The Internal Senses in Latin, Arabic, and Hebrew Philosophic Texts," in *Studies in the History of Philosophy and Religion*, ed. I Twersky and G.H. Williams, (Cambridge: Harvard University Press, 1973), vol. I: 250–314. Carla de Martino, *Ratio particularis. La doctrine des sens internes d'Avicenne à Thomas d'Aquin* (Paris: Vrin, 2008).

61. Aristotle, *On the Soul* III, 4; 429b6 and 9–10 (trans. Hett).

62. Aristotle, *On the Soul* II 11; 423b1–4 (trans. Hett).

63. Aristotle, *On Sense and the Sensible* IV, 442b1 (trans. Hett).

64. Aristotle, *On the Soul* III 13; 435a17–18 (trans. Hett).

65. Enrico Berti, *Aristotele. Dalla dialettica alla filosofia prima* (Padova: Cedam, 1977), 380 (translation is mine).

66. Richard K. Sorabji, "Aristotle on Demarcating the Five Senses," in *Articles on Aristotle*, eds. J. Barnes, M. Schofield, R. Sorabji, vol. 4: *Psychology and Aesthetics* (London: Duckworth, 1979). 76–92.

67. Plato, *Philebus*, 51a–52a, trans. Dorothea Frede, *Plato. Complete Works*, (Indianapolis: Hackett, 1997).

68. Aristotle, *Protrepticus*, fragment B24, *Protrepticus. An Attempt at Reconstruction* (Göteborg: Studia Graeca et Latina Gothoburgensia, 1961), 57.

69. Aristotle, *On Generation and Corruption*, 329b13 (*On Coming-to-Be and Passing-Away*, trans. E.S. Forster and D.J. Furley, Cambridge: Harvard University Press / Classical Loeb, 1955).

70. Aristotle, *Metaphysics*, A 1; 980a, trans. W. D. Ross (Oxford: Clarendon Press, 1908). See also *On Sense and Sensible* II, 437a12 (trans. Hett).

71. Aristotle, *Nicomachean Ethics*, 1118a10, trans. H. Rackham (Cambridge: Harvard University Press / Classical Loeb, 1990).

72. Was Aristotle thinking of the famous glutton Philoxenus mentioned in the *Eudemian Ethics* (III, 2, 1; 231a17) who was said to be longing to have a throat as long as that of a crane?

73. Aristotle, *On the Soul* III, 13; 435b16–17 (trans. Hett).

74. See Aristotle, *On the Soul* II, chapters 7–11.

75. Aristotle, *On the Soul*, II, 7, 419a20; *On Sense and Sensible* II, 438b3 ff.

76. Themistius, *In Libros Aristotelis De anima Paraphrasis*, Corpus Aristotelicum Graecum vol. 5.3, ed. Richard Heinze (Berlin: Reimer, 1899), 73, 27.

77. Aristotle, *On the Soul* II, 7; 419a12–14 (trans. Hett)

78. Aristotle, *On the Soul* II, 7; 419a15–17 (trans. Hett).

79. Aristotle, *On the Soul* II, 7; 419a20–21 (trans. Hett).

80. Alloa, "Der Tastsinn als Grenze der Medientheorie" in *Das durchscheinende Bild. Konturen einer medialen Phänomenologie* (Berlin/Zurich: diaphanes, 2011), 124–133. See also Alloa, 'Metaxu. Figures de la médialité chez Aristote,' *Revue de Métaphysique et de Morale* 63 (2009): 247–262.

81. Aristotle, *Parts of Animals* II, 8; 653b25–2 (trans. Peck).

82. Aristotle, *Parts of animals* II, 10; 656b35–36 (trans. Peck).

83. Aristotle, *On the Soul* II, 11; 423b23 (trans. Hett).

84. In his in many respects remarkable analysis, Johansen comes to the conclusion that "in the case of both taste and touch the sense-organ is flesh." T. K. Johansen, *Aristotle on the Sense-Organ* (Cambridge: Cambridge University Press, 1998), 193.

85. Averroes, *Commentarium Magnum in Aristotelis De anima Libros*, ed. F. Stuart Crawford, Cambridge, MA: Mediaeval Academy of America, 1953 (*Long Commentary on the* De anima *by Aristotle*, trans. Richard C. Taylor [New Haven/London: Yale 2009], 230).

86. Nicolas d'Oresme, *Expositio liber II, tractatus quartus*, ad 423b17. Nicolas d'Oresme, *Expositio et questiones in Aristotelis De anima*, ed. Benoît Patar (Leuven, Editions Peeters, 1995), 58.

87. Francisco Suárez, *Commentaria una cum quaestionibus in libros Aristotelis De anima*, disp. 7: De sensibus exterioribus in particular, a. 5. See also Chrétien, "Body and Touch," in *The Call and the Response*, trans. Anne Davenport (New York: Fordham University Press, 2004), 83–131.

88. Aristotle, *On the Soul* II, 10; 422a13–16 (trans. Hett).

89. Thomas Aquinas, *Sentencia libri On the Soul*, Opera Omnia, vol. XLV, Rome: Leonina-Vrin 1984, *Lectio* XXI, 502. *Commentary on Aristotle's On the Soul*, trans. by K. Foster and S. Humphries (New Haven: Yale University Press, 1951), 158.

90. Aristotle, *On the Soul* II, 10; 422a14 (trans. Hett).

91. Averroes, *Commentarium Magnum in Aristotelis De anima Libros*, 102 (*Long Commentary on the* De anima *by Aristotle*, 221).

92. Albertus Magnus, *De homine*, q. 32, a. 3 and 4, 278b–280b, ed. Henryk Anzulewicz and J.R. Söder, Latin/German (Hamburg: Meiner, 2004).

93. Aristotle, *On the Soul* II 11; 420a4f. In the twentieth century, Merleau-Ponty will speak of the fleshly body as "innate complex" (*complexe inné*).

94. Aristotle, *On the Soul* II 11; 423b8–15 (trans. Hett).

95. Cynthia Freeland, "Aristotle on the Sense of Touch," in *Essays on Aristotle's De Anima*, eds. Martha C. Nussbaum and Amélie Oksenberg Rorty (Oxford: Oxford University Press, 1992), 227–248, 230.

96. Jean-Louis Chrétien, "Body and Touch," 89.

97. Aristotle, *On the Soul* II, 9; 421a20–23 (trans. Hett).

98. Aristotle, *On the Soul* II, 9; 421a23–27 (trans. Hett).

99. Friedrich Schleiermacher, *Über die Religion* III [1799] (*On Religion. Speeches to its Cultured Despisers*, ed. Richard Crouter [Cambridge: Cambridge University Press, 1996], 59): "With anguish I see daily how the rage of the understanding does not allow this sense to arise at all." See also Dieter Mersch, *Posthermeneutik* (Berlin: Akademie Verlag, 2011). I think personally there may be enough reasons to give up this loaded term.

Between Vision and Touch: From Husserl to Merleau-Ponty
Dermot Moran

1. Jean-Louis Chrétien, *L'Appel et la réponse* (Paris: Minuit, 1992), trans. Anne Davenport, *The Call and the Response* (New York: Fordham University Press, 2004), 86.

2. Immanuel Kant, *Anthropologie in pragmatischer Hinsicht abgefaßt* (Königsberg: Friedrich Nicolovius, 1798; 2nd corrected edition: Königsberg: Nicolovius, 1800), Academy edition ed. Oswald Külpe (2nd ed. Göttingen, 1917), vol. VII, 323; English translation by Robert Louden as *Anthropology from a Pragmatic Point of View* (Cambridge: Cambridge University Press, 2006), 227–228.

3. Edmund Husserl, *Ideen zu einer reinen Phänomenologie und phänomenologischen Philosophie. Zweites Buch: Phänomenologische Untersuchungen zur Konstitution*, hrsg. Marly Biemel, Husserliana IV (Dordrecht: Kluwer, 1991), trans. R. Rojcewicz and A. Schuwer as *Ideas pertaining to a Pure Phenomenology and to a Phenomenological Philosophy, Second Book* (Dordrecht: Kluwer, 1989). Hereafter "*Ideas* II" followed by English pagination, Husserliana (hereafter "Hua") volume and German pagination.

4. An earlier version of this paper was presented at the Thirty-Ninth Meeting of the Husserl Circle, Husserl-Archives, Paris (Thursday 25 June 2009). I am

grateful to my commentator, Pat Burke, for his critical comments and also to Sara Heinämaa, Tom Nenon, Thane Naberhaus, Raymond Kassis, and John J. Drummond, for their helpful comments. This paper was also presented to the Centre for Phenomenological Philosophy, Philosophy Faculty, Russian State University for the Humanities, RGGU (Moscow), Moscow (Monday 16 November 2009). I am grateful to Victor Molchanov, Anna Yampolskaya, Mikail Belous, and the other participants, for their critical comments.

5. M. Merleau-Ponty, *Le Visible et l'invisible*, texte établi par Claude Lefort (Paris: Gallimard, 1964), trans. Alfonso Lingis, *The Visible and the Invisible* (Evanston, IL: Northwestern University Press, 1968). Hereafter "*The Visible and the Invisible*" followed by the pagination of the English translation and then the pagination of the French original.

6. Merleau-Ponty writes, "*se toucher = le touchant-touché*" (Husserl, *The Visible and the Invisible*, 254; 302).

7. The terms "*le chiasme*" (Husserl, *The Visible and the Invisible*, 130; 171) and "*le chiasma*" (Husserl, *The Visible and the Invisible*, 214; 264) come from the Greek χιασμός, "criss-crossing") and are found in Merleau-Ponty's *Visible and Invisible* (the terms do not appear in his essay, "Eye and Mind"). Chiasm refers to a rhetorical figure of speech (in English termed "chiasmus") where elements are repeated in a reversed pattern, e.g., Cicero's "one should eat to live and not live to eat," and also to an anatomical feature whereby the nerves in the eye cross over to the opposite side of the brain. Merleau-Ponty does not refer to the rhetorical figure as such and it is often assumed he is employing the term in its anatomical sense, see the Editors' Introduction to Fred Evans and Len Lawlor, eds, *Chiasms. Merleau-Ponty's Notion of Flesh* (Albany, NY: SUNY Press, 2000), esp. 17–18 n. 2.

8. See also David Brubaker, "Merleau-Ponty's Three Intertwinings," *The Journal of Value Inquiry* 34 (2000), 89–101, and Leonard Lawlor, "*Verflechtung*: The Triple Significance of Husserl's Course Notes on Husserl's "Origin of Geometry," in *Husserl at the Limits of Phenomenology*, ed. Len Lawlor and Bettina Bergo (Evanston, IL: Northwestern University Press, 2002).

9. See Merleau-Ponty, *L'Oeil et l'esprit*, ed. Lambert Dousson (Folio Plus, Philosophie), 13; "Eye and Mind," trans. Carleton Dallery, in *The Primacy of Perception and Other Essays on Phenomenological Psychology, the Philosophy of Art, History and Politics* (Evanston, IL: Northwestern University Press, 1964), 162. Hereafter "Eye and Mind" followed by pagination of English translation and then French edition.

10. See Merleau-Ponty, "Eye and Mind," 163; 16.

11. Merleau-Ponty, "Eye and Mind," 169; 25. Here Merleau-Ponty says that the metamorphosis of seeing and the visible "defines" flesh.

12. Merleau-Ponty, "Eye and Mind," 168; 24. See also Beata Stawarska, "Mutual Gaze and Social Cognition," *Phenomenology and the Cognitive Sciences* 5 (2006), 17–30.

13. ". . . *toute chair, même celle du monde, rayonne hors d'elle-même*," Merleau-Ponty, "Eye and Mind," 186; 55.

14. Merleau-Ponty, *The Visible and the Invisible*, 133; 173.

15. In "Eye and Mind" Merleau-Ponty illustrates this claim with a quotation from the French painter André Marchand (who in turn is citing Paul Klee)— sometimes rather than feeling that I look at the forest, I feel I am being looked at by the forest, see Merleau-Ponty, "Eye and Mind," 167; 23. Merleau-Ponty is here drawing on Marchand's interview with Georges Charbonnier in George Charbonnier, *Le Monologue du peintre*, 2 vols., (Paris: Juillard, 1959/1960) which had only recently appeared.

16. Merleau-Ponty, *The Visible and the Invisible*, 139; 181.

17. Merleau-Ponty, *The Visible and the Invisible*, 193; 243.

18. David Katz was born in Kassel on 1 October 1884 and studied at Göttingen where he studied under the experimental psychologist and psychophysicist and researcher on color perception Georg Elias Müller (1850–1934), who himself had been a student of Wilhelm Wundt. Katz also attended Husserl's lectures and seminars and Husserl was one of his doctoral thesis examiners in 1907. His *Die Erscheinungweisen der Farben* appeared in 1911 and later was expanded into *Die Farbenwelt* (1930), trans. as *The World of Color*, trans. R. B. McLeod and C. W. Fox (London: Routledge, 1999). He published his study of touch *Der Aufbau der Tastwelt* in 1925, in *Zeitschrift für Psychologie und Physiologie der Sinnesorgane*, Ergänzungsband, vol. 11, 1–270 (reprinted: Darmstadt: Wissenschaftliche Buchgesellschaft, 1969); trans. Lester Krueger as *The World of Touch* (Hillsdale, N.J: Lawrence Erlbaum Publishers, 1989). Katz continued to work in experimental and developmental psychology at Göttingen until 1919 when he moved to the University of Rostok. He grew close to the Gestalt psychologists but was not a member of their group. He was forced to leave Germany in 1933, first for England, and then, in 1937, he took a position at the University of Stockholm where he remained until his death in 1953. He had a major influence on the ecological theories of perception of J. J. Gibson, see the obituary of R. Arnheim, "David Katz, 1884–1953," *American Journal of Psychology*, vol. 66 no. 4 (Oct. 1953), 638–642, and Lester Krueger, "Tactual Perception in Historical Perspective: David Katz's World of Touch," in *Tactual Perception: A Sourcebook*, ed. William Schiff, Emerson Foulke (New York: Cambridge University Press, 1982).

19. M. Merleau-Ponty, *Phénoménologie de la perception* (Paris: Gallimard, 1945), trans. C. Smith as *Phenomenology of Perception* (London: Routledge & Kegan Paul, 1962). Hereafter "*Phenomenology of Perception*" followed by the English pagination and then the pagination of the French original. David Katz already receives a brief mention in Merleau-Ponty's *La Structure du comportement* (Paris: Presses Universitaires de France, 1942), trans. A.L. Fisher, *The Structure of Behavior* (Boston: Beacon Press, 1963).

20. See C. Freeland, "Aristotle on the Sense of Touch," in Martha Nussbaum and Amelie O. Rorty, eds, *Essays on Aristotle's De Anima* (Oxford: Oxford University Press, 1995), 227–248 and Jean-Louis Chrétien, *The Call and the Response*, op. cit., esp. 83–112.

21. The first two editions of Berkeley's *An Essay towards a New Theory of Vision* were published in Dublin in 1709. Revised versions of the *Essay* were also pub-

lished in 1732 with the first and second editions of *Alciphron*. Here I am using the edition by David R. Wilkins (Dublin: Trinity College, 2002).

22. Étienne Bonnot de Condillac (1715–1780), *Traité des sensations* (1754) in Condillac, *Oeuvres philosophiques de Condillac*, vol. 1, Corpus général des philosophes français tome XXXIII (Paris: Presses Universitaires de France, 1947), 219–335. Born in Grenoble, Condillac was a Catholic priest who did no pastoral work, associated with Diderot and Rousseau and published widely on philosophy and psychology, including *Essai sur l'origine des connaissances humaines* (1746), *Traité des systèmes* (1749), *Traité des sensations* (1754), *Traité des animaux* (1755), and a 15-volume *Cours d'études* (1767–1773). An admirer of Locke, he translated Locke's *Essay* into French, and advocated sensationalism, according to which all ideas including memory and reflection are modifications of sensations ("sensation contains within it all the faculties of the soul"). Condillac knew Berkeley's *New Theory of Vision* in the French translation of Joncourt (1734) and in the summary of Voltaire in his *Elements of the Philosophy of Newton*.

23. Condillac writes: "L'oeil a donc besoin des secours du tact, pour se faire une habitude des mouvemens propres à la vision ; pour s'accoutumer à rapporter ses sensations à l'extrémité des rayons, ou à peu près ; et pour juger par-là des distances, des grandeurs, des situations et des figures" *Traité des sensations*, Book III Chapter iii §2.

24. For a general summary of nineteenth-century empirical psychological studies of touch (including discussions of Wundt, Weber, James, et al.), see F. B. Dresslar, "Studies in the Psychology of Touch," *The American Journal of Psychology* vol. 6 no. 3 (1894), 313–368. Dresslar discusses studies of the accuracy of space as revealed by active touch, the assessment of weights, and other typical themes of empirical research of the time.

25. Brentano and his students played an important role here. See Carl Stumpf, *Über den psychologischen Ursprung der Raumvorstellung* (Leipzig, 1873).

26. See especially Kevin Mulligan, "Perception," *Cambridge Companion to Husserl* (Cambridge: Cambridge University Press, 1995), 225 n. 3.

27. Erich R. Jaensch completed his doctorate with G. E. Müller (1850–1934) in 1908. He conducted research on visual acuity and eidetic imagery. He later became a defender of Nazi racial types in the study of personality and, on that basis, took over the editorship of the *Zeitschrift für Psychologie*. He died in 1940. He corresponded with Husserl and sent him his early studies on perception of faces.

28. Heinrich Hofmann, "Untersuchungen über den Empfindungsbegriff," *Archiv für die gesamte Psychologie*, vol. XXVI (Leipzig, 1913), 1–136. Hofmann wrote his doctoral dissertation with Husserl and is mentioned by Husserl at *Thing and Space*, § 41, see H. Spiegelberg, *Phenomenology in Psychology and Psychiatry: A Historical Introduction* (Evanston, IL: Northwestern University Press, 1972), 56. I have not been able to determine when Hofmann died.

29. See Wilhelm Schapp, *Beiträge zur Phänomenologie der Wahrnehmung* (Halle: Niemeyer, 1910; reprinted with a new Foreword by Carl Friedrich Graumann, Wiesbaden: B. Heymann, 1976). Schapp studied with Rickert in Freiburg

and Dilthey and Simmel in Berlin before going in 1905 to Husserl at Göttingen where he completed his doctorate in 1909. He subsequently had a career in law and published on legal philosophy and the philosophy of history. His book on perception is quoted approvingly by Merleau-Ponty in *Phenomenology of Perception* (see esp. 229–230; 265).

30. Jean Hering, born in Alsace, studied under Husserl at Göttingen, writing a dissertation on the a priori in Lotze, and later published an important essay on essence, *Bemerkungen über das Wesen, die Wesenheit und die Idee*, for the *Jahrbuch* vol. 4 (1921), 495–543. He later studied theology and wrote a number of texts on dreaming: "La réprésentation et le rêve," in *Revue d'histoire et de philosophie religieuse* (1946), 193–206; "Concerning Image, Idea, and Dream," *Philosophy and Phenomenological Research*, 8 (1947), 188–205; "Quelques thémes d'une phénoménologie du rêve," in *For Roman Ingarden. Nine Essays in Phenomenology*, ed. A.-T. Tymieniecka (The Hague: Nijhoff, 1959), 75–89. For a brief biography, see Roman Ingarden, "Jean Hering 1890–1966," *Philosophy and Phenomenological Research* 27 (1967), 308–309.

31. David Katz, *Die Erscheinungsweisen der Farben und ihre Beeinflussung durch die individuelle Erfahrung, Zeitschrift für Psychologie* Ergängzungsband 7 (Leipzig: Johann Ambrosius Barth, 1911). A revised and expanded edition was published in 1930 as *Der Aufbau der Farbenwelt*.

32. See H. Spiegelberg, *Phenomenology in Psychology and Psychiatry: A Historical Introduction*, op. cit., 40. Georg Elias Müller (1850–1934) was born near Leipzig, where he studied from 1868–1869. He then moved to Berlin to continue his studies, but soon volunteered for the Prussian army. In 1871, he returned to his studies, moving in 1872 to work with Hermann Lotze (1817–1881) at Göttingen. He was appointed to a position in Göttingen in 1876, where he stayed, for the most part, for the next 40 years. He developed a theory of memory, using Hermann Ebbinghaus's (1850–1909) techniques with nonsense syllables, in which forgetting is caused by interference from later-learned material, rather than from the "fading away" of an original memory trace. He also espoused a version of Heinrich Ewald Hering's (1866–1948) "opponent-process" theory of color vision, the main rival to Hermann von Helmholtz's (1821–1894) "trichromatic" theory. Müller appears to have been quite hostile to Husserl and never mentions him in his publications. See Spiegelberg, *Phenomenology in Psychology and Psychiatry*, op. cit., 34–35.

33. E. Husserl, *Ding und Raum. Vorlesungen 1907*, ed. Ulrich Claesges, Hua XVI (The Hague: Nijhoff, 1973), trans. by R. Rojcewicz, *Thing and Space: Lectures of 1907*, Husserl Collected Works VII (Dordrecht: Kluwer, 1997). Hereafter "*Thing and Space*" with English and then Husserliana volume number and pagination of German edition.

34. Husserl, *Thing and Space*, 257; XVI 298.

35. Husserl at times does not want to speak specifically of a kinaesthetic "sense" (Husserl, *Thing and Space*, XVI 298).

36. The concept of "phantom" is developed in *Ideas* II, where it is primarily considered as a consideration of the sensibly appearing thing, abstracting from

causality. Husserl however also thought there were concretely occurring individual phantoms in the world, e.g., rainbows.

37. Husserl, *Thing and Space*, § 65, 195; XVI 230–31.

38. Husserl, *Thing and Space*, § 69.

39. Husserl, *The Visible and the Invisible*, 7; 22.

40. Husserl, *Thing and Space*, § 73.

41. Merleau-Ponty, *The Visible and the Invisible*, 255; 303.

42. Husserl, *Thing and Space*, § 48, 141; XVI 166.

43. The term "pre-empirical" is particularly unfortunate if it suggests an intermediary veil between perceiver and perceived or a two-dimensional domain out of which three-dimensionality is constituted.

44. Husserl, *Thing and Space*, § 51, 149; XVI 177.

45. Hua IV 66.

46. I have benefited greatly from reading John J. Drummond's essay "On Seeing a Material Thing in Space" reprinted in Dermot Moran and Lester Embree, eds. *Phenomenology. Critical Concepts* (London: Routledge, 2004), vol. 2, 43–55. See also Filip Mattens, "Body or Eye: A Matter of Sense and Organ," *The New Yearbook for Phenomenology and Phenomenological Philosophy* VIII (2008), 93–125.

47. The concept of a perceptual field will be developed by Aron Gurwitsch in his *The Field of Consciousness* (Pittsburgh: Duquesne University Press, 1964).

48. Husserl, *Thing and Space*, § 25.

49. Hua XVI 83. Edith Stein is more definite: for her, not all sensory data are organized into fields. She states: "There is certainly no olfactory and flavor field analogous to the visual and auditory field, and we prefer to leave aside the question whether a field of touch can be spoken of in the same sense," see her *Philosophy of Psychology and the Humanities*, trans. M. C. Baseheart and M. Sawicki, Collected Works of Edith Stein 7 (Washington, DC: ICS Publications, 2000), 13.

50. Husserl, *Thing and Space*, § 46, 135; XVI 159.

51. Husserl, *Thing and Space*, § 48.

52. Husserl, *Thing and Space*, § 83.

53. Husserl, *Thing and Space*, § 45.

54. See Husserl, *Thing and Space*, § 46, 136; Hua XVI 160. Elizabeth Behnke has commented on these terms in her "Edmund Husserl's Contribution to the Phenomenology of the Body in Ideas II" in Thomas Nenon and Lester Embree, eds, *Issues in Husserl's Ideas II* (Dordrecht: Kluwer, 1996), 148 n. 23.

55. In the background clearly are Hermann Lotze's (1817–1881) "feelings of movement" (*Bewegungsgefühle*) and "positional signs" (*Lokalzeichen*), as discussed in his *Microkosmos*. See H. Lotze, *Microcosm: An Essay Concerning Man and His Relation to the World*, trans. E. Hamilton and E. E. C. Jones (Edinburgh: T. & T. Clark, 1885) and William R. Woodward, "From Association to Gestalt: The Fate of Hermann Lotze's Theory of Spatial Perception, 1846–1920," *Isis*, Vol. 69, No. 4 (Dec., 1978), 572–582. The idea is that certain qualitative feelings attach themselves to non-spatial experiences in order to act as "local signs" signaling that these experiences are taking place somewhere in the body.

56. Sometimes these are called "motor sensations" and John J. Drummond has suggested they should more properly be called "somoaesthetic sensations." The term "kinaesthetic sensations" is somewhat inexact and Husserl himself is not consistent in his terminology. He speaks of "sensations," "complexes," "circumstances," "appearances," processes, and so on. With regard to the "kinaesthetic" Husserl is not referring to the physiological movements of the body (the physical range of movements of which the body is capable) but rather our first-person experiential sense of the moving of our eyes, tilting and turning the head, looking up or down, and so on, especially insofar as those movements are *freely* undertaken or voluntary. In this sense, for Husserl, the body is a "freely moved sense organ" (Husserl, *Ideas* II, 61; IV 56), see Filip Mattens, "Perception, Body, and the Sense of Touch," op. cit., 100. Of course, when the barber moves my head with his hands, there is still an element of freedom in that I choose to *cooperate* and not stiffen the neck muscles but his act of turning and tilting my head is not the same as a similar act I undertake myself. Husserl is not precise about the nature of these "kinaesthetic sensations": does moving my head *feel different* to me than when my head is moved by someone? Furthermore, if I just imagine turning my head without actually turning it, do the same kinaesthetic sensations come into play? How exactly these kinaesthetic sensations relate to what is now called proprioception (which does not necessarily relate to the body in its self-movement) is also problematic. For a helpful discussion, see Shaun Gallagher, "Bodily self-awareness and object perception," *Theoria et Historia Scientiarum: International Journal for Interdisciplinary Studies*, vol. 7 no. 1 (2003), 53–68. Anatomists suggest that sense of a joint moving is very complex, involving not just muscle and positional sensations but also tautness on the skin, etc.

57. Hugo Münsterberg (1863–1916) for instance was an important German psychologist who went to Harvard at the end of the nineteenth century on the invitation of William James. He corresponded with Husserl.

58. See for instance Katz, *World of Touch*, op. cit., 232–3, who cites G. E. Müller, *Abriss der Psychologie* [*Outline of Psychology*] (Göttingen, 1924) as distinguishing between muscle sensations and sensations of position that are communicated largely by cutaneous touch sensations. The discussion continues; see Antonio Damasio, *The Feeling of What Happens: Body, Emotion and the Making of Consciousness* (London: Heinemann, 1999).

59. See Husserl's 1921 remark (Ms D 13 IV, 4) as quoted by Ulrich Claesges, *Edmund Husserls Theorie der Raumkonstitution* (The Hague: Nijhoff, 1964), 76 n. 3.

60. For an interesting discussion see Claesges, *Edmund Husserls Theorie der Raumkonstitution*, op. cit., 93.

61. The issue is complex. Clearly any temporal moment can accommodate any object (e.g. any musical note, C, D, E etc.,) so the "matter" must be the specific matter that individuates the note as such. There appears not to be a specific matter for the temporal dimension itself, see John Brough, "Husserl's Phenomenology of Time-Consciousness," reprinted in Dermot Moran and Lester Embree,

eds, *Phenomenology. Critical Concepts* (London: Routledge, 2004), vol. 2, 56–89. Similarly, visual space can accommodate any "image" or color.

62. The lived body is experienced as a bearer of sensations (Husserl, *Ideas* II § 36) and as an organ of the will (ibid., § 38), as the vehicle of my "I can's." In particular, the lived body is the "zero point of orientation" from which all directions (up, down, near, far, etc.) get their sense. Husserl claims the body is present in all our perceptual experience and is involved in all other conscious functions (ibid., § 39), and this view is embraced also by Merleau-Ponty.

63. Katz, *World of Touch*, op. cit., 40–41, quotes Ewald Hering to the effect that the term "sensation" should not be applied to colors since sensations refer to intrabody experiences and color is always experienced as outside the body. Later in *Thing and Space*, § 64 Husserl will say that we determine visual distance from some zero-point we locate somewhere in the head behind the eyes.

64. See Merleau-Ponty, "Eye and Mind," 166; 19.

65. Katz, *World of Touch*, op. cit., 41, refers to touch as "bipolar" since there is both a touching experience and a touched quality (smoothness, etc.) that is revealed. Katz also maintains we need to change our "set" (*Einstellung*)—the translation "set" became popular in Anglo-American psychology, e.g. mind-set—in order to attend to the sensings as opposed to the objectified sensory qualities. Pain sensations, on the other hand, are never objectified in the object but always experienced in the body. Descartes makes the same point, stating that one does not construe the felt quality of tickling as a property of the feather.

66. Husserl, *Thing and Space*, § 47, 137; Hua XVI 162.

67. Husserl, *Ideas* II § 36.

68. *Treatise on the Sensations*, Bk II, ch. V § 4 (a). Condillac writes: "C'est donc à cette sensation que commencent pour la statue, son corps, les objets et l'espace. à quoi elle reconnoît le sien. Elle apprend à connoître son corps, et à se reconnoître dans toutes les parties qui le composent ; parce qu'aussi-tôt qu'elle porte la main sur une d'elles, le même être sentant se répond en quelque sorte de l'une à l'autre; c'est moi. Qu'elle continue de se toucher, par-tout la sensation de solidité mettra de la résistance entre les manieres d'être, et par-tout aussi le même être sentant se répondra, c'est moi, c'est encore moi." *Traité des Sensations*, Bk II, ch. V § 4 (a).

69. For instance, it can be found in the work of psychologists Weber, Wundt, and Titchener. The phenomenon of fingers touching each other, or one hand touching the other, is already discussed by E. H. Weber, Wilhelm Wundt, and others. For instance, there is mention of it in Section 56 of Titchener's *Manual of Experimental Psychology* (1924), 383–84.

70. E. H. Weber (1795–1879), published two studies of touch: *De Tactu* (1834) and *Tastsinn und Gemeingefühl* (1846), published in R. Wagner, ed., *Handwörter-buch der Physiologie (Pocket dictionary of physiology)*, vol. III, part 2, 481–588. Both works are translated in *E. H. Weber on the Tactile Senses*, ed. and trans. Helen E. Ross and David J. Murray, 2nd ed. (Hove, East Sussex: Erlbaum, Taylor & Francis, 1996). Weber and Gustav T. Fechner (1801–1887) were founders of psychophysics, the attempt to systematically relate physical phenomena, e.g., sound or weight,

with the perception of them. Psychophysics can be considered the earliest form of experimental psychology in the modern sense. Weber carefully documented the different sensitivities to touch in various parts of the body, the perception of weight, heat, cold, etc., and the ability of the perceiver to distinguish when being touched by two points of a compass at the same time. In *Der Tastsinn*, for instance, Weber discusses the issue of whether two sensations arise when sensitive areas of the body touch each other. He claimed that the two sensations do not merge into one: a cold limb touching a warm limb (e.g., a hand touching the forehead) reveals both heat and cold.

71. See E. H. Weber, *Tastsinn und Gemeingefühl*, in *E. H. Weber on the Tactile Senses*, op. cit., 212.

72. E. H. Weber, ibid., 207.

73. Husserl, *Ideas* II, § 36 152–54; Hua IV, 144–47.

74. Hua IV 151; 161 The noun "*Verflechtung*" is reasonably uncommon in Husserl's *Ding und Raum* (e.g. XVI 162) and *Ideen* II and, besides its occurrence in relation to the "double sensation" is also occasionally used to refer to the interweaving of motivations, *Erlebnisse*, or of protentions and retentions (see Hua IV 256). The verb "*verflicht*" and the past participle "*verflochten*" occur in the First Logical Investigation § 1 and § 9 (and Derrida has commented on this). The term *Verflectung* occurs several times in *Cartesian Meditations* and particularly in his *Phenomenological Psychology* lectures, often used to express the complex intertwining of different *Erlebnisse*, e.g., perception, imagination, remembering, etc. (see, e.g., Hua IX 9, 199, 354) Merleau-Ponty acknowledges that he is inspired by Husserl's term in his essay "The Philosopher and His Shadow," M. Merleau-Ponty, *Signes* (Paris: Gallimard, 1960), 222–223; trans. R. McCleary, *Signs* (Evanston, IL: Northwestern University Press, 1964), 176–77. In his footnote attached to this text Merleau-Ponty references Marly Biemel's introduction to Husserliana IV (xvii) which cites a passage from (the then unpublished) Husserliana V 124 which reads "*ein wichtiges Ergebnis unserer Betrachtung, daß die Natur*" *und der Leib, in ihrer Verflechtung mit diesem wieder die Seele, sich in Wechselbezogenheit aufeinander, in eins miteinender konstituieren.*"

75. Husserl, *Thing and Space*, § 49.

76. Husserl raises some interesting questions here which, however, he passes over. Are these kinaesthetic sensations, basic or "simple" sensations or do they indicate very "complex products of associative fusion" (Husserl, *Thing and Space*, XVI 171)?

77. Husserl, *Thing and Space*, 271; XVI 315.

78. Merleau-Ponty, *Phenomenology of Perception*, 255; 295.

79. Husserl, *Thing and Space*, § 49, 147; XVI 174.

80. See also Husserl, *Thing and Space*, § 64: "The word 'depth' . . . should awaken thoughts of a presentation in relief" (194; XVI 228).

81. Husserl, *Thing and Space*, § 58.

82. See his remarks on Riemannian visual space at Husserl, *Thing and Space*, XVI 315.

83. Hua IV § 32.

84. Hua § 32.

85. Hua § 34; Hua IV 139.

86. Husserl, *Ideas* II, 153; IV 145.

87. Husserl's neologism: *Empfindnisse*, see Hua V 8–10.

88. Husserl, *Ideas* II, 152–53; IV 145. Merleau-Ponty will quote this phrase "*es wird Leib, es empfindet*" in "The Philosopher and His Shadow" *Signs*, 166; 210.

89. Husserl, *Ideas* II, 153; IV 145.

90. In a recent paper, "Touch and the Sense of Reality," presented to the Embodied Subjectivity Conference, Royal Irish Academy Dublin (26 May 2010), Matthew Ratcliffe has argued for an identity of experiences in cases where, for instance, both hands are clasped together as in prayer or when both hands are rubbed together as in the act of warming one's hands through friction. Ratcliffe states: "the experience does not involve alternation between perceiving and perceived hands but a unitary perception of the rubbing." While it is the case that the salient experience in these cases appears to be unified, in fact, one can place one's attention in one hand or the other and experience also the doubling and distinctness of the experiences. I am grateful to Matthew Ratcliffe for providing me with a draft of his paper.

91. Hua IV 146.

92. Husserl, *Ideas* II, 153; IV 146.

93. Husserl, *Ideas* II, 154; IV 146.

94. See Hua IV 335. See U. Klaesges, *Husserls Theorie der Raumkonstitution*, op. cit., and Tadashi Ogawa '"Seeing" and "Touching": or Overcoming the Soul-Body Dualism," *Analecta Husserliana* vol. XVI (1983), 77–94.

95. Husserl, *Ideas* II § 37, 155; IV 147.

96. Husserl, *Ideas* II § 37, 155; IV 148.

97. Husserl, *Ideas* II § 37, 156; IV 148.

98. Husserl, *Ideas* II, 158; IV 150.

99. For relevant discussions of the primacy of touch, see Steven Crowell, "The Mythical and the Meaningless: Husserl and the Two Faces of Nature," in Thomas Nenon and Lester Embree, eds, *Issues in Husserl's Ideas II* (Dordrecht: Kluwer, 1996), esp. 93–97 and Edith Wyschogrod, "Doing before Hearing: On the Primacy of Touch" in François Laruelle, ed., *Textes pour Emmanuel Levinas* (Paris: Editions Jean-Michel Place, 1980), 179–202.

100. Who, in order to attempt to answer Molyneux's question, studied sight in patients born blind but with newly restored vision (also see Merleau-Ponty, *Phenomenology of Perception*, 222–225; 257–260). Marius Von Senden, *Raum- und Gestaltauffassung bei operierten Blindgeborenen vor und nach der Operation* (Leipzig: J. A. Barth, 1932), translated by Peter Heath as *Space and Sight* (London: Methuen, 1960).

101. Merleau-Ponty (*Phenomenology of Perception*, 229; 265) refers to Schapp, *Beiträge zur Phänomenologie der Wahrnehmung*, 23ff.

102. Merleau-Ponty, *Phenomenology of Perception*, 216; 250.

103. See, Merleau-Ponty, *Phenomenology of Perception*, 226; 305–308; 352–355.

104. See esp., Merleau-Ponty, *Phenomenology of Perception*, 315–17; 366–68.

105. Merleau-Ponty, *Phenomenology of Perception*, 312; 361.

106. Merleau-Ponty, *Phenomenology of Perception*, 315; 363.

107. Merleau-Ponty, *Phenomenology of Perception*, 315; 364.

108. Merleau-Ponty, *Phenomenology of Perception*, 315; 364.

109. Merleau-Ponty, *Phenomenology of Perception*, 314; 363.

110. Merleau-Ponty, *Phenomenology of Perception*, 316; 365. Katz, *World of Touch*, op. cit. 28. Merleau-Ponty cites this remark: "It is not consciousness which touches or feels, but the hand, and the hand is, as Kant says, 'an outer brain of man,'" (Merleau-Ponty, *Phenomenology of Perception*, 316; 365). Merleau-Ponty remarks in a footnote that this statement is "quoted without reference" in David Katz's *Der Aufbau der Tastwelt* (1925). Katz himself writes: "Kant once used a very apt figure of speech when he called the hand, man's outer brain" (*World of Touch*, op. cit., 28). This precise remark ("Die *Hand* ist das auessere Gehirn des Menschen") cannot be found in Kant's complete works, but see, "Was heißt, sich im Denken zu orientieren?" trans. "What is *Orientation* in Thinking" in Kant, *Political Writings* (Cambridge: CUP) and the quotation from his *Anthropology from a Pragmatic Point of View* at the top of this paper. See Peter Woelert, "Kant's Hands, Spatial Orientation, and the Copernican Turn," *Continental Philosophy Review* 40 (2007), 139–150. For a general study of the role of the hand, see Frank Wilson, *The Hand: How It Shapes the Brain, Language and Culture* (New York: Random House, 1998).

111. Merleau-Ponty, *Phenomenology of Perception*, 316; 365.

112. Merleau-Ponty, *Phenomenology of Perception*, 316; 365.

113. Merleau-Ponty, *Phenomenology of Perception*, 317; 366.

114. Merleau-Ponty, *Phenomenology of Perception*, 316; 365.

115. Merleau-Ponty, *Phenomenology of Perception*, 256; 296.

116. Merleau-Ponty, *Phenomenology of Perception*, 257; 298.

117. Merleau-Ponty, *Phenomenology of Perception*, 257; 297.

118. Merleau-Ponty, *Phenomenology of Perception*, 266; 308.

119. Merleau-Ponty, *Phenomenology of Perception*, 267; 309.

120. Merleau-Ponty, *Phenomenology of Perception*, 318; 367–68.

121. Merleau-Ponty, *Phenomenology of Perception*, 319; 368.

122. Merleau-Ponty, *Phenomenology of Perception*, 320; 369.

123. Merleau-Ponty, *The Visible and the Invisible*, 130; 171.

124. Merleau-Ponty, *The Visible and the Invisible*, 138; 180.

125. Merleau-Ponty, *The Visible and the Invisible*, 131; 171.

126. Merleau-Ponty, *The Visible and the Invisible*, 133; 174.

127. Merleau-Ponty, *The Visible and the Invisible*, 184–185.

128. Merleau-Ponty, *The Visible and the Invisible*, 131n; 171n.

129. Merleau-Ponty, *The Visible and the Invisible*, 140; 183.

130. Merleau-Ponty, *The Visible and the Invisible*, 143; 185–186.

131. Merleau-Ponty, *The Visible and the Invisible*, 143; 186.

132. Merleau-Ponty, *The Visible and the Invisible*, 141; 183.

133. Merleau-Ponty, *The Visible and the Invisible*, 141–142; 184.

134. The mutual touching of the handshake is an example of intercorporeality (Merleau-Ponty, *The Visible and the Invisible*, 142; 184).

135. Merleau-Ponty, *The Visible and the Invisible*, 144; 187.

136. Merleau-Ponty, *The Visible and the Invisible*, 141; 184.

137. Merleau-Ponty, *The Visible and the Invisible*, 147; 191.

138. Merleau-Ponty, *Signs*, 166; 210.

139. Husserl, *Ideas* II, 152; IV 145.

140. See Hua IV 5.

141. Merleau-Ponty, "Eye and Mind," 163; 16.

142. Merleau-Ponty, "Eye and Mind," 163; 16.

143. See Dermot Moran, "Sartre on Embodiment, Touch, and the 'Double Sensation,'" Proceedings of 48th Annual SPEP Meeting, *Philosophy Today* (Supplement 2010), and idem, "Sartre's Ontology of the Body," in Vesselin Petrov, ed., *Ontological Landscapes—Recent Thought on Conceptual Interfaces between Science and Philosophy* (Frankfurt: Ontos-Verlag, 2010).

144. Husserl, *The Visible and the Invisible*, 141; 183.

145. See Jacques Derrida, *Le toucher, Jean-Luc Nancy* (Paris: Editions Galilée, 2000), trans. Christine Irizarry as *On Touching—Jean-Luc Nancy* (Stanford: Stanford University Press, 2005).

146. See Luce Irigaray, *An Ethics of Sexual Difference*, trans. Carolyn Burke and Gillian Gill (Ithaca, NY: Cornell University Press, 1984), 175. This critique has generated a large scholarly literature. See Elizabeth Grosz, "Merleau-Ponty and Irigaray in the Flesh," *Thesis Eleven*, vol. 36, no. 1 (1993), 37–59; Cathryn Vasseleu, *Textures of Light: Vision and Touch in Irigaray, Levinas, and Merleau-Ponty* (London: Routledge, 1998); and Tina Chanter, "Wild Meaning: Luce Irigaray's Reading of Merleau-Ponty," in Fred Evans and Leonard Lawlor, eds, *Chiasms. Merleau-Ponty's Notion of Flesh* (Albany, NY: SUNY Press, 2000), 219–236. See also Claude Lefort, "Flesh and Otherness," in his *Ontology and Alterity in Merleau-Ponty* (Evanston, IL: Northwestern University Press, 1990).

147. Merleau-Ponty, *The Visible and the Invisible*, 154; 199.

148. Merleau-Ponty, *The Visible and the Invisible*, 154; 200.

149. Merleau-Ponty, "Eye and Mind," 175; 37.

150. Merleau-Ponty, *The Visible and the Invisible*, 210; 260.

151. September 1959, in Merleau-Ponty, *The Visible and the Invisible*, 210; 260.

Biodiversity and the Diacritics of Life
Ted Toadvine

1. Jacques Derrida, *L'Animal que donc je suis* (Paris: Galilée, 2006), 53; *The Animal That Therefore I Am*, trans. David Wills (New York: Fordham University Press, 2008), 31.

2. Giorgio Agamben, *L'Aperto: L'uomo e l'animale* (Torino: Bollati Boringhieri, 2010), 33–34; *The Open: Man and Animal*, trans. Kevin Attell (Stanford: Stanford University Press, 2004), 26–27.

3. See Ted Toadvine, "Le temps des voix animales," *Chiasmi International* 15 (2013): 269–282.

4. See Derrida, *L'Animal*, 95/ *The Animal*, 133; Leonard Lawlor, *This Is Not Sufficient: An Essay on Animality and Human Nature in Derrida* (New York: Columbia University Press, 2007), 60–63; and Ted Toadvine, "Life beyond Biologism," *Research in Phenomenology* 40, no. 2 (2010): 243–266.

5. For a concise survey of such endorsements, see Donald Maier, *What's So Good about Biodiversity? A Call for Better Reasoning about Nature's Value* (Dordrecht: Springer, 2012), 2.

6. David Takacs, *The Idea of Biodiversity. Philosophies of Paradise* (Baltimore: Johns Hopkins University Press, 1996), 3. See also 37.

7. David Tilman, "Biodiversity & Environmental Sustainability amid Human Domination of Global Ecosystems," *Daedalus* 141, no. 3 (2012), 109.

8. For a more developed treatment of this critique of biodiversity, see Nicolae Morar, Ted Toadvine, and Brendan Bohannan, "Biodiversity at Twenty-Five Years: Revolution or Red Herring?" (forthcoming).

9. Julia Koricheva and Helena Siipi, "The Phenomenon of Biodiversity," in *Philosophy and Biodiversity*, ed. Marrku Oksanen and Juhani Pietarinen (Cambridge, MA: Cambridge University Press, 2004), 29–30.

10. See, for example, Koricheva and Siipi, 35; James Maclaurin and Kim Sterelny, *What Is Biodiversity?* (Chicago: University of Chicago Press, 2008), 7; and Bryan Norton, "Biodiversity: Its Meaning and Value," in *A Companion to the Philosophy of Biology*, ed. Sahotra Sarkar and Anya Plutynski (Malden, MA: Blackwell, 2008), 373.

11. Diane Srivastava and Mark Vellend, "Biodiversity-Ecosystem Function Research: Is It Relevant to Conservation?" *Annual Review of Ecology, Evolution, and Systematics* 36 (2005): 267–294.

12. Maier, *What's So Good about Biodiversity?*, 3.

13. Maier, *What's So Good about Biodiversity?*, 2.

14. Maier, *What's So Good about Biodiversity?*, 3.

15. Maier, *What's So Good about Biodiversity?*, 423, 416.

16. Richard Kearney, "What Is Diacritical Hermeneutics?," *Journal of Applied Hermeneutics* (2011), 1.

17. Kearney, "What Is Diacritical Hermeneutics?," 1. My emphasis.

18. Kearney, "What Is Diacritical Hermeneutics?," 3.

19. Merleau-Ponty, *Signes* (Paris: Gallimard, 1960), 49; *Signs*, trans. Richard McCleary (Evanston, IL: Northwestern University Press, 1964), 39.

20. Merleau-Ponty, *Signes* (Paris: Gallimard, 1960), 50; *Signs*, trans. Richard McCleary (Evanston, IL: Northwestern University Press, 1964), 39.

21. See Emmanuel Alloa, "La chair comme diacritique incarné," *Chiasmi International* 11 (2009), 249–261; and Emmanuel Alloa, "The Diacritical Nature of Meaning: Merleau-Ponty with Saussure," *Chiasmi International* 15 (2013): 167–181.

22. This is also the typical description for how we should proceed in the case of biodiversity as well. See, for example, Maclaurin and Sterelny, 9.

23. See Kearney, "What Is Diacritical Hermeneutics?," 2.

24. Merleau-Ponty, *Signes* (Paris: Gallimard, 1960), 49; *Signs*, trans. Richard McCleary (Evanston: Northwestern University Press, 1964), 39.

25. Merleau-Ponty, *Signes* (Paris: Gallimard, 1960), 49; *Signs*, trans. Richard McCleary (Evanston: Northwestern University Press, 1964), 39.

26. Merleau-Ponty, *La Prose du monde* (Paris: Gallimard, 1969), 161; *The Prose of the World*, trans. John O'Neil (Evanston, IL: Northwestern University Press, 1973), 115.

27. Merleau-Ponty, *La Prose du monde* (Paris: Gallimard, 1969), 41; *The Prose of the World*, trans. John O'Neil (Evanston, IL: Northwestern University Press, 1973), 28.

28. Merleau-Ponty, *Signes* (Paris: Gallimard, 1960), 51; *Signs*, trans. Richard McCleary (Evanston: Northwestern University Press, 1964), 41.

29. Merleau-Ponty, *La Prose du monde* (Paris: Gallimard, 1969), 50; *The Prose of the World*, trans. John O'Neil (Evanston, IL: Northwestern University Press, 1973), 35.

30. Merleau-Ponty, *La Prose du monde* (Paris: Gallimard, 1969), 47; *The Prose of the World*, trans. John O'Neil (Evanston, IL: Northwestern University Press, 1973), 33.

31. Merleau-Ponty, *Signes* (Paris: Gallimard, 1960), 53–54; *Signs*, trans. Richard McCleary (Evanston, IL: Northwestern University Press, 1964), 42; See also Kearney, "What Is Diacritical Hermeneutics?," 2.

32. Merleau-Ponty, *Signes* (Paris: Gallimard, 1960), 54; *Signs*, trans. Richard McCleary (Evanston: Northwestern University Press, 1964), 43.

33. Merleau-Ponty, *Signes* (Paris: Gallimard, 1960), 58; *Signs*, trans. Richard McCleary (Evanston: Northwestern University Press, 1964), 46.

34. Merleau-Ponty, *Le visible et l'invisible* (Paris: Gallimard, 1964), 267; *The Visible and the Invisible*, trans. Alphonso Lingis (Evanston, IL: Northwestern University Press, 1968), 213–214.

35. Merleau-Ponty, *Le monde sensible et le monde de l'expression* (Genève: Mētis Presses, 2011), 206.

36. Merleau-Ponty, *Le visible et l'invisible* (Paris: Gallimard, 1964), 277; *The Visible and the Invisible*, trans. Alphonso Lingis (Evanston, IL: Northwestern University Press, 1968), 224.

37. David Morris, "Merleau-Ponty, Movement and Development: On the Difference between Being and Determinate Being," presented at the 2013 International Merleau-Ponty Circle (unpublished), 1.

38. Morris, "Merleau-Ponty, Movement and Development," 3.

39. Merleau-Ponty, *Le visible et l'invisible* (Paris: Gallimard, 1964), 233; *The Visible and the Invisible*, trans. Alphonso Lingis (Evanston, IL: Northwestern University Press, 1968), 179. See also Richard Kearney, "Ecrire la chair: L'expression diacritique chez Merleau-Ponty," *Chiasmi International* 15 (2013), 183.

40. Martin Heidegger, *Nietzsche*, Erster Band (Pfullingen: Verlag Günther Neske, 1989), 520; *Nietzsche*, Volume III, trans. Joan Stambaugh, David Farrell Krell, and Frank Capuzzi (San Francisco: HarperCollins, 1991), 41.

41. Merleau-Ponty, *La Nature* (Paris: Seuil, 1995), 302; *Nature*, trans. Robert Vallier (Evanston, IL: Northwestern University Press, 2003), 238.

42. Arne Naess, *Ecology, Community and Lifestyle*, trans. and ed. by David Rothenberg (Cambridge, MA: Cambridge University Press, 1989), 36.

43. See Donald Worster, *Nature's Economy: A History of Ecological Ideas* (Cambridge, MA: Cambridge University Press, 1977), 205–220, 291–315; Donald Worster, *The Wealth of Nature: Environmental History and the Ecological Imagination* (Oxford: Oxford University Press, 1993), 156–170.

44. For an insightful analysis of Merleau-Ponty's account of expression, see Veronique Foti, *Tracing Expression in Merleau-Ponty: Aesthetics, Philosophy of Biology, and Ontology* (Evanston, IL: Northwestern University Press, 2013).

45. George C. Williams, *Natural Selection: Domains, Levels, and Challenges* (Oxford: Oxford University Press, 1992), 72–73.

46. Merleau-Ponty, *La Nature* (Paris: Seuil, 1995), 243; *Nature*, trans. Robert Vallier (Evanston, IL: Northwestern University Press, 2003), 186.

47. Merleau-Ponty, *La Nature* (Paris: Seuil, 1995), 240; *Nature*, trans. Robert Vallier (Evanston: Northwestern University Press, 2003), 184.

48. Elizabeth Grosz, *Chaos, Territory, Art: Deleuze and the Framing of the Earth* (New York: Columbia University Press, 2008), 9.

49. Grosz, *Chaos, Territory, Art*, 7.

50. See Maier, *What's So Good about Biodiversity?*, 121.

51. Williams, *Natural* Selection, 76.

52. Grosz, *Chaos, Territory, Art*, 6.

53. Jared Diamond has recognized this point to a certain extent in *The World until Yesterday* (New York: Penguin Books, 2012), 369–409. Concerning the overall problems with his account, see James C. Scott, "Crops, Towns, Government," *London Review of Books* 35, no. 22 (2013): 13–15.

The Passion According to Teresa of Avila
Julia Kristeva

1. *Thoughts on God's Love*, from the Critical Edition of P. Silverio de Santa Teresa, C.D., Chapter 5:5. Also available as *Conceptions of the Love of God* in *The Complete Works of St. Teresa*, vol. 1–3, trans. E. Allison Peers (New York: Bloomsbury Academic, 2002).

2. *Thoughts on God's Love*, from the Critical Edition of P. Silverio de Santa Teresa, C.D., 1:10. Also available as *Conceptions of the Love of God in The Complete Works of St. Teresa*, vol. 1–3, trans. E. Allison Peers (New York: Bloomsbury Academic, 2002).

3. *The Life of St. Teresa of Avila*, from the Critical Edition of P. Silverio de Santa Teresa, C.D., Chapter 10:1. Also available as *The Complete Works of St. Teresa*, vol. 1–3, trans. E. Allison Peers (New York: Bloomsbury Academic, 2002).

4. *The Life of St. Teresa of Avila*, from the Critical Edition of P. Silverio de Santa Teresa, C.D., Chapter 18:1. Also available as *The Complete Works of St. Teresa*, vol. 1–3, trans. E. Allison Peers (New York: Bloomsbury Academic, 2002).

5. *The Life of St. Teresa of Avila*, from the Critical Edition of P. Silverio de Santa Teresa, C.D., Chapter 18:4. Also available as *The Complete Works of St. Teresa*, vol. 1–3, trans. E. Allison Peers (New York: Bloomsbury Academic, 2002).

6. *The Life of St. Teresa of Avila*, from the Critical Edition of P. Silverio de Santa Teresa, C.D., Chapter 18:13. Also available as *The Complete Works of St. Teresa*, vol. 1–3, trans. E. Allison Peers (New York: Bloomsbury Academic, 2002).

7. *The Life of St. Teresa of Avila*, from the Critical Edition of P. Silverio de Santa Teresa, C.D., Chapter 29. Also available as *The Complete Works of St. Teresa*, vol. 1–3, trans. E. Allison Peers (New York: Bloomsbury Academic, 2002).

8. St. Teresa of Avila, *The Way of Perfection* in *The Complete Works of St. Teresa*, vol. 2, trans. E. Allison Peers (New York: Bloomsbury Academic, 2002), 28:10.

9. Cf. D. W. Winnicott, «L'esprit et ses rapports avec le psyché-soma» in *De la psychiatrie à la psychanalyse* (1958) Payot, 1969, 135–149. Cf. D. W. Winnicott, "The Mind and Its Relation to the Psyche-Soma," in *From Painting to Psychoanalysis*.

10. From the Greek *aisthesis*: a single term that signifies touch and sensitivity, like the German word *Gefühl*.

11. *The Life of St. Teresa of Avila*, from the Critical Edition of P. Silverio de Santa Teresa, C.D., Chapter 11:6. Also available as *The Complete Works of St. Teresa*, vol. 1–3, trans. E. Allison Peers (New York: Bloomsbury Academic, 2002).

12. *The Life of St. Teresa of Avila*, from the Critical Edition of P. Silverio de Santa Teresa, C.D., Chapter 11:7. Also available as *The Complete Works of St. Teresa*, vol. 1–3, trans. E. Allison Peers (New York: Bloomsbury Academic, 2002).

13. Edmund Husserl, *Ideen* I, trans. Paul Ricoeur (Paris: Gallimard, 1971), 227.

14. See the magnificent interpretation of touch by Jean-Louis Chrétien in his *L'appel et la réponse* (Minuit: 1992), 103.

15. Thérèse d'Avila, *Chemin de Perfection*, trans. Jeannine Poitrey (Paris: Éditions du Cerf, 2011), 754.

Refiguring Wounds in the Afterlife (of Trauma)
Shelly Rambo

1. Cathy Caruth, *Literature in the Ashes of History* (Baltimore: Johns Hopkins University Press, 2013), 92.

2. Gert Buelen, Samuel Durrant, and Robert Eaglestone, eds., *The Future of Trauma Theory: Contemporary Literary and Cultural Criticism* (New York: Routledge, 2013), xvii.

3. Ibid., xii.

4. Cathy Caruth, *Unclaimed Experience* (Baltimore: Johns Hopkins University Press, 1995).

5. Dori Laub, "Bearing Witness or the Vicissitudes of Listening," in *Testimony*, 58. In the preface to *Trauma: Explorations in Memory*, Caruth also presents trauma

research in terms of sound: "there is no single approach to *listening* to the many different traumatic experiences and histories we encounter" (ix).

6. Shoshana Felman and Dori Laub, *Testimony: A Crisis of Witnessing in Literature, Psychoanalysis, and History* (New York: Routledge, 1991).

7. Julian Wolfreys, "Trauma, Testimony, Criticism," ch. 6 in *Introducing Criticism at the 21st Century* (Edinburgh: Edinburgh University Press, 2002), 129.

8. Jacques Derrida, "Rams: Uninterrupted Dialogue—Between Two Infinities, the Poem," ch. 5 in *Sovereignties in Question: The Poetics of Paul Celan* (New York: Fordham University Press, 2005), 135–163. Note Derrida's reflections in "Rams" and "The Truth that Wounds." Derrida's reflections here: "But survival carries within itself the trace of an ineffaceable incision" (139).

9. Buelens, Durrant, and Eaglestone note in *The Future of Trauma Theory*, "Many have argued that there is something profoundly traumatic in the impulse that underlies deconstruction and Derrida's work, and that this work both enacts and responds to trauma (see Critchley; Eaglestone; Ofrat)," 2.

10. In turn, Elie Wiesel claimed that the twentieth century birthed a new genre of literature—that of testimony and witness. For him, the task of the survivor—and writer—was to witness to wounds that do not surface into language. See "The Holocaust as a Literary Inspiration," in *Dimensions of the Holocaust* (Evanston, IL: Northwestern University Press, 1977), 9.

11. See Dominick LaCapra's reading of the Tancred and Clorinda parable and his critique of Caruth's work in *Writing History, Writing Trauma* (Baltimore, Johns Hopkins University Press, 2000), 181–220. The extent to which trauma can be "working through" is at the heart of his critique; see 21–22.

12. Cathy Caruth, "Parting Words: Trauma, Silence, and Survival," *Cultural Values*, 5, no. 1 (2001): 7–26.

13. Cathy Caruth, *Literature in the Ashes of History*, 7.

14. The authors of *The Future of Trauma Theory* refer to trauma theory at the end of the twentieth century—Caruth, Felman, Laub, etc—as "classical trauma theory," xii.

15. See Shelly Rambo, *Spirit and Trauma: A Theology of Remaining* (Louisville, KY: Westminster John Knox Press), 2010.

16. Examples within theology and biblical studies include works by Jennifer Beste, Cynthia Hess, Serene Jones, Dirk Lange, Samuel Ballentine, Dan Mathewson, David G. Garber, and Kathleen M. O'Connor.

17. Caravaggio, *The Incredulity of St. Thomas*, 1601–1602, http://www.wga.hu/frames-e.html?/html/c/caravagg/06/34thomas.html.

18. Richard Dawkins, British evolutionary biologist and prominent figure in what is referred to as the "new atheism," tweeted, "If there's evidence, it isn't faith. Doubting Thomas, patron saint of scientists, wanted evidence. Other disciples praised for not doing so." http://www.religiondispatches.org/wire/7152/doubting-thomas-a-patron-saint-for-scientists.

19. Grace Jantzen, *Foundations of Violence. (Death and the Displacement of Beauty series)* (London: Routledge, 2004). She writes, "The fundamental thesis of

the project is that the choice of death, the love of death and of that which makes for death, has been characteristic of the west from Homeric and Platonic writings, through centuries of christendom, and takes particularly deadly shapes in western postmodernity," vii.

20. See Rita Nakashima Brock and Rebecca Parker, *Proverbs of Ashes: Violence, Redemptive Suffering, and the Search for What Saves Us*, (Boston: Beacon Press, 2002); Delores Williams, *Sisters in the Wilderness: The Challenge of Womanist God-Talk*, (Maryknoll, NY: Orbis Books, 1995).

21. Richard Kearney, "Writing Trauma: Narrative Catharsis in Homer, Shakespeare, and Joyce," http://www.abc.net.au/religion/articles/2012/07/19/3549000.htm

22. See Patricia Ticineto Clough, ed., *The Affective Turn: Theorizing the Social*, (Durham, NC: Duke University Press, 2007). In the introduction, Clough provides a description of the relationship between affect studies and trauma theory, 1–33.

23. Kearney, "Writing Trauma."

24. Kearney, "Writing Trauma."

25. Gregory of Nyssa, "The Life of St. Macrina," in *The Fathers of the Church: St. Gregory Ascetical Works, Vol. 58*. Translated by Virginia Woods Callahan. (Washington, DC: The Catholic University of America Press, 1999), 181–186.

26. Virginia Burrus, "Macrina's Tattoo," *Journal of Medieval and Early Modern Studies* 33 (2003), 403–417.

27. Francine Cardman, "Whose Life Is It? The Vita Macrinae of Gregory of Nyssa," *Studia Patristica* 37 (2001), 33–50.

28. Gregory of Nyssa, *The Fathers of the Church*, 195–272.

29. Gregory of Nyssa, *The Fathers of the Church*, 185.

30. Her name connects to Lampedes, the torchbearing nymphs of the underworld, who are the companions of Hecate, the Greek titan goddess of witchcraft and crossroads. They are spirits of the underworld who bear light.

31. Gregory of Nyssa, *The Fathers of the Church*, 186.

32. Immediately after childbirth, Emmelia receives a vision, prompting her to assign a secret name (Thecla) to Macrina. Thecla was an early Christian martyr, famed, Gregory notes, for her virginity (164).

33. Georgia Frank, "Macrina's Scar: Homeric Allusion and Heroic Identity in Gregory of Nyssa's Life of Macrina," *Journal of Early Christian Studies*, vol. 8, no. 4, Winter 2000, 513.

34. Virginia Burrus, "Macrina's Tattoo," *Journal of Medieval and Early Modern Studies*, vol. 33, no. 3, Fall 2003, 414.

35. Cardman writes, "My hopes are to find some traces of Macrina in the scant clues and tantalizing absences of the *Life*; my fears are that she is so veiled in Gregory's web of words that only the phantoms of memory survive" (35). Cardman is taking up concerns raised by Elizabeth A. Clark in "The Lady Vanishes: Dilemmas of a Feminist Historian after the 'Linguistic Turn'," in *Church History*, vol. 67, no. 1, March 1998, 1–31.

36. Gregory of Nyssa, *The Fathers of the Church*, 182.

37. Judith Herman, *Trauma and Recovery: The Aftermath of Violence—from Domestic Abuse to Political Terror* (New York: Basic Books, 1992).

38. This scene depicts the Tuesday sessions conducted by neurologist Jean-Martin Charcot, and it depicts the work of early psychoanalysis. See Herman's description in ch. 1, "A Forgotten History," *Trauma and Recovery*, 7–32. Broullet's painting can be accessed at http://www.aly-abbara.com/museum/medecine/pages_01/picture/Charcot_lecon.html

39. Judith Butler, *Precarious Life. London: Verso, 2004; Frames of War: When Is Life Grievable?* (London: Verso, 2009).

40. Note especially ch. 1, "Exploration and Exoneration or What Can We Hear," in *Precarious Life* in which she presents the problem of lives that do not count in the public sphere.

41. Amy Hollywood, *Sensible Ecstasy: Mysticism, Sexual Difference, and the Demands of History* (Chicago: University of Chicago Press, 2002), 276.

42. Luce Irigaray, *Marine Lover of Friedrich Nietzsche* (New York: Columbia University Press, 1991), 171.

43. Catherine Keller, *Face of the Deep: A Theology of Becoming* (New York: Routledge, 2003), 221.

44. Amy Hollywood, *Sensible Ecstasy*, 270.

45. I am indebted to Cameron Partridge here who emphasizes the importance of clothing in Gregory of Nyssa's interpretation of resurrection. He writes, "so fond is Gregory of clothing imagery that it serves as one of the chief metaphors through which he envisions resurrection embodiment. Clothing imagery was uniquely able to reflect both radical change and continuity of identity" (60). Building on Partridge's insights, the Macrina scene can be understood as a burial "sewing/dressing" room in which new garments are being woven. The scar is the new cloth—resurrection skin—that woven (witnessed) at this curious crossing (trans-). The scar is the sign of resurrection skin, the first fruits of that restoration of the *imago Dei*. Macrina's body is a visible sign *of what is always already here* (eschatological dimension). Cameron Partridge, ch. 1, "'Form Blossoming in an Unusual Manner': Reclothing Sexual Difference in Gregory of Nyssa," in *Transfiguring Sexual Difference in Maximus the Confessor* (Unpublished doctoral dissertation, Harvard University, Cambridge, MA, 2008).

46. Following Cardman's suggestion that the scene offers a "resistant reading," the scar might also offer a disruption in Gregory's negation of the flesh.

47. Partridge, "Form Blossoming in an Unusual Manner," 64.

48. Hollywood, *Sensible Ecstasy*, 270.

49. Note their essays written in honor of scholar Nancy Eisland, a forerunner in disability theology. This rich exchange of essays is located in *Journal of Feminist Studies in Religion*, 26, no. 2 (2010).

50. Hollywood, *Sensible Ecstasy*, 277.

51. Gregory of Nyssa, *The Fathers of the Church*, 185.

52. Gregory of Nyssa, *The Fathers of the Church*, 185. Drawing from Caruth's imaginary in the epigraph, this also alludes to the closing scenes in the Gospel

of John in which the disciples gather along the shores of the Sea of Tiberius (John 21).

53. Gregory of Nyssa, *The Fathers of the Church*, 164.

54. Gregory of Nyssa, *The Fathers of the Church*, 176.

This Is My Body: Contribution to a Philosophy of the Eucharist
Emmanuel Falque

Emmanuel Falque, professor and chair of philosophy at the Institut Catholique de Paris, and one of the most original voices in the younger generation of French philosophers, brings together his training in patristic and medieval studies with the vibrant phenomenological tradition in France, forging a much closer synthesis between phenomenology and theology than many previous thinkers while also pushing their work further. His main critique of the phenomenological tradition and especially such thinkers as Emmanuel Lévinas, Michel Henry, and Jean-Luc Marion concerns precisely the topic of the flesh, although he is also interested in the status of hermeneutics. He argues that the phenomenological distinction (in Husserl, Merleau-Ponty, Henry, and Marion) between "body" and "flesh" (*Leib* and *Körper*) reinscribes the traditional philosophical dualism between mind and matter or soul and body on a phenomenological level and does not take the materiality and "animality" of our flesh sufficiently seriously. He hence seeks to recover the "organicity" of the body (in its concrete "flesh and bones") and to take full account of its animal nature (the chaos or "abyss" of our passions, drives, and impulses). His phenomenological trilogy, which tries to take a radically secular starting point but arrives at deeply theological conclusions, tries to work this out on multiple levels: The first volume concerns suffering and death by employing Christ's humanity and anguish in the garden and arguing that he fully shares our human condition; the second volume explores the topics of birth and resurrection (translated as *The Metamorphosis of Finitude*); the third volume develops the account of animality and organicity more fully, arriving at a phenomenology of marriage and the Eucharist. The paper included in this volume (first presented at the Australian Catholic University in Melbourne, Australia, then at the 2014 American Academy of Religion conference in Baltimore, Maryland) carries further the argument about the flesh and carnality via a radical examination of Christ's portrayal as the "lamb" on the altar, of what it means to say that the Eucharist is the "body" of Christ that is meant to be "eaten," and by exploring the heritage, content, modality and aim of the Eucharist, while also drawing out implications for the topic of sexual difference.
—Trans. Christina M. Gschwandtner

1. I here take up again the major lines of my work *Les noces de l'Agneau: Essai philosophique sur le corps et l'eucharistie* (Paris: Cerf, 2011) in order to synthesize them. This necessarily brief paper can only point back to this work in order to justify the theses set forth here fully and to note the references that are announced there.

2. *Opening Remarks for the Second Vatican Council (John XXIII)*. Cited by B. Sesboüé and Ch. Theobald, eds. *La parole du salut: Histoire des dogmes*, vol. 4 (Paris: Desclée, 1996), 479.

3. Charles Péguy, *Note conjointe sur M. Descartes* (Paris: Pléiade, 1992), 1307.

4. I refer here to the entirety of my triptych: *Le passeur de Gethsémani: Angoisse, souffrance et mort: Lecture existentielle et phénoménologique* (Paris: Cerf, 1999); *Métamorphose de la finitude: Essai philosophique sur la naissance et la résurrection* (Paris: Cerf, 2004), trans. by George Hughes as *Metamorphosis of Finitude: An Essay on Birth and Resurrection* (New York: Fordham University Press, 2012); *Les noces de l'agneau: Essai philosophique sur le corps et l'eucharistie* (Paris: Cerf, 2011), translation forthcoming with Fordham University Press. [The French version alerts the reader throughout to connections to these works. These references have been eliminated in the interest of space. Some other cuts have also been made. The translation is hence slightly shorter and not strictly identical to the French original. All cuts have been approved by the author.—Trans.]

5. Tertullian, *On the Flesh of Christ* (*De carne Christi*) in *Anti-Nicene Fathers*, vol. 3 (Peabody, MA: Hendrickson Publishers, Inc., 1994), chap. IX, 530. See on this point my analysis and commentary on *De carne Christi* in *Dieu, la chair, et l'autre* (Paris: Presses Universitaires de France, 2008), chap. V, 252–88: "The consistency of the flesh (Tertullian)," especially 269–86: "the flesh as my sister" (§35) and "the hypothesis of flesh for my death" (§36).

6. I.e., the distinction between the historical Jesus and the risen Christ. Cf. the hypothesis of Michel Henry's reading in *Incarnation* (Paris: Seuil, 2000), §24, 180–89 ("The Fundamental Problematic in Irenaeus and Tertullian") and my critical remarks "Y a-t-il une chair sans corps?" in *Phénoménologie et christianism chez Michel Henry*, ed. Philippe Capelle (Paris: Cerf, 2004), 95–133.

7. Cf. P. Ide, "L'homme et animal: Une altérité corporelle significative," in *L'humain et la personne* (Paris: Cerf, 2009), 281–99 (traits quoted on 287).

8. Friedrich Nietzsche, *Beyond Good and Evil*, trans. Walter Kaufmann (New York: Vintage, 1989), §36, 48.

9. Nietzsche, *Posthumous Fragments*, ("the leading thread of the body"), *Beyond Good and Evil*, §230 ("the primitive text of the natural human"), and ("the body that philosophizes").

10. Council of Trullo, called Quinisext Council, held in Constantinople in 692, "under the cupola," which is why the council of the palace called it "de troulos" or "in trullo." Canon 82, in *Acta conciliorum*: "We decree that henceforth Christ our God must be represented in his human form but not in the form of the lamb." (*Christi Dei nostri humana forma characterem etiam in imaginus deinceps pro veteri agno erigi ac depingi jubemus* [col. 1691]).

11. *Corps-à-corps* is an idiomatic expression that means "hand-to-hand," as in "hand-to-hand combat." There is no equivalent English idiomatic expression that involves the word "body" instead of the hand. Despite its awkwardness the expression will be translated as "body-to-body" throughout the paper to capture the author's emphasis on the body in this context.—Trans.

12. Respectively, Martin Heidegger, *Nietzsche I* (Paris: Gallimard, 1971), 438 ("The concept of chaos") and Immanuel Kant, *Critique de la raison pure* (Paris: Presses Universitaires de France, 1980), 124/A 111 ("Transcendental Deduction,

Principle of the Possibility of Experience [recognition of the concept]"). I prefer the translation "mix of sensations" (Heidegger [Klossowski], *Nietzsche I*, 138 ["Chaos"]) to the "crowd of phenomena" (PUF) or the "mass of phenomena" (G–F), leading necessarily to the operation of "synthesis."

13. Benedict XVI, *Encyclical* Deus caritas est (*God is Love*) (Ijamsville, MA: The Word Among Us Press, 2006), §5, 13.

14. Thomas Aquinas, *Summa Contra Gentiles*, vol. IV (Revelation), chap. 88 ("The sex and age of those raised").

15. Maurice Blanchot, "The Secret of Golem," in *Le livre à venir* (Paris: Gallimard, 1959), 130–31 ("The symbolic experience"), trans. by Charlotte Mandell as *The Book to Come* (Stanford, CA: Stanford University Press, 2003), 87.

16. St. Augustine, *Ennarationes in Psalmos*/*Commentary on the Psalms*, I, 33, §8; I, 34, 11.

17. Thomas Aquinas, *Summa Theologiae*, trans. by the Fathers of the English Dominican Province (Westminster, MA: Christian Classics, 1911), IIIa q.75, a.5, respectively ("Whether the Accidents of the Bread and Wine Remain in This Sacrament after the Change?"), 2443.

18. Anthropophagy would certainly have been enough to discourage us from that cf. Henri de Lubac, *Corpus mysticum: L'eucharistie dans l'Eglise au Moyen Age* (Paris: Aubier, 1941), 305ff. ("Amalarius's Threefold Body and What Became of It"), trans. Gemma Simmonds as *Corpus Mysticum: The Eucharist and the Church in the Middle Ages* (Notre Dame, IN: Notre Dame University Press, 2006).

19. IV. Lateran Council (1215), repeated by the Council of Trent (1551), "Decree on the Sacrament of the Eucharist," in G. Dumeige, *La foi catholique*, n.739 (Dz 1642), chap. IV, 407: "Transubstantiation."

20. Respectively, Thomas Aquinas, *Summa Theologiae*, Ia, Q.3, Art. 4, ad. 2 (being as "act of being" and as "predicate"); Georg Wilhelm Friedrich Leibniz, *Principles of Nature and of Grace founded in Reason* (1714), §1 (Substance as "being capable of action").

21. Cf. Benedict Spinoza, *Ethics* (Paris: Vrin, 1983), Book III, Prop. VI, 261 ("The effort for persevering in being" [*in suo esse perseverare conatur*]); also Book III, Prop. II, Scholia, 251 ("No one has determine what *the Body can do*").

22. Georg Wilhelm Friedrich Hegel, *Lessons on the Philosophy of Religion* (Paris: Vrin, n.d.), III, 1 ("Absolute Religion"), 77.

23. *Cited and explained by X. Lacroix, "Connaître au sens biblique," Christus* (January 2007): 13.

24. J. Ratzinger, "Letter to the Bishops of the Catholic Church on the Collaboration of Man and Woman in the Church" (May 31, 2004), §12.

25. Dietrich Bonhoeffer, *Creation and Fall* (1932 Berlin course), trans. John C. Fletcher (London: SCM Press, 1959), 60–61.

26. lit. "the deacon"—Trans.

27. From the Preparation of the Gifts in the Eucharistic Liturgy.

28. Thomas Aquinas, I *Sentences*, D.8, Q.1, A.2, reply 2. See my article "Limite théologique et finitude phénoménologique chez Thomas d'Aquin," in *Revue*

des sciences philosophiques et théologiques, Revue du Centenaire (July–Sept. 2008): 527–36 (especially 549–51: "L'adage de la proportion limitée").

29. A. Kojève, *Introduction à la lecture de Hegel* (Paris: Gallimard, 1947/1993), 13. Commentary on G.W.F. Hegel, Phenomenology of Spirit, vol. 1, (B) "Self-Consciousness," beginning of the master-slave dialectic ("Independence and Dependence of Self-Consciousness: Domination and Servitude"): "self-consciousness is in itself and for itself when and because it is in itself and for itself for a consciousness other than the self; that is to say, that it is only inasmuch as it is recognized . . . Each extreme is for the other the middle term with whose help he enters in relation with himself . . . They recognize themselves as they recognize each other reciprocally."

30. *Noces de l'agneau*, 100 and 229, respectively.

31. *Cf.* John Paul II, *The Theology of the Body: Human Love in the Divine Plan* (Boston: Pauline Books, 1997), 355. Cf. *Code of Canon Law*, Canon 1142: "For a just cause, the Roman Pontiff *can dissolve a non-consummated* marriage between baptized persons or between a baptized party and a non-baptized party at the request of both parties or one of them, even if the other party is unwilling."

32. Cf. Jean-Jacques Olier (responding to Saint John Eudes), "Mémoires" (1642–1652), *Traité des Saints Ordres*, 1984 vol. IV, 123: "our Lord is not only host in the holy sacrament, but he is also communion, because he comes *to communicate to us the religious and respectful feelings* he bears toward his Father . . . As our Lord has formed his Church by his holy Spirit and by the vivifying spirit, our Lord now wants to reform his Church *in taking on the qualities and dispositions of the spirit which are his condition in the very holy sacrament of the altar.*"

33. Jean-Luc Marion, "The Present and the Gift," in *God without Being*, trans. Thomas A. Carlson (Chicago: University of Chicago Press, 1995), 178.

34. Romano Guardini, *Le Seigneur* (Paris: Alsatia, 1954), vol. II, 126; trans. as *The Lord* (Washington, DC: Regnery Gateway, 1954).

35. *"Rituel du mariage" (édition française)*, IVème bénédiction nuptiale, *Manuel des Paroisses* (n.p.: Ed. Tardy, 1992), 140.

Original Breath
Karmen MacKendrick

1. No one can write or think except in debt to others, but in the case of this paper, my debts are unusually direct and clear, and so demand some acknowledgement. The essay arises from a series of meetings with Patricia Cox Miller, for the purpose of reading Jean-Christophe Bailly's *The Animal Side*, and from reading her paper "Adam, Eve, and the Elephants." I am profoundly in her debt for both, and lastingly grateful to Helen Tartar, who handed me a copy of Bailly and said rightly that I would like it. (Helen was usually right.) Lesser friends than Virginia Burrus and Jennifer Glancy would have been bored to tears by my repeated and anxious discussions of "where the paper stands now." Catherine Keller, upon my mention to her of some passages that did not make it into this version, supplied me with the epigraph by sending a lovely paper of her own in which she made

use of it ("Dark Anointments," from a presentation at the American Academy of Religion, 2012).

2. Except where otherwise noted, I have used the New American Bible translation (In *Catholic Study Bible*, Oxford University Press, 2011).

3. For an important discussion of the "face of the deep" over which this wind sweeps, in contradistinction to the insistence on creation *ex nihilo*, see Catherine Keller, *Face of the Deep: A Theology of Becoming* (New York: Routledge, 2002).

4. In Jean-Luc Nancy's *The Sense of the World*, the world as sense is precisely the world that is not divinely framed—but the sense of divinity he opposes there is one of certainty, even predetermination, not one of open responsivity as an ever-shifting sense-making. Trans. Jeffrey S. Librett (Minneapolis: University of Minnesota Press, 2008).

5. The Spirit is said to *move* in the American Standard Version, Bible in Basic English, Douay-Rheims, Good News Translation, King James Version, New American Standard, New Century, Webster, Third Millennium, and Tyndale Bible. It *hovers* in the New International Version, Complete Jewish Bible, English Standard Version, God's Word Translation, Hebrew Names Version, Lexham English Bible, New International Reader's Version, New King James Version, New Living Translation, Darby, Today's New International, World English translation. The Common English Bible and the New Revised Standard both translate *ruach elohim* as "a wind from God," which in both instances *sweeps* over the waters. Finally, in Young's Bible the Spirit *flutters*; the Wycliffe Bible offers the waters more agency as the Spirit is *borne upon* them, and The Message reads, perhaps a bit freely and to my mind a little terrifyingly, "Earth was a soup of nothingness, a bottomless emptiness, an inky blackness. God's Spirit brooded like a bird above the watery abyss." All of these are available at the highly useful Online Parallel Bible at http://www.biblestudytools.com/parallel-bible/

6. Christian interpreters tend to be tempted to read the Trinitarian "Holy Spirit" here. Despite the ambiguous numbering of God, it is challenging to justify this reading textually.

7. Hildegard of Bingen, Letter 41, "Letter to the Prelates of Mainz," in *The Book of Divine Works: Ten Visions of God's Deeds in the World and Humanity*, trans. Ronald Mille, ed. Matthew Fox (Santa Fe, NM: Bear and Company, 1987), 358.

8. In the first *Duino Elegy*, Rainer Maria Rilke writes strikingly of this difference: "already the knowing animals are aware / that we are not really at home in / our interpreted world." ("die findigen Tiere merken es schon / daß wir nicht sehr verläßlich zu Haus sind / in der gedeuteten Welt.") In *The Selected Poetry of Rainer Maria Rilke*, ed. and trans. Stephen Mitchell (New York: Vintage, 1982), 150–51. In a text that extensively considers Rilke, Jean-Christophe Bailly writes, "[Animals] all have it, this precedence, an air of seniority, the look of having been there before, and this is what we see when we see them looking at us and when we see them simply being among themselves, in their own domains. Although the pretentious ideology of humankind as the pinnacle of creation implies the destruction of all the respect for this precedence that would normally be due . . .

we recognize the seniority of animals at least implicitly." Jean-Christophe Bailly, *The Animal Side*, trans. Catherine Porter (New York: Fordham University Press, 2011), 62.

9. Patricia Cox Miller, "Adam, Eve, and the Elephants: Asceticism and Animality," in *Ascetic Culture: Essays in Honor of Philip Rousseau*, ed. Blake Leyerle and Robin Darling Young (Notre Dame, IN: University of Notre Dame Press, 2013).

10. Miller cites particularly "the Hexaemeron tradition as exemplified by Basil of Caesarea, Ambrose, and John Chrysostom." Miller, ibid.

11. See, for a few examples, Louis Ginzberg, *The Legends of the Jews* (1901–1938), trans. Henrietta Szold, vol. 1, *From the Creation to Jacob* (Digireads.com, 2004), vol. 1, "The Angels and the Creation of Man;" "The Ideal Man." See also vol. 5, *From the Creation to the Exodus: Notes for Volumes One and Two* (Baltimore: Johns Hopkins University Press, 1998), 69, n.12; 83, nn. 29–30. Qur'an, 2.29–34. Citations from the Qur'an from *The Holy Qur'an*, trans. M.H. Shakir (Tahrike Tarsile Qur'an, Inc., 1983) Online via Online Book Initiative at http://quod.lib .umich.edu/k/koran/. See also Dag Nikolaus Hasse, "Influence of Arabic and Islamic Philosophy on the Latin West," *Stanford Encyclopedia of Philosophy*, 2008, at http://plato.stanford.edu/entries/arabic-islamic-influence/; Chittick, "The Divine Roots of Human Love;" Moses Maimonides, *The Guide for the Perplexed*, trans. M. Friedländer (London: Routledge and Kegan Paul, 1904), available at http://www.sacred-texts.com/jud/gfp/gfp012.htm, 1.2; Thomas Aquinas, *The Summa Theologica of St. Thomas Aquinas*, trans. Fathers of the English Dominican Province, 1920, available at http://www.newadvent.org/summa/1094.htm, Kevin Knight, 2008, Part 1, Question 94, Article 3.

12. Dante, 1.2.1–2. On angels, 1.2.3. On animals' shared instincts, 1.2.5. Cutting off in advance the possible argument that the animals might have wanted to speak outside their own kind, Dante adds, "Between creatures of different species, on the other hand, not only was speech unnecessary, but it would have been injurious, since there could have been no friendly exchange between them." 1.2.5. "Since, then, human beings are moved not by their natural instinct but by reason, and since that reason takes diverse forms in individuals, according to their capacity for discrimination, judgment, or choice . . . I hold that we can never understand the actions or feelings of others by reference to our own, as the baser animals can. Nor is it given to us to enter into each other's minds by means of spiritual reflection, as the angels do, because the human spirit is so weighed down by the heaviness and density of the mortal body." Dante, 1.3.1. Dante must acknowledge that God and animals are both said to speak in Genesis, the first in world-creation (and then in conversation with the humans), the second in the serpent's discussion in chapter 3. Both modes of speaking, he declares, are indirect, and animal speaking is actually a sort of possession, the manipulation of the animal body by angel or demon: "[If] the air can be moved at the command of the lesser nature which is God's servant and creation . . . can it not also, at God's command, so be moved as to make the sound of words?" Dante, 1.4.6. On animals as something like ventriloquists' dummies for God or for demons, see Dante, 1.2.6.

13. Dante, 1.4.4. Dante finds it reasonable to suppose that this was the very first speaking, because it is the most proper possibility: "Thinking, therefore . . . that the first man addressed his speech to God Himself, I say, equally reasonably, that this first speaker spoke immediately—as soon, indeed, as God's creative power had been breathed into him." Dante, 1.5.1.

14. *Seducing Augustine: Bodies, Powers, Confessions*, with Virginia Burrus and Mark Jordan (New York: Fordham University Press, 2010), conclusion, 115–27; *Divine Enticement: Theological Seductions* (New York: Fordham University Press, 2013), esp. chapter 4, 141–67.

15. Bailly, 60–61.

16. Thus in Bailly, 49. Citing Maurice Merleau-Ponty, *Nature: Course Notes from the College de France*, ed. Dominique Seglard, trans. Robert Vallier (Evanston, IL: Northwestern University Press, 2003), 155, 188.

17. Bailly, 70.

18. Bailly, 55.

19. Miller, citing Georges Bataille, *Theory of Religion*, trans. Robert Hurley (New York: Zone Books, 1989), 24, 22.

20. Miller, citing *Historia monachorum in Aegypto*, 6, "On Theon," ed. A.-J. Festugière, *Subsidia Hagiographica* 34 (Brussels: Société des Bollandistes, 1961), 44; English translation in *The Lives of the Desert Fathers*, trans. Norman Russell (Kalamazoo, MI: Cistercian Press, 1981), 68.

21. Humpty Dumpty to Alice, in Lewis Carroll, *Through the Looking Glass and What Alice Found There* (London: Puffin Books, 1948), 88: "'The question is,' said Alice, 'whether you can make words mean so many different things.' 'The question is,' said Humpty Dumpty, 'which is to be master—that's all.'"

On the Flesh of the Word: Incarnational Hermeneutics
John Panteleimon Manoussakis

1. Patočka, *Heretical Essays in the Philosophy of History*, trans. Erazim Kohák (Chicago: Open Court, 1996).

2. For a further discussion on this point see my essay "The Philosopher-Priest and the Mythology of Reason" in *Analecta Hermeneutica* (special issue Refiguring Divinity) 4, 2012, 1–18.

3. On Gnostic *sige* (silence), see St. Irenaeus, *Adversus Haereses*, II. 12 (where he emphatically affirms that "where Logos is, there certainly cannot be Sige").

4. See, for example, Slavoj Žižek, *The Puppet and the Dwarf: The perverse Core of Christianity* (Cambridge: MIT Press, 2003), 32.

5. M. Heidegger, *Being and Time*, trans. Joan Stambaugh (New York: SUNY Press, 1996), 252 [273].

6. "Contrary to Christianity's basic incarnational thrust, a gradual unbodying became the model, not only for asceticism, but especially for mystical theory. . . . It would be good to think back on Augustine, who, while vigorously denouncing the Neoplatonists' lack of Christ's descending humility in the *Confessions*, sets forth in his treatise on mysticism a decidedly ascending model—from bodily to

imaginative to purely spiritual visions—which remained authoritative for the whole period that followed." Von Balthasar, *Theo-Logic*, vol. II: Truth of God, trans. Adrian J. Walker (San Francisco: Ignatius Press, 2004), 110–111.

7. Richard Kearney, "What Is Diacritical Hermeneutics?" in *Journal of Applied Hermeneutics* (December 2011), 1–14.

8. This reversal is best illustrated by comparing the two "visions" (of which only the first can properly be called so) in VII. 17. 23 and IX. 10. 25. Their multiple and significant differences are captured at their culmination: for the first contemplation (atemporal and individual) culminates in a vision ("et pervenit ad id, quod est in ictu trepidantis *aspectus*," [16–17]), while the second (temporal and communal) culminates in a touch ("nunc extendimus nos et rapida cogitatione *attingimus*"). After this, in the lengthy treatment of the senses that forms the core of Book X, the senses are ranked as follows: touch (X. 30. 41–42); taste (X. 31. 43–47); smell (X. 32. 48); hearing (X. 33. 49–50); and finally sight (X. 34. 51–53).

9. Augustine, *The Confessions*, trans. Maria Boulding, O.S.B. (Hyde Park, NY: New City Press, 1997), I. 18. 28, p. 58.

10. Augustine, *The Confessions*, VIII, 9.21, p. 201.

11. Augustine, *The Confessions*, III. 1.1, p. 75.

12. E. Levinas, *Existence and Existents*, trans. Alphonso Lingis (The Hague: Martinus Nijhoff, 1978), 44.

13. Augustine, *The Confessions*, VII. 10.16, p. 173.

14. Augustine, *The Confessions*, X. 14.21.

15. Augustine, *The Confessions*, I.1.1.

16. Augustine, *The Confessions*, II.3.6.

17. It is of interest to see how this term is used elsewhere in the Scriptures and especially in the eschatological parables of the Gospel of St. Matthew. In the parable of the two sons, the father sends his first son to work in the vineyard but he refuses; "but later [ὕστερον] he changed his mind and went" (Matt. 21:29). Here the term "later" is used together with a verb denoting repentance, or changing one's mind [μεταμεληθείς]. In the parable of the tenants that follows immediately after this one, the term is employed as an indicator of the time the father sent his own son to the vineyard (Matt. 21:37)—a reference to the incarnation, and thus to the eschatological fullness of times.

18. Augustine, *The Confessions*, X. 27. 38.

19. Richard Kearney, "What Is Diacritical Hermeneutics?" 4.

20. Augustine, *The Confessions*, I. 6.10, p. 44.

21. Augustine, *The Confessions*, I. 6.8, p. 44.

22. Augustine thinks throughout the *Confessions* of his relation to God in terms of distance and proximity. See also "non enim pedibus aut spatiis locorum itur abs te aut reditur ad te" (Augustine, *The Confessions*, I. 18.28). This phrase illustrates the movement of the narration in the *Confessions*: moving away from God and returning to God.

23. Augustine, *The Confessions*, I. 6. 9.

24. Augustine, *The Confessions*, I. 6.7, p. 43.

25. Augustine, *The Confessions*, I. 6.8, p. 43.

26. Augustine, *The Confessions*, I. 13. 20, p. 52.

27. ". . . inasmuch as language distinguishes and interrelates presence and absence" (Ricoeur, *Freud & Philosophy*, 368–369). Ricoeur is thinking here of the original absence, the absence of the absent mother, which, in Freud's famous example, becomes regulated by—and, in turn, necessitates—the birth of language (fort/da). See also, ibid., 385.

28. Cf., ibid., 385.

29. Edmund Husserl, *Ideas Pertaining to a Pure Phenomenology*, 111 (see note 15 above). Robert Sokolowski, *Introduction to Phenomenology* (Cambridge: Cambridge University Press, 2000), 17–21.

30. Edmund Husserl, *On the Phenomenology of the Consciousness of Internal Time*, trans. John Barnett Brough (Boston: Kluwer Academic Publishers, 1991) and Maurice Merleau-Ponty, *Phenomenology of Perception*, trans. Donald A. Landes (London: Routledge, 2012), especially 432–457.

31. Maurice Merleau-Ponty, Preface to A. Hesnard, *L'Oeuvre de Freud et son importance pour le mode modern* (1960), cited by Ricoeur in *Freud & Philosophy*, 417, note 99. The insight itself is discussed by Ricoeur on 382.

32. Ricoeur, *Freud & Philosophy*, 383.

33. Ibid., 370.

34. Ibid., 383.

35. The phrase "this is my body" must be understood (and it can only be understood) as an erotic declaration—more so, as an erotic performance. "This is my body" makes little or no sense if one were to approach it as an informative proposition like "Paris is the capital of France." Rather, it is more akin to the sentence "I love you." I am indebted for this insight to Fr. Patrick Royannais who writes: "Si vous voulez comprendre quelque chose à l'eucharistie, n'imaginez pas que la parole de Jésus répétée à chaque eucharistie est une information qui vise à dire ce qu'est le pain, vraiment son corps. Il s'agit bien davantage d'une déclaration d'amour. Lorsque Jésus dit, c'est mon corps pour vous, il dit, je vous aime, « Ayant aimé les siens qui étaient dans le monde, il les aima jusqu'au bout » (Jn 13) Le repas eucharistique est nuptial s'il s'agit d'alliance, comme l'enseigne Cana, festin des noces de l'agneau. Les amants se disent: prends, ceci est mon corps pour toi."

Contributors

Emmanuel Alloa is Assistant Professor at the Philosophy Department of the Universität St. Gallen (Switzerland) and Senior Research Fellow at the NCCR eikones. His research areas are German and French phenomenology and ancient philosophy, and he has worked on issues like perception, embodiment, and visuality. Among his publications are *La résistance du sensible. Merleau-Ponty critique de la transparence* (Kimé, 2014), *Das durchscheinende Bild. Konturen einer medialen Phänomenologie* (Diaphanes, 2011), as well as a coedited volume on embodiment: *Leiblichkeit. Geschichte und Aktualität eines Konzepts* (Mohr/Siebeck–UTB, 2012).

Edward S. Casey is Distinguished Professor at the State University of New York, Stony Brook, where he works in aesthetics, philosophy of space and time, ethics, perception, and psychoanalytic theory. His published books include *Imagining: A Phenomenological Study* (Indiana University Press, 2000), *Remembering: A Phenomenological Study* (Indiana University Press, 2000), *Getting Back into Place* (Indiana University Press, 1993), *The Fate of Place* (University of California Press, 1997), and *The World at a Glance* (2007).

Jean-Louis Chrétien teaches philosophy at the University of Paris IV. His books, as translated into English, include *The Unforgettable and the Unhoped For* (Fordham University Press, 2002), *Hand to Hand* (Fordham University Press, 2003), and *The Call and the Response* (Fordham University Press, 2004). He is one of the coeditors of *Phenomenology and the "Theological Turn": The French Debate* (Fordham University Press, 2000), as well as the author of the follow-up volume

Phenomenology "Wide Open": After the French Debate (Fordham University Press, 2005).

Emmanuel Falque is the Dean of the Department of Philosophy at The Catholic Institute of Paris. His published work includes *Saint Bonaventure et l'entrée due Dieu in théologie*; *Dieu, la chair et l'autre: D'Irénée à Duns Scot*; and the trilogy *Le passeur de Gethsémane, Métamorphose de la finitude*—which has been translated as *The Metamorphosis of Finitude* (Fordham University Press, 2012)—and *Les noces de l'agneau*.

Michel Henry (1922–2002) was Professor of Philosophy at the Université Paul Valéry, Montpelier. Among his many works are *The Essence of Manifestation* (Nijhoff, 1973), *Incarnation. Une philosophie de la chair* (Seuil, 2000), *I Am the Truth* (2002), *Material Phenomenology* (2008), *Seeing the Invisible: On Kandinsky* (Bloomsbury, 2009), and *From Communism to Capitalism* (Bloomsbury, 2014).

Richard Kearney is the Charles Seelig Professor of Philosophy at Boston College. He is the author of over 20 books, among them the trilogy *The God Who May Be* (Indiana University Press, 2001), *On Stories* (Routledge, 2002), and *Strangers, Gods, and Monsters* (Routledge, 2003), as well as works including *Debates in Continental Philosophy* (Fordham University Press, 2004), and *Anatheism* (Columbia, 2011). In 2008 he launched the Guestbook Project, an ongoing artistic, academic, and multi-media experiment in hospitality.

Julia Kristeva is a philosopher, psychoanalysist, and novelist who teaches at the University of Paris VII (Diderot). She is the author of many books, including *In the Beginning was Love* (Columbia University Press, 1987), *Black Sun* (Columbia University Press, 1989), *Strangers to Ourselves* (Columbia University Press, 1991), *Female Genius* (Columbia University Press, 2001), and *Hatred and Forgiveness* (Columbia University Press, 2010).

Karmen MacKendrick is Professor of Philosophy at Le Moyne College. Her work touches on questions of language, corporeality, and temporality as they relate to theology and religious studies. She is the author of *Counterpleasures* (SUNY, 1999), *Immemorial Silence* (SUNY Press, 2001), *Word Made Skin* (Fordham University Press, 2004), *Fragmentation and Memory* (Fordham University Press, 2008), and *Divine Enticement* (Fordham University Press, 2012).

John Panteleimon Manoussakis is Associate Professor of Philosophy at the College of the Holy Cross, and an Honorary Fellow at the Faculty of Theology and Philosophy of the Australian Catholic University. He is the author of two books, editor of five volumes and he has published over thirty articles in English, Greek, Russian, Serbian, and Ukrainian.

Jean-Luc Marion teaches at the University of Paris IV (Sorbonne) and is Andrew Thomas Greeley and Grace McNichols Greeley Professor of Catholic Studies at the University of Chicago Divinity School. His foci include modern philosophy, phenomenology, patristics, and mystical theology. Among his many books are *God Without Being* (Chicago University Press, 1991), *Reduction and Givenness* (Northwestern University Press 1998), *Being Given* (Stanford University Press, 2002), *In Excess* (Fordham University Press, 2002), and *The Erotic Phenomenon* (Chicago University Press, 2007).

Dermot Moran is Professor of Philosophy (Metaphysics & Logic) at University College Dublin, Ireland, and Sir Walter Murdoch Adjunct Professor at Murdoch University, Perth, Australia. His books include: *The Philosophy of John Scottus Eriugena. A Study of Idealism in the Middle Ages* (Cambridge, 1989), *Introduction to Phenomenology* (Routledge, 2000), *Edmund Husserl. Founder of Phenomenology* (Polity, 2005), and *Husserl's Crisis of the European Sciences: An Introduction* (Cambridge University Press, 2012). Professor Moran was awarded the Royal Irish Academy Gold Medal in the Humanities in 2012.

Jean-Luc Nancy is Distinguished Professor of Philosophy at the Université Marc Bloch, Strasbourg as well as a respected commentator on art and culture. His wide-ranging thought is developed in books including *Listening* (Fordham University Press, 2007), *Dis-Enclosure* (Fordham University Press, 2008), *Noli me Tangere* (Fordham University Press, 2008), *Corpus* (Fordham University Press, 2008), and *Corpus II* (Fordham University Press, 2013).

Anne O'Byrne is Associate Professor of Philosophy at the State University of New York, Stony Brook, where she works on twentieth century and contemporary European philosophy. Professor O'Byrne also maintains an interest in Irish Studies and has written philosophical work concerning the functioning of sovereignty in Northern Ireland and the inheritance of the Irish language. She is the author of *Natality and Finitude* (Indiana University Press, 2010) and the translator of Jean-Luc Nancy's *Corpus II* (Fordham University Press, 2013).

Shelly Rambo is Associate Professor of Theology at Boston University School of Theology. A constructive theologian, she engages the textual tradition of Christianity with particular attention to literary analysis and criticism. Her book, *Spirit and Trauma: A Theology of Remaining* (Westminster John Knox Press, 2010), forges a theology of the Spirit through engagements with postmodern biblical hermeneutics, a theology of Holy Saturday, and contemporary trauma theory.

Paul Ricoeur (1913–2005) was among the most respected philosophers of the twentieth century. He was awarded the Kyoto Prize in 2000 for his revolutionary work in phenomenology and hermeneutics. His books include *The Conflict* *of Interpretations* (Northwestern, 1974), *The Rule of Metaphor* (Routledge. 1978), the three volumes of *Time and Narrative* (Chicago University Press, 1984, 1985, and 1988), *Oneself as Another* (Chicago University Press, 1992), *The Just* (Chicago University Press, 2000), and *Living up to Death* (Chicago University Press, 2009). During his long career he taught at the Sorbonne, Nanterre, and the University of Chicago, among other appointments.

Ted Toadvine is Associate Professor of Philosophy and Environmental Studies at the University of Oregon. He is author of *Merleau-Ponty's Philosophy of Nature* (Northwestern University Press, 2009) and editor or translator of eight books, including *The Merleau-Ponty Reader* (Northwestern University Press, 2007) and *Eco-Phenomenology: Back to the Earth Itself* (SUNY Press, 2003). His current research interests include the immemorial past of nature, the phenomenology of human animality, and the disclosure of the end of the world through works of art.

Brian Treanor is Professor of Philosophy and Director of Environmental Studies at Loyola Marymount University. He is the author of *Aspects of Alterity* (Fordham, 2006) and *Emplotting Virtue* (SUNY Press, 2014), and the coeditor of *A Passion for the Possible* (Fordham University Press, 2010), *Interpreting Nature* (Fordham University Press, 2013), and *Being-in-Creation* (Fordham University Press, 2015). Current projects include the development of an "earthy" hermeneutics, and a monograph on the experience of joy.

David Wood is W. Alton Jones Professor of Philosophy at Vanderbilt University, where he teaches continental and environmental philosophy. His books include *Thinking after Heidegger* (Polity, 2002), *The Step Back* (SUNY Press, 2005), and *Time after Time* (Indiana University Press, 2007). *Reinhabiting the Earth*, and *Deep Time* are due out from Fordham in 2015. He is also an earth artist.

Index

Perspectives in Continental Philosophy
John D. Caputo, series editor

John D. Caputo, ed., *Deconstruction in a Nutshell: A Conversation with Jacques Derrida*.

Michael Strawser, *Both/And: Reading Kierkegaard—From Irony to Edification*.

Michael D. Barber, *Ethical Hermeneutics: Rationality in Enrique Dussel's Philosophy of Liberation*.

James H. Olthuis, ed., *Knowing Other-wise: Philosophy at the Threshold of Spirituality*.

James Swindal, *Reflection Revisited: Jürgen Habermas's Discursive Theory of Truth*.

Richard Kearney, *Poetics of Imagining: Modern and Postmodern*. Second edition.

Thomas W. Busch, *Circulating Being: From Embodiment to Incorporation—Essays on Late Existentialism*.

Edith Wyschogrod, *Emmanuel Levinas: The Problem of Ethical Metaphysics*. Second edition.

Francis J. Ambrosio, ed., *The Question of Christian Philosophy Today*.

Jeffrey Bloechl, ed., *The Face of the Other and the Trace of God: Essays on the Philosophy of Emmanuel Levinas*.

Ilse N. Bulhof and Laurens ten Kate, eds., *Flight of the Gods: Philosophical Perspectives on Negative Theology*.

Trish Glazebrook, *Heidegger's Philosophy of Science*.

Kevin Hart, *The Trespass of the Sign: Deconstruction, Theology, and Philosophy*.

Mark C. Taylor, *Journeys to Selfhood: Hegel and Kierkegaard*. Second edition.

Dominique Janicaud, Jean-François Courtine, Jean-Louis Chrétien, Michel Henry, Jean-Luc Marion, and Paul Ricoeur, *Phenomenology and the "Theological Turn": The French Debate*.

Karl Jaspers, *The Question of German Guilt*. Introduction by Joseph W. Koterski, S.J.

Jean-Luc Marion, *The Idol and Distance: Five Studies*. Translated with an introduction by Thomas A. Carlson.

Jeffrey Dudiak, *The Intrigue of Ethics: A Reading of the Idea of Discourse in the Thought of Emmanuel Levinas*.

Robyn Horner, *Rethinking God as Gift: Marion, Derrida, and the Limits of Phenomenology*.

Mark Dooley, *The Politics of Exodus: Søren Kierkegaard's Ethics of Responsibility*.

Merold Westphal, *Overcoming Onto-Theology: Toward a Postmodern Christian Faith*.

Edith Wyschogrod, Jean-Joseph Goux, and Eric Boynton, eds., *The Enigma of Gift and Sacrifice*.

Stanislas Breton, *The Word and the Cross*. Translated with an introduction by Jacquelyn Porter.

Jean-Luc Marion, *Prolegomena to Charity*. Translated by Stephen E. Lewis.

Peter H. Spader, *Scheler's Ethical Personalism: Its Logic, Development, and Promise*.

Jean-Louis Chrétien, *The Unforgettable and the Unhoped For*. Translated by Jeffrey Bloechl.

Don Cupitt, *Is Nothing Sacred? The Non-Realist Philosophy of Religion: Selected Essays*.

Jean-Luc Marion, *In Excess: Studies of Saturated Phenomena*. Translated by Robyn Horner and Vincent Berraud.

Phillip Goodchild, *Rethinking Philosophy of Religion: Approaches from Continental Philosophy*.

William J. Richardson, S.J., *Heidegger: Through Phenomenology to Thought*.

Jeffrey Andrew Barash, *Martin Heidegger and the Problem of Historical Meaning*.

Jean-Louis Chrétien, *Hand to Hand: Listening to the Work of Art*. Translated by Stephen E. Lewis.

Jean-Louis Chrétien, *The Call and the Response*. Translated with an introduction by Anne Davenport.

D. C. Schindler, *Han Urs von Balthasar and the Dramatic Structure of Truth: A Philosophical Investigation*.

Julian Wolfreys, ed., *Thinking Difference: Critics in Conversation*.

Allen Scult, *Being Jewish/Reading Heidegger: An Ontological Encounter*.

Richard Kearney, *Debates in Continental Philosophy: Conversations with Contemporary Thinkers*.

Jennifer Anna Gosetti-Ferencei, *Heidegger, Hölderlin, and the Subject of Poetic Language: Toward a New Poetics of Dasein*.

Jolita Pons, *Stealing a Gift: Kierkegaard's Pseudonyms and the Bible*.

Jean-Yves Lacoste, *Experience and the Absolute: Disputed Questions on the Humanity of Man*. Translated by Mark Raftery-Skehan.

Charles P. Bigger, *Between Chora and the Good: Metaphor's Metaphysical Neighborhood*.

Dominique Janicaud, *Phenomenology "Wide Open": After the French Debate.* Translated by Charles N. Cabral.

Ian Leask and Eoin Cassidy, eds., *Givenness and God: Questions of Jean-Luc Marion.*

Jacques Derrida, *Sovereignties in Question: The Poetics of Paul Celan.* Edited by Thomas Dutoit and Outi Pasanen.

William Desmond, *Is There a Sabbath for Thought? Between Religion and Philosophy.*

Bruce Ellis Benson and Norman Wirzba, eds., *The Phenomenology of Prayer.*

S. Clark Buckner and Matthew Statler, eds., *Styles of Piety: Practicing Philosophy after the Death of God.*

Kevin Hart and Barbara Wall, eds., *The Experience of God: A Postmodern Response.*

John Panteleimon Manoussakis, *After God: Richard Kearney and the Religious Turn in Continental Philosophy.*

John Martis, *Philippe Lacoue-Labarthe: Representation and the Loss of the Subject.*

Jean-Luc Nancy, *The Ground of the Image.*

Edith Wyschogrod, *Crossover Queries: Dwelling with Negatives, Embodying Philosophy's Others.*

Gerald Bruns, *On the Anarchy of Poetry and Philosophy: A Guide for the Unruly.*

Brian Treanor, *Aspects of Alterity: Levinas, Marcel, and the Contemporary Debate.*

Simon Morgan Wortham, *Counter-Institutions: Jacques Derrida and the Question of the University.*

Leonard Lawlor, *The Implications of Immanence: Toward a New Concept of Life.*

Clayton Crockett, *Interstices of the Sublime: Theology and Psychoanalytic Theory.*

Bettina Bergo, Joseph Cohen, and Raphael Zagury-Orly, eds., *Judeities: Questions for Jacques Derrida.* Translated by Bettina Bergo and Michael B. Smith.

Jean-Luc Marion, *On the Ego and on God: Further Cartesian Questions.* Translated by Christina M. Gschwandtner.

Jean-Luc Nancy, *Philosophical Chronicles.* Translated by Franson Manjali.

Jean-Luc Nancy, *Dis-Enclosure: The Deconstruction of Christianity.* Translated by Bettina Bergo, Gabriel Malenfant, and Michael B. Smith.

Andrea Hurst, *Derrida Vis-à-vis Lacan: Interweaving Deconstruction and Psychoanalysis.*

Jean-Luc Nancy, *Noli me tangere: On the Raising of the Body.* Translated by Sarah Clift, Pascale-Anne Brault, and Michael Naas.

Jacques Derrida, *The Animal That Therefore I Am.* Edited by Marie-Louise Mallet, translated by David Wills.

Jean-Luc Marion, *The Visible and the Revealed.* Translated by Christina M. Gschwandtner and others.

Michel Henry, *Material Phenomenology.* Translated by Scott Davidson.

Jean-Luc Nancy, *Corpus.* Translated by Richard A. Rand.

Joshua Kates, *Fielding Derrida.*

Michael Naas, *Derrida From Now On.*

Shannon Sullivan and Dennis J. Schmidt, eds., *Difficulties of Ethical Life.*

Catherine Malabou, *What Should We Do with Our Brain?* Translated by Sebastian Rand, Introduction by Marc Jeannerod.

Claude Romano, *Event and World.* Translated by Shane Mackinlay.

Vanessa Lemm, *Nietzsche's Animal Philosophy: Culture, Politics, and the Animality of the Human Being.*

B. Keith Putt, ed., *Gazing Through a Prism Darkly: Reflections on Merold Westphal's Hermeneutical Epistemology.*

Eric Boynton and Martin Kavka, eds., *Saintly Influence: Edith Wyschogrod and the Possibilities of Philosophy of Religion.*

Shane Mackinlay, *Interpreting Excess: Jean-Luc Marion, Saturated Phenomena, and Hermeneutics.*

Kevin Hart and Michael A. Signer, eds., *The Exorbitant: Emmanuel Levinas Between Jews and Christians.*

Bruce Ellis Benson and Norman Wirzba, eds., *Words of Life: New Theological Turns in French Phenomenology.*

William Robert, *Trials: Of Antigone and Jesus.*

Brian Treanor and Henry Isaac Venema, eds., *A Passion for the Possible: Thinking with Paul Ricoeur.*

Kas Saghafi, *Apparitions—Of Derrida's Other.*

Nick Mansfield, *The God Who Deconstructs Himself: Sovereignty and Subjectivity Between Freud, Bataille, and Derrida.*

Don Ihde, *Heidegger's Technologies: Postphenomenological Perspectives.*

Suzi Adams, *Castoriadis's Ontology: Being and Creation.*

Richard Kearney and Kascha Semonovitch, eds., *Phenomenologies of the Stranger: Between Hostility and Hospitality.*

Michael Naas, *Miracle and Machine: Jacques Derrida and the Two Sources of Religion, Science, and the Media.*

Alena Alexandrova, Ignaas Devisch, Laurens ten Kate, and Aukje van Rooden, *Re-treating Religion: Deconstructing Christianity with Jean-Luc Nancy.* Preamble by Jean-Luc Nancy.

Emmanuel Falque, *The Metamorphosis of Finitude: An Essay on Birth and Resurrection.* Translated by George Hughes.

Scott M. Campbell, *The Early Heidegger's Philosophy of Life: Facticity, Being, and Language.*

Françoise Dastur, *How Are We to Confront Death? An Introduction to Philosophy.* Translated by Robert Vallier. Foreword by David Farrell Krell.

Christina M. Gschwandtner, *Postmodern Apologetics? Arguments for God in Contemporary Philosophy.*

Ben Morgan, *On Becoming God: Late Medieval Mysticism and the Modern Western Self.*

Neal DeRoo, *Futurity in Phenomenology: Promise and Method in Husserl, Levinas, and Derrida.*

CPSIA information can be obtained
at www.ICGtesting.com
Printed in the USA
BVOW03s0605190917
495237BV00001B/65/P